TRAINING FOR SOFTWARE ROLLOUTS

TRAINING FOR SOFTWARE ROLLOUTS

The Definitive Guide to Developing and Implementing
Software Training Programs

CHARLES H. TREPPER

McGraw-Hill

New York San Francisco Washington, D.C. Auckland Bogotá
Caracas Lisbon London Madrid Mexico City Milan
Montreal New Delhi San Juan Singapore
Sydney Tokyo Toronto

Library of Congress Cataloging-in-Publication Data

Trepper, Charles H.
    Training for software rollouts / Charles H. Trepper.
        p.   cm.
    Includes index.
    ISBN 0-07-134923-5
    1. Information services industry—Employees—Training of.   I. Title.
HD9999.I492T74   1999
658.3'1243—dc21   99-056224
                                                    CIP

McGraw-Hill

A Division of The McGraw·Hill Companies

1 2 3 4 5 6 7 8 9 0   DOC/DOC   0 9 8 7 6 5 4 3 2 1 0

ISBN 0-07-134923-5

The sponsoring editor for this book was Richard Narramore, the editing supervisor was Janice Race, and the production supervisor was Elizabeth J. Strange. It was set in Palatino per the IPROF design specs by Kim Sheran, Paul Scozzari, Joanne Morbit, Deirdre Sheean, and Michele Pridmore of the Hightstown McGraw-Hill Desktop Publishing Unit.

Printed and bound by R. R. Donnelley & Sons Company.

McGraw-Hill books are available at special quantity discounts to use as premiums and sales promotions, or for use in corporate training programs. For more information, please write to the Director of Special Sales, Professional Publishing McGraw-Hill, Two Penn Plaza, New York, NY 10121-2298. Or contact your local bookstore.

This publication is designed to provide accurate and authoritative information in regard to the subject matter covered. It is sold with the understanding that neither the author nor the publisher is engaged in rendering legal, accounting, or other professional service. If legal advice or other expert assistance is required, the services of a competent professional person should be sought.
—*From a Declaration of Principles jointly adopted by a Committee of the American Bar Association and a Committee of Publishers.*

 This book is printed on recycled, acid-free paper containing a minimum of 50% recycled de-inked fiber.

Important Guidelines for Photocopying or Downloading Pages From This Publication

CONTENTS

APPENDIXES

INTENDED AUDIENCE

Information technology (I/T) managers and training personnel, I/T training consultants, and human resource (HR) professionals will find this book to be an excellent handbook for defining, developing, and implementing highly successful information technology training programs and courses, with emphasis on the area of training for software rollouts.

UNIQUE FEATURES OF THIS BOOK

This book is unique in its approach to defining, developing, and implementing I/T training programs, using a running case study to demonstrate the tasks involved. The topics are presented in a sequence likely to occur in the "real world." Beyond the mechanics of performing the tasks, however, I discuss why each step is necessary, and how it fits with other steps in the development process.

The process detailed in this book to develop training programs is a derivative of the widely used instructional systems development/design (ISD) model. I chose this model because it's very similar to the standard systems development life cycle model with which most I/T staff are familiar. If this book is used by an HR professional, this model can help the HR professional relate the training process to I/T staff, and will provide a common ground for discussion during the development of the training program.

Important features of the book are:

- Dozens of downloadable, customizable forms, checklists, and document samples for a quick start.
- Hot teaching tips from the best professional trainers in the business.
- Directions for producing training programs that utilize both purchased and custom-developed training materials and courses. Many I/T shops don't have the resources to develop full-blown training programs, and so they purchase either materials or courses from external vendors. This book details how to get the most out of purchased courseware.
- The use of industry-standard instructional systems development techniques and processes to create a methodology that flows smoothly from phase to phase.

- Process maps that show the training developer his or her "position" in the process and the next steps.
- The seamless progression of documents and other training materials from one phase to the next.
- State-of-the-art techniques for each phase, such as multilevel needs analysis and organizational and financial impact analysis. These are included to help training developers ensure significant return on their training dollars.
- Employee performance measurement techniques that provide methods of continually improving the training management process.
- A consideration of EEO and other legal matters in each phase to ensure proper regulatory compliance.

HOW TO USE THIS BOOK

This book can be used as a reference guide, a comprehensive manual, or a textbook for courses taught in a classroom setting. It contains step-by-step instructions, deliverable samples (blank and completed), tips and pitfalls, references, and a case study. The case study runs throughout Part One of the book, giving the reader the opportunity to use the skills learned to solve a "real-life" problem. Experienced trainers will find this book to be a handy reference guide to the training development process. Readers at all levels of experience will find the references helpful in broadening the scope and depth of their knowledge.

The first part of this book is a basic guide to the entire process of I/T training. It begins with assessing I/T training needs in an organization, and runs through the entire process of designing, delivering, and evaluating the effectiveness of training. The second part of the book focuses on the special issues involved in training users on the most important business software—from Windows to SAP.

THE CASE STUDY

The case study in this book details the development of a training program for the rollout of the Widget Control System (WCS) ERP package at Acme Widgets. I/T managers, I/T trainers, and the Acme Widgets' HR department are all involved in various aspects of the case. Some training will be purchased, and some developed in house. Examples of how to use techniques to accomplish the rollout are included at each point in the process. Sample forms and checklists are progressively complete at each phase of the process.

Questions, comments, and other feedback may be directed to:

Charles H. Trepper
The Trepper Group
250 Carlson Parkway, Suite 322
Minnetonka, Minnesota 55305
Phone: (612) 449-9725
E-mail: chtrepper@uswest.net

Acknowledgments

A book of this size would be impossible without the help of many people. I attempt to name everyone here, and if anyone is left out, I sincerely apologize.

Professor Kathryne A. Newton of Purdue University provided me with content structure and guidance on the book.

Equally important is the staff at McGraw-Hill, including Richard Narramore, who led me through the project, and Janice Race, who coordinated the edit. Obviously, there are lots of other people at McGraw-Hill who got this project through and out the door, and I thank them for their help as well. Rick Williamson and Mike Hayes got me started with McGraw-Hill, and I appreciate their contacts.

Professor Jeffrey Whitten of Purdue University pointed me in the right direction.

The content providers and consultants—Susan Boyd of Susan Boyd Associates, Paul Fox of Fox Performance, Raja Thiagarajan of Workshops by Thiagi, Inc., and Warren S. Reid, Managing Director of WSR Consulting, LLC—supplied great information for the book.

The vendors were also very helpful. My thanks go to Tina Szoka and Elizabeth Hart at Lotus Corporation, Amy Stuhlberg at Microsoft, Bernhard Hochlehnert at SAP, and Andrea Ward and Rosanna Loo of Oracle Corporation.

Of course, friends and family gave me the support and, occasionally, the will to finish this effort.

A special thanks to Superior Expeditions for the weekend scuba breaks that helped me decompress.

INTRODUCTION

For many organizations, the single largest capital expense is computer systems. However, organizationwide rollouts of new computer applications such as proprietary systems, Windows 98, Lotus Notes, or SAP often take much more time and money to implement than anyone originally planned. The culprit is nearly always inadequate employee training on the new software for both technical and business staff. Many successful books have been published on the MCSE certification, Windows, MS Office, and enterprise resource planning (ERP) systems. Huge amounts of money have been spent on training for these initiatives. But no book has been written that guides the information technology (I/T) manager, training manager, or consultant responsible for software rollouts through designing, developing, and implementing a training program for a major rollout. This book is a comprehensive guide to developing and delivering training to support a software rollout. There is detailed advice on widely used applications, including Lotus Notes, Windows 98/NT, and MS Office, and ERP packages such as SAP and Oracle.

Professionals creating a training program for custom software or ERP packages usually face five major challenges in an organization:

1. Selling training to management and the organization as a whole
2. Finding an affordable training solution, whether developed in house or purchased
3. Getting people to attend training
4. Supporting staff after training
5. Measuring training success

Each of these obstacles can be overcome using standard, time-tested methods, techniques, and tools.

I.1 SELLING TRAINING TO MANAGEMENT AND THE ORGANIZATION AS A WHOLE

Selling the idea of training is difficult for two major reasons: time and money. Employees must be allowed to take time for training. Managers often view the training time for employees as unproductive—as time that could be better spent on daily work tasks. Most training is provided on the job (OJT), and a formal training program is often seen as a waste of organizational resources. Successful training design for strategic software programs includes:

- Working with the business strategy and goals that are driving the technology deployment
- Understanding the impact of the new business processes on people's day-to-day jobs and careers
- Developing tools to measure the contribution of training over time

All these factors are critically important in determining the learning model and posttraining support that will make your training investment pay off. Chapter 1, "Getting Started—Political and Organizational Issues," provides tips and techniques for selling management on the need for a training program, as well as an organizational structure for the rollout project to ensure proper coordination of the effort. The chapter presents approaches for justifying training programs, and tips for overcoming management objections and challenges to your presentation. A sample presentation template is also included to provide a "jump start."

The best way to convince management to spend time and money on training is to clearly document the needs, costs, and benefits of the required training. Chapter 2, "How to Conduct a Training Needs Analysis," presents a simple, structured approach for determining what the overall training needs for staff are and which staff must attend which training for which software. Sample forms and templates are included to save time and effort on the part of the training team.

Producing a sound financial analysis of the training program includes hard and soft costs, benefits, and the likely consequences in terms of cost if training is not provided. Often, showing the costs associated with doing nothing is enough incentive to galvanize management into funding the training effort. Chapter 3, "Creating a Budget and Time Line for the Training Program," provides a step-by-step layout of a project plan for the training program, time estimates for each task, and tips and techniques for estimating the dollars needed for each step. A sample project plan and work breakdown structure are included to facilitate a quick start. Once the training needs, audience, budget, and time line are set, you are ready for Chapter 4, "Designing the Training Program." This chapter shows you how to use the needs analysis to design the training program, and provides sample forms and checklists for the design.

I.2 FINDING AN AFFORDABLE TRAINING SOLUTION

Once you've decided what training must be supplied to whom, the next challenge is to find a training solution that meets the project budget and time line. Several types and combinations of training are available. Training can be delivered by traditional means, e.g., classroom or self-study, by computer-based training (CBT), by distance learning via the Internet, or by some combination. Chapter 5, "Self-Directed Training versus Classroom Training," presents the various advantages and disadvantages of each option.

Another decision to be made is whether to build the training program in house or to purchase training. Chapter 6, "Make or Buy—Purchasing Training versus Developing and Delivering Training In House," provides a toolkit for both deciding what you can do yourself and evaluating your internal training development capabilities. When deciding how to approach training, it is important to understand the advantages of using professional trainers versus subject matter experts, such as business end users or software specialists. Chapter 6 presents a process and criteria for making that determination.

Chapter 7, "Purchasing Training," presents evaluation templates for deciding what you need if the decision is made to purchase training. The chapter offers advice on finding vendors, evaluating courseware, and selecting training materials. Tips and techniques are also presented on bidding out the project and negotiating with training vendors for the best prices on training and related services.

If training is purchased, especially in the form of a packaged solution, it often must be modified for a particular organization, and sometimes even a specific group of users or I/T staff. Chapter 8, "Customizing Packaged Training to Meet the Needs of Your Organization," guides the training developer through the process of changing the purchased training to ensure that it meets the organization's requirements discovered during the needs analysis. Customizing training solutions to meet specific learning needs is the key to success. Chapter 8 shows you how to refine the needs, identify skill gaps, and design the perfect solution working with vendors to assure success.

I.3 GETTING PEOPLE TO ATTEND TRAINING

How the training program is implemented will significantly affect how participants perceive the training. There are several decisions to be made when implementing a training program, including whether to conduct the training on-site or off-site. In addition, the trainer assigned to the class may well be the most significant determinant of success or failure. Chapter 9, "Implementing the Training Program," covers these issues and more to ensure a successful implementation.

In any effort that involves significant change in an organization, communication is the key. Training is often seen by "long-timers" as being a threat to their job security. Chapter 10, "Communicating the Training Rollout to the Organization," shows how to build enthusiasm for the program, provide real incentives to attendees, and sustain excellent attendance at training classes.

Even the best trainers can learn from others with more experiences. Chapter 11, "Tips for the Trainer," combines common-sense tips with expert advice from training designers and developers, as well as experienced trainers. Activities to keep attendees coming back are included in the chapter.

I.4 SUPPORTING STAFF AFTER TRAINING

Part of implementing a training program is understanding the long-term needs of participants, posttraining. Help desks are often swamped after a training class. Chapter 9 offers a complete program for identifying and assigning ongoing support tasks. The chapter includes tips on incorporating the new training material in your help desk, developing "power users" to support other, less experienced users, and helping all system users develop a sense of independence to reduce their support requirements. Chapter 7 also helps you work with vendors to get great support on purchased training.

I.5 MEASURING TRAINING SUCCESS

Evaluating and continually improving training is perhaps the most important task in training. Showing a significant payback for training dollars spent will do more to build the case for future training than anything else. Chapter 12, "Measuring Training Success by Measuring On-the-Job Trainee Performance," presents a simple, complete process for designing and using course evaluations to continually improve the quality of your training program.

I.6 USING THE INFORMATION FOR YOUR ROLLOUT

All the information detailed in Chapters 1 to 14 (Part One) can be used to improve the quality of training in your organization. The chapters in

Part Two, "Application-Specific Training Issues," provide useful training-related information on various software products. The training process map and checklist found in Appendix B provide a step-by-step "action item" or "punch" list to check off as you proceed. Chapters 1 to 14 provide training tips and pitfalls to watch for, as well as resources for purchasing and/or developing training for the rollout of the software to ensure success.

I.7   THE PROCESS MAP

At the start of each chapter a process map indicates where you are in the process of developing a training program (see Figure I-1). The process map allows you to start anywhere in the process by letting you see where you are and where you're going. It provides you with a step-by-step guide that can be used to develop a project plan in MS Project 98 or in another format. The process map begins with selling the project to develop the program, and runs through the entire process to evaluation and continual improvement. At a high level, the needs analysis really drives the rest of the process. When all the needs are known, the trainer has an idea (albeit rough) of the required effort, and can construct the program plan. The program plan details the work to be done, and at a high level, the classes to be constructed.

The design phase actually consists of three steps. The first step is to use the information from the needs analysis to design a curriculum. The curriculum document may have varying levels of detail with regard to specific classes. Once the curriculum design is done, the next step is to decide

FIGURE I-1

Process Map

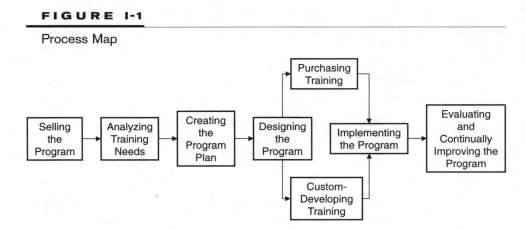

whether to make or buy training. Usually, there will be some of both. The last step in the design phase is to work with either vendors or internal staff to design the class materials, etc. Implementation is also critical, and tips are presented for increasing attendance (both mental and physical!).

I.8 INTRODUCTION TO THE RUNNING CASE— ACME WIDGETS INC. ERP ROLLOUT

Acme Widgets Inc. (AWI) recently purchased the Widget Control System (WCS) ERP package for client/server architectures. This package is designed to automate all of Acme Widgets' major business systems. Some business functions are currently running on legacy mainframe systems, and other business functions are performed manually. The WCS is designed to automate all business functions into a single, integrated system that will provide the company with a significant competitive edge. The major functions to be automated are purchasing, manufacturing, sales, finance/accounting, and human resources. To facilitate productivity and information sharing among all employees, both technical and nontechnical, AWI is installing a new knowledge-sharing system called KIS (knowledge and information sharing).

The transition from both old legacy systems and manual processing will involve many changes, and corporate management must be convinced that an integrated, complete training program will be needed to address the needs of various types of I/T staff and various levels of end users. Some I/T staff are primarily hardware-oriented and will need training on the WCS and KIS installation requirements, while others are mostly concerned with the software and will need training on the customization of both. Business users have skill sets ranging from personal computer (PC) novice to expert/power system user.

The I/T training manager, Bob, has put Mike, the training team lead, in charge of the effort to develop and design a training program that integrates the use of both products and that helps both I/T and end users become proficient, productive users. Mike will work with:

- Shawn and Dave, who are trainers
- Kathy, a training developer
- Jack, a technical writer
- Trudy, the company's human resources (HR) training specialist

Acme Widgets' corporate management is not convinced that a formal training program is needed. Most of the executives feel that the staff should be able to learn the two software products from the systems development team or through manuals and on-line help screens. Besides, some of the executives argue, a formal training program for both pieces of software would be too expensive. The chief information officer (CIO) for Acme Widgets, Connie, believes that a formal training program is the best way to train the I/T staff to install and maintain the WCS effectively. She also feels that users will need heavy training for a major change in the way they do their work. The vice president of human resources, Richard, also thinks that a formal program is necessary for end users, but is unsure of how to sell it. Connie and Richard have asked Bob to put together a presentation to sell the program and to have Mike manage the project.

Examples of how to use techniques to solve this problem are included in each chapter. Sample forms and checklists are progressively completed at each phase of the process. The process of selling, designing, and implementing the WCS and KIS training programs is detailed in each chapter.

PART ONE

DESIGNING, DEVELOPING, AND IMPLEMENTING A SOFTWARE TRAINING PROGRAM FOR YOUR ORGANIZATION

CHAPTER 1

Getting Started—Political and Organizational Issues

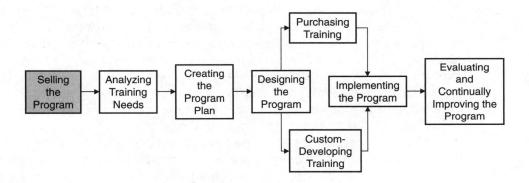

In This Chapter

OVERVIEW

Implementation of an effective training program will never occur unless it is supported at all levels within the organization. Management must first be shown that existing training practices do not meet all of its requirements. This may be because the current program doesn't reflect the organization's operations, or it may be due to a change in the type of training needed to support management decisions in today's ever more competitive environment. Management can then be shown how the new, integrated training program can be used to effectively fulfill those unmet requirements. Management, particularly senior management, must be persuaded that training belongs on top of everyone's agenda.

The benefits of proper training for both I/T and business staff for new software rollouts are too compelling to ignore: improved productivity, higher employee morale, increased flexibility and less resistance to change, and cost savings. Without proper selling and planning, however, these benefits can be reduced or eliminated by controversy caused by ongoing political issues. Such problems are often at least partially the fault of differences between two opposing executive mindsets. One type of executive believes that training is very important and that a formal training program is the way to get users up to speed on new software. The other type of executive doesn't want to spend any money if possible and would prefer that system users learn on the job.

There is also a potential conflict of interest between management and trainees in that knowledge is portable—it is not in management's interests to provide training that will be of benefit to competitors if the employee moves on (the "free-rider" problem). Some managers are particularly unhappy at providing high-demand skills in ERP and MCSE, which are seen as highly portable. The training team must persuade managers that retraining reduces turnover.

1.1   SELLING MANAGEMENT ON THE NEED FOR A TRAINING PROGRAM

While it's usually easy to convince management that some kind of training is necessary for new software, it's not as easy to convince management to spend the time and money on establishing a formal training program. To justify your existence, there are six basic steps to follow.

Step 1. Find an Executive Sponsor

Without someone at the top to back the training program, it will almost certainly fail. The executive sponsor knows the political landscape and can guide you through the potential landmines. A sponsor also has the ability to lobby and champion your cause among those who can fund it and ensure attendance of participants. To get an executive sponsor you must first cover your potential exposures and be aware of management's concerns. That leads to Step 2.

Step 2. Know the Training Management Issues

One major issue is the need to offer incentives to employees to attend training. While I/T staff may be happy to go to training on software because it increases their mobility and market value, end users may not see the value as easily. It may be necessary to offer visible incentives, such as cash, recognition, or promotions, to make the newly skilled employee feel valuable. The obvious benefit of incentive programs is to keep the employee on whom you just spent all that training money!

Another management issue is management and organizational education. Employees must be educated to understand the relevance of the training to business issues. Also, there must be a conscious respect for budgets. Training programs do not come cheaply, and management and staff must understand clearly how the money will be spent and what the payback will be. The training team must never assume that everyone knows what the training is all about. The training team needs to give thorough attention to overcoming this lack of knowledge through staff and client education.

Ownership, both short and long term, is also a major issue. Who will own the new training program initially and on an ongoing basis? Ownership of the new program should be consistent with its primary objective. In many situations, it will be desirable for someone outside of I/T to take ownership. For example, HR or an independent corporate training group might assume responsibilities. In such an event, the program is more likely to be properly maintained and used.

Perhaps the biggest issue is the cost. Where will the money for the program come from? Is the training team going to be budgeted from a central pool, or will it be funded from the software rollout project? If it is funded on a project basis, who will maintain the materials? These are all questions that must be answered before a management presentation because they will be asked. These questions and more are addressed in Chapter 3, "Creating a Budget and Time Line for the Training Program."

Step 3. Find Out *How* Your Management Thinks

The process of selling management on the idea of a formal training program for a software rollout has a number of steps, but the constant in the process is continual communication. Understanding the communication styles of senior management and other key stakeholders is critical to selling the concept. If you know how people think, you can customize your approach to their thought process. Learn everything you can about them. What projects have they funded or killed before? Do those projects have anything in common? For example, did they kill projects that had a weak project plan? Did they kill projects that had a vague scope and objective declaration? *Remember:* Forewarned is forearmed.

So how do you get all this great preparatory information? Talk to other staff members who have worked with each of the managers you must sell. One great resource is the manager's secretary. That person usually knows a lot about the manager's work and communication style, and may even have some insight into the manager's pet peeves.

When I worked at a large food wholesaler, I once had to sell the VP of I/T on training six mainframe experts on client/server technology for a data warehouse project. This was back in 1992, when client/server was just starting to really take off. This VP was an adamant supporter of mainframe technology and wasn't particularly thrilled with the idea of a PC on everyone's desk. In fact, he saw the PCs mostly as game machines and waited as long as possible before upgrading desktops.

I got to know his executive secretary over time, and asked her lots of questions. What time of day was he most receptive? What didn't he like about presentations he'd heard before? Was there anything he really liked? By the time we got around to talking about the project funding, I'd been able to get a feel for his communication style without even touching on the project. By tailoring my style to his, I was able to secure the funding I'd asked for. If you get to know people before you ask for something, you're much more likely to get it than if you just show up on their doorstep asking for money.

Step 4. Find Out *What* Your Management Thinks

As mentioned before, some executives don't think much of formal training programs and don't want to put the money into the infrastructure necessary to build one. What are their issues with training? What problems do they see with the program? What do they think of training and training programs in general? What good and bad experiences have they had with training programs in the past?

One effective way of persuading senior managers to back a training program is to emphasize the value to managers individually. Try to find out what they want and don't want in a training program. Find out what their needs are before you do a general presentation. You probably won't end up being all things to all people, but you may be able to meet most of everyone's basic needs. Interview managers extensively so you can incorporate their concerns into the sales document.

The attitude of I/T management is also extremely important to the process of training for software rollouts. The crucial question to be answered is whether current I/T staff members are willing and able to change with the times; specifically, do they have the skills necessary to deal effectively with end users in all business areas? During the participative planning process, other department heads can become sensitive to the anxiety that I/T staff are possibly experiencing. Other department managers can make the idea of the new software more palatable to I/T staff by pointing out that this endeavor is a formidable challenge that represents an experience-building opportunity. In becoming a partner in the project's success, the I/T staff contribute toward a new organizational structure that is equipped to respond to competition.

Step 5. Get to Their Peers

Like all professional employees, senior managers are concerned about how their peers perceive them and what their peers are thinking—peers both within and outside the organization. Executives talk among themselves. The best way to defuse emotional and political time bombs that can jeopardize success is to include all affected parties in the planning process. This means other executives at the same level as your primary sponsor. The planning process should be participative and start with an articulation of the organizational goals targeted by the effort and an outline of anticipated costs and benefits. This stage of the planning process should also address the most critical concern of the participants, which is how they will be affected. If the executives are comfortable with the process and proposed product, they are more likely to ask their divisions and departments to attend training.

If you can, find some examples of other executives and/or senior managers at other organizations who have sponsored efforts like yours. This gives your executive the opportunity to talk to other people at an executive level, and also indicates that you've done your homework. If you can find an organization in the same industry (manufacturing, banking, etc.), all the better. Your sponsor will then have some foundation for backing your effort because he or she can point to success at similar organizations.

Step 6. Sell, Sell, Sell!

To be able to sell something, you *must* believe in it. If the people you're selling to think, even for a minute, that you're hesitant about the program, their enthusiasm will dry up. And you must sell people at all levels of the organization. Try to build demand from grass roots. Try to find people in your organization who really want the training you're offering. A common groundswell of support can be very helpful to your cause. If senior managers are being told by their staff that their staff have certain needs, and you can meet those needs at reasonable cost, you have a pretty good chance of succeeding. If you must, take a selling skills course to improve your sales abilities.

One little known fact about selling is that it involves more listening than talking. *Remember:* You can't learn if you're talking. My father has been in sales for over 40 years. I used to marvel at how he could build rapport with a customer so fast while talking so little. Years later, he told me that by listening he could adapt his sales pitch on the fly. The main point is that the more your customer tells you, the more you know about your customer's needs. By listening carefully, you can pick up on the needs of the largest number of people and then customize your program to meet those needs.

1.2   APPROACHES TO JUSTIFYING TRAINING PROGRAMS

There are many ways to justify training programs, but all have one thing in common: They must demonstrate that the training program adds some *real value* to the organization. Real value is defined as either increasing revenue or decreasing costs in an organization. Real value can only be assessed by structured performance indicators and good evaluation programs. Experienced trainers will justify their existence by giving the company's management accurate performance indicators (revenue versus cost, etc.) to evaluate their effectiveness. Chapter 12, "Measuring Training Success by Measuring On-the-Job Trainee Performance," presents several approaches to evaluating training programs. Some specific factors that cause management to back a training program include:

1. Employee hiring data—new employees must learn the new software.
2. Worker skill, ability, and knowledge inventories.
3. Laws and regulations requiring training. (*Example:* Auditors must know the financial piece of any ERP package.)

4. Competitors are doing it. (This can be a major incentive for management!)
5. Entry-level training in ERP software can be attractive to new employees.
6. Why waste money on a software rollout if nobody can use it?

Each of these factors must be presented in a way that meets your management's expectations. And each of these factors must assist your employees in improving the quality or quantity of their work as well as implement skills to meet your customers' needs.

Putting training's contribution to the organization in terms of learning provides a more robust position in the face of budget pressures. The reality is that I/T organizations need their people to learn things all the time. This has never been more true in these days of rapid-fire change, and never more critical than in the field of I/T. If the training department has a reputation for operating cost-effectively, it will more readily get management to support funding for the learning that management knows is needed. Training's ultimate deliverable—learning for performance—is often expensive. It is, however, not nearly as expensive as the one thing a business absolutely cannot afford: ignorance on the part of its people, ignorance of what the business requires them to know in order to achieve its plans and goals.

It's important to gather data on how other organizations that are installing the same software have set up training programs and how much the programs cost. You can usually work with the software vendor to get contacts at other clients. The software vendor can provide you with data on the success rates of organizations that rolled out their software without training their employees in a formal program versus those that set up and delivered a structured training program. The other clients can tell you how they've justified the training and, if they couldn't get management to fund a formal program, what some of the typical problems were they experienced. Other clients can also give you valuable data on cost estimates and ROI analyses for the program. (Also, see Chapters 3 and 12 for budgeting and measurement information, respectively.)

1.3 TIPS FOR OVERCOMING MANAGEMENT OBJECTIONS AND CHALLENGES TO YOUR PRESENTATION

Be sure that the training program integrates your organization's policies, procedures, and business practices into the software training. The content of each course should address relevant policies and procedures along with software operation and use. Instruction should move beyond the "how to" and incorporate common business problems and issues related to the system. Instructors may find it helpful to partner with other administrative departments as well as current system users in framing realistic scenarios. This will go a long way to helping management understand the value of training.

In terms of the actual sales presentation, preparation is the first critical element in any successful sale. Preparing yourself to hurdle the barriers of objections is critical. You can give the most informative, energetic presentation and still encounter objections. Top salespeople often use the following five techniques to help them leap over objections.

- *Think of objections as questions.* Objections may often sound like verbal attacks on you or your project, but you don't want to sound defensive. You can deflect any hostility in your answer by rephrasing the objection as a question in your mind. For instance, if an executive says, "The cost is too high," mentally change the statement into the question, "Why does the project cost so much?" Responding calmly and sensibly to the question makes your challenger more receptive to your answer.

- *Discover the hidden objections.* Prevent some objections by asking the right questions at the beginning. Make a list of objections your customer might make (see above general management issues), and then think of a question for each that will help you eliminate it right away.

- *Acknowledge objections.* Even the best project will have some potential problems. Nobody's perfect. If you don't know something, be honest, and let the person know you'll get back to him or her. The project may not be perfect, but it may still be a terrific idea. However, if you acknowledge the validity of the objection, it can help you build rapport.

- *Reroute and rephrase.* Often you can direct the objection back to the customer with the question, "Why do you feel that way?" If the customer answers with a more precise reason, you are one step closer to addressing the objection and possibly eliminating it. You can also rephrase the objection in your own words, showing the person that you're listening and you understand the person's concerns. This gives you time to think about your answer.

- *Turn the negative into the positive.* An objection is no longer an objection if it becomes a reason for your customer to buy. If a manager says, "Your cost is too high," you could reply, "The cost reflects the high quality of the end product, and there are no hidden extras. Good value is important to you, isn't it?" Of course, these techniques must be used and phrased in a professional manner.

Using these five simple techniques will help you through the presentation. Preparation, however, is still the best tool. Find out everything you can about everyone and everything, and be prepared!

1.4 GETTING ORGANIZED—SETTING UP THE TRAINING TEAM AND PROJECT TEAM STRUCTURE

Organizing the Team

It's extremely important to set up the training and project teams so that they work closely together. The training must be developed in tandem with the system and/or software as it's rolled out. Often, training teams come from a part of the company that has little or no contact with I/T prior to the software development effort. This is a big mistake because few generic trainers have seen projects with the size or scope of a large enterprisewide software rollout. While the specific team and level of involvement of the various members would depend on the specifics of the project, it is extremely important to have trainers who specialize in I/T training and understand the complexities of software rollouts. The main point is that all affected functions of the organization must participate in the program's development and implementation in order to foster commitment to the new program throughout the organization and also to improve the design of the new program.

Organizing the project team involves developing the concept and vision; dividing labor; understanding that you will need many skills, more than can be found in one person; and recognizing and planning for constraints from the start. It's also important to account for resources, both human and otherwise. You may need time logs, scheduling software, and other software and documentation tools. It's also important to develop standard procedures. (Administration is not a four-letter word!) Other specifics that are essential to keeping the project team moving ahead include creating objectives, developing an organization chart (for larger teams), filling out time sheets, and creating and keeping meeting notes. Also, remember to schedule regular meetings by type (status versus action). Establish rules of engagement with the boss, client, gurus, facilities staff, etc., now and save trouble later.

Recruiting among a pool of resources is an activity the training project manager will find to be absolutely critical. Depending on the structure of the organization and the competition process between various projects, this may include interviewing people and assessing their skill sets. An important thing to realize is that the project will be only as successful as the manager and the project team are. Incompetence kills the best of plans each and every time.

Staff on a project would ideally be static. The project manager and the teams should be part of the birth and final completion of a project. However, this is rarely the case. Some turnover is expected among team members, but, again, a key person leaving a project can be devastating. What is usually not expected, but does frequently happen, however, is a change of project managers in midcourse. This can be particularly bad since the reasons behind such changes usually involve politics. Be extremely careful and thorough in documentation efforts in case a team member leaves. Documentation can also ease the learning curve of new hires in midproject.

The responsibilities of the training project manager are significant. They include all aspects of project success criteria completion: that is, on time, within budget and scope. Ultimately, the project manager bears the responsibility of failures and successes. It is thus important that the selection of a candidate project manager be based on relevant evidence of past successes and breadth of expertise.

The typical project staff is divided into three categories. There are project managers, the core teams, and the contracted teams. The core team members are those who see the project through, while the contracted team members are those who will perform particular project tasks. In organizing the project team, the following characteristics are critical to look for in good I/T trainers:

- Excellent communication and people skills
- Commitment
- Shared responsibility
- Flexibility
- Task-oriented
- Ability to work within schedule and constraints
- Trust and mutual support
- Team-oriented

- Open-minded
- Ability to work across structure and authorities
- Facility with project management tools
- Familiarity with use of training material development tools

Certainly the most important is communication skills. Regardless of skill level, if trainers cannot communicate the information well, they are essentially useless. This topic will be covered more in Chapter 6 in the section discussing whether to use professional trainers or subject matter experts.

Setting Up the Team Structure

Ideally, members of the I/T training staff would be combined on a project team with some HR folks. This team would report to a training team leader, who would report to the head of the software rollout project. Even if the I/T training staff report within the CIO's purview, it's important to have the training team members who are responsible for the software rollout report to, or work closely with, the project team. After all, it's the project team that will suffer and be both the subject and object of complaints if the training goes badly. Figure 1-1 shows an ideal layout.

Note that although the training team leader technically reports to the I/T training manager, that person also has a "dotted-line" reporting relationship to the software rollout project manager. Because the materials produced by the training project team serve and reflect the software rollout team, these two groups must work closely together. Detailed job descriptions are included in Appendix B and can be found on McGraw-Hill's

FIGURE 1-1

Training Program Project Team Organization Chart

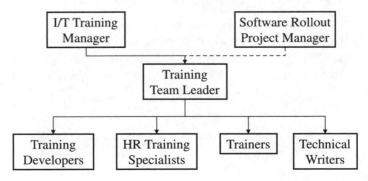

TABLE 1-1

Training Project Team Job Description Summary

Title	Responsibilities	Deliverables
Training team leader	Sell, manage, and coordinate the training program	Project plan, executive summary, status reports, presentations
Training developer	Perform needs analysis, design training program, work with technical writers to produce materials	Training materials, evaluation plan and materials, feedback forms
HR training specialist	Monitor the training program for regulatory compliance, participate in training and evaluation designs	Regulatory compliance state ments, HR follow-up plans, employee development impact statements
Trainer	Deliver the training effectively	Usability and participant feed-back on training materials
Technical writer	Create and maintain training documentation and other materials	Training manuals, documenta-tion, updates, project document library

website at www.books.mcgraw-hill.com/training/download. The forms can then be opened, edited, and printed using Microsoft Word or other word processing software. Table 1-1 briefly summarizes the responsibilities of each team member. Each of the positions shown in the table contributes a unique set of deliverables to the process and program. More than one of each position on this team may be needed, depending on the project size.

1.5 COORDINATING TRAINING AND SOFTWARE PROJECT TEAM ACTIVITIES

Once the project team members have been selected and the project team has been organized, it's important to keep the activities closely aligned with the software project team. Some easy methods for ensuring that the training program serves the needs of the software rollout are:

- Have training team leaders and members attend the software team's meetings and vice versa.
- Hold joint status meetings at least weekly.
- Use groupware tools such as Lotus Notes.

- Make sure that the training team participates in the systems analysis for the new software.

The delivery of quality training is a team effort. The instructors must be knowledgeable of the subject matter and be skilled in the techniques of training preparation and delivery. Software project team members must be prepared to receive the initial training and must be capable of assisting the training team in developing training for users. When these mutually supportive objectives are in place, the training will be effective.

To ensure that all training is thorough, existing partnerships with the I/T and business departments should be strengthened and others established. Offices responsible for policy, procedure, and system operation should establish effective partnerships. Partners may include multiple divisions within the same department. Customer interests must also be represented in the partnership to guarantee that any unique items and relevant case studies are presented in the training. The partners must develop training that incorporates not only the "how to" and "why," but also "hands-on" activities to reinforce skill development.

The training team must work hand in hand with the software rollout team to be successful. The training team needs the knowledge of the product from the rollout team, and the rollout team needs the training to help their users be comfortable and productive with the new software. A good synergy can produce great results, but if the two groups are at odds, disaster is pretty much assured!

The first imperative for any staff department is responsiveness to what its customers see as their needs. What they see as needed may be 100 percent tactical in nature. It may be entirely short term. It may even be shortsighted. Software project teams usually operate in "management-by-crisis" mode, and training users is going to be a last-minute, "Oops! Almost forgot!" task. Sealing the relationship between the software and training teams will help the software rollout team understand that training must be developed right alongside the software.

One of the key outcomes of dealing well with the internal training customer's training needs is that it makes it possible to suggest other needs that the customer has not thought of. Once the customer's tactical requirements for training have been successfully met, the training manager can bring up issues and needs that are not tactical in nature but may be more important in the long run. Such issues might include making sure professionals know something of the businesses in which they work and managing the staff and communicating with their customers on their own terms.

Discovering these kinds of strategic training needs adds a proactive dimension to the training department's responsibilities. The training team should see this as both a right to be earned and an obligation to be met. That is, you must earn the right to bring up strategic, long-term, nonurgent issues to a customer. And you must make sure you meet the obligation to do so—it's easy to lose sight of these issues that are less urgent, but more important, amid the tactical preoccupations of the line manager/customer.

The training manager must also build relationships with internal training customers. This means spending time with them that is not transaction-oriented or issue-oriented, that is not focused on finding or suggesting needs and dealing with them. In fact, the whole point of building a relationship with a customer is to establish a productive environment for issues and transactions, to build a backdrop for dealing with specific needs in the future. The goal is to create a context of knowing each other on a person-to-person basis, a context in which issues and transactions can be handled with confidence and trust.

Thus, the training manager establishes a program of regular contacts with customers, a mutual "what's going on" update from time to time, a quick drop-in visit now and again. These meetings should always be on the customer's turf, though done in a planned and managed way. Above all, the contact should be built on the foundation of previous success in handling training needs. Creating relationships with customers cannot be done if a history of solid training service is not there to build on.

1.6   COORDINATING TRAINING AND HR TEAM ACTIVITIES

Training is part of the human resource development (HRD) process, and so it's important to make sure that the training team works closely with the organization's human resource department during the analysis, design, and implementation of the training program. HR departments are usually staffed with people who provide training in the workplace but for whom training is not their primary responsibility. HR people should play key roles in training and raising the competency of the work force.

HR people can assist the training team by helping to change employer and employee attitudes toward training and to develop an environment in which employees can grow and learn. HR staff can also provide tools and ideas for ongoing mentorship. If the senior HR person (usually a vice president) has considerable influence in the organization, HR may be able to motivate employers to be open and receptive to working with the training team. As the training team creates courses, classes, programs, and certifications, the HR staff can document and measure organizational development initiatives. HR can also help track recurring training requirements to maintain employee competence.

HR can help training teams build training around organizational and individual objectives and strategies. This makes training more relevant and gets everyone focused on applying the new skills to the organization's key priorities and goals. HR teams are also responsible for the assessment and development of professional competencies, based on the new requirements.

There is a growing awareness by managers of the lost productivity that occurs when line employees leave normal work duties for training, especially for time lost in travel. The HR staff can help the training team demonstrate the ROI of training to reduce management anxiety. HR can also help lessen concern over high overall costs of traditional classroom training by raising the visibility of productivity gains in many operational areas. And HR can help the training team cope with the increased complexity of software resulting in a greater need for training for employees.

Though they may never become expert in ISD, members of the HR team know enough about the ins and outs of the organizational climate, culture, and work processes to become great allies. They can offer information about who is new or tenured, who is the "guru" and on what subject, and who needs to be convinced to get on board. By partnering with training, HR staff may gain credibility with participants over time. People in the organization view the training team as a trusted guide and helper. HR is often looking for a way to improve its image. HR tends to stay in touch with employees and the culture. While the training team concentrates on deliverables and measurements, the HR team can work to ensure employee cooperation.

To begin building a relationship with HR, choose an HR person who makes you feel comfortable. Share information about both the formal and informal structures within the training organization. Involve the HR staff early in the process when assessing and defining training needs. Introduce the HR staff to the training team and the staff to be trained. Also, involve the HR staff with employees at all levels represented in the training program(s) in order for the HR staff to get multiple perspectives and a feel for what's happening.

Becoming real partners takes time and consistency; it doesn't happen on the first day. Over time, however, the trust, knowledge, and continual learning on the part of both the training and HR teams will help make the HR staff members "honorary" members of your staff.

CASE: ACME WIDGETS—PRESENTING THE PROGRAM PROPOSAL TO MANAGEMENT

Bob (the training manager) recently met with Connie (the CIO). Connie and Richard (VP of human resources) are both convinced that there must be a formal, integrated training program for the two products (WCS and KIS). Connie and Richard realize that it would be extremely difficult for systems and end-user personnel to learn both of these software packages through on-the-job training. Bob has created a proposal that would address both the unique needs of the two packages and the different levels of technical proficiency required by I/T staff versus end users. Bob also talked to several other executives and got a list of some of their issues with training programs, including:

- Cost
- Vague or badly defined benefits and payback statements
- Unclear or lacking evaluation methods
- Lack of employee enthusiasm
- Employees learning new skills and then leaving for more money

By talking to the executives directly, Bob learned that some managers were feeling productivity pressure and that they thought that good training could help relieve this pressure. Bob also talked to Carol, a senior manager, who felt that training could compensate for some other significant factors affecting AWI, including:

- Employee turnover
- Technical breakthrough/internal adjustment
- Rightsizing—internal adaptation to external change
- Fast growth
- Integration of new team members
- Culturally diverse coworkers
- Structural adjustments to do more with less

After interviewing many people, Bob felt that the impact of these factors on AWI could be lessened with a good, effective training program. He put together a training program that addressed the overall needs (to be detailed in Chapter 2), and he also developed a high-level budget and time line (to be detailed in Chapter 3). He stated clearly the benefits, noting how the training program would serve the specific needs of the organization. He carefully covered each of the major issues that management had with training programs in general. Bob also worked with the software rollout teams to find out the hardware and software requirements for the training workstations and included them in the presentation to avoid surprises. He was very successful and received a "go" decision.

Note: This presentation is found in Appendix C and on McGraw-Hill's website at www.books.mcgraw-hill.com/training/download. The forms can then be opened, edited, and printed using Microsoft Word or other word processing software.

Coming Up in Chapter 2

With the decision to move ahead, Bob will tell Mike (the training team lead) and the training team to begin the process of analyzing the training needs and gathering the training program requirements of the I/T staff and business users at Acme Widgets.

R E F E R E N C E S

Brier, T. F. (1993, April 26). Follow the business leaders. *Information Week* (517), 60.

Briggs, L. J., & Gagne, R. M. (1979). *Principles of instructional design* (2d ed.). New York: Holt, Rinehard and Winston.

Chaturvedi, A. (1996). *Class notes for management 683; advanced concepts in information systems.* West Lafayette, IN: The Krannert School of Management in-house press, Purdue University.

Davenport, T. R. (1995). Wanted: Business savvy developers. *Information Week* (551), 64.

Carey, L., & Dick, W. (1996). *The systematic design of instruction* (4th ed.). New York: HarperCollins.

Ebert, R. J., & Griffin, R. W. (1995). *Business essentials.* Englewood Cliffs, NJ: Prentice Hall.

Glaser, Perry. (1996, December). Forrester view column. *CIO, 10* (5), 32–36.

Herbst, P. (1995, September). R-e-s-p-e-c-t, what do you mean to management? *Application Development Trends, 2* (9) 18–20.

Leshin, C. B., Pollock, J., & Reigeluth, C. M. (1992). *Instructional design strategies and tactics.* Englewood Cliffs, NJ: Educational Technology Publications.

McGee, M. K. (1996). Careers column. *Information Week* (642), 98.

Posner, G. J., Rudnitsky, & A. N. (1986). *Course design: A guide to curriculum development for teachers* (3d ed.). New York: Longman.

Springer, W. P., Jr. (1996). I/S-Business dialogue. *Application Development Trends, 3* (9), 50–52.

Stokes, S. L. (1993). Blueprint for business literacy. *Information Systems Management, 10,* 73–76.

Tate, C. E., Jr., Megginson, L. C., Scott, C. R., Jr., & Trueblood, L. R. (1985). *Successful small business management* (4th ed.). Plano, TX: Business Publications, Inc.

Trepper, C. H. (1996, July). Academia needs to respond to I/S demand for business savvy. *Application Development Trends, 3,* (7), 26–29.

Trepper, C. H. (1996, October). Learning toward the cutting edge. *Application Development Trends, 3* (10), 33–37.

Trepper, C. H. (1996). *Business literacy for computer information systems* (2d ed.). West Lafayette, IN: Learning Systems, Inc.

CHAPTER 2

How to Conduct a Training Needs Analysis

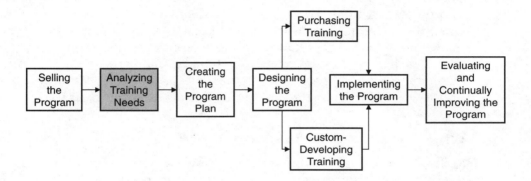

In This Chapter

OVERVIEW

After the program has been sold to management, a needs analysis must be done to determine the required training, the current organization/staff skill set, and methods for addressing the gap. Once the needs are known, the program plan can be prepared.

What Is a Training Needs Analysis?

A training needs analysis (TNA) identifies who requires training (and who doesn't) and in what. A training needs analysis also identifies deficiencies in skills and knowledge in workplace performance and defines training solutions to meet organizational learning requirements. A needs analysis is a major organizational task. The process often requires input from jobholders, managers, and training personnel and therefore needs to be carefully structured and directed.

The training department's job is to make sure the right people learn the right things at the right time. So in terms of a training department's activity, the process of searching out who needs to learn what (and who doesn't), and when they need to, is a top priority. Ongoing needs analysis should be a rolling, evolving process that moves as the business does, constantly gathering data about what sort of learning is needed and what sorts of priorities there are in terms of topics and people. Needs analysis should be a high-priority task the training team performs on a constant, regular basis.

Why a Training Needs Analysis?

Rolling out software without considering user needs is like building a house on sand. By carrying out effective user needs analyses at a very early stage in the life cycle of the rollout, you ensure that you produce what your customer wants and how your customer wants it. Performing a complete, accurate user needs analysis will strengthen your rollout by allowing you to:

- Accurately determine specific user needs
- Which makes your users central to the process
- Which increases their buy-in to the rollout
- Which in turn reduces resistance to change
- Thus smoothing and lessening the learning curve

The members of the software rollout team will thank you for helping them. Users who are well trained are much more comfortable in the new environment of an ERP system, which makes the rollout team "look good." I/T staff who are comfortable in their new software environment are more likely to use the new software to improve their productivity, which drives down overall I/T costs.

The TNA also identifies who does *not* need training. While this may seem obvious, you might be surprised at the number of people who are sent to training even though they don't need it. Corporations waste enormous amounts of money each year sending employees to training on subjects that they already know or will never use. A TNA can help reduce or even eliminate that problem.

The Needs Analysis Process

The process of discovering and documenting training needs for a software rollout involves four major steps:

1. Identify what knowledge, skills, abilities, and experiences (KSAEs) employees need to perform.
2. Measure what KSAEs an employee (group) currently has.
3. Compare the current KSAEs with required KSAEs and document the gaps.
4. Using the gap data, create the training specifications (to be done in Chapter 4).

Since the purpose of this book is to create a training program that teaches people how to use new software, there are several questions to ask at the beginning of the process, including:

- Which employees need to learn what?
- Why do they need to learn it?
- At what depth do they need to learn it?
- What is the priority of the training in the eyes of management and employees?
- What are the priorities in terms of topics?
- What are the priorities in terms of time? (When does the training need to be completed? This is detailed further in Chapter 3.)

Answering these questions will provide the basis for the training needs analysis process. Appendix F contains the TNA process and deliverables checklist from which the following tasks are drawn:

1. Document the overall needs.
2. Document the business tasks accomplished for each feature/function.
3. Document timing.
4. Document new knowledge/skill requirements.
5. Define *who* will do *what* in the new world.

6. Document current audience KSAEs.

7. Analyze the gap in competencies between current skills and required skills.

8. Present new business tasks and job design to management.

These eight tasks are part of a standard needs analysis, and are integrated into the process outlined in this chapter. Each of the following sections (2.1–2.4) uses some of the above tasks. The forms shown in this chapter and in the casework at the end of this chapter can be found in Appendix G, "Sample Forms."

2.1   WHAT SOFTWARE IS BEING INSTALLED? DETERMINING THE OVERALL NEEDS

There are several steps in determining the training needs for a software roll-out. The first step is for the training staff and the I/T staff to work together and document the software's features and functions. Any technology training requirements, such as how to operate new hardware, must be documented. The timing of the rollout must also be factored in to ensure timely delivery of the training. The I/T resources responsible for each part of the software must be determined to ensure access to the proper subject matter experts during training development. The last step in this section is to document which positions, but not necessarily which person, will do what in the new world.

With this information in hand, the training team can determine who will use which parts of the software, and work with HR to design the training necessary to make the incumbents or new employees productive in the new or redesigned jobs. This section only deals with the tasks necessary to identify the training needed in the new world. Sections 2.2, 2.3, and 2.4 present the tasks necessary to examine the current world and help employees cross the gap between old and new work environments.

Step 1. Document the Feature/Function Hierarchy

The feature/function hierarchy must be completed down to a level of detail that allows the training developer to determine concrete learning objectives. Sometimes this means working with a systems analyst and documenting the software flows down to the screen level. Because the I/T staff and business users will need to know their specific areas thoroughly, it is necessary to document the overall needs and the business tasks that correspond to each feature/function.

To begin this step, make a feature/function hierarchy diagram like the one shown in Figure 2-1. Descriptions (about a paragraph long) must be written for each box on the chart to provide perspective from an overall view of the system down to the function of each field and shortcut key, if any. A sample descriptive paragraph for the F1 function key might be as follows:

> The F1 key is located in the upper left-hand corner of the keyboard. It allows a user to get help at the screen or field level. If a user presses the F1 key while the cursor is in a specific field, help about that field will be displayed first. A user may then select more options from the help menu across the top of the help screen. To exit help, click the X button in the upper right-hand corner of the help screen.

In addition to a narrative paragraph, it's often helpful to have screen shots with arrows and "balloons" to help the user (both I/T and business) understand the context of the training material.

Once the feature/function set of the software has been documented, the business task for each feature/function must be correlated with the software, with the exception of access and help-related features (see Step 2). This is important because the organization staff members must understand how the training will help them use the software to improve their job performance and satisfaction. That correlation usually takes the form of a matrix like the one in Table 2-1, filled out with a sample from the Widget Control System software.

FIGURE 2-1

Feature/Function Hierarchy

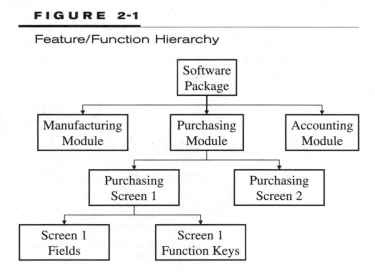

TABLE 2-1

Item	Function	Screen	Module	Business Task	Organization Unit
1.	Update widget description	WMD01	Inventory	Maintain inventory master file	Inventory control
2.	Change employee title	WHR02	HR	Promote employee	HR
3.	Transmit order	WPO01	Purchasing	Order raw material	Manufacturing

In the table, each of the functions within a screen corresponds to a screen ID, a module in which the screen exists, and a business task within an organizational unit or department. This information is critical to training development because it enables the trainer to provide the trainee with both the "big picture" and detailed information on why the training is necessary and how it will change the way people work. This form will drive the design phase detailed in Chapter 4. This matrix also brings together the training team, the software rollout team, and the user community, thus enhancing the collaborative nature of the rollout effort.

If the software being rolled out is nonbusiness software, such as groupware or a suite like Microsoft Office, there probably won't be a direct correlation of features or functions to any specific business function. It is useful, however, to classify the features into various levels of users, whether in I/T or a business area. An example classifying Microsoft Office features is shown in Table 2-2.

The function or skill to be used in the software, the screen, and the product can be described in as little or much detail as necessary. The skill levels can be determined based on a broad survey of staff. This type of table could be used with an ERP package as well, but it's usually more helpful to break ERP usage down by business function, as shown in Table 2-1. This form will be used in classifying the training sessions and determining content and trainees for specific features.

When you have properly classified the software feature/function set, you must determine the timing and sequence of the rollout, because this will drive the sequencing of the training. It's usually necessary for the training team to produce a project plan for the training program, and then work with the rollout project manager(s) to integrate the training schedule with the rollout plan. These schedules can be produced in any viable project management tool, such as Microsoft Project. The process checklists

TABLE 2-2

Item	Function	Screen	Product	Level/User Type
1.	Cut/copy and paste	Main window	MS Word	Beginner
2.	Center cell contents	Main spreadsheet	MS Excel	Beginner
3.	Group objects	Slide	MS PowerPoint	Beginner
4.	New doc via template	Main window	MS Word	Intermediate
5.	Center across columns	Main spreadsheet	MS Excel	Intermediate
6.	Slide special effects	Slide sorter/show	MS PowerPoint	Intermediate
7.	Word macros	Main window	MS Word	Advanced
8.	Excel visual basic mod	VB script sheet	MS Excel	Advanced
9.	MS Word to HTML document conversion	Main window or template	MS Word	Power user

contained in Appendix F can serve as the task lists to incorporate into a project plan. Remember that any changes in the timing of the rollout must be accounted for in the training program plan.

Step 2. Document Security, Help, and Access Factors

Issues such as security, help (on-line versus manuals versus help desk), and how to access the software (by clicking on an item in a menu or by clicking on an icon) must be documented and resolved. While these issues are not directly related to the use of the software, they certainly impact its use. The business users or I/T staff members must have access to the software as needed to perform their jobs. It's important to gather needs and develop training on how to:

- Obtain a user ID and password
- Resolve password problems (e.g., expired or forgotten passwords)
- Log on to the system
- Start and exit the software
- Get help and report bugs
- Request changes or maintenance to the software

In many cases, the approach to these tasks changes drastically with the rollout of new software. For example, if the new software is running on a different server or new type of hardware (e.g., IBM versus Unisys), the procedure for logging into and out of the system may change completely.

Or if the software support has been outsourced to the vendor, the procedure and phone number for getting help may change.

Step 3. Document Technology Training Issues

Some software vendors assume that a user (business or I/T) has a certain level of techno-literacy before using their software. Unfortunately, the assumed level is often much higher than the actual level. So it's important to document issues related to hardware or other technology training needs. For example, if a new electronic time-reporting system is being installed as part of an HR package rollout, employees must know how to "badge in" and "badge out" on the electronic time clock.

If employees are making the transition from mainframe "dumb terminals" to PCs, it's extremely important to teach them how to use the hardware properly. Inserting disks or CDs in the machine incorrectly can cause permanent damage. With regard to laptops, it's extremely important to teach first-time users how to handle the machine and how to insert spare batteries and disk drives. Specific technology training requirements will become clear when the current skills audit and job analysis is done, as discussed in Section 2.2.

Step 4. Document Who Will Use Which Parts of the Software

When all the new tasks and requirements are documented, the next step is to determine who will use which parts of the software. The job/position-to-feature/function-and-business-task matrix presents the vision of who will use specific feature/functions of the software. Notice that this matrix does not have specific names, but simply positions. Because the person in the specific position can change, it is usually more useful to document the training needs by job rather than person. This matrix shows which users will be involved in which business tasks.

This document doesn't have to be prepared by the training team. It may be prepared by the rollout team or by senior management in combination with HR. But no matter who prepares it, the training team must have access to this information to complete the needs analysis. A sample document for both business and I/T staff might resemble Table 2-3.

In the table, jobs 3 and 4 are I/T staff. Job 3 is the security manager, and job 4 supports the accounting department. Be sure to sort this table according to either business task or module once all positions are entered. That way, the number of people in each class becomes more clear, and train-

TABLE 2-3

Item	Job/Position	Function	Screen	Module	Business Task
1.	Billing clerk	New invoice	Inv. Master	Billing	Enter invoices
2.	Dock supervisor	Update item	Item Master	Inventory	Maintain item status
3.	I/T security anal.	New user	User Master	Security	N/A
4.	Sr. P/A—credit	New credit	A/R Master	A/R	Support accounting

ing can be planned more accurately. This form will be used to schedule people in each of the jobs for training.

Another advantage of classifying training by module is that the business users get the same information as the I/T staff. There is often a disconnect between what the users learn about operating the software and what the I/T staff learns about maintaining it. By putting the business users in the same operational classes as the I/T staff, the I/T staff learn how users operate the system. Thus, when there are problems or support issues, communication is clearer, and all parties start with the same frame of reference.

Step 5. Document Training for the New Jobs

Designing training for the rollout begins with using the results of the needs analysis to determine the characteristics of the new jobs. In order to analyze jobs and skills, it is necessary to break the task down into the identification of smaller units. Jobs are described in terms of tasks, and functionally in terms of roles. The key question in functional analysis is: How do the job components and required competency units meet organizational and operational objectives? The key question in job analysis is: What are the components of the job (tasks, roles, etc.)? What units of competency does the job require? The key question in skill auditing is: Does the performance of individuals demonstrate the competencies required by the job? The training team members may be involved in actually designing the new jobs, or they may simply be customers or the HR team.

Regardless of who produces the actual job descriptions, the training team must have complete information about the new jobs. This includes work activities and software modules or features to be used, any automated forms or materials needed, and the various workplace environment factors that affect workers each day. Information about work activities that must be obtained includes:

- What is accomplished
- How, why, and when an employee performs an activity
- Processes, procedures, and records
- Materials processed
- Documentation or other written materials produced (format, size, complexity, etc.)
- Services rendered
- Related jobs that may give information or may need analysis if the job is significantly changed

It's also important to specify or obtain information about work performance measurement and standards for the new jobs and tasks. In some ERP packages, it's very difficult to back out of a completed transaction, and so performance standards become very important with respect to error counts.

When new software is implemented that dramatically changes the way a business functions, there are often factors that change within the job context, including:

- Working conditions
- Work schedule
- Organizational context
- Social context
- Incentives
- Financial factors
- Nonfinancial factors

These factors can often deeply affect employees. The training team has a major opportunity to help the organization through a difficult time by preparing the work force for the new environment in a smooth, seamless, comfortable manner.

The final outcome of the job training design process is a training description for each job, approved by HR, which could be expected to include an outline of:

- The overall accountabilities and the training needed to ensure that the employee is competent
- The skills required before commencement of the job
- Any skills to be learned on the job with OJT

Some basic characteristics of well-designed job training descriptions include meeting individual needs for psychological growth, especially responsibility, job challenge, and achievement. Also important is identifying training needs that will provide the jobholder with:

- *Direct feedback.* Evaluation of performance should be timely and direct.
- *New learning.* Training enables people to feel that they are growing.
- *Scheduling.* People should be aware of exactly when or how often they'll be in training.
- *Control over resources.* Individuals should have some control over when their training occurs so they'll be able to schedule resources to cover for them.
- *Personal accountability.* People should be held accountable for the training.

Problems associated with job training design include the fact that a good job training program is time-consuming and costly. As workers are told to expect better job satisfaction, they may raise their expectations beyond what's possible. Also, the new jobs won't produce tangible performance improvements for some time after the beginning of the effort, which is likely to raise the ire of management, particularly if lots of money was spent on the training program development.

Avoiding problems during the training design process can be accomplished by ensuring that this process, above all others, is a collaborative one. Establish agreement that the job descriptions will define the future working of the job. Arrange for experienced employees to help with the job description process themselves. Involve management in reviewing the prepared job description. Finalize the job descriptions with representatives of workers, unions, and management. Once the broad functions of a position are identified, it will be easier to set goals for employees holding that position.

The last step before assessing the current work force is to identify the specific training needs for the new world. This information is best stored in some kind of database because you will no doubt want to sort and view it in various ways. Regardless of how the data are viewed, the key information that must be entered must, at a minimum, include:

- Job/position
- Department/organizational unit
- Software module
- Software screen
- Software feature/function (includes possible paths and errors— may be flowcharted)

- Estimated number of classes
- Estimated number of hours

A sample view of the data by software module for WCS might resemble Table 2-4. The information in the table can be sorted by any of the columns to make it more useful. For example, a senior manager in purchasing may want to know how many classes his purchasing agent must take so that the manager can estimate lost time on the job. To facilitate this "query" the data could be sorted by job or organization unit. It is best to store the data in a database if possible. A spreadsheet will eventually become too cumbersome, and is not capable of custom-reporting needs that may be necessary throughout the project.

2.2   DECIDING WHO NEEDS TRAINING, IN WHAT AREAS—AND WHO DOESN'T

The first major needs analysis step, then, is defining the skill requirements of each job to properly use the new software. The next step is to determine whether the individuals who are available for these jobs have the competencies demanded of them in order to do the jobs effectively. The odds are that most current employees will need significant training. There are various techniques for assessing the current work force, one of which is the skills audit/skills analysis, which is an assessment of the competencies possessed by individuals in performing the job.

A skills audit may indicate an almost complete overlap between the demands of the job and the skills required. If the existing skills and the new skills seen to be required as a result of the audit have some overlap, but by

TABLE 2-4

Item	Software Module	Software Function	Screen	Job	Org. Unit	Est. Classes	Est. Hours
1.	Purchasing	Update widget description	WMD01	Purchasing agent	Purchg.	2	6
2.	Accounting	Enter new G/L acct.	ARM01	Accounting clerk	Accting. —G/L	3	12
3.	Manufacturing	Let down	MSH03	Forklift driver	Whse.	1	8
4.	HR	Enter new candidate	HRA02	Recruiter	HR	1	8

no means a complete overlap, it will be possible to bridge the gap through training. If there is virtually no overlap, as is often the case in new software rollouts, training will be difficult, and will require a complete program plan as specified in this book.

It is important to remember that simply asking workers if they have the skills needed to do the job may elicit a less than truthful response. Some workers feel if they do not respond affirmatively to such questions, desired opportunities will go to others. Others may hide their lack of skill or understanding to avoid embarrassment.

An assessment of worker competence needs to be conducted so workers perform independently, rather than leaning on someone else's abilities. Opportunities for employees to demonstrate practical skills should be provided without demeaning the workers or endangering their job security. Some questions to ask during a skills audit are:

- Which skills are possessed and used by a person in his or her current job?
- Which skills are possessed but not used?
- How well do the person's skills match each of the new jobs?
- Which skills need to be acquired by an individual to suit a particular job?
- What are the main skill gaps for a particular group of workers?
- How big is the gap between what workers need to know and what they currently know?

If possible, the information that results from these questions should be quantified. For example, the size of the gap could be rated on a scale of 1 to 10, where 1 is a small gap and 10 is a large gap. Information for current employee skill assessments may be gathered from sources such as:

- Employee selection data
- Reviews of employee performance
- Worker skill, ability, and knowledge inventories
- Plans for future vacancies or promotions (e.g., corporate politics)
- Laws and regulations requiring training

If formal gathering methods are needed, it's important to use a well-recognized, proven tool to gather data on current capabilities. There are several time-tested methods of gathering current skill data:

- Questionnaires are the most commonly used method of extracting information from users—and the most commonly misused.

- Observational analyses provide direct information about user requirements. However, effective observation is not simple. Behaviors take place in real time. Effective observation techniques capture and analyze these behaviors to understand the work being done. This can be difficult.
- Interviews provide opportunities for investigators to pursue specific areas of interest in detail. The interviews can be unstructured, semistructured, or structured—the difference relates to the extent to which the questions are preplanned, in both content and order. The interview data can also be subjected to attribution and/or content analyses.
- Rating scales provide opportunities to address a range of behavioral aspects, including attitudes. There is a large body of research information that deals with the nature of different kinds of rating scales, scaling analyses, and attitude development and measurement.

Each of these methods has its upside and downside. The method chosen should result from a consensus of users, I/T staff, and training team members, as all will need to participate.

The software and technology being rolled out is new to the organization, so it's unlikely that current staff will have any real expertise in the specific product. The two forms shown in Figures 2-2 and 2-3, respectively, provide samples that can be used to gather both specific software and technology experience and general technology aptitudes and experience for use in designing the training program to make sure that it meets the needs of the staff.

The first form, Figure 2-2, inventories experience with a specific package, in this case WCS. Notice that in the forms there are places to record both years of experience and skill level. These two are *not* always equivalent. An employee may have 3 years of experience in a particular software module, but in those 3 years the employee may have only performed simple functions. Never assume that 5 years of experience means the employee is an expert. The comfort level, the last item in Figure 2-3, is very important, particularly if the person filling out the form doesn't have much experience with the new software. Interestingly, this person might as likely be a member of the I/T staff as she or he would be a business user. There are many I/T professionals who had a difficult time moving from the mainframe to PCs, so new software can often be as much of a shock to an I/T person as to a business user.

FIGURE 2-2

Name:								
Title:								
Organization Unit:								
Date:								
Item	Software Module	Software Function	Screen	Years of Experience	Skill Level: 1 – 5 (1=Beginner, 5=Expert)			
1.	Purchasing	Update widget description	WMD01		1	2	3	4	5
2.	Accounting	Enter new G/L acct.	ARM01		1	2	3	4	5
3.	Manufacturing	Let down	MSH03		1	2	3	4	5
4.	HR	Enter new candidate	HRA02		1	2	3	4	5

To make the rollout more effective, it is imperative that the training team and management have a thorough understanding of the strengths and weaknesses of all staff members. Awareness of both the business goals and each person's strengths and weaknesses will allow teams to be formed that are better equipped to deliver. A skills audit examines the needs of the business and the skills of each individual and presents the results in a concise way. While sometimes controversial, this information has a number of important benefits:

- The right staff with the most suitable skills can be placed in the right positions.
- Areas can be identified in which internal cross-training can take place.
- Overcapacity or underutilization can be identified and addressed.

FIGURE 2-3

Name:
Title:
Organization Unit:
Date:
Years of Overall Computer Experience:

Overall Skill Level

Beginner   Expert

1   2   3   4   5

Yrs Legacy Computer Experience:

Legacy Computer Skill Level

Beginner   Expert

1   2   3   4   5

Years PC Experience:

PC Skill Level

Beginner   Expert

1   2   3   4   5

How comfortable are you learning new software?

Very Uncomfortable   Very Comfortable

1   2   3   4   5

- Skill and knowledge gaps can be accurately identified, increasing the effectiveness of training.
- Individual staff development plans will be better, resulting in higher morale and lower turnover.
- External recruitment becomes better targeted.

Obviously, these benefits go beyond just the software rollout, and most of the information gathered for the training program development will have far-reaching benefits across the organization. The information gathered during this effort can be used to address organizational communication problems, employee performance issues, and software development/rollout process effectiveness. The forms completed in this step will be the basis for the gap analysis and needs statement when compared with training requirements.

2.3 CREATING A SKILLS INVENTORY DATABASE

To more effectively gather, store, and utilize the current skill base, it's a good idea to store skill inventories in a database. Organizations can effectively and easily determine the number of individuals who have the skills, abilities, and expertise each of the new jobs demands, and the gaps that exist, by entering the information into the database and then extracting it in various forms and sorts. The first step in creating a skills inventory database is to decide what information will be stored. Generally, all the information gathered in this chapter should be stored. This includes:

- Name
- Title
- Organization unit/department
- Years with the organization
- Years of experience with various technologies
- Expertise level with various technologies
- Training classes completed (to be filled in later)

Other information can be added as needed. This database not only can be very helpful in the training area, but also can assist management in making decisions on promotions, replacements, and other HR and organizational matters.

Once you determine what data will be stored, you must determine how the data will be stored. For this task, you may want to request help from your I/T department. If the structure of the database is set up incorrectly, it will make both access and updates difficult. One method of avoiding data obsolescence is for training to partner with another department such as HR.

2.4 CREATING THE GAP ANALYSIS AND TRAINING NEEDS DOCUMENT

Once the future needs and current skill sets are known, the last step is to create the final needs analysis document. This document presents the required training, with the gap between current skills and future needs as the foundation. To formalize the gaps, it's important to match levels of analysis and levels of training content. Content has three levels: organizational, task, and personal. These need to be considered in relation to the three functional levels—organizational, subunit, and individual.

A TNA based on the assumption that individuals are automatically aligned with organizational goals will be inherently unsound. Training should lead to some observable gain in what learners are able to do, and ability can be seen as a combination of knowledge, skills, and attitudes. A gap between the competencies revealed by functional/job analysis and the skills demonstrated by individuals indicates a training need. Table 2-4 and Figures 2-2 and 2-3 provide the information necessary to complete the form in Table 2-5. Note that not all of the people require all of the classes. Sheri only really needs two of the three available classes in WCS because she's been helping the rollout team and thus understands more than a beginner.

It's easy to build the document and justify the training if the current skills assessment and training design were done thoroughly and correctly.

TABLE 2-5

Item	Software Module	Software Function	Screen	Person(s)	Org. Unit	Est. Classes	Est. Hours
1.	Purchasing	Update widget description	WMD01	Jeff Smith	Purchg.	2	6
2.	Accounting	Enter new G/L acct.	ARM01	Sheri Jones	Accting. —G/L	2	8
3.	Manufacturing	Let down	MSH03	Tom Jahnke	Whse.	1	8
4.	HR	Enter new candidate	HRA02	Kirby Smith	HR	1	8

It's important to have a sufficient level of detail to justify the program, but not overwhelm the reader, who is likely a senior manager. An outline might be as follows:

1. Introduction/overview
2. New training needs
   a. Feature/function hierarchy
   b. Feature/function-to-business-task matrix (or difficulty-level list)
   c. Job/position-to-feature/function matrix
   d. Class outline
3. Current staff assessment
   a. Software package skills assessment
   b. General computer skills assessment
4. Gap analysis
   a. Brief explanation of how the classes fill the gaps
   b. Class needs by employee
5. Appendixes with survey details and high-level class descriptions

It's extremely important to correlate the training requirements for the new software with the results of the current assessment. There is often a disconnect between the forms completed and the use of the data. Each of the forms completed in this chapter is used to construct the needs and gap document, which will, in turn, be used to complete the project plan in Chapter 3 and the design in Chapter 4.

CASE: ACME WIDGETS—PRODUCING THE TRAINING NEEDS STATEMENT

With the decision to move ahead, Bob tells Mike (the training team lead) and the training team to begin the process of analyzing the training needs and gathering the training program requirements of the I/T staff and business users at Acme Widgets. The first piece of WCS to be implemented will be the HR part. This is being done so that both HR and management can track the progress of employees through the remainder of the project. Working with the HR department and software rollout team(s) to determine the needs for WCS and KIS, Mike, Shawn, Dave, and Kathy have produced a preliminary task list based on the steps detailed in this section. Jack started putting together a set of forms for the staff to fill out. Trudy in HR has agreed to review and critique the forms.

The first step was to obtain the information necessary to document the major parts of the software packages (WCS and KIS) and break the functions down to the level of detail necessary to develop a training program. For the purpose of this book, the scope of the detailed working example will be limited to developing training for the employee master screen. The feature/function hierarchy for the WCS human resources module is shown in Figure 2-4.

FIGURE 2-4

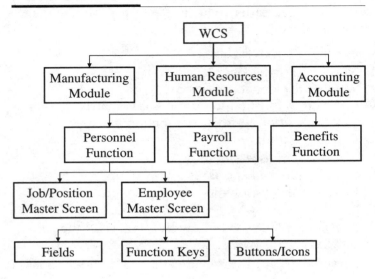

FIGURE 2-5

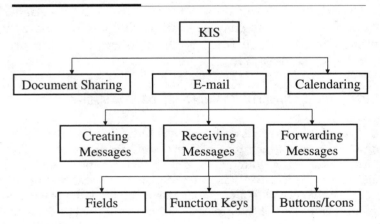

The scope of the detailed working example for KIS will be limited to developing training for the screen that allows users to receive e-mail. Figure 2-5 shows the feature/function hierarchy for KIS.

Kathy contacted with Gary, one of the WCS software team leaders. She sat down with him to talk about the systems analysis documents and how the software functions match up with the human resource business functions. Together,

TABLE 2-6

Item	Function	Screen	Module	Business Task	Organization Unit
1.	Enter new employee	HRM01	HR	Hire employee	HR
2.	Change employee pay	HRP02	HR	Raise/lower pay	HR
3.	Select employee benefits	HRB03	HR	Benefits selection	HR

they came up with a software-feature/function-to-business-task matrix, shown in Table 2-6. The table will be used to ensure that the HR people who are trained on WCS understand how much faster and easier WCS will allow them to do their jobs. In addition, it will help the HR department understand how the new software and training fit in the business.

Shawn met with Lauren, the KIS software rollout team leader, to set a level for each of the features in KIS. Shawn and the rest of the team want to make sure that those employees with very little computer experience don't end up in a class where they're clearly over their heads. Shawn and the other team members also want to make sure that advanced users don't waste time in easy classes. Table 2-7 shows the software feature/function difficulty level by user type for the KIS e-mail feature. The first three features are fairly simple, but there are some enhanced features that are part of the "receive message" function that require some training. Item 6 is a function that allows users to create a custom message template for all messages sent. If there's a standard memo or form used to request information or purchase something, the form can be created and used as needed. This is an advanced function and would only be rolled out to those wishing to become power users.

TABLE 2-7

Item	Function	Screen	Product	Level/User Type
1.	Create message	New memo	KIS	Beginner
2.	Receive message	Folder view	KIS	Beginner
3.	Forward message	Read message	KIS	Beginner
4.	Recover deleted message	Read message	KIS	Intermediate
5.	Shortcut keys	Folder view	KIS	Intermediate
6.	Create message template	Folder view	KIS	Power user

Dave worked with Raj, a network security analyst, to develop a list of possible training needs on what to do when logging on to the system, especially if password problems are encountered.

Once the general features have been outlined and matched to business tasks, the matrix linking the job/position to feature/function to business task must be completed. This helps trainers, software rollout team members, and users understand how the software, training, job, and business task all fit together. It also helps the training and rollout teams ensure that the software and training are aimed at the right job and task. Mike talked to Richard in HR to find out if the rollout and training teams' vision of the training matched the HR department's view. Table 2-8 is the result of those discussions. Note that there is no corresponding grid for KIS. Table 2-7 is sufficient to produce a table like Table 2-8 for KIS.

All the actual needs are gathered and documented, so the training team has a rough idea of the needs by software module. In Chapter 4, the detailed design will be done. Table 2-9 presents a high-level view of the amount of training required to become proficient in the WCS HR module.

TABLE 2-8

Item	Job/Position	Function	Screen	Module	Business Task
1.	HR recruiter	Enter new employee	HRM01	HR	Hire employee
2.	Payroll manager	Change employee pay	HRP02	HR	Raise/lower pay
3.	BPA clerk	Select employee benefits	HRB03	HR	Benefits selection

TABLE 2-9

Item	Software Module	Software Function	Screen	Job	Org. Unit	Est. Classes	Est. Hours
1.	HR	Enter new employee	HRM01	HR recruiter	HR	2	6
2.	HR	Change employee pay	HRP02	Payroll manager	HR	2	12
3.	HR	Select employee benefits	HRB03	BPA clerk	HR	2	8

TABLE 2-10

Item	Software Module	Software Function	Screen	Person(s)	Org. Unit	Est. Classes	Est. Hours
1.	HR	Enter new employee	HRM01	Trudy	HR	1	3
2.	HR	Change employee pay	HRP02	Jane	HR	2	12
3.	HR	Select employee benefits	HRB03	Marsha	HR	1	4

As a team, the members of the training group administered the current skills assessment form for software packages to gauge WCS training needs, and they administered the current skills assessment form for general computer skills for KIS. Table 2-10 is a list of potential students by class for WCS.

Mike and Bob took all the material and facts and figures and put them in a three-ring binder with tabbed dividers. They had the duplicating department make copies for the training team and the software rollout managers. Sharing the information is critical to ensure that the training team provides training that's really needed on the software being rolled out.

Note: The forms and checklists referenced in this chapter (found in Appendixes F and G) are available for use as starting points in the appendixes and on McGraw-Hill's website at www.books.mcgraw-hill.com/training/download. The forms can then be opened, edited, and printed using Microsoft Word or other word processing software.

Coming Up in Chapter 3

Now that the training needs have been documented, the next step is to convert the training needs analysis into a specification for training. But first you must document the remaining tasks and begin building the project plan and budget for the program. The number and approximate complexity of the classes, as well as the number and levels of users, will play a big role in determining the project size and budget.

REFERENCES

Briggs, L. J., & Gagne, R. M. (1979). *Principles of instructional design* (2d ed.). New York: Holt, Rinehart and Winston.

Carey, L., & Dick, W. (1996). *The systematic design of instruction* (4th ed.). New York: HarperCollins.

Leshin, C. B., Pollock, J., & Reigeluth, C. M. (1992). *Instructional design strategies and tactics.* Englewood Cliffs, NJ: Educational Technology Publications.

Posner, G. J., & Rudnitsky, A. N. (1986). *Course design: A guide to curriculum development for teachers* (3d ed.). New York: Longman.

Rothwell, W. J., & Cookson, P. S. (1997). *Beyond instruction: Comprehensive program planning for business and education.* San Francisco: Jossey-Bass.

Wager, W. W., Gagne, R. M., & Briggs, L. J. (1992). *Principles of instructional design.* Fort Worth, TX: Harcourt, Brace, Jovanovich.

CHAPTER 3

Creating a Budget and Time Line for the Training Program

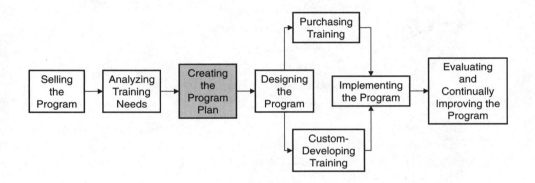

In This Chapter

OVERVIEW

Once the needs are known, the program plan can be prepared. The program plan details the steps, effort (time and manpower), dates, and dollars necessary to produce the training for the software rollout. Relevant items from the training needs analysis provide a clear profile of organizational and employee training needs. Those needs drive the planning activity for the remainder of the program development. The steps taken to complete this activity include:

- Identify critical path activities
- Identify critical path players
- Document drop-dead date ranges
- Estimate the remaining activity hours and costs
- Factor in the elapsed time ranges
- Estimate hardware/software costs
- Calculate the total budget
- Generate alternatives
- Communicate the program plan to partners
- Gain management approval

These steps appear in a process checklist in Appendix F and on McGraw-Hill's website at www.books.mcgraw-hill.com/training/download. The forms can then be opened, edited, and printed using Microsoft Word or other word processing software.

In designing the training program, priorities and overall need can be assessed. Time and money can be saved by seeing from the outset how the whole pattern fits together and what the cycle of need will be. Are there external short courses that can be taken advantage of on a regular basis? Is there a foreseeable need for an induction program or for entry-level training? These questions must be answered to ensure a cohesive training program.

3.1 WHEN MUST TRAINING BE COMPLETED? DETERMINING THE CRITICAL PATH AND DROP-DEAD DATES

Critical Path Planning

Most of the time, the development and delivery of training for software rollout is driven by the rollout schedule. Usually, the training team must meet or even beat the software rollout deadlines because training must be ready to go when the software is ready. Critical path planning allows the training team to stay ahead of the work done by the rollout team, thus giving the team an edge in adapting the training development schedule to the inevitable bumps in the road during software rollouts. Critical path planning done well enables a project team to answer such questions as:

- How long will the project take?
- What are the critical tasks that must be completed?
- What are the dependencies between the tasks?
- How long will each task take?
- When must each task start and end?
- Who will be responsible for each task?
- What resources will be required to complete each task?
- How will delayed tasks affect the project?
- What is the impact of a modification to the project scope?
- What is the cost of the project and the cost of each task?
- Is the project on schedule?
- How can slippage problems be corrected?
- What is the project's cost at any point in time?
- What is the best way to speed up the project?

These questions appear in Appendix F and on McGraw-Hill's website at www.books.mcgraw-hill.com/training/download. The forms can then be opened, edited, and printed using Microsoft Word or other word processing software.

These questions provide a starting point for planning the remainder of the training development program. However, in the management of any development project, the unexpected will always happen. Not even the best team can predict everything that could possibly go wrong. Critical path management makes it much easier to deal with any contingency that may arise. Critical path management enables the team to examine surprises and their effect on the project. It makes it possible to reallocate or redirect resources to deal with a problem before it becomes more serious and to minimize its effect on the project. Some of the factors that affect critical path management include:

- Key user availability
- Software (SW) team availability as subject matter experts (SMEs)
- The possibility that managers who must sign off may be unavailable

- The likelihood that if consultants are used part time, some resources may be restricted
- Other resources currently involved in the SW rollout(s)
- Budgets

Other factors can also affect training project management. It's important to account for staffing and technology issues as well, because they seem to pop up when least expected.

Critical paths can be planned in several ways, but the major issue is knowing on whom (or what) you're dependent to complete at least the core tasks of a project. For example, in a software rollout, one of the core tasks is installing the new software so that it can be modified. While the programming teams are likely to be part of the core project team, someone such as an operations person who may actually load the software on the computer may be an ancillary player. Early identification and allocation of resources on the critical path is vital to the success of the project. Appendix F contains the Training Program Plan Estimating Guide, which provides a list of activities for the rest of the project. Check this list to determine the major critical path activities for your project. This guide is also available on McGraw-Hill's website at www.books.mcgraw-hill.com/training/download. The forms can then be opened, edited, and printed using Microsoft Word or other word processing software.

There are also factors that are unique to training and documentation projects that aren't easily found in standard project management books. JoAnn T. Hackos is president of Denver, Colorado–based Comtech Services (www.comtech-serv.com), and the author of *Managing Your Documentation Projects*. According to Hackos, some of the issues to be considered in planning a training rollout include:

- *Rollout schedule fluctuations.* Training contingency plans are needed in case there are dramatic changes in the software rollout schedule.
- *What is the source of the new training material?* Because of the amount of work on rollout projects, there is often difficulty getting rollout resources to help with training.
- *Are there a sufficient number of subject matter experts to help with the training?* Even if rollout staff are available, they must still have the knowledge to be able to train others.
- *Facility planning.* Rollout schedule changes may affect the availability of rooms or outside facilities, and a significant shift in the date may cause an organization to lose deposits.

- *Stability of the rollout project overall.* Is the project going according to plan? Does the rollout team continually assess its position and communicate it to the training team?

As an extra tool to help, Hackos's website has a dependency calculator that is available at http://www.comtech-serv.com/toolpage.htm. It's important to recognize both standard project management issues and issues that are unique to training projects.

Running Alongside the Rollout

It's essential for the scheduling of the training development effort to parallel the rollout schedule, and even better to get slightly ahead. By paralleling the rollout schedule, changes to the training schedule will be easier, and the training staff will maintain some familiarity with the software rollout process. Particularly in the early stages of the software development and rollout process, it's important for the training team to establish itself as a full partner with the rollout team. As the project progresses, the training team should continually exchange information with the rollout team. This enables the training team to stay up-to-date with changes to the rollout schedule.

Staying ahead of the software rollout team means managing your lead times for task completion. Lead times, and the program plan in general, are often affected by personnel constraints, user time availability, and other factors. Many times, classes are scheduled without sufficient notice to students, and either instructors or students who really need to be there can't make it. Lead times are also heavily affected by other organizational happenings. Ongoing projects may possess resources you need to complete your project. It's important to be aware of other projects occurring in the organization, particularly if any resources on your critical path are currently in use by other projects.

To find the critical dates (or date ranges) for the training project, talk to the rollout team, and try to get a copy of the project plan. If there isn't an electronic version of a plan, try to get at least a spreadsheet such as that shown in Table 3-1. The dates in the table provide the training team with rough estimates of when development on the screens or functions will be complete. That means that the software will be stable enough to lock down the requirements on training. Knowing how large the module or function is gives the training team an idea of how much training will be required. For example, ARM01 will take over six weeks to complete, and so it's one of the

TABLE 3-1

Item	Software Module	Software Function	Screen	Est. Start Date	Est. Finish Date
1.	Purchasing	Update widget description	WMD01	1/15/2000	2/15/2000
2.	Accounting	Enter new G/L acct.	ARM01	1/15/2000	3/2/2000
3.	Manufacturing	Let down	MSH03	2/17/2000	3/17/2000
4.	HR	Enter new candidate	HRA02	1/15/2000	2/15/2000

larger parts. This is a complicated screen, and will require a significant amount of training development. WMD01 and HRA02 are both smaller and thus should require less training. Once you have the dates of the rollout milestones, you can begin creating a program plan, time line, and budget.

3.2 CREATING A PROGRAM PLAN AND TIME LINE

A program is a planned sequence and combination of activities designed to achieve specified goals. It is important to distinguish between a program and a project. A program can be made up of one to many projects. Also, programs may be ongoing and actually sponsor projects. For this book, a program is described as a series of projects designed to create a training program, with each set of deliverables (classes, materials, etc.) making up smaller projects. Programs involve:

- Equipment
- Materials
- Money
- Personnel
- Time

Typically, the program manager (in this case the training lead) looks at each of these resources and allocates them as needed. The training lead also develops a strategy that serves as the road map for program execution from program initiation through support. The execution strategy evolves through an iterative process and becomes increasingly more definitive in describing the relationship of the essential elements of a program.

Elements in a training program include:

- Information sources
- Risk management
- Costs
- Contract approach (if training is purchased)
- Management approach
- Method of support when the training is complete

Properly tailored program strategies form the basis for sound management, and provide a historical record of the program's maturation and decision process. Program strategies are based on the exercise of good judgment and common sense, and include innovative ways to achieve program success.

Before beginning the program design process, there are a number of questions you need to address. For example, who is involved or should be involved in the program design process? Be sure, when you design the program, to include appropriate members of *all* departments that will be affected by the program. History shows that programs are less likely to succeed if these parties are not involved in the planning.

Another issue is the review process as the design proceeds. Consult as broad a range of people as possible to build consensus, support, and awareness of what you are doing. More review is better than less review, but try to avoid "analysis paralysis." As part of the review process, it's also important to determine what persons or departments need to approve the program design. This depends very much on the nature of your authorization to carry out the program. When in doubt, get advice from appropriate consultants or authorities.

There are many other issues, questions, and common problems in program planning. Program planning is not an exact science. The following questions frequently pop up in the planning process:

- How far ahead can you plan when carrying out a program that is dependent on so many variables?
- How can you be sure that a given strategy will work?
- How do you make plans when you do not know whether or when resources will be available?
- How do you know how long it will take to carry out a particular activity?
- What happens if the program is too successful and grows beyond what the funds will support?

Regardless of these uncertainties, it is better to plan and then change that plan when necessary than to wait to make a plan until "all variables are under control." In the world of training and HR development, it is assumed that plans will not unfold exactly as planned. As far as possible, you should consult with those people who have had more experience in order to test the appropriateness of your program design.

The funding issue always has a certain amount of uncertainty. If you do not develop a program plan, it is certain that needed resources will not be available. On the other hand, developing a program plan creates a reality for your program that gives you a chance to go after needed resources. You need to be aware, however, that preparing and circulating a funding proposal does not guarantee that funding will become available. Budgeting is covered in Section 3.4, and Section 3.7 gives tips on avoiding budget cuts once the projects are under way.

In program planning, initial designs typically turn out to be sketchy. As the program begins to unfold, more and more activities surface which need to be carried out. This pattern is normal, not exceptional. Every program needs to be designed in such a way that new activities and even new program components can be added as the program evolves.

Program planning also needs to be understood as a mobilizing or consensus-building task. A part of the task of designing the program is seeking to ensure that the plan is viable. Viability, in turn, is dependent on the actions and reactions of the intended participants in the program. If the intended participants of the program do not like the program and refuse to participate, the program design is defective, no matter how conceptually and technically brilliant the design appears to be.

A carefully planned program can help members express their wants. During program-planning meetings you can facilitate participation from team members by:

- Explaining that you need ideas from each member, because the programs are for the members and they share the responsibility to help plan meaningful programs.
- Reviewing objectives. Members should understand that programs are designed to help them answer questions and provide good services.
- Encouraging members to think of ideas for programs in their areas.
- Asking what information would help each member at the present time.

- Discussing trends that affect the project or rollout as a whole. What new ideas, products, and information are important to your members?
- Exploring possible resources for programs and information.

This program will be successful only if you can get members to participate. Encourage members to talk and share ideas.

In Appendix F and on McGraw-Hill's website at www.books.mcgraw-hill.com/training/download is the Training Program Plan Estimating Guide, which provides a list of activities for the rest of the project. This list and the average times and percentages can be used to complete a project plan in products such as MS Project, or can be entered into a form or spreadsheet. The estimating guide gives you an idea of how long each task will take per unit of work. For example, the time to specify learning objectives for a class is about 1.5 elapsed days. While this may seem like a lot of time for one class, it isn't if you count the time the trainer must take to analyze the needs, think through and document the desired behaviors, and get the material approved. It may not take 12 hours of work by the training developer, but the total elapsed time to get feedback on the objectives and route the material for approval is about 1 to 2 days.

Developing metrics to measure learning can be a very difficult task. The training developer must state exactly what behaviors the student will exhibit when the class is completed, how the behavior will be measured, and what the measures will mean. According to the estimating guide, developing metrics for a single class can take 2 to 5 days, which includes routing and approval times. The task of selecting and sequencing course content takes about 1 to 2 days. If we combine these tasks, we have a basic course design. Table 3-2 presents an example of how these tasks might be estimated for the new G/L account function in the accounting module of WCS. The information in the table was taken from Tables 2-5 and 3-1.

The needs analysis revealed that there were two classes, about 4 hours each, needed to train someone on this function. As an aside, two-part classes are slightly more difficult than single classes to create because there must be a logical break between the classes or students get lost or can't "make the connection" between the two classes. In any case, the classes for this function must be ready by March 2, 2000, and so the amount of effort allocated to create the classes must be sufficient to complete them by that date. The classes are already grouped for the function, so we don't have to do that task.

Creating a set of objectives for two half-day classes should take about 3 days. However, because both of these classes are tied together, the time

TABLE 3-2

From Table 2-5

Item	Software Module	Software Function	Screen	Org. Unit	Est. Classes	Est. Hours
2.	Accounting	Enter new G/L acct.	ARM01	Accting. —G/L	2	8

From Table 3-1

Item	Software Module	Software Function	Screen	Est. Start Date	Est. Finish Date
2.	Accounting	Enter new G/L acct.	ARM01	1/15/2000	3/2/2000

needed is probably closer to 2 days. Creating a set of metrics will likely take about 3 days, and selecting and sequencing content should take about 4 days because of the dual-course requirement. These numbers assume one full-time person or equivalent labor unit (FTE) working on the courses. The total number of "working days" is 9. If we know the drop-dead date is March 2, 2000, then the course design must begin no later than February 18, 2000. Back-timing is almost *never* the best way to estimate, but since the rollout team determines its deadlines and yours, back-timing is one way of meeting the required rollout dates.

This process is repeated for each need from the needs analysis. Once the calculations are complete, you'll have a spreadsheet for each class or function that resembles Table 3-3. Notice the extra-day lead time. It's important to build in some breathing space for corrections, additions, etc. A complete blank form is available in Appendix G and on McGraw-Hill's website at www.books.mcgraw-hill.com/training/download. The forms can then be opened, edited, and printed using Microsoft Word or other word processing software.

Once all the classes are estimated, they are totaled into a task spreadsheet that is derived from the estimating guide such as the one shown in Table 3-4. This form, with room to estimate the remaining tasks, is included in Appendix G and can be found on McGraw-Hill's website at www.books.mcgraw-hill.com/training/download. The forms can then be opened, edited, and printed using Microsoft Word or other word processing software. Notice that the days estimated do *not* include weekends or holidays. The worksheet in Appendix G must be completed for all tasks for all needs and classes. It is likely that there will be some variance and required changes to the plan over time, and these documents tend to be "living documents" over the life of the program.

The program plan document must also contain other standard sections found in most project plans. These include a statement of benefits, a program purpose statement, a schedule with deliverables and dollars, and a list of impacted organizational units. A sample outline is available in Appendix G and on McGraw-Hill's website at www.books.mcgraw-hill.com/training/download. The forms can then be opened, edited, and printed using Microsoft Word or other word processing software.

TABLE 3-3

Class/Needs Work Estimates Sheet

Item	Software Module	Software Function	Screen	Org. Unit	Est. Classes	Est. Days	Est. Start	Est. Complete
2.	Accounting	Enter new G/L acct.	ARM01	Accting. —G/L	2	9	2/17/2000	3/1/2000

TABLE 3-4

Task Group	Task	Est. Days	Est. Start	Est. Complete
Design	Develop objectives	22	1/4/2000	2/3/2000
	Develop metrics	35	2/4/2000	3/17/2000
	Select/sequence content	8	3/18/2000	3/29/2000
	Create groups/tracks	3	3/30/2000	4/1/2000
Task group total		**68**	**1/4/2000**	**4/1/2000**

3.3　COMMON PLANNING MISTAKES THAT TRAINING MANAGERS MAKE

The single biggest mistake that most program or project managers make is not accounting for elapsed time versus hours needed to complete a task. Even if a task only takes a total of 2 working hours, it may take days or even weeks to get time from the software teams and/or subject matter experts who are needed to develop the training for the rollout. Not factoring in user availability and the willingness to take time away from work to help develop the training, as well as to participate in it, can extend project deadlines. Also, not factoring in vacations, sick time, etc., can be a huge mistake. Some staff plan vacations well in advance of taking them, and these longer vacations are typically more expensive. If you ask an employee to cancel or postpone a trip, be prepared to reimburse that employee for the prepaid costs and penalties.

Thinking you don't need a plan is the second biggest mistake. If you don't plan your work, you can't work your plan. Training programs for software rollouts are usually enormous efforts, and *not* efforts that can be managed by the seat of your pants. Even if a plan is put together, most people greatly underestimate the size and complexity of the program because they fail to consider the number of people required to make the program succeed. Also, not keeping deadlines flexible enough to account for the inevitable changes in both the software rollout schedule and the requirements is a major problem. The rollout schedule *will* change, and so will the requirements, and the training program plan must adapt to the changes.

Inappropriate staffing and staff loading poses still another big mistake. Managers must understand intimately the skills and work capacity of their staff. Schedules on software rollout projects are typically very tight, and putting a "greenie" or even a new manager in charge of the training will likely lead to a disaster. Try to use performance history as a guide to loading staff with work. If someone has a history of not functioning well under pressure, do *not* place that person in the critical path.

Not building partnerships with users and the software rollout team(s) and allowing politics to affect the development and execution of the plan are two other very common mistakes. Well-built partnerships typically preclude political problems, but that isn't universally true. Be sure to understand the needs of *all* organization players before asking for the support of a plan. Another mistake along these lines is not understanding how to get and keep funding (see Section 3.7).

Not having a contingency plan in case something goes wrong is also a major problem. Nothing ever goes as planned, and sooner or later, your plan and reality will part ways. A contingency plan allows you to manage the bumps in the road and bring the project back on course quickly. The main issue here is that some managers feel that experience is a substitute for planning. This may be true on small, bite-sized projects, but not for an effort of this magnitude.

Bad communication is last, but certainly not least. A lack of communication about what's being developed is just as bad as inaccurate communication. It's important to keep all parties who are involved in the development and delivery of training informed of the project status. One easy way to do this is to start a weekly or bimonthly newsletter. This lets others know where you are and what you're doing. Communication provides an awareness of the training development effort, as well as gives other areas the chance to ask questions and help the training team if they have something to contribute.

3.4   GETTING FUNDING—WHERE DOES ALL THE MONEY COME FROM?

The program and all costs associated with it must be funded. There are two basic choices for getting funding. The first is to place the organization's total budget for I/T training under the I/T training manager, who pays all the training bills. This approach provides centrally funded I/T training for all the departments in that training manager's scope of responsibility. The second is to have the organization's customer departments put the money for training programs in their budgets. The training department then charges for its services in order to pay the bills for training, known as the chargeback method. There are, of course, advantages and disadvantages of each of these ways of managing training budgets.

The most obvious benefit of funding I/T training centrally is that it keeps things more tightly focused and easier to manage. Since the money for I/T training is under the control of the I/T training manager, it is easier to direct training dollars to wherever the I/T training manager thinks the training belongs. The nuts and bolts of training activities can be steered to the target areas that the training manager and/or rollout team judges to be important. It is easier for a centrally funded group to devote attention and resources to issues that are important for the rollout as a whole, and to focus on the tactical urgency of helping people learn what their jobs and projects require.

The major problem with centralized funding is that a centrally funded I/T training group sometimes ignores reality and tries to run a training department based on a theoretical philosophy that ignores day-to-day needs. It is easy for such a group to turn inward. Also, like any autonomous group, the measure of I/T training performance becomes the accomplishment of planned activities rather than the achievement of needed business results.

The advantage of operating an I/T training department in charge-back mode is that it provides an excellent chance for business needs to drive the training activity. If the organization's department managers have the I/T training funds in their budgets, they obviously have a larger say in making decisions about what programs get implemented, when they are implemented, for whom, and for what purposes. The I/T training department and its customers will inevitably work more closely together under these conditions.

The problem with running chargebacks is that the training team runs the risk of implementing programs that are popular in order to justify the team's continued existence. The goal can become filling seats to meet the budget, rather than helping people learn the software. Worse yet is the possibility that user departments could withhold training funds if they don't like the software being rolled out.

3.5 BUDGETING

Training in the use of information technologies is a requirement if investment in these technologies is to pay off. Budgeting for training programs is the single most important part of adopting a new technology. The question of how to arrange funding for I/T training programs is an important one, and it makes considerable sense to think the issue through before the pressure of planning a budget arrives on the calendar. Remember, you get what you pay for. You have to define what you want and what your requirements are just as you do in the needs analysis. Some organizations can get away with a several thousand dollar investment and are very happy with the outcome—they are fulfilling their strategic objective for their training. Others invest millions of dollars to meet their strategic objective. Questions to ask that help training teams achieve their goals include:

- Is there a clear overall cost?
- Is there a breakdown of what is included in the cost (analysis, development, delivery, etc.)?

- Is there information about any additional training costs (time, salaries, travel, materials)?
- Is there information regarding the cost to customize the program to the business needs?
- Is there an outline of the cost of any finances involved (such as premises, travel, accommodation, etc.)?
- Is there a cost measure of the training results in past similar programs?
- Is there an estimate of the cost per student day?
- Have all corporate policies been complied with?
- Is there financial justification of the program?
- Have maintenance costs been estimated on a yearly basis and included in the overall project cost?

These questions are available as a checklist in Appendix F and on McGraw-Hill's website at www.books.mcgraw-hill.com/training/download. The forms can then be opened, edited, and printed using Microsoft Word or other word processing software.

Some costs are incurred only once in the development of the course. Others, such as workbooks or facility rentals, are repeated for each participant or each time the course runs. Typical costs include:

- Course design, development, or purchase
- Salary of instructor, consultant, and/or staff
- Off-site travel, lodging, and meals
- Facilities rented or allocated
- Equipment and hardware
- Instructional materials
- Loss of productivity while trainees are attending training

A professional training process can pay big dividends, and a well-designed training budget gets the most out of each dollar. Training expenditures are too costly to waste, and cost-effective training is within reach and within budget. A simple question to ask, which may help you maintain your budget, is: If no one knows how to use the software, how much is it worth? While this may seem like an obvious question, senior managers typically choke on large training dollar requests. It's helpful to remind them from time to time what you're actually doing—making sure the software is used.

Training budgets for ERP and application-specific software can range from 6 to 15 percent of the total budget, with the majority being around 6 to 10 percent. That means that in an $80 million ERP rollout, the cost of training is likely to be around $5 million. This is a *really* big number for a CIO to swallow, and it's going to require a significant amount of detail to justify.

To figure the cost of the labor for the training program, take the total number of hours per task in the Task Group Total Worksheet (found in Appendix G and on McGraw-Hill's website at www.books.mcgraw-hill.com/training/download. The forms can then be opened, edited, and printed using Microsoft Word or other word processing software.) and break down the hours by labor type. For example, if you have 150 days of course design, then you probably need a training developer or course designer for those tasks (unless your trainers double as developers). If software must be installed, you'll need help from technical support and/or operations. For each set of tasks, make sure you have the required expertise on your labor worksheet. A partial example (by task group only) is given in Table 3-5.

Notice in the table that training team, rollout team, and end-user costs were factored in. It's important to remember that the costs of lost time on the job (salary) must be factored in. This ensures that the benefit received will be calculated properly, as all costs will be included. Benefit information

TABLE 3-5

Phase	Labor Type	Hours	Cost/Hour	Total Cost
Design	Training project leader	50	$110	$5,500
	Training developer 1	120	$150	$18,000
	Training developer 2	120	$150	$18,000
	Rollout team member	40	$150	$6,000
	Business user/adviser	70	$80	$5,600
Choose delivery options	Training project leader	40	$110	$4,400
	Training developer 1	20	$150	$3,000
	Business user/adviser	20	$80	$1,600
Make or buy decision	Training project leader	20	$110	$2,200
	Senior manager	10	$300	$3,000
Grand total (partial)		510		$67,300

can be gathered from the rollout team. The worksheet in the table is available at the task level in Appendix G and on McGraw-Hill's website at www.books.mcgraw-hill.com/training/download. The forms can then be opened, edited, and printed using Microsoft Word or other word processing software.

Once the labor costs are known, the other costs listed must be added in as well. Table 3-6 presents an example of a high-level, overall budget worksheet. One thing worth noting is that lost productivity of trainees will often be the largest single cost. That's why it's very important to have management brought into this process (see Chapter 1).

Some of the items in Table 3-6 are hard to calculate early in the program, but benchmarking will help. Talk to other organizations that have done the same implementations, or even the vendors themselves. They may have some numbers that are "typical" of one of their installations. Be wary of numbers that sound too good to be true though, because those numbers may be "best case" and not reflect the average reality.

3.6 CONTROLLING TRAVEL AND OTHER EXPENSES

Travel and expenses (T&E) have become major areas that corporate bean counters are now trying to get under control. As the tax benefits that corporations derive from T&E deductions shrink, corporate accountants are going to get tougher and tougher on class and conference participants. To get maximum results from your training budget, take a hard look at your

TABLE 3-6

Item	Cost
Labor	$1,500,000
Travel, lodging, meals	800,000
Facilities	400,000
Hardware	100,000
Software	250,000
Purchased instruction materials	150,000
Salary/lost job time	2,300,000
Grand total	**$5,500,000**

current training resources and suppliers. Buy lots of books. The right $25 book or $95 videotape can be very effective for individual learners. Build a company library, and pass training materials around. You can make plenty of mistakes as you buy publications that miss the mark, but your expenditures are low in total.

Use local resources to avoid travel at all. If you're within a reasonable distance of a major university, the odds are that the classes there are cheaper per student day than any commercial training class. And the material may well be more up-to-date, the result of a local professor's research. Local training firms often do an outstanding job in building computer skills. Also, go to local conventions. If you are in or near a major city, you should be able to avoid sending staff to faraway places (e.g., Scottsdale in February) simply as a reward for being good.

Use internal resources to avoid travel. Some of the best trainers in the country for your people are your people. They know your market, your strengths, your customers, your suppliers, and your competitors. Many of your highly skilled employees can share their expertise with several others. In addition to on-the-job training, a classroom environment can be structured to take advantage of the capabilities of your very talented people. Train your best producers to be trainers. One of the most cost-effective expenditures for learning is training the trainers. Instead of always using outside trainers, hire a consultant to design a program that will train your best staff to be expert trainers.

Send teams to seminars and require solutions in return. One person sitting in a program may have dozens of ideas, some good, some not so good, about how the new seminar concepts could be implemented in the company. Too often, however, the best concepts die when the attendee gets home to his or her "real job." On the other hand, three seminar participants from the same company can have a continuing dialogue over several days to focus on a seminar's content. In ongoing conversations, they can determine just how the techniques presented could best be used by their firm. Many firms require that their participants come back from seminars with a written outline containing a recommended action plan.

Bring the program to your place. When you go to a program and develop a new understanding or build better skills, return as a teacher. You learn and retain more when you teach your skills to others. That's an effective way to spread the cost for a few attendees over a dozen others in the company. Or bring the seminar program to your location. If the tuition costs were the same, the travel bill might be for two instructors instead of twenty attendees. Also, the instructors should be able to modify the session to achieve your specific goals. You might even get the seminar tailored with examples that are directly related to your situation.

As a last resort, if your staff must travel, work with local travel agents to find package deals. Also, if something (like a hotel room) sounds too high-priced, either ask the travel agent to negotiate a lower rate, or do it yourself. Many hotels will come down in price when asked. With regard to flights, it's often to the organization's advantage to allow training participants to stay over a Saturday night. Most airlines offer significantly reduced fares with a Saturday night stay. In many cases, the combined costs of additional car rental and hotel days will still be less than leaving prior to midnight Saturday.

3.7   AVOIDING TRAINING BUDGET CUTS

Cutting the training budget may seem to be an effective method of relieving a company's cashflow crisis, but in the long term this tactic is bound to stifle company productivity and employee initiative, with a long-term impact on the bottom line. The question you will probably be asked is if training money is being well invested. Some estimates indicate that only about 20 or 30 percent of all training is being used on the job a month later, resulting in billions of wasted dollars.

The problem is not that training is ineffective, but that it is poorly planned and implemented. Managers request courses without assessing what their employees' real needs are, and supervisors neglect to reinforce employees' new skills. Either way, there is waste. Whether your training budget is large or small, there are ways to make sure that you're spending that money wisely. Some simple tips are:

- Stay visible! Publicize your successes, and make the obvious really obvious. Most managers know that training is important, but sometimes they must be reminded.
- Use the spending history as a starting point. If you have just set up the budget, you may want to keep track of expenses for several months before beginning your budget.
- Be realistic. Do not underestimate your expenses simply to gain favor with management.
- Budget for fixed expenses first, and then determine your variable or discretionary expenses.

- Estimate a yearly amount for unusual expenditures (such as repairs to equipment), and budget an equal portion for each budget period.
- Do not forget periodic expenses like licenses for software such as CBT.

Avoiding these mistakes will help ensure that your budget is sufficient to complete the work, especially if you can convince management that training budget cuts may be a short-term solution, but will result in more harm than good in the long-term perspective.

Training ensures that staff become more productive in the workplace and thus more valuable to the organization. An employee who works "smart" can save and even generate money for the company. In the long run, skilled and competent staff members will take their company to the forefront, but heavily cut training budgets can only yield short-term financial relief. Because training makes no immediate contribution to the bottom line, the training budget generally appears to be the obvious one to slash. However, management needs to shed the expectation of instant results from courses. Management should anticipate a learning curve before the individual and the company truly reap the benefits of training.

This means that when considering training, management needs to factor in the additional time that learning must be actively applied in the workplace, on top of the hours or days spent on coursework. Another argument commonly presented when training budgets are under discussion is that employees who have been trained and have enhanced skills levels become attractive targets for headhunters and are likely to be lured to greener pastures. In fact, these employees are far more likely to remain loyal because they feel that their interests are being looked after by their employer.

It makes no sense to invest in technology to achieve a competitive advantage and then fail to match that with a similar investment in training. Training is vital if users are to tap into the full potential of a software package, and even self-taught users will acquire additional skills that enable them to perform their jobs more efficiently.

CASE: ACME WIDGETS—CREATING THE PROGRAM PLAN AND BUDGET DOCUMENT

In Table 2-7 Shawn created a set of needs for KIS that span the skill levels of most users. Because each user will only be required to pass the beginner courses, there isn't a need to assign the advanced courses at this time. However, those courses must still be designed and be available for both I/T and users as needed. In Table 2-9 Mike and the team created a series of courses designed to get HR staff up to speed on the three principal areas of human resource management—personnel, payroll, and benefits. For each major function, two classes of varying duration are required in order to become proficient in operating the screens.

Using these needs, the team went back to Gary, WCS's software rollout team leader, and Lauren, KIS's software rollout team leader, to get the planned completion dates for each software package. Table 3-7 has the dates for KIS, and Table 3-8 has the dates for WCS.

Notice that in Table 3-7 there is only one row for the KIS e-mail system. Because KIS is a canned package, no modifications are made during installation. So there is only one beginning and ending date for the installation of that module of KIS. The KIS module will be installed by 2/15/2000.

The WCS HR module will be complete by 3/2/2000. This is possible because there are staff working on each part (personnel, payroll, and benefits). The package is integrated, and all HR functions use the same employee database. Thus development can run parallel, and no one piece is completely dependent on the other. Since the KIS and WCS rollouts are happening together, training will not be required until WCS is complete. This means that the training team will have time to properly design and implement the program.

TABLE 3-7

Completion Dates for KIS

Item	Software Module	Software Function	Screen	Est. Start Date	Est. Finish Date
1.	E-mail	All e-mail functions	E-mail	1/15/2000	2/15/2000

TABLE 3-8

Completion Dates for WCS

Item	Software Module	Software Function	Screen	Est. Start Date	Est. Finish Date
1.	HR	Enter new employee	HRM01	1/15/2000	2/15/2000
2.	HR	Change employee pay	HRP02	1/15/2000	3/2/2000
3.	HR	Select employee benefits	HRB03	1/15/2000	2/15/2000

By looking back at Tables 2-7 and 2-9, Mike and Bob figured that there were three KIS classes (beginner, intermediate, and power user) and six WCS classes. With the aid of the estimating guide, an example is given in Table 3-9.

Mike, Dave, and Shawn can work with Kathy to keep the class development moving on parallel tracks. As the work gets done, it must be approved by users and the rollout team, so that while the training team is waiting for approvals for some classes, it can develop others.

These classes must be combined, which then forms a composite of all the work in all the phases, which in turn drives the dates for the projects. A partial example is shown in Table 3-10.

By using the information in Table 3-9 to feed the budgeting process based on standard rates, Mike calculated the budget for the design phase. Dave, Kathy, and Shawn account for the bulk of the charges for the 165 days of work, though some user charges are built in as well. Table 3-11 presents the totals for the design phase of the program.

The last piece of the budget puzzle is to add in other costs besides labor. Though costs vary because of many factors, it's important to at least "guesstimate" the totals.

TABLE 3-9

Item	Software Module	Software Function	Screen	Org. Unit	Est. Classes	Est. Days	Est. Start	Est. Complete
1.	KIS	E-mail	Beginner	All	1	35	1/11/2000	3/12/2000
2.	KIS	E-mail	Intermed.	All	1	20	1/18/2000	2/12/2000
3.	KIS	E-mail	Power	All	1	20	1/18/2000	2/12/2000
4.	WCS	Personnel	HRM01	HR	2	30	2/15/2000	3/19/2000
5.	WCS	Payroll	HRP02	HR	2	40	2/15/2000	3/26/2000
6.	WCS	Benefits	HRB03	HR	2	40	3/15/2000	5/12/2000

TABLE 3-10

Task group	Task	Est. Days	Est. Start	Est. Complete
Design	Develop objectives	85	1/11/2000	3/12/2000
	Develop metrics	50	2/4/2000	3/17/2000
	Select/sequence content	20	3/18/2000	3/29/2000
	Create groups/tracks	10	3/30/2000	5/12/2000
Task group total		165	1/4/2000	4/1/2000

The best way to do this is to partner with the right organizational units and staff. Travel agents and even training vendors can help you calculate some of the T&E dollars. Technical support and computer operations folks can help figure up the costs for new hardware and software required to run the new program. Most organizations do put limits on spending, so it's important to have an idea or general range for costs. Mike and Bob put together a plan, shown in Table 3-12, based on a total limit given to them by Connie of $8 million. This represents about 8 percent of the $100 million allocated for implementing both KIS and WCS enterprisewide.

The results of the planning activity can be seen in Appendix D in the program plan completed for the case study. Putting the pieces together into one cohesive, easily read document is probably the most important part of planning. Too often, great plans are made well, but presented badly. This can cause even the best and most complete plan to be rejected by management because the document is unreadable!

TABLE 3-11

Phase	Labor Type	Hours	Cost/Hour	Total Cost
Design	Training project leader	240	$110	$26,400
	Trainer 1	320	$150	$48,000
	Trainer 2	320	$150	$48,000
	Training developer	320	$150	$48,000
	Rollout team member	240	$150	$36,000
	Business user/adviser	240	$80	$19,200
Grand total (partial)		1680		$55,200

TABLE 3-12

Item	Cost
Labor	$2,500,000
Travel, lodging, meals	1,200,000
Facilities	400,000
Hardware	500,000
Software	400,000
Purchased instruction materials	300,000
Salary/lost job time	2,500,000
Grand total	$7,800,000

Coming Up in Chapter 4

Now that the remaining tasks and project plan and budget for the program are known, the next step is to take the needs analysis (i.e., requirements) and use the results to design a curriculum.

REFERENCES

Hackos, JoAnn T. (1999). President, Comtech Services. 710 Kipling Street, Suite 400, Denver, CO, 80215. Phone: (303) 232-7586. www.comtech-serv.com.

Hackos, JoAnn T. (1994). *Managing your documentation projects.* New York: John Wiley.

Hickel, James K. (1993). *The cost-effective organization: How to create it, how to maintain it.* United Kingdom: Glenbridge Pub Ltd.

Leshin, C. B., Pollock, J., & Reigeluth, C. M. (1992). *Instructional design strategies and tactics.* Englewood Cliffs, NJ: Educational Technology Publications.

Tracy, John A. (1996). *Budgeting ala carte: Essential tools for harried business managers.* New York: John Wiley.

Welsch, Glenn A., et al. (1988). *Budgeting: Profit planning and control.* New York: Prentice-Hall.

CHAPTER 4

Designing the Training Program

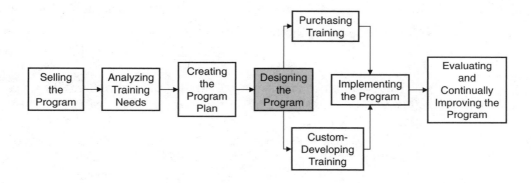

In This Chapter

OVERVIEW

Design is actually a circular process. Once a design has been implemented, it is evaluated, and this evaluation becomes part of the next design phase. Further, design and delivery are interrelated, in that delivery questions have to be addressed at the planning phase. Design involves stating the training program's objectives, instructional methodologies, and structure and sequence for each position. The end result of the design phase is the training plan and overall curriculum. The training plan makes extensive use of the training needs analysis information to produce training for each of the needs analyzed. The training plan design incorporates a number of identifiable steps that include:

- Preparation and sequencing of learning objectives
- Review and/or creation of training materials except those that may be purchased
- Determination of skills and knowledge requirements

These steps are designed to result in a training plan or high-level program—the detail may be purchased or created, as seen in later chapters. These steps are designed to answer at least the following questions:

- Is the purpose of the training documented?
- Do the objectives match requirements gathered during the needs analysis?
- Is there a balance ensuring a diversity of learning activity types (exercises, case studies, opportunities for skills practice) to support adult learning?
- Have all delivery systems, appropriate for the objectives, been considered and the one(s) selected clearly documented?
- Does the selection of learning methods and materials support the module objectives?
- Has the team checked that content matches critical job performance requirements?
- Does the content include a description of the expertise level of the training event (basic, medium, advanced)?
- Has the team determined objectives at the module level (knowledge, skills, and attitude) that support the overall training objectives?
- Has the team discussed the length of each event and of the overall program?
- Has the team created quality training documentation and detailed learning exercise descriptions?

These questions appear in a checklist in Appendix F and on McGraw-Hill's website at www.books.mcgraw-hill.com/training/download. The forms can then be opened, edited, and printed using Microsoft Word or other word processing software.

While these questions seem obvious, it's important to remember that it is equally dangerous to oversimplify training as it is to make it too complex.

If you oversimplify the training and people do not understand either why the system has been configured as it has, or the relevance of modifications, or the use of defaults, or the reference fields, etc., their input will reflect this lack of understanding. Another issue is the level of skill required. For example, managers need to understand the new chart of accounts, but obviously not in the same way as the data entry people. This example is an obvious distinction, but many are more subtle, and it comes down to a judgment call about whether people with different levels of skill requirements should all attend the same course or whether two (or more) different courses are justified.

Training notes should be adapted to reflect modifications to standard products. However, the major challenge is the classroom exercises. We all learn best by doing, so for every critical competency identified, an exercise should be designed using a familiar scenario from the client's own business environment. (See the section on building learning activities later in this chapter.)

Among the most important course decisions is the identification of course goals. If goals have not been articulated adequately, subsequent decisions will have no foundation. If clear goals are lacking, it will be impossible to evaluate a course efficiently, and there will be no sound basis for selecting appropriate subject matter, materials, and training methods. What is more, evaluation will not be rooted in common understanding.

Unless the goals of the course are clearly understood by both parties, students will find evaluation procedures confusing and, perhaps, unfair. Without clear course goals, students may find that the course is irrelevant and that the material is not related to their personal goals, or to any other goals they can recognize as being important. They often complain that they do not know what to concentrate on when they study, since no topic priorities are set. In a worst case, they may decide the course is disorganized, that topics do not fit together, and that there is no direction. On the other hand, clear goals ensure that:

- Training will be more focused and precise. Instructors will have subjected the course to a thorough analysis and selected what they expect the students to learn in the course.
- Points where learning needs to be monitored or tested can be identified easily.
- The training team can confirm that student needs are being met.
- Instructors will be aware of different training and learning styles. One can specify the product and make an intelligent choice of the appropriate training and learning process.

Students will always have a clear statement of the purpose and aims of the course to turn to when they are studying or are unsure of the course's aims. They will find it easier to progress through the course in an organized manner. There is a clear communication of intent on the part of the trainer regarding what he or she is trying to train, what the students are going to be expected to be able to do, how their achievement will be measured, and what will be accepted as evidence that they have achieved the goals.

4.1   DECIDING WHAT KNOWLEDGE MUST BE TRANSFERRED

Deciding what knowledge must be transferred is driven by the training needs analysis (TNA), described in Chapter 2. What must be taught, who needs to learn it, and how success will be measured are determined in the TNA. Once they are determined, you are ready to establish the specific learning objectives. In Section 4.4, these objectives (which now roughly describe a class) will be grouped into logical tracks, which in turn make up a curriculum. Section 4.4 also separates the classes by level (e.g., beginner, etc.).

It is easy to determine what knowledge must be transferred if you are operating in an environment where there are competency standards or specific job descriptions (see Chapter 2). These will let you know what the industry or enterprise requires employees to learn in a given area. They will also let you know the level to which it is to be learned and the kind of background that is required. For example, it may be impossible to ask an employee to learn to operate the statistical capabilities of Excel if that employee does not have some background in simple statistics.

Knowledge transfer generally consists of explaining and demonstrating correct task performance, helping workers under supervision the first time, allowing personnel to perform alone, evaluating performance, and providing feedback. There is an important difference between telling workers how to do a task and successfully transferring skills, ability, or knowledge. Even after demonstration, misunderstanding by employees may lead them to delete records or send e-mails to the wrong person. With software training, there is a large variance in the ease of learning and use. Some concepts are hard to learn and require practice.

While training personnel, you want to continually measure their level of understanding. With large software packages, each piece builds on, and interfaces with, other pieces. It's important to make sure that nobody gets lost during training. You should also gear training to the participants based on their levels. Presenting beginners with advanced material will result in frustration. Try to structure the objectives so that only a few concepts are presented at a time. This helps prevent information overload. Where needed, divide tasks into components, since ERP software can be overwhelming at times.

While explanations and demonstrations are important in training, workers are more likely to retain information when they can put it to use. Especially at the lower end of skills acquisition, training methods are more effective when they emphasize practice over theory. Explanations should be limited in length and complexity. When showing a video (e.g., entering a new customer), you will want to encourage workers to ask questions, and as well, it is important that you ask questions of them. This way you can check worker comprehension of the materials covered. Besides reinforcing the employee's own skills, having employees help each other can reduce total training time and can free supervisors to do other work. Many employees appreciate and enjoy the added responsibility and status of helping coworkers.

Writing Learning Objectives

Once the employees' training needs have been identified, employers can then prepare objectives for the training. Instructional objectives, if clearly stated, will tell employers what they want their employees to know, to do, to do differently or better, or to stop doing. Having clearly defined objectives will enable the employer to evaluate whether those objectives have been reached.

When writing learning objectives, it's important to understand the difference between purpose and outcomes. One purpose of training is to change behavior. Is it enough to develop understanding if there are no outcomes of this understanding? Competency-based training is based on the concept that learning has behavioral outcomes. That means that learning is demonstrated by changed or demonstrated behavior. The capacity to do something is proof that the student has learned successfully.

Learning objectives do not necessarily have to be written, but in order for the training to be as successful as possible, clear and measurable objectives should be thought out before the training begins. For an objective to be effective it should identify as precisely as possible what the individuals will do to demonstrate that they have learned it, or that the objective has been reached. The objectives should also describe the important conditions under which the individual will demonstrate competence and define what constitutes acceptable performance.

A learning objective is a brief, clear statement of what the participant should be able to do as a result of training. It should look at how the learning relates to successful completion of the task or job. A well-written objective is specific and measurable. It forms the basis for the training program design and evaluation. Generally, objectives are given in writing to the participants. It's also important to review the objectives orally at the beginning of the session in order to allow participants an opportunity to ask questions and allow you to make necessary modifications.

It's important to follow some guidelines for writing learning objectives. Write objectives from the viewpoint of what the specific trainee or participant will do. Use active voice. Be as specific as possible. Avoid vague terms such as *know, learn, comprehend, study, cover,* and *understand.*

Through specific, action-oriented language, the instructional objectives should describe the desired knowledge, practice, or skill and its observable behavior. Objectives are most effective when worded in sufficient detail that other qualified persons can recognize when the desired knowledge or behavior is exhibited. There are three basic steps to writing learning objectives.

1. *Review the need (from the TNA) to determine the desired behavior, purpose, and/or outcome.* For example, one of the needs might be for a student to send a group e-mail. The student would need to understand how to create a group, insert the group name address into the e-mail, create the e-mail, and send the e-mail.

2. *Break the need or objective into small, easily demonstrable and measurable parts.* The first small piece of the need mentioned in step 1 is to create a group using a group address facility. One specific, small piece of that task is to create a blank group entry that can contain names. The next step is to insert the names into the group entry, and the last step is to save the group entry.

3. *Determine the metrics.* How many errors are permissible when learning? Are these errors stated in numbers or percentages? Should the student be able to perform the task within a specific time limit? (Metrics are covered in more detail in Section 4.2.)

Specificity is extremely important because it allows trainers to measure participant success, and enables the participants to benchmark and improve their skills throughout the course. Thus, objectives must be very clear, concise, and measurable. Examples of vague or unclear learning objectives would be:

- Each participant will understand how to fix a customer problem.
- Each participant will know the procedure for e-mailing a vendor.

Nowhere in these objectives is there any mention of a specific activity, demonstrable behavior, or way of measuring success. These objectives can be restated more clearly in the following way:

- Each participant will reverse a customer transaction with zero errors in 2 minutes or less.
- Each participant will create and send an e-mail to a vendor following company policy.

Learning objectives also need to take into consideration the audience, the level at which the participant is to use the information, and the standards of acceptable performance. The target audience (participants or trainees) must be considered, because the same topic may be approached differently depending on the background of the groups to be trained. Will they need to be able to apply the information and solve problems? If so, will the participants need to apply knowledge to actual cases or problems? How well must the trainee perform the objective, and how will performance be measured?

To ensure that the objectives created correspond to the needs gathered, it's useful to have a form that correlates the need and objective to specific parts of the software, or the rollout. It's also important to include the level or type of need, which helps place the objective in the right context. An example form is shown in Table 4-1, which provides a quick cross-reference of needs and objectives, allowing training developers to keep the training aimed at the right goals. It also feeds the course outline, which usually has the following sections:

- *Prerequisites.* Any courses or KSAEs that a student must have prior to the course
- *Description.* A brief description of the course
- *Value of the course.* A short summary of why the course is important to the student/organization
- *Objectives.* What the student should learn or be able to do as a result of the class
- *Course topic/session outline.* What will be done in the course
- *Additional readings.* Any reference material such as manuals, handouts, etc.

A good course description allows potential participants to make an intelligent decision about taking the course, and sets their expectations of the course appropriately.

TABLE 4-1

Item	Software Module	Software Function	Level or Type	Need	Objective(s)
1.	HR KIS-e-mail	Enter new employee e-mail	Business— HR KIS— beginner	Enter a new employee into employee database	1. Enter employee data in 3–4 minutes with four errors or less 2. Send an e-mail to the employee's manager notifying the manager of the entry
2.	HR	Change employee pay	Business— HR	Update employee pay details	Change the employee's tax withholding to the correct number with zero errors
3.	HR	Select employee benefits	Business— HR	Enter/select and create employee benefits package	Enter employee benefit selections in 10 minutes with two or fewer errors

How to Get the Knowledge Transferred—Building Learning Activities

After the objectives for the training program are set, learning activities can be identified and developed. To ensure that employees transfer the skills or knowledge from the learning activity to the job, the learning situation should simulate the actual job as closely as possible. Thus, employers may want to arrange the objectives and activities in a sequence that corresponds to the order in which the tasks are to be performed on the job.

A few factors will help to determine the type of learning activity to be incorporated into the training. One aspect is the training resources available to the employer. Can a group training program be used, or should the employer train the employees on a one-to-one basis? The training activity can be group-oriented, with lectures, role play, and demonstrations; or it can be designed for self-paced instruction, such as interactive video training programs.

The methods and materials used for the learning activity can be as varied as the trainer's imagination and available resources will allow. The trainer may want to use charts, diagrams, manuals, slides, films, viewgraphs (overhead transparencies), videotapes, audiotapes, or blackboard and chalk, or any combination of these and other instructional aids. The learning activities should be developed so employees can demonstrate that they have acquired the desired skills or knowledge.

Determining the instructional techniques is also part of building learning activities. What techniques will work best to learn the behavioral objectives? Examine the behavior and content areas of the learning objectives. For example, if the behavior describes "doing," then an exercise, not a lecture, would be a more appropriate training method. If objectives are mostly cognitive skills, then oral presentations may be more appropriate. Keep in mind that adult learners retain:

- 10 percent of what they read
- 20 percent of what they hear
- 30 percent of what they see
- 50 percent of what they see and hear
- 65 percent of combined hearing, reading, and seeing
- 80 to 90 percent of what they hear, see, and apply

Use appropriate vocabulary and terminology for the audience as indicated by your assessment of entering behaviors. Review the advantages and disadvantages of each learning activity in your specific course. Review media related to the content area for correlation with the behaviors and content of the objectives.

4.2   DEVELOPING COMPETENCY MEASUREMENTS OR A CERTIFICATION TEST

Increasingly, training is seen as an investment that will provide beneficial returns, rather than a cost center. Training is finally being seen as a tool to affect strategic change and a means to achieve a competitive edge. Once organizations become aware of the directions that they need to take to survive or grow, the shaping of strategy to achieve the desired directions may involve considerable training. With such an important investment, organizations see the value of monitoring how the investment is paying off.

Measurement must link directly with the organization's business and confirm training's impact on business. Training has become increasingly linked with an organization's strategic business plan. This is partly the result of the recognition that training pays off in terms of the business objectives if appropriately targeted and focused. The linkage results from a perceived lack of direction and control of training, with training viewed as an end in itself. The evolution of training as a partner in business has many benefits, but business requirements must be accounted for in all steps of training development.

Developing Objective Metrics

For each learning outcome or objective you must write the measurement criteria and the conditions of measurement using established measurement methods. Accurate technical skills assessment almost definitely requires a global knowledge of the various skill levels of a large population to reduce tendencies to rate technicians' skills relative only to coworkers. Raters need training so that they know what constitutes objectivity and subjectivity. Raters need to know how to obtain and distinguish between quantitative and qualitative data, and they need to know what to do with the data. Factors that must be accounted for include:

- A collaborative approach to data gathering and interpretation of data
- Measurement of multiple aspects of the program
- Consideration of multiple levels of the program
- Inclusion of perspectives from different stakeholders
- Use of both formative and summative questions
- A management information system for sharing evaluation and program information
- Reliance upon multiple and repeated measures over time

These factors are common to most measurement and evaluation projects within training development programs. They must be addressed for the program to be successful, particularly those that involve managing stakeholder expectations and showing the value of the training program.

It's important to note that clear measurements express how you will quantify the level of competency your students must reach. The training developers must ask themselves: How will students show us they've gained these skills and competencies? How will we grade student achievement of these skills and competencies? A simple three-step approach for stating measurements is:

1. Associate measurements with competencies.
2. State the method or conditions you will use to measure each competency.
3. State the criteria or standards you will use to pass or fail students.

The first step is to decide what will be measured and how (per each need or competency), and what the benchmarks will be. The standards by which a student will be measured in training must match the standards by which a student will be measured on the job. For example, an employee may be measured by the number of customer service calls taken per hour. The new software may make it 30 percent easier for employees to solve customer service problems. If that's true, then a normal metric of four calls per hour would now be expected to grow to five or six calls per hour using the new software. Thus an objective metric would be "The student will be able to log at least five calls in an hour using the software."

The next step stating the methods or conditions used to measure competency really depends on what's being measured. If you are trying to find out if the student knows all of the modules in an ERP package, a simple multiple-choice question will measure the results. However, if you want to know if the student can actually enter a new employee, it's best to measure the student's success in performing that task. If there are times when conditions change, such as higher call volumes at certain hours of the day, it's a good idea to test how well the employee can use the software when under stress.

Once the conditions and metrics are set, a decision must be made about what constitutes "pass/fail" criteria. Like the actual metrics, these criteria can come from many sources. In any case, however, the criteria must satisfy the employee's performance standards on the job. It's important to distinguish criteria for an individual objective from the overall test, or even the program pass/fail benchmark. An employee might have to perform certain tasks correctly to pass the test at all. If an ERP user can't log on properly, it makes no difference how well the user can enter data. Most tests use 70 to 80 percent pass rates, but there is certainly a degree of variability based on the level of criticality of the task.

It's extremely important to set up metrics so they solidify the assessment process. Failing a student in an ERP training class could be very unpopular politically, and may cause management to question the metric used. However, many organizations are using assessment to support the achievement of corporate purposes. They link training and assessment to their strategic objectives. They use simple assessment tools to gauge transfer of learning to the job and to corporate objectives. This allows trainers to be a little tougher, because the employees must show that they can support the organization's mission by doing their work quickly, efficiently, and accurately.

Metrics are often viewed as providing inconsequential reaction data and costly and time-consuming outcome data. The training team faces additional challenges in ensuring adequate assessment of "soft" training/learning and sometimes operates in a climate of weak management support for evaluation. However, a new trend in training assessment links assessment to performance, organizational competencies, and core values, rather than to training. Evaluation is linked to performance, to organizational competencies, and to core values, rather than to training. More specifically, the aim is to assess how the organization is able to adapt.

Developing a Certification Test

Certification-based training is a proven system that enables an organization to deliver a training program composed of professional reusable components via the corporate intranet, in self-paced modules, or in a classroom or a one-on-one environment. The organization evaluates the trainees through one or more written certification tests and observation of the trainees through a "live" run of their work. Like developing individual tests for objectives, there are a specific set of steps to be taken when developing groups of tests for a certification. This set of steps is similar to, but more complex than, the three-step approach specified earlier.

A module is a set of material with specific learning objectives; it may be made up of an intranet subsite, material on the world wide web, or five pages in a company manual. Each module contains a study guide that the employee uses to study for a written test, in addition to a checklist of specific skills that are to be evaluated during the qualification run. Modules have specific attainable objectives, are self-paced, and contain a study guide that highlights the material tested. Modules break material up into components that contain foundation skills and job-specific skills. Foundation components cover material that is applicable for all employees in skills such as company history, computer skills, or guest service techniques. Job-specific modules train skills that employees need to carry out their day-to-day tasks.

Microsoft, Novell, Lotus, and others have spent millions of dollars convincing the I/T industry of the value of certification. People, especially managers, perceive that there is value and importance in certification. An internal certification program (made up of several tests) allows those staff and managers who value certification to see that an employee has attained a specific skill level. It's also important to remember that, just like any other product, certification tests must be branded to create perceived value in the organization. The training department must develop testing materials, standards, and a review methodology, as well as a tangible way to recognize professionals earning certification.

One disadvantage of a certification test is that courseware must be more comprehensive than is usually produced for internal software roll-outs. It is possible that if a certification test is to be developed, some entity outside might sell courseware that training departments can use. This has been done extensively with the MCSE program. To keep current with the recent release of updates to, or new features of, a software package, the certified professional (whether business or I/T staff) must stay current on the latest feature/function set. By staying certified, the professional is showing continued competency.

Benefits of a Certification Test

There are many benefits to be gleaned from an internal certification test. It provides an organizational path for students. Students who want to learn about the software may not even know where to start. They can read an introductory book, but where do they go from there? Some people can learn well on their own with a book or CD, while others find greater benefit in instructor-led classes. But what books? What classes? Students who want to learn about NT have a nice, easy path—just follow the MCSE track through either classes, CDs, or books. The certification helps the professional know where to begin.

A certification test also provides a continuing justification for training departments. Training departments can set up a program that entices students to sign up for blocks of classes at a time. Training departments can also administer and maintain materials for both ongoing training for current employees and also entry-level training for new recruits. A certification test allows a training department to provide training that can generate productivity gains by guiding staff through a clear, concise path to job success.

A certification test can also turn students into advocates. If students learn about the software being rolled out, they will then become advocates for the software as they move within the organization. This is both due to the knowledge learned during the course of preparing for certification and also due to the fact that since certification candidates have invested a serious amount of time, energy, and money into the product, they will likely be cheerleaders for the product. This can really help smooth the implementation for the rollout team.

Certifications can also assist in the promotion and hiring process, although this can be controversial. There are lots of stories about people who were passed over for promotions or projects because they didn't have the appropriate certifications. Other arguments are about "certified" individuals who passed exams but had little practical experience. Novell's program at one point became so diluted that you could find "paper CNEs" who had become a CNE through reading books without ever touching a NetWare server!

To show real effectiveness and quality, a certification program must be exam-based, and the exams must be difficult. If it's easy to become a certified (software name here) professional, then there is no value. The problem of making it too difficult, however, is that it limits the number of people who can obtain the certification, and therefore the certification does not become widely recognized. A balance must be struck between making the program worthwhile and making it prohibitively difficult.

The program must have multiple levels. Not all Lotus Notes users (including I/T staff) need to know how to develop databases and LotusScript. A beginner level might only involve learning how to create and edit documents and send e-mail. Intermediate courses could add simple database design and implementation, and advanced courses could involve administrative tasks. The same is true for ERP software. SAP business users certainly don't need to know how to write ABAP code (the SAP programming language), but they do need to understand how their entries affect other systems. The levels can also correspond to various parts of the product. It's possible that a user only needs to know the financial side of the Oracle ERP suite, and not the procurement part.

All these factors must be accounted for when creating a certification program and its associated tests. It's also important to manage the expectations of stakeholders, and to ensure participation of those stakeholders in the certification development process. If senior managers aren't aware of the development effort, it's unlikely that the program will meet their expectations, which means employees will not be performing as expected. This is sure death for a training program.

Steps to Create a Certification Test

Creating a certification test is a significant process that can be heavily influenced by organizational politics. Individual managers will likely have their own opinion of what employees should be tested on and how the test should be measured. If possible, political pressure should be listened to, but it should *not* dictate the creation of the test or the metrics associated with it.

A performance test allows the learner to demonstrate a skill that has been learned in a training program. Performance tests are also criterion-referenced, in that they require the learner to demonstrate the required behavior stated in the objective. The evaluator should have a check sheet to go by that lists all the performance steps that the learner must perform to pass the test. If the standard is met, the learner passes. If any of the steps is missed or performed incorrectly, the learner should be given additional practice and coaching and then retested. There are three critical factors in a good performance test:

- The learner must know what behaviors (actions) are required in order to pass the test. This is accomplished by providing adequate practice and coaching sessions throughout the learning sessions. Prior to the performance evaluation, the steps required for a successful completion of the test must be understood by the learner.
- The necessary equipment and scenario must be ready and in good working condition prior to the test. This is accomplished by prior planning and a commitment by the leaders of the organization to provide the necessary resources.
- The evaluator must know what behaviors are to be looked for and how they are rated. The evaluator must know each task and the parameters for the successful completion of each step.

To meet these critical factors, there are a set of standard steps that are followed to create a complete program, with multiple tests and tracks. This 10-step approach is as follows:

1. Use the objectives, along with the metrics for each objective, to create a test bank of items. The first step in putting together a simple course test, or a more complex certification test, is to create a large number of test items. These items can be either written or performance (task-based) items. Questions generally reflect a statement of the objective.
2. Determine which test items can be answered in written form and which test items can be answered by performing a task. This should be fairly obvious. For example, if the student is required to perform a task, the test item would be performance-based with metrics for time and error rates.
3. Determine which test items can be used for each type of student (e.g., I/T versus business user). It's important to decide which items are best suited to each type of student. This is usually done by categorizing students as technical and nontechnical students.

4. Classify the test items by difficulty and type (e.g., finance versus sales and distribution). The test items should be rated according to the depth of knowledge required to perform the task. For example, creating an e-mail message in Lotus Notes is a simple task and thus would be rated at the beginner level. Designing and creating a Lotus Notes database would require considerably more knowledge of the product and would be rated as an advanced concept. The items must also be divided by type. For ERP software, this is usually by module.

5. Group the test items into logical units for a test or part of a test. Grouping the items can be done according to difficulty, type, level, and other methods. For more information, see Section 4.4.

6. Group the units and/or tests into tracks and certificates (e.g., finance versus sales and distribution). Certificates can be awarded based on completion of grouped units by level or difficulty, by business function, etc. The tracks and certificates help the students understand what they've accomplished, as well as reassuring management that the training is organized and aligned with the business.

7. Determine the pass/fail criteria or score. This will obviously depend on the level of criticality of the task or training need or objective. As mentioned above, the pass/fail criteria depend in large part on the severity of the risk of failure. Is 70 or 80 percent good enough? How much will a failure cost? How difficult is it to fix the problem created by the failure?

8. Determine test and/or program administration guidelines. Test and program administration involves tasks such as scheduling courses and tests, guarding the answers or changing the tests periodically, and regulating the environment in which the test is administered. Is a test computer required?

9. Develop incentives that will encourage employees to participate. Maybe even more importantly, develop incentives for management to give employees the time to participate. Following is a list of questions to ask regarding incentives. The list also appears as a checklist in Appendix F and on McGraw-Hill's website at www.books.mcgrawhill.com/training/download. The forms can then be opened, edited, and printed using Microsoft Word or other word processing software.

- Is the task seen to be worthwhile?
- Do the employees believe they can perform the task?
- Is there incentive for performing well?
- Do the incentives really matter to the participants?
- Is the incentive contingent upon good performance?
- Do the participants know the link between incentive and performance?
- Are incentives scheduled to prevent discouragement?
- Are all available incentives being used?
- Do the participants find the work interesting?
- If incentives are mixed, is the balance positive?
- Is "punishment for good performance" prevented?
- Is "reward for poor performance" prevented?
- Is there peer pressure for good performance?
- Is task unpleasantness or stress within acceptable levels?
- Does poor performance draw attention?

10. Use some kind of test bank software or database to manage test items and results. A number of packages are available that will store test items and generate tests.

This 10-step approach appears as a process checklist in Appendix F and on McGraw-Hill's website at www.books.mcgraw-hill.com/training/download. The forms can then be opened, edited, and printed using Microsoft Word or other word processing software. Additional steps or changes to these steps should be made based on the needs of the individual organization.

4.3 SELECTING AND SEQUENCING PROGRAM AND COURSE CONTENT

The scope of a course is a curriculum decision and, as such, is broadly identified through a process of dialogue that involves the instructor, department, and organization at large. Although the organization's course approval process is the originating point for content decisions, instructors have latitude within the bounds of the final approved course description in deciding the specific content that will be part of a particular course offering. If the course is part of a sequence that builds on skills and knowledge from a previous course or is standardized across the department, the course will include the expected content.

It is usually advisable that instructors think about underlying assumptions throughout the process of planning a course. For example, instructors should think about whether their content is inclusive or concentrates on a very narrow perspective, whether their approach takes developments in the field into consideration, and how their course will complement other courses in the department.

Selecting Content

Selecting content begins by asking some questions about what information will help students meet the objectives and/or pass the tests. These simple questions can make a big difference in how you select the content:

- How does your course fit into the knowledge base of the organization?
- Should students be taught not only substantive knowledge but also the evidence for this knowledge and the procedures by which it was obtained?
- If students do have to know and apply knowledge and skills from other than what you consider to be your discipline, do you consider yourself able to teach, where necessary, the information and skills to students who lack them?
- What (1) information, (2) processes, and (3) attitudes and values constitute the subject matter or content of the course?
- Does the vendor have material that is recommended for the class?

These questions will lead the training developer (and trainer) in the right direction in terms of the material. It's useful to also consider the manuals surrounding the material to be taught. While software manuals are rarely easy to use, they do provide a good checklist of material to cover.

Making a Concept Map or Content Web

Make a random list of the concepts, values, skills, processes, theories, etc., that you want to cover in your course by asking yourself the question: What are the important "things" I want my students to learn in this course? Looking at your list, what two to six (approximately) key concepts or ideas are central to what you want students to learn? Place these on your concept map. Arrange the other concepts, values, skills, processes, and theories from your initial list on your map by making links using terms such as *leads to, is influenced by, depends upon, caused by,* and *related to* between these and the key concepts. Look carefully at your map and decide if:

- The most general and fundamental concepts are front and center.
- The other concepts are related in logical fashion.

- There are no omissions.
- There is no duplication.
- The various content elements are related to the course's learning objectives.

Ask yourself what values and assumptions are implicit in the decisions that have been made regarding content selection and emphasis.

Next, broad content areas are determined. To accomplish this, potential content is reviewed in relation to the selected theme. For example, if HR is the theme, information gathered about personnel, payroll, and benefits should be examined. Available HR-related curricula and content sources may also be studied. Finally, consider related focus areas. For example, in manufacturing, these might encompass the fiscal, economic, marketing, distribution, and management areas. As with the broad content areas, it must be decided which focus areas exemplify and define the broad theme. Questions to ask include:

- Which focus areas actually exist within the theme and assist in defining the theme more comprehensively?
- To what extent might the organization be able to assist with class- and work-based learning in related focus areas?
- To what degree can the focus areas be readily incorporated into the curriculum?

These questions are really about making sure that the course content is what should be there, and also that the content ties directly to the organization's goals. Focus areas are important because they provide the foundation for creating the "core" concept of a specific course. For example, the core concept of a class about an employee data entry screen is getting the data into the system. An example of a concept map for the employee master data screen might resemble Figure 4-1. In this figure, the core concept is at the center of the picture, and the necessary ancillary tasks surround it as context. Laying these tasks or objectives out in a picture allows you to visualize how the course will look when it's complete. These maps can also be used to sequence content later in the process.

Sequencing Options

The next step in the design phase is to determine the program sequence and structure to ensure the learning objectives are met. A proper sequence provides the learners with a pattern of relationship so that each activity will have a definite purpose. The more meaningful the content, the easier it is to

FIGURE 4-1

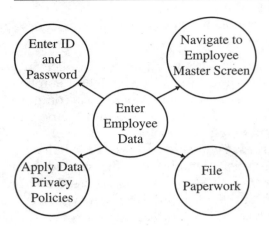

learn and, consequently, the more effective the instruction. Proper sequencing also helps to avoid inconsistencies in the content of the instruction. When material is carefully sequenced, duplication is far less likely. Some of the techniques and considerations used in sequencing are:

- Go from the familiar to the unfamiliar, from the known to the unknown. Lay down a familiar frame of reference before introducing foreign concepts.
- Move from the concrete to the abstract, from the general to the specific. Fill the students' minds with concrete examples before emphasizing general abstractions.
- Use a historical episode in which the problem was resolved.
- Proceed according to a logical or conceptual outline.
- Avoid introducing abstract, formal, and unfamiliar words, terms, or phrases until you have made them concrete, familiar, and intelligible.

Take the objectives you have developed and organize them in the sequence of instruction by chunking them into related groups and then determine a logical sequence.

If there are many objectives, they should be organized into clusters that are conducive to learning. The sequencing performed earlier is the basis for breaking the objectives down into clusters based on the class relationship between them. If the training program is long, reinforcement also has to be accounted for. If a task is taught in the instructional program and then is not used for some time after the learners return to their duties, some decay is likely to take place. The remedy for this is to ensure that the learners perform their newly acquired skills as soon as possible upon returning to the job.

4.4   DEVELOPING TRAINING TRACKS AND HIGH-LEVEL LESSON PLANS

Developing Training Tracks

Because there are several types and levels of users who will be participating in the courses, it's a good idea to have multiple "tracks" that are complete learning plans for various types of students. These tracks can be shown in a format such as flow diagrams. Figure 4-2 shows a training program with two different tracks. Both tracks start out training ERP HR basics, but then split, with the upper track becoming more technical and the lower track becoming more focused on business.

Tracks can also be developed based on levels of skill. A groupware training program may have beginner, intermediate, and advanced tracks,

FIGURE 4-2

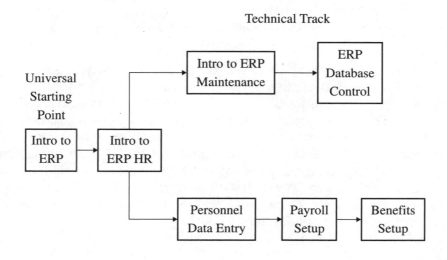

as well as technical administration tracks. The key is to understand the students' needs and expectations well enough to separate the training into logical divisions. The tracks should reflect the objectives for each course and the program. The measurement or assessment of the program's value will also be affected by the track layouts.

The High-Level Lesson Plan

The purpose of a lesson plan is really quite simple; it is to communicate. The lesson plans you develop guide you in helping your students achieve intended learning outcomes. Whether a lesson plan fits a particular format is not as important as whether it actually describes what you want, and what you have determined is the best means to an end. If you write a lesson plan that can be interpreted or implemented in many different ways, it is probably not very good. Following are some common mistakes:

- The objective does not specify what the student will actually do that can be observed.
- The lesson assessment is disconnected from the behavior indicated in the objective.
- The materials specified in the lesson are extraneous to the actual described learning activities.
- The instruction is not efficient or effectively targeted at the level of intended student learning.
- The student activities described do not contribute in a direct and effective way to the objective.

A lesson plan that contains one or more of these mistakes needs rethinking and revision, particularly when the fate of the organization rests on the ability of the employees to use the new software effectively.

The development of a lesson plan has to begin somewhere, and a good place to start is with a list or description of general information about the plan. This information sets the boundaries or limits of the plan. Here is a brief but good list of these information items: (1) the skill level of the students for whom the plan is intended; (2) the specific subject matter (finance, manufacturing, etc.); and (3) if appropriate, the name of the unit of which the lesson is a part.

Each part of a lesson plan should fulfill some purpose in communicating the specific content, the objective, the learning prerequisites, the expected outcome, the sequence of student and trainer activities, the materials required, and the actual assessment procedures. At the conclusion of a lesson, the assessment tells the trainer how well students actually attained the objective. For each lesson, there are inputs, processes, and outputs or expected outputs.

Inputs refer to the physical materials, other resources, and information that will be required by the process. If you have thought about what the lesson is supposed to accomplish, the inputs become easy to describe. In general categories, inputs consist of:

- Information about the students for whom the lesson is intended. This information includes how old the students are and what they already know about what you want them to learn.
- Information about the amount of time you estimate it will take to implement the lesson.
- Descriptions of the materials that will be required by the lesson.
- Information about how you will acquire the physical materials required.
- Information about how to obtain any special permissions and schedules required.

The process is the actual plan. If you have done the preliminary work (thinking, describing the inputs), creating the plan is relatively easy. There are a number of questions you answer in creating the plan:

- What are the inputs? This means you have the information (content description, student characteristics, list of materials, prerequisites, time estimates, etc.) necessary to begin the plan.
- What is the output? This means a description of what the students are supposed to learn.
- What do I do? This means a description of the instructional activities you will use.
- What do the students do? This means a description of what the students will do during the lesson.
- How will the learning be measured? This means a description of the assessment procedure.

The outputs are the learning results and student behaviors exhibited when the course is complete. In addition, there may also be results of evaluations (course and instructor) which can be stored for further use in continually improving the course or program. This is discussed more in Chapter 12.

The high-level lesson plan actually evolves into a syllabus, or course summary. A syllabus is the vehicle for communicating the structure of the course and operating procedures. It will help students know what is expected from the start of the course. A positive image will be presented to the students because a well-prepared syllabus is evidence that the instructor takes training seriously. A syllabus also provides the departmental supervisor with pertinent information about the course.

One can begin by studying syllabi from other instructors or syllabi that have been used previously in the course being taught. Instructors might also check with their departments for specific guidelines they may have about a syllabus format. The following are generally included in the syllabus:

- *Relevant information about the course and instructor.* The information should include the current session, the purpose, etc. These facts are normally placed at the beginning of the document.
- *A clear statement of course goals.* The course goals should be as clear as possible and should describe what the students will be expected to know, rather than what the instructor plans to do.
- *A statement of grading criteria that explains the pass/fail criteria.* This is likely to be somewhat controversial if a failure is even an option. Management commitment is critical here.
- *A statement of course policy.* This is best expressed in a clear, non-threatening form. Policies should be set for such events as missing an exam, turning in a late assignment, or missing class. It is a good idea to go on record with a fairly stringent policy that can be informally tempered at a later date, if and where circumstances so warrant.

Beyond the content of the syllabus is its tone, which can be welcoming or hostile. A brief syllabus with strong warnings about policy infringements and no encouraging words about the excitement of the course content may be off-putting. Syllabi that contain humor and enthusiasm can create good first impressions. Some studies suggest 10 rules for syllabus construction:

1. Convey enthusiasm for the subject.
2. Convey the intellectual challenge of the course.
3. Provide opportunities for students to personalize the content.
4. Convey respect for the ability of students.

5. State course goals positively so that they appear attainable.
6. Convey the possibility of success in stating grading policy.
7. Adequately specify assignments.
8. Vary assignments according to the type of expertise required.
9. Make provisions for frequent assessment of student learning.
10. Convey the trainer's desire to help students individually.

Similarly, spatial layout can make a difference. Syllabi that are well designed will certainly be more effective than those that are tossed together the day before the class.

It is important to check over the final typed copy for mistakes and typos. If the instructor does not catch them, it is certain that the students will. It is good policy to hand out the syllabus on the first day of class, unless the instructor wants to engage students in participating in course planning. The instructor will need to review and discuss the syllabus with the students, answering any questions that they may have and providing appropriate clarification.

It is vital to have enough copies of the syllabus—that includes extras to hand out to students who have lost their copies and to accommodate students who have registered for the class but do not appear on the initial roster. If changes are made in the syllabus subsequently, it is a good idea to give them to students in writing. Much ambiguity and confusion can result from half-remembered spoken promises.

CASE: ACME WIDGETS—DESIGNING THE TRAINING PROGRAM

In Chapter 2, Bob, Mike, and the rest of the team put together a needs analysis for the HR portion of WCS and for several levels of KIS user. The next step is to use the process in this chapter to complete the specifications of the course design. For the purpose of this book, we'll look at the employee master data screen entry process in WCS. Kathy, the training developer, will be creating the WCS employee master data screen classes (there are two).

Creating the Employee Master Training

The first step for Kathy is to decide what knowledge must be transferred to the new users. Since both business users and I/T staff must understand how the screens work, the classes will be generic to the product, and not tailored to either a technical or a business level. Recall from Chapter 2 that the employee master data class for the screen was listed as shown in Table 4-2.

TABLE 4-2

Item	Software Module	Software Function	Screen	Job	Org. Unit	Est. Classes	Est. Hours
1.	HR	Enter new employee	HRM01	HR recruiter	HR	2	6

The two classes represent a logical division between simply entering the data and coping with errors. The first class presents the necessary material to enter a complete new employee record. The class takes about 2 hours. The second class helps the user solve error messages and other problems commonly encountered when entering data. Kathy talked with Trudy, the HR specialist, and received some guidance on establishing objectives for the classes. Kathy was given some metrics, as established by the quality goals of the HR department, regarding the timeliness and accuracy of their data. The concept map Kathy produced is shown in Figure 4-1. From this concept map, Kathy produced some objectives for the first class, which are listed in Table 4-3.

For this class, there will be few "concept questions" although a knowledge of company policies on new employee announcements would be useful. Most of the metrics will be performance-related.

For the error-handling class, Kathy created the concept map pictured in Figure 4-3. This figure shows a logical sequence of handling errors from the simple and known to the complex, which is likely beyond the capabilities of the operator. The resulting objectives are listed in Table 4-4. Note that the time frame for completion (10 minutes) didn't change. The operator and help desk must work together to solve the problem.

The learning activities for the data entry classes consist of a brief orientation and overview of the module and screen, a step-by-step walk-through of the data entry procedures, and a simulated problem-solving session for the errors. The "test" for the employee master data entry class simply consists of a procedural simulation for each type of error message, as well as various types of employees (hourly, salaried, etc.). The types of certificates are personnel, payroll, and benefits operator. Each of these constitutes a single level, which is by module. An employee who completes all three is certified as a WCS HR specialist user. The tracks resemble Figure 4-4. These tracks help employees understand the requirements for certification, provide them with incentives to perform and work toward promotions, and help management evaluate employee progress.

Another format that works well for classes set by level is the hierarchy chart. For example, suppose you wanted to create a certification plan for the KIS system. The starting point or foundation consists of the basic skills of using e-mail and reading documents in a knowledge database. The next level of skill, geared to the interme-

TABLE 4 - 3

Item	Software Module	Software Function	Level or Type	Need	Objective(s)
1.	HR	Enter new employee	Business—HR	Enter a new employee into employee database	1. Log on to the HR part of WCS 2. Enter all new employee data in 5 to 10 minutes with two errors or less 3. Save the data
2.	HR	Enter new employee	Business—HR	Notify all involved parties of new employee	1. Create e-mail list 2. E-mail involved parties within 2 hours of data entry

FIGURE 4 - 3

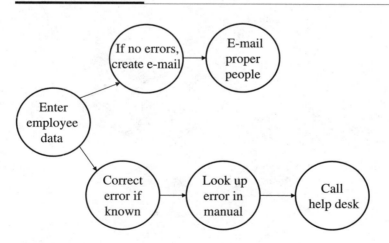

diate user, would be to know how to create databases. The top level, or power user, would add some administrative skills. A possible layout is depicted in Figure 4-5. In the figure, each of the levels above beginner builds on the skills acquired at the level below. For example, the intermediate-level database administration skill builds on the beginner-level document editor skill. Each of these levels provides a

TABLE 4-4

Item	Software Module	Software Function	Level or Type	Need	Objective(s)
1.	HR	Enter new employee	Beginner	Solve data entry problems	1. Find the source of the problem 2. Solve it if possible without assistance 3. Find the problem in the manual if needed 4. Call the help desk if the problem is complex or systematic 5. Employee master should still be complete within 10 minutes

FIGURE 4-4

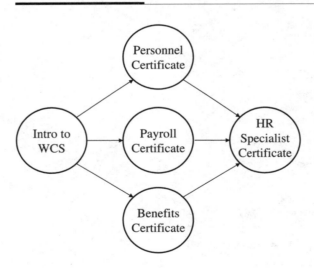

certificate that both gives the employees a sense of accomplishment and tells them and the next instructor that they're ready for the next course.

Using the information created for the WCS course, Kathy put together a syllabus containing a lesson plan and other relevant information. The sample course description is presented in Figure 4-6. This is obviously an abbreviated course description. More or less detail may be required to meet the needs of each class. This outline may change if training is purchased or if students are sent off-site to a third-party trainer.

FIGURE 4-5

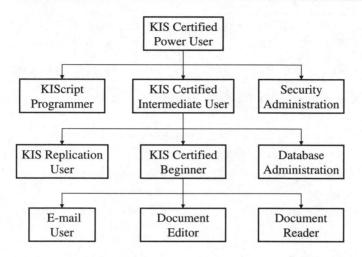

FIGURE 4-6

WCS HR Employee Master Screen Course (Two Parts)

Course Purpose

This course is designed to provide the student with the ability to enter a new employee record and fix any errors that occur during the entry. Should errors occur that are outside the scope of normal entry problems, the student will know when to call the help desk.

Prerequisite

None

Instructor

Shawn Jones is a professional trainer with 5 years of experience in WCS HR fundamentals.

Objectives

Upon the completion of this course, the student will be able to:

- Log on to the HR part of WCS
- Enter all new employee data in 5 to 10 minutes with two errors or less

---

FIGURE 4-6

WCS HR Employee Master Screen Course (Two Parts)
(Continued)

- Save the data
- Create an e-mail list of the people who need to know about the new employee
- E-mail involved parties within 2 hours of data entry
- Find the source of any problems
- Solve the problems, if possible, without assistance
- Find the problem in the manual if needed
- Call the help desk if the problem is complex or systematic

Course Approach

The student will be using a simulated WCS system for both parts of the class. The performance metrics will be based on the data entry accuracy and speed. The student must meet the criteria specified in the objectives to receive the certificate of completion.

Course Schedule

The course will run in two parts: (1) data entry and error correction and (2) problem solving. Data entry training will take about 2 hours, and problem solving will take about 4 hours.

Course Policies

Because of the amount of work to be done in the classroom, class will start and end on time. Students are asked to comply with the break time limits to facilitate learning. Students should feel free to help each other as we are all going to learn together.

Coming Up in Chapter 5

With the curriculum designed, it's time to make some decisions about the delivery method. There are several options, including self-study, classroom, computer or web-based training, facilitated computer-based learning, and live distance learning options. As Chapter 5 will explain, the delivery method depends on the type and critical nature of the training needs.

REFERENCES

Briggs, L. J., & Gagne, R. M. (1979). *Principles of instructional design* (2d ed.). New York: Holt, Rinehart and Winston.

Carey, L., & Dick, W. (1996). *The systematic design of instruction* (4th ed.). New York: HarperCollins.

Davis, J. R. (1995). *Interdisciplinary courses and team training: New arrangements for learning.* Phoenix, AZ: Oryx Press.

Day, R. S. (1980). Training from notes: Some cognitive consequences. In W. McKeachie (ed.), *Learning, cognition, and college training. New directions for training and learning, No. 2.* San Francisco: Jossey-Bass.

Diamond, R. (1991). *Designing and improving courses and curricula in higher education.* San Francisco: Jossey-Bass.

Gaines Robinson, Dana, & Robinson, James. (1989). *Training for impact.* San Francisco: Jossey-Bass.

Kirkpatrick, Donald L. (1996). *Evaluating training programs: The four levels.* San Francisco: Berrett-Koehler.

Leshin, C. B., Pollock, J., & Reigeluth, C. M. (1992). *Instructional design strategies and tactics.* Englewood Cliffs, NJ: Educational Technology Publications.

Phillips, Jack. (1997). *Handbook of training evaluation and measurement methods.* Houston, TX: Gulf Publishing Company.

Posner, G. J., & Rudnitsky, A. N. (1986). *Course design: A guide to curriculum development for trainers* (3d ed.). New York: Longman.

Rothwell, W. J., & Cookson, P. S. (1997). *Beyond instruction: Comprehensive program planning for business and education.* San Francisco: Jossey-Bass.

Todesco, Angie. (1997). *From training evaluation to outcome assessment: What trends and best practices tell us. A progress report from the learning services directorate to the public service commission.* Texas: Learning Resources Network.

Wager, W. W., Gagne, R. M., & Briggs, L. J. (1992). *Principles of instructional design.* Fort Worth, TX: Harcourt, Brace, Jovanovich.

York, Dan. (1998, October). Creating a linux certification and training program. *Linux Gazette.*

CHAPTER 5

Self-Directed Training versus Classroom Training

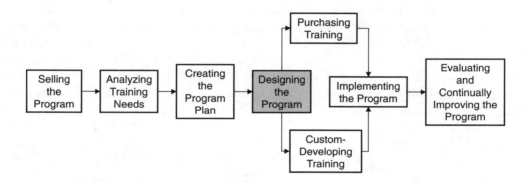

In This Chapter

OVERVIEW

This chapter is concerned with the design process, because the decision on the delivery method(s) will determine much of how the training development process proceeds. The decision is dependent on the results of both needs analysis and design.

Good training programs, regardless of delivery method, take advantage of the latest learning technologies and best practices. Recent developments in best practices include the decreased use of centralized "event" training and the increased use of more local, on-site training. Training is often needed for one or a few individuals, not necessarily for a large group. Waiting until there is a sufficient number to train in a traditional group can be costly in terms of lost productivity. As software rollouts progress, various types of individuals will need different types of training, though users may need it as a group when the software is implemented at the end of development. On-site, customized training addresses this need.

Other best practices include the increased use of short, task-oriented modules and powerful training sessions available during the normal workweek which are immediate and consistent. Web-based technologies are becoming prevalent, as is computer-based training (CBT) and interactive video. Newer concepts in training also provide learners with the training they need when they need it. Some participants in the software rollout may be technically adept; others may not. The main, important theme is proximity and realism, where training is available either on or as close to the job as possible.

One issue of considerable concern is that of the different qualities of interaction. It seems to be a very important issue, often neglected in training. The key to maximizing learning is to individualize it. This is achievable through a high level of interaction. The ability to achieve quality learning is very much dependent on paying close attention to what the student is doing, what the student's strengths and weaknesses are, and what the student needs additional help with. This is essential in every learning environment. The different technologies discussed here generally lead to very different results as far as the quality and quantity of interaction, so it's important to address that issue.

5.1   SELF-STUDY OR CLASSROOM?

The decision whether to use classroom or self-study methods to deliver the training is based on several factors that account for both the audience and the course content. Some of the specific factors that must be examined are:

- Analysis of your target audience, including their educational levels and degrees of computer literacy. This was completed in the needs analysis.
- Content possibilities. This includes whether the content must be presented in linear or free-form.
- How the program will be used. Does the audience need to take the material home to study?

- What types of computers your audience will have available.
- Talent and technical support needed and available, e.g., instructional designer, programmers, etc.
- Budget and time lines, determined in Chapter 3.
- The software itself.

These factors and others affect both the way the material is presented and the environment in which it's presented. The advantages and disadvantages of classroom and self-study follow.

The Traditional Classroom

The conventional classroom includes all activities and interactions in and out of class which are generally facilitated by an instructor or trainer. Classrooms can now be both real and virtual, as discussed in Section 5.4 on live distance learning (DL) options. Traditional classrooms, however, have the most structure and formality of the learning methods discussed in this chapter. The classroom environment has both advantages and disadvantages. Some key advantages are:

- Instruction can be easily customized and revised.
- Broad proficiency is gained in a short period of time.
- The learning process is directed and focused on specific objectives.
- Course content is quickly developed.
- Development costs are minimal.
- Trainees can ask questions.
- Trainees learn from each other and have an interactive environment.
- Employers consider completion of formal training as evidence of knowledge.

Some of these advantages are obviously dependent on the type of course, the duration of the course, and the difficulty of the material to be presented. This leads to some of the key disadvantages:

- Slow learning rate
- Low knowledge retention
- Inconsistencies from class to class
- Scheduling difficulties
- Facilities costs

The major difference between self-study classes and classroom training is the interaction between students and instructors. In the traditional classroom, the high level of interaction often leads to a discovery of new knowledge derived from the class's collective knowledge. With software roll-outs, this can be especially helpful, particularly if students experiment as they learn. Both student and instructor stand to benefit from the collaboration.

The Self-Study Route

If your company cannot or will not send you to training for whatever reason, or if you cannot afford a formal course, self-study is the choice. The major disadvantage of self-study training methods is that the student must find out if something in the material has changed. For some students, self-study is the right choice because these students internalize the material better and faster than having someone else tell them how to do things.

It's probably safe to say, though, that for most people, formal training is still perceived as better. Most people believe that you cannot learn everything through self-study. Also, formal training is better for beginners because it makes learning easier and the students learn to do things right from the start. Despite these unfavorable points, do not entirely discount self-study. It's still useful, and may be helpful after formal training. It can enhance your knowledge, and you can experiment and try out things that were not discussed in class. It also helps students develop self-confidence and makes them proud that they can learn new things on their own. Some other advantages of self-study are:

- Students can work when they want. There is no need to wait for a scheduled training course.
- Students can work at their own pace.
- Students can target specific topics for study without having to plod through an introductory course to reach the necessary topic.
- The training is consistent. With audio and video it can also be both entertaining and enjoyable.
- Courses are particularly suited to adults who wish to learn but don't want to sit in a classroom.

Of course, there are many different types of self-study delivery media, including print, video, and CD-ROM. Each of these presentation methods has its own advantages and disadvantages (see Table 5-1).

TABLE 5-1

Advantages and Disadvantages of Self-Study Delivery Media

Media	Advantages	Disadvantages
Print (books, manuals, workbooks)	Can be quickly developed	Expensive to revise
	Portable	Bulky to store and transport
	Self-paced	Low completion rates
	Can be referenced later	Requires literate learners
Video (videotapes, teleconferences)	Efficient for large groups or multiple locations	High production costs
	Does not require trainer or trainee travel	Requires complex planning
	Controlled, consistent content	Requires playback equipment
	Able to demonstrate as well as explain	Risk of technical malfunction
CD-ROM	High-quality, interactive approach	Can be very expensive
	Can be easily installed	May become obsolete quickly
	Takes up little room to store	May require large amounts of disk storage space
	Can be used on employee's PC	

Application Considerations

Because ERP software is so complex, it is usually recommended that formal classroom training be used for at least the basics. Training can make the difference between an ERP implementation that meets its goals on time and on budget and one that gets seriously messed up. Some leading ERP vendors have recently begun to move into the midmarket and the end-user training arena. To succeed in these two new markets, a number of these vendors offer flexible technology-based alternatives to their traditional technical classroom training programs. This can work if the trainee is very computer literate, but is less likely to be successful with computer novices. Self-study materials can be supplied as reference material, but it's better to have students learn together in a facilitated classroom CBT setting (see Section 5.3).

5.2 COMPUTER OR WEB-BASED TRAINING OPTIONS

Computer-based training is the delivery of learning by computer or through multimedia, typically as self-paced learning; however, some CBT is facilitated in a classroom setting. Many companies are turning to CBT to better utilize training dollars by providing employees with materials that don't require additional instructor or travel costs. There are many companies providing CBT materials both on CD-ROM and over the Web, but most provide only the materials, not implementation strategies.

As with any technology, however, there are good and bad reasons for buying. When organizations purchase CBT courses because of the low per-employee cost, these courses can receive extremely low usage, for reasons including:

- The materials available do not meet the employee's needs.
- Training time is limited because of staff shortages.
- There is no formal plan for implementing, delivering, and evaluating the training.

New technologies are often implemented because they're new. If the technology implementation isn't properly planned, it is unlikely that any real value will be realized from the investment. Intranet-based CBT is no different, and organizations must plan for its use and implementation first.

Present-day CBT technology allows each student to learn at his or her own pace. The underlying premise of this methodology is that highly motivated individuals can master a subject given adequate time and carefully designed materials. Through the use of innovative computer technology, designed specifically for education and training, trainees set their own pace for learning, thus enabling them to master each lesson, program, unit, and subject before moving to the next. Trainees who need to repeat the instruction can do so with the press of a key. Students who learn quickly can progress rapidly through a review of basic knowledge and skills toward more challenging learning at their own pace. CBT offers all the advantages that are common to other forms of flexible learning, including:

- Consistent presentation of material
- The flexibility for the learner to work at his or her own pace
- The opportunity for the learner to study at a convenient place and time
- Interactivity, which can improve motivation and retention
- Immediate feedback to questions and practice exercises

- The greater realism that results from graphics, sound, moving images, and simulations

CBT is not the best choice, however, for some organizations, because:

- Special equipment is needed, sometimes including noisy sound cards.
- It is not easily portable.
- Learning material is more costly.
- The program may take up too much space on computers.

The relative costs of technology-based and paper-based classes depend upon a number of factors. In general, CBT has higher costs, but can be more exciting for students. Some success factors are:

- Choosing the right vendor
- Ensuring the materials are relevant
- Properly managing the implementation and use of the courseware
- Motivating employees to use the courseware
- Demonstrating the results to management

To ensure that courseware materials are relevant, managers and project leaders from all areas of the organization should be involved, including various applications development and support groups as well as end users. As the curriculum is developed, managers and training leaders review the materials and ensure that the employees will have the skills needed to be productive when they've finished training.

There are three general approaches to implementing CBT: (1) traditional, (2) one in which the student uses the material alone, as preparation for an instructor-led classroom experience, and (3) a facilitated CBT session with an instructor present for help and coordination. Each of these approaches has value and its unique advantages and disadvantages. Deciding on the approach means considering the difficulty of the materials, the level of the students, and the time available for students to use the courseware.

The traditional approach works for students who have some basic skills in the topic, but need additional information to help them in their work. This is the least expensive alternative. As a basic skills course (for which CBT is often used), CBT may not work if the material is unclear, or the student needs someone to answer questions. For advanced students, the CBT-only approach may not be able to provide a learning experience that challenges their skills.

There are also hundreds of on-line courses now being offered via the Internet and web by dozens of colleges and universities worldwide. These include both independent study and instructor-led courses. Within these courses, the Internet and web are being used for on-line course marketing, student registration, administration, student-instructor communication via e-mail and conferences, transfer of student assignments and materials, and on-line research, testing, and "field trips" to other websites. The Internet is also beginning to be used in conjunction with other DL methods and media (discussed in Section 5.4). In summary, the key advantages of interactive multimedia training are that:

- Self-paced instruction encourages students to take the most efficient path to content mastery. They'll skip areas they already know and concentrate on areas they're weak in.
- Instruction can be personalized to accommodate different learning styles and maximize a student's learning efficiency.
- It may be cheaper. The biggest costs of interactive instruction are in the design and production of the material. So the more students who use the program, the lower the cost per student.
- It's more consistent. Human instructors can have bad days and get tired. A machine doesn't, so instruction does not vary in quality from day to day or from one class to another.
- Students tend to ask more questions and explore more areas when they are not in a group setting. Machines never lose patience when students keep asking the same question until they've got it.
- It ensures students have mastered current material before they move onto the next subject.
- Programs can be structured so the student has to answer a number of review questions correctly before the new material can be accessed.

It's also safer. Learning some skills involves some risk, particularly of destroying data. In some cases, the basis for many of these skills can be taught from the safety of a computer or TV screen, without endangering development or production environments.

Application Considerations

One potentially big advantage of web-based ERP training is that ERP clients can access the ERP software company's website for training. This means that customers don't have to constantly update their CBT library on-site. They simply have their employees access the ERP vendor's training library via the Internet, which will always be current. Other advantages include no travel costs, access anytime, and the potential to participate in discussion groups or chat rooms for help. The major disadvantage is the lack of live interaction between student and instructor. This is more important for those with a lower level of computer literacy than for students who are I/T staff. The other disadvantage is that the training can't be customized to a particular organization's configuration since many organizations access the same site.

5.3   FACILITATED COMPUTER-BASED TRAINING

The facilitated approach combines the benefits of CBT with the advantages of having an instructor present to answer questions. Concepts and rules can be derived more readily and internalized faster from active play, exploration, and investigation than from listening to or reading about them. The major drawback to having an instructor lead and pace the class is the potential to hold back advanced students. This may not happen if the instructor is flexible in managing the classroom and if the material doesn't require teamwork among students. Another disadvantage of using CBT in a classroom setting is the technology maturity: the technology isn't stable because it's new.

Whether because of equipment failure or operator error, program malfunctions become a major source of embarrassment and frustration to teachers and trainers, who often refuse to use the technology again. Even trainers who are enthusiastic about the Internet and are teaching others to use it find that it's too unreliable to demonstrate "live" and instead capture screens to their hard drives or make overhead transparencies of web pages. In today's environment that emphasizes learner evaluations of their instructors, trainers and teachers are afraid to look foolish or unprepared, since that might result in unfavorable written student evaluations that would follow them forever and could negatively impact their careers.

In the facilitated CBT approach, students learn through discovery while also setting the pace of their learning. To facilitate learning, instructors coach students and design individual experiences through which students develop new skills. This approach creates an environment in which knowledge is shared through the collaboration of individuals while being guided by instructors. In facilitated CBT, expertise and prior experience are incorporated into the learning process as students use the information provided by the CBT material to form their own skills, as well as to share the skills learned with others. The instructor's role in this approach is to facilitate maximum sharing of information and knowledge among learners rather than control the delivery and pace of the content. The instructor also acts as a problem solver when mistakes are made or technology glitches occur.

An advantage of facilitated CBT is that a human voice narrating course material is often a comfort to students and can reassure them if they make a mistake. The student can go over the same materials many times until it's grasped and can be tested at frequent intervals to make sure the information is sinking in, and the instructor can facilitate that process. Another advantage of facilitated CBT is that the equipment needed to run it is often already available. Many companies have personal computers with CD-ROM drives which could be used to run programs. Facilitated CBT is also not restricted by location, because the instructor can go wherever there's a need. The training can take place wherever there is a computer, and with laptops, students can even be moving while they're learning.

5.4   LIVE DISTANCE LEARNING OPTIONS

The success of distance education is highly dependent on various factors. The primary concern is the way in which information is imparted to the student and the way in which the student uses the new knowledge from the material. As such, the media to transmit the learning materials should be chosen based on the actual needs and not the latest bells and whistles. The two primary forms of distance learning are (1) videoconferencing or teleconferencing and (2) web-based distance learning.

In designing an effective distance class, you must consider the goals and the content requirements of the class, as well as the technical constraints. If common delivery systems are required, they must be made accessible to all participants. As the Internet conforms to this requirement, it is likely to be the common medium of delivery.

Today, the quality of distance education depends on technology. Recent improvements in the costs and capabilities of hardware and software, combined with the growth of the Internet and improvements in connectivity, encourage the development of new classes that can be delivered via the web. Distance learning allows students to manage their time and learn while interacting with other students and instructors. For organizations, distributed learning is a way to increase the speed, flexibility, and reach of training and education, reduce costs associated with offering classroom training as the only delivery vehicle, leverage instructor resources, and leverage team learning and collaboration.

Videoconferencing and Teleconferencing

Interactive videoconferencing is an effective medium that may be used in distance education settings. This system can be integrated into the distance education program without much disruption to the curriculum and course. It is designed to support two-way video and audio communication between multiple locations. Most systems utilize compressed digital video for the transmission of motion images over data networks such as high-capacity phone lines with various special services.

Videoconferencing is probably one of the best known methods for distance learning. It allows a high level of interaction between students and instructors. Instructors may actually present the course material on the fly and do not need to ship the materials to the students prior to the class session. Students can actually see the instructors and raise questions and get immediate feedback.

However, the major problem of deploying videoconferencing as a usable method for distance learning is cost. Most videoconferencing setups rely on proprietary hardware and software. The cost for this hardware and software is so prohibitive that it is not feasible for an individual to purchase the entire system. Though videoconferencing may have a significant effect on reducing the cost of instruction, it still leaves significant scope for improvement.

Still, the latest information is often best delivered in face-to-face meetings, and the cost of sending a trainer to a number of locations can be prohibitive. A number of companies are solving that problem with satellite video teleconferencing. To receive a teleconferencing session you need a satellite dish at your location. A dish runs anywhere from $2,500 to $4,000 installed. You can call your local TV station for guidance, or simply look through the yellow pages. Broadcasting time isn't cheap (around $2,200 an hour), but that's for several or many people. And it's still much cheaper than travel expenses, which can run around $2,000 per person. Furthermore, broadcast costs may go down in the future as satellite capacity increases. Table 5-2 sums up the advantages and disadvantages of videoconferencing and teleconferencing.

Web-Based Distance Learning

When incorporating the Internet into a distant delivered course, it is anticipated that all students in the course will have Internet access. This is to ensure equal opportunities for computer interaction and feedback. Students will be subjected to challenges of learning basic computer skills, new software, and appropriate on-line communication skills. Troubleshooting student computer

TABLE 5-2

Advantages	Disadvantages
Efficient for large groups or multiple locations	High use costs
Does not require trainer or trainee travel	Requires planning and central groups
Controlled, consistent content	Requires expensive equipment
Able to demonstrate as well as explain	Risk of technical malfunction
Allows "real-time" visual contact between students and the instructor or among students at different sites	Unless a sincere effort is made by the instructor, students may remain unresponsive in the course
Supports the use of diverse media like media-boards, handwritten documents, and videos	If visuals, like handwritten or copied materials, are not properly prepared, students may encounter difficulty in reading them off the screen
Enables communications with experts in other geographical locations	If the transmission line capacity among sites is not large enough, the students may observe disrupted signals when movement occurs in real time
Can provide access to students who have special needs	If the audio system is not properly configured, students may observe an audio "echo." The result is audio interference that detracts from the learning environment

problems will probably become an integral part of normal instructional responsibilities, and thus a help desk proves very useful. There are significant advantages to using web-based distance learning methods. Some of these are:

- Live voice and interactivity across the Internet
- Choice of real-time or "asynchronous" (on-demand) training
- No geographical constraints
- Inexpensive, simple technical requirements, accessible to students and instructors with limited help from professional engineering or technical staff
- Simple and powerful testing and evaluation, ideal for compliance-based training needs
- Quick to get up and running and to gain organizational momentum
- No entrenched opposition, plenty of allies

- Little or no new investment in infrastructure beyond standard intranet and PCs
- Reduced travel time of conventional training delivery
- Good use of experts' time, leverages their expertise

Internet/web on-line interactive capabilities can also be used in conjunction with CD-ROM-based multimedia training. These emerging "hybrid" systems offer a glimpse of the possibilities of distance learning for the near future. Some advantages of Internet/web-based training combined with centrally loaded CD-ROMs are:

- Fast learning curve, high retention
- Consistent
- Interactive, immediate feedback
- Ease of record keeping
- Easy updates—just reconnect!

The flip side of the advantages is that not everyone has Internet access, even at businesses that do provide it to some employees. Other disadvantages are that students need a moderate degree of computer literacy, training requires additional security measures, and the high level of current Internet hype makes it difficult to determine what's practical for the near future.

Application Considerations

Both video and web-based distance learning provide some benefits. These approaches are good, but they fall short in two specific areas that affect the productivity of the ERP user. First, business procedures within the enterprise can vary based on geographical location and legal requirements. As a result, training has to be localized to accommodate these variances. It is difficult to provide customized, localized business procedures via the traditional training methods.

Expanded bandwidth and capabilities at the access and backbone level have created an environment that can serve more users faster—and with sophisticated applications requiring high processing speed and responsiveness. ERP training can be conducted in a distance learning environment. If the DL environment is primarily self-study, though, many of the same concerns exist as mentioned in Section 5.1. And the number of ERP vendors providing both live and self-study DL experiences will continue to expand with the overall growth of the Internet. Beginners, however, are still better off in a classroom that provides "hand-holding."

5.5 COMBINING METHODS FOR MAXIMUM EFFECTIVENESS AND EFFICIENCY

A decision on delivery methods can result in the use of one or more types of training delivery. Advanced ERP students and beginning groupware or office suite trainees can use self-study or distance learning facilities. As the needs for training evolve, students and their organizations can utilize the best technology, instead of just one. The delivery method depends on factors such as cost (overall and per student), the desired level of interaction between students and the instructor as well as among students, and the current skill level of the students. Table 5-3 presents a comparison based on these factors.

As you can see from the table, the primary criteria are interaction levels, simply getting the knowledge across, ease of use of training materials, and cost. These methods can be combined in many cases to suit varying combinations of priorities of primary criteria. It should also be noted that none of these delivery methods is exclusive of the others. They can be combined (as indicated in the case below) to maximize the effectiveness and efficiency of the training effort.

To maximize the impact of training, try to tailor the delivery method to the need. Combinations of training content can be delivered to your organization through a variety of media. Overall results of studies find that instructor-led training provided the most learner feedback and media richness (extent of two-way communication). Computer-based training, which allows for a "communications feedback loop" but lacks immediate interpersonal interactions, is rated a close second, with video rated third.

TABLE 5-3

Primary Criteria	Secondary Concerns	Delivery Method
Interaction	Skill level	Classroom lecture and software use
Interaction	Individual learning speed	Facilitated CBT
Interaction	Cost per student, ongoing	Live DL (video)
Knowledge transfer	Individual learning speed	Self-study web-based DL/CD
Knowledge transfer	Portability, cost	Print or CDs on laptops
Ease of use	Advanced material	Facilitated CBT
Ease of use	Beginner/intermediate material	Automated help or self-study CD
Cost	Skill level, interaction	Print, videotape, CDs

Thus, individuals and organizations should evaluate their preference for dependent or self-directed learning.

If styles tend toward dependent learning, a more media-rich training method should be utilized to provide participants with a meaningful, interactive process. On the other hand, preferences toward self-directed learning allow participants to take advantage of the flexibility and cost benefits associated with CBT or other multimedia training. Furthermore, minimal significance between preferences for CBT or instructor-led training, coupled with advances in technology, makes a compelling point for including CBT alternatives in any training curriculum, especially if such methods can maximize a participant's ROI.

CASE: ACME WIDGETS—CHOOSING THE DELIVERY METHOD(S)

With the curriculum designed, Mike, the I/T training team lead; Kathy, the training developer; and Shawn and Dave, the trainers, must decide how each of the classes should be delivered. It's important to remember, though, that any training purchased from a vendor will likely be delivered in the vendor's preferred method. As explained so far, the delivery method depends on the class content requirements and the student's skill level, as well as cost and other factors. To help facilitate the decision on delivery methods and media, the team created a decision matrix with the factors and courses needed (limited to the HR and KIS classes for this case study). Both products will require similar types of training, according to some of the criteria shown in Table 5-3.

WCS CONSIDERATIONS

The I/T staff will use classrooms with facilitated CBT for beginner classes, and will attend with business users. The I/T staff will then move on to self-study CBT for the advanced classes, but may also use the DL modules hosted by WCS on its website for updates and knowledge-base searches. For some administrative classes, the I/T staff will have WCS personnel on-site as needed, and WCS will supply just-in-time training via CD-ROM or DL to facilitate advanced learning.

Business users will attend the beginner classes with the I/T staff. This ensures that both the I/T staff and business users will learn the same things the same way. This will aid in communication during support issue resolution. Power users will also have some classroom advanced training in the form of facilitated CBT.

Table 5-4 shows how the decisions were made based on factors such as cost, class type (audience), ease of use of the delivery method, and portability. This table is also available as a form in Appendix G. The advanced administrative functions build naturally on the basics. Since the I/T staff have a technical background, the training team felt that the WCS rollout team should be able to learn most of the administrative functions via a CD-ROM either locally or at WCS's website. Instructors are available to answer questions as needed. If Acme Widgets required more "hand-holding," an advanced class could be taught live through videoconferencing or on-site as needed.

KIS CONSIDERATIONS

The rules for KIS training follow the same guidelines as WCS. In this case, the KIS "beginner" features are simple enough to learn via CBT, but hand-holding is necessary to make the end users comfortable. This means that facilitated CBT is probably the best way to go, with some introductory material presented in a formal classroom setting, as indicated in Table 5-5. It is possible that the I/T staff could learn the introductory material on their own because of their technical proficiency, thus saving some instructor costs. In many cases, the I/T staff require

TABLE 5-4

Training Class Delivery Method Assessment Matrix

Class	Audience	Factors	Delivery Method(s)
Employee master maintenance	I/T and business users	Beginner class Interaction needed Ease of use important	Classroom or facilitated CBT
Employee payroll setup	I/T and business users	Slightly advanced material Interaction needed Critical business function	Facilitated CBT
Employee benefits setup	I/T and business users	Beginner class Interaction needed Ease of use important	Classroom or facilitated CBT
WCS HR administration	I/T staff only	Advanced material Sophisticated audience Need to keep current	Web-based DL or self-study web-based CBT Instructors on call as needed

TABLE 5-5

Class	Audience	Factors	Delivery Method(s)
E-mail	I/T and business users	Beginner class Interaction needed Ease of use important	Classroom or facilitated CBT
Document authoring	I/T and business users	Slightly advanced material Interaction needed Critical business function	Facilitated CBT
Database access	I/T and business users	Beginner class Interaction needed Ease of use important	Classroom or facilitated CBT
Administration	I/T staff only	Advanced material Sophisticated audience Need to keep current	Web-based DL or self-study Web-based CBT

much less formal training on the easy features, but more training on the administrative functions because of the potential impact of mistakes made by system administrators.

The training team knows that these are only possibilities, but it's important to assess what methods would be acceptable to AWI. If a vendor were to propose DL for a beginning WCS class, the training team must know that an approach with little interaction won't meet a beginner's needs. On the other hand, a vendor proposing straight classroom CBT for a group of I/T staff on beginning KIS would be seen as just as bad.

Coming Up in Chapter 6

With the curriculum designed and the delivery method possibilities determined, it's time to decide on who will do what. Will the Acme Widgets training team deliver the training, or will the training be purchased? How will the organization decide? How do you determine what training your organization can deliver on its own, and in what areas it will need help? Should the software rollout subject matter experts do the training, or should professional trainers be used? Chapter 6 will answer these questions.

REFERENCES

Abola, Titus. (1995, April). Computer training: Surviving the software deluge. *PC Digest.*

Alessi, Stephen M., & Trollip, Stanley R. (1991). *Computer based instruction: Methods and development* (2d ed.). Englewood Cliffs, NJ: Prentice-Hall.

Brown, Ann E., & Orwig, Gary W. (1995). *Multimedia technologies for training.* Englewood, CO: Libraries Unlimited.

Clyatt, Bob. (Spring 1998). Web-based distance learning: Tool for change. *Learning Magazine* (2), 1.

Gayeski, Diane (Ed.). (1993). *Multimedia for learning: Development, application, evaluation.* Englewood Cliffs, NJ: Educational Technology Publications.

Hall, Brandon. (1997). *Web-based training cookbook.* New York: John Wiley & Sons.

Holloway, R. E., & Ohler, J. (1991). Distance education in the next decade. In G. J. Anglin (Ed.), *Instructional technology, past, present, and future* (pp. 259–266). Englewood, CO: Libraries Unlimited.

Jonassen, D. H. (1993, January). Thinking technology. *Journal of Educational Technology,* 35–37.

Loosmore, Judy. (1996, February). Developing a multimedia CD-ROM. *New Currents Newsletter 3* (1).

Massie, Elliot. (1995). *The computer training handbook: Strategies for helping people to learn technology.* Minneapolis, MN: Lakewood Books.

Trepper, Charles. (1997, July). New technologies require structured methodologies. *Application Development Trends Magazine 4* (7).

Trepper, Charles. (1997, September). Employees should be held accountable for training. *Application Development Trends Magazine 4* (9).

Trepper, Charles. (1997, December). Companies benefit from intranet-based CBT. *Application Development Trends Magazine 4* (12).

Willis, B. (1992). *Instructional development for distance education.* (ERIC Document Reproduction Service No. ED 351 007).

Make or Buy—Purchasing Training versus Developing and Delivering Training In House

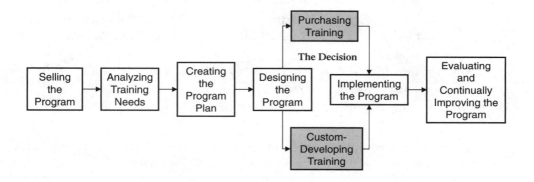

In This Chapter

6.1 Deciding what you can do yourself

6.2 A training capability assessment form

6.3 Using trainers versus subject matter experts

Case: Acme Widgets—Assessing AWI's training capabilities

OVERVIEW

The decision to develop training internally, outsource the development, or outsource the entire training effort is a question frequently faced by organizations developing a training program. The decision is not an easy one and depends on a number of factors. Regardless of the length, complexity, or objectives of the program, you need to consider the same basic factors in the make-or-buy decision. The basic factors are the cost (internal versus external), the staff availability, the staff skill levels and knowledge bases, the timing, the audience size and type, and the program size, type, complexity, and objectives.

Organizations have historically thought of the "hire versus contract" question as simply a matter of filling roles for nonstrategic services. And the standard project dependencies still exist when making the decision, such as cost, capacity, quality, speed, reliability, and extensions. However, organizations are using contractors for project management, program development, and other strategic roles. Newer ideas include looking for consultants who:

- Understand your specific business and application training areas.
- Know how to manage a training project to produce a quality product on time and on budget.
- Are proficient in leading-edge training technologies. These proficiencies may not exist in-house and are difficult to find in a new hire.
- Eliminate the myriad of administration tasks you face every day with full-time employees.
- Eliminate the concern about how to use full-time employees after a specific project is completed.

Perhaps the greatest benefit of outsourcing is that it allows management to focus its attention on strategic parts of the business, while the outsourcer focuses on improving the training services and infrastructure. Be aware, however, that there are certainly disadvantages, such as loss of control, loss of knowledge after a project is completed, security risks, and potentially higher costs. It's important to balance the costs and benefits and understand the implications of both. This topic is covered in more detail in Section 6.2.

6.1 DECIDING WHAT YOU CAN DO YOURSELF

Decision Factors

The decision about what can be done in house begins with this question: Does appropriate training exist internally or in the marketplace? *Appropriate* means more than just a product in a category. The training must also offer the features required to meet the specific needs of the organization, and it must be capable of supporting the organization long term. Many training vendors today offer some form of both custom development and off-the-shelf delivery capability.

Even when the product does not have some specific required feature, if the product is customizable, limited development can provide a richer product and the uniqueness of a custom solution. For instance, if the organization requires training not supported by any replication vendor, a training development kit may be available. This allows the organization to use the base of the prebuilt product, while building just the required changes for its unique organization.

To improve efficiency, save resources, and help focus energy, most corporate training departments are combining internal and external training expertise. For example, an organization may undertake its own performance and training needs analysis but contract with an external provider to design and deliver the actual training program. There are several explanations for increased outsourcing of training activities.

First, like all other parts of a business, corporate training departments are being asked by senior management to do more with less. This pressure to do more work with the same resources and less money is forcing training professionals to outsource training in order to make costs, specifically labor costs, less fixed and more variable. Variable cost structures allow training professionals to focus on delivering training as it is needed, where it is needed, and when it is needed, "just in time."

One point about outsourcing training requires mention. The decision to outsource may rest with training professionals but is most likely influenced by senior line and staff executives (i.e., the training group's customers) as they demand training that will meet their needs and be delivered in a timely manner. It is reasonable to assume that some training professionals, in an effort to perpetuate their usefulness, may present a barrier to the outsourcing option.

Second, the role of training professionals within corporate environments is changing. While the training professionals continue to spend a significant amount of their time on traditional activities such as program development and delivery, corporate trainers are spending increasingly more time on nontraditional activities such as consulting and strategic planning. One of the main reasons for this role shift is that training professionals are working in organizational development or effectiveness departments.

Some companies prefer not to rely on an outside party to train their personnel. These companies usually have a separate department whose sole task is to teach personnel the skills required in their various functions within the company. Specifically, in-house computer training is designed to help employees learn how to use the hardware and software that is standard in the company. Some of the software might be commercially available, while some might be customized and specially developed for the company's use. The decision factors and other information included in this chapter are applicable to both.

In some cases, in-house training is cheaper and more practical than outside training. Why send employees to school if you have the equipment and people to train them? With in-house training, you can monitor the progress of the trainees, and are assured that the users are well-trained because you were the one who trained them. By training users in house, you give training a personal touch. If the trainer is an officemate, people may find it easier to open up; it's easier to learn with someone you know.

Overall, however, there has been a realization that the costs of transactions between organizations may well be less than the benefits to be obtained by carrying out work internally. The need to meet higher quality standards and respond to the use of just-in-time (JIT) training techniques has produced a requirement to stay current with the fast changes in office and process technology, and an imperative of dealing with structural change, including the necessity of deciding whether to integrate or dispose of acquired activities. If these reasons seem applicable to your organization, outsourcing training may be a good idea.

Time or Money—Which Is More Important?

Both time and money are critical when considering the make-or-buy decision. Cost is not only a key consideration, but one that must be justified to management. Time is often a critical factor. If you can find external resources that meet your needs, it's usually faster to use them. However, modifying or tailoring an off-the-shelf product can considerably increase your time commitment. Consultants can often do the tailoring for you, but the learning curve while they get to know your organization and/or industry adds more time.

Audience numbers and levels must also be considered. If the number to be trained is small, a public seminar may be the way to go. If the audience is large and the training need will continue for a long time, it may be more cost-effective to build an in-house program. If the audience is large and dispersed, an off-the-shelf or self-study program will probably work best. If the audience is at a high level, if outsider credibility is necessary, or if a lot of people need to be trained quickly, a program delivered by an outside consultant will work well.

In most cases, the cost of externally produced programs is usually easier to calculate than internally produced programs, because of invoices received and tracked. Some costs to consider are:

- Purchase price of materials and classes (sometimes these are separate)

- Facility rental costs, if any
- Train-the-trainer costs
- Licensing fees, conditions of use
- Update costs when material becomes outdated
- Custom-tailoring costs
- Consulting fees in addition to training costs

Measuring external costs also includes tracking recurring costs over time. This includes ongoing licenses, "update classes" to keep staff current, and any travel and meal costs. While external training may seem cheaper in the short term, eventually costs may catch up to, and even surpass, internal training costs.

There is often a false idea that contracted resources are better because they're released when the project is complete. The cost of using external training developers and trainers for 6 months may, in fact, be more than the cost of hiring full-time employees for as much as 2 years. It's extremely important to do a thorough cost analysis before making this decision.

It's important to not underestimate your training requirement or undervalue your training resources. Many sites choose to have internal resources deliver their training. The advantage of this is that they have someone familiar with their environment who has the appropriate business focus. One of the major concerns with this approach is that training is normally scheduled at just the time when internal resources are least likely to have the time to devote to it.

An alternative is to select a specialized resource: a training consultant with a background in both the presentation of training and a knowledge of the product you are implementing. Integrate this consultant into your project team and this person will add enormous value to your project because he or she will focus exclusively on your business. Customized courses are designed in conjunction with the project team to produce material relevant for the different audiences you wish to train. The courses are conducted on site, with your setup, your data, and your business scenarios and examples—and you integrate your policies and procedures to the degree necessary to assist your audience.

When comparing purchasing training against developing it in house, the organization must decide how to price in-house resources. The usual approach is to use salary costs plus an overhead burden for staff. In some cases, capital equipment, such as PCs and other computer resources, that is already owned by the company may not be factored into the cost of development. This approach may lead to less than optimal decisions, particularly if the accounting department can't offer total-cost-of-ownership numbers.

In an organization that must work with a preset personnel and capital budget, *opportunity cost* is a much more appropriate measure. Economists and accountants define opportunity cost as (1) the benefit that would have been obtained from an alternative if that alternative had been accepted; or (2) the cost of forgone revenue by choosing a particular alternative. Where an organization must allocate I/T resources from a preset budget, using a resource on one development project means you cannot use that resource on another project. Deciding to develop data replication capabilities in house means that the organization must, at best, defer other applications, or, at worst, not undertake them at all. The correct cost to use in deciding whether to undertake in-house development is, then, the forgone benefit of the project not chosen. It's just as important to calculate internal costs thoroughly as it is to monitor external costs. Internally produced program costs to consider are:

- Staff salaries and benefits (including support staff)
- Media costs (slides, overheads, video)
- Production (typesetting, printing, storage)
- Facilities
- Consultants
- Utilities, if unusual

Internal costing models often neglect to measure opportunity cost, or the lost time from other assignments. When training developers, subject matter experts, and other staff are dedicated to developing a training program, they are by definition unavailable for other tasks. This can have a significant impact on the organization if the tasks neglected are mission critical.

Identification of total outsourcing costs and savings can be a full-time job. The degree to which the staff monitor and report outsourcing costs, in comparison with in-house costs, seems to vary depending on how much staff expertise and time are available for that effort. In addition, anyone who has been involved in the implementation process for a new training program knows that there are numerous start-up costs in the initial stages of implementation. The same holds true for launching an outsourcing program. All these factors have an impact on the process of assessing outsourcing costs and savings. It's extremely important to work with your organization's accounting department to find the true value of developing an in-house program or using outsourcing.

Two methods for capturing cost data periodically are to measure unit costs and savings and to monitor aggregate costs and savings. It is likely that there will be substantial savings for one class or type of class that's outsourced, moderate savings for others, and little or no savings in some. In many cases, the impact of outsourcing is most obvious when examining the bottom line and assessing the net effect of outsourcing within an organization as a whole. The estimated time to assess outsourcing costs and savings is about 3 to 6 months for the initial training, 6 months to 1 year for further classes, followed by periodic monitoring on an ongoing basis for the life of the outsourcing program.

The expertise of both external and internal resources must be carefully evaluated to provide a fair base for decision making. Some of the factors against which resources should be evaluated are:

- Subject matter knowledge
- Industry knowledge
- Specific company knowledge
- HRD knowledge
- Presentation skills
- Credibility with the audience

As a general rule, there may be some instances where the needs of an organization are so special as to require custom-developed training. But many vendors offer a single solution for providing this capability for different areas to meet the needs of the increasingly heterogeneous environments found in today's organizations. The benefits gained from in-house development come in the areas of customizing the training for the specific needs and environment of the organization. The benefits from buying training derive from taking advantage of the vendor's support, maintenance, and upgrade capabilities, along with taking advantage of the opportunity to allocate internal resources to meeting other needs that are unique to the organization, as well as leveraging the vendor's investment in research, development, skills, and continuous enhancement of the training products.

Avoiding Risks and Mistakes

Some specific risks are associated with outsourcing training development and delivery. While these are not necessarily disadvantages, they are some "things to watch out for" when making the decision. Some of the risks associated with outsourcing include:

- Lack of management control over the training development process
- Lack of management control over the delivery of training
- Reduced financial commitment from the organization
- Imprecise definition of outsourcing service
- Inadequate documentation of the responsibilities of both parties
- If necessary, the subsequent prohibitive cost of insourcing

To minimize these risks, an appropriate management structure for defining strategic direction and accepting responsibility is vital. The organization should also appoint an experienced contract/outsourcing manager to handle and manage the outsourcing relationship. It is suggested that this manager should be involved from the initial scoping of the outsourcing project through the duration of the outsourcing agreement. An important additional point is that the outsourcing process *is* a project and should be managed as such, with all the tools, procedures, and monitoring that any significant project would require.

Even when these risks are monitored and controlled, there are still common mistakes made on many unsuccessful outsourcing projects. Sometimes the wrong people dominate the process. This might be the legal or finance departments, or a single manager or vendor. This causes the organization to choose price over content. Also, vendor capabilities and qualifications are not fully investigated by the organization, and unsuitable vendors aren't weeded out of the selection process.

There is also a high risk to outsourcing projects when internal training staff do not understand the program and/or content that is being contracted out. While external experts may seem to be a perfect remedy for overworked staff with little time to learn new concepts, experience shows they are not. It is clearly preferable for anyone outsourcing a training program to have some understanding of the program and content requirements.

6.2 A TRAINING CAPABILITY ASSESSMENT FORM

Table 6-1 presents a form designed to assist you in the decision-making process. All the factors, risks, costs, and benefits mentioned so far are contained in this form. Each item must be assigned a priority, from 1 to 5, with 5 being the most important and 1 the least. There is also a place on the form to indicate whether your organization believes that item is best suited for internal training (I), outsourcing (O), or either (E). The form is also available for use in Appendix G and on McGraw-Hill's website at www.books.mcgraw-hill.com/training/download. The forms can then be opened, edited, and printed using Microsoft Word or other word processing software.

All of the items in Table 6-1 are important and are dependent on the individual organization. The training team must work with management and users to assess the capability of training resources, the organization's readiness, management's commitment to training (time, staff, and money), and other factors specific to a particular organization. The use of this form is detailed in the case study.

TABLE 6-1

Training Capability Decision Matrix

Item	Factor	Priority (1–5)	Develop Internally	Outsource	Either
1.	Staff salaries				
2.	Train-the-trainer costs				
3.	Material purchase costs				
4.	Material licensing costs				
5.	Facility costs				
6.	Media costs				
7.	Equipment costs				
8.	Consulting costs (for internal)				
9.	Current staff skill levels				
10.	Staff skill acquisition time				
11.	Program complexity				
12.	Audience credibility				
13.	Project deadline(s)				
14.	Access to leading-edge expertise				
15.	Risk mitigation				
16.	Development process control				
17.	Delivery process control				
18.	Quality control				
19.	Service-level agreements				
20.	Documentation management				
	Total				

6.3 USING TRAINERS VERSUS SUBJECT MATTER EXPERTS

The decision to use trainers or subject matter experts from the software roll-out teams or user areas is another potentially difficult decision. Dedicated instructors are essential to ensure that the work force is capable of performing accurate and timely financial transactions. SMEs are generally not resourced adequately with time, and the time spent on the preparation and delivery of quality training often puts them behind in their other job responsibilities. It's very important that if SMEs are used, a program is established to support them. Through skill development training opportunities, SMEs should be allowed a release from other duties to allow time for training related responsibilities.

Professional Trainers

Usually a professional trainer has experience delivering training person-to-person or person-to-group. This training, typically in a classroom- or lecture-style setting, may be formal or informal. SMEs frequently have little training experience but know the subject matter well. The problem with SMEs is that they often have a difficult time communicating their thoughts. Professional trainers are usually excellent communicators and can get the message across to their audiences fairly easily.

Technical training personnel usually have a working-level knowledge of the systematic approach to the training process, as well as a knowledge of the training program organization, administration, and infrastructure. They also know how to plan, conduct, and document a training needs assessment or job analysis of a position(s) to determine the training requirements associated with that position. One of the other advantages is that technical training personnel have the ability to design a training course or curriculum to satisfy the training requirements identified by a needs assessment, job analysis, or other regulations or requirements. Professional training personnel can also help develop training materials to support the presentation of classroom, OJT, self-study, or laboratory training.

Subject Matter Experts

It is possible to train subject matter experts to become trainers. It's rather difficult, though, because most subject matter experts tend to overwhelm trainees with technical details that may not be necessary in some cases.

The focus of the SMEs must be shifted from expounding on the details and from digging into the "guts" of the product to educating trainees and to motivating good learning behavior.

One way of beginning the transition of their thought processes is to involve the SMEs in the design of the instructional package. It's also important to explain that the materials are geared toward supporting the trainees in their jobs, and not necessarily turning them into developers. As the SMEs work with the training team on the training package, it's important to create and deliver "train-the-trainer" sessions to provide the SMEs with both teaching and learning skills. In train-the-trainer sessions, don't overwhelm the SMEs with the gory details of training methodologies and interactive activities. You must set a tone and method of behavior that is consistent with the way you want the SMEs to act as trainers.

The SMEs should observe an expert trainer in action. Make sure that the SMEs understand how trainers focus on learning rather than on lecturing and details. You can also involve the SMEs in practice-teaching role plays. Videotape these sessions and provide specific feedback to improve their behavior. You should also provide lesson plans to support the training activity. This will help the SMEs feel more like trainers. If they are told to follow the outlines, they will be less likely to offer up unnecessary detail.

Another approach to shifting the SMEs' thought processes away from lecturing on details is to give them a different job title, at least for the duration of the training. One possibility is "application coach." Help the "coaches" understand that their role is to assist the trainers in improving the job performance of the members of their team using the new software. Train the SMEs on the essential steps of the teaching process, and role play teaching situations. Also, stress the importance of guided practice and explain why it helps trainees. Often, SMEs are so comfortable with their work that they don't understand why others just don't "get it." The SMEs can also organize individual and small-group training sessions (e.g., brown bag lunch classes) after the formal training.

Either or Both?

Finally, there is no rule that says you must use one or the other. It is possible, and even advantageous, to partner trainers and SMEs to develop and deliver training. The trainers can use the SMEs' knowledge to develop quality content, while structuring that knowledge in a manner appropriate to adult learning. In the classroom, the trainer is the lead, and the SME is present to help answer questions and solve any problems that occur during the training. In this case, both trainer and SME gain. The trainer learns about the business, and the SME develops skills for transferring knowledge effectively.

CASE: ACME WIDGETS—ASSESSING AWI'S TRAINING CAPABILITIES

COMPLETING THE ASSESSMENT FORM

AWI is implementing both groupware and an ERP system, so there is going to be a large amount of training to develop and deliver. To determine AWI's training capability for this big workload, Bob, the I/T training manager, and Mike, the I/T training team lead, met with Richard, the vice president of human resources, and Trudy, the human resources training specialist. Together, they assessed the current staff, as shown in Table 6-2. This table is available as a form in Appendix G.

The next step was to fill out the training capability decision matrix. To complete this form, Mike and Bob worked with Richard, as well as other key staff from the user areas, including:

- Dennis, the vice president of manufacturing
- Diego, the vice president of sales
- Jeff, the vice president of finance
- Sandra, the vice president of purchasing

They firmed up the budget and the time line from Chapter 3. Once there was general agreement on the information, and how it would impact each area, the assessment matrix form looked as it does in Table 6-3. With a staff this small, and a crunch time line, the members of the training team realized that their ability to develop complete programs for KIS and WCS was very limited. Therefore, they decided to either purchase or outsource most of the training. Mike and the team

TABLE 6-2

Staff Name	Department	Area of Expertise	Skill Level (1–5)
Bob	Training	Training management	4
Mike	Training	Training management	4
Shawn	Training	Training delivery	3
Dave	Training	Training delivery	4
Kathy	Training	Training development	5
Jack	Training	Technical writing	3
Richard	HR	HR management	4
Trudy	HR	HR training	4

will work with Gary, the WCS software rollout team leader, and Lauren, the KIS software rollout team leader, to find vendors (see Chapter 7) and get the right training. Kathy specifically spent time with Gary and Lauren to determine which classes might need modification for their environment and which could be delivered generically. Table 6-4 summarizes their discussion for the HR modules. This table is available as a form in Appendix G.

TABLE 6-3

Item	Factor	Priority (1–5)	Develop Internally	Outsource	Either
1.	Staff salaries	4		X	
2.	Train-the-trainer costs	4		X	
3.	Material purchase costs	5		X	
4.	Material licensing costs	5		X	
5.	Facility costs	5		X	
6.	Media costs	4		X	
7.	Equipment costs	3			X
8.	Consulting costs (for internal)	4		X	
9.	Current staff skill levels	3	X		
10.	Staff skill acquisition time	3	X		
11.	Program complexity	5		X	
12.	Audience credibility	2	X		
13.	Project deadline(s)	5		X	
14.	Access to leading-edge expertise	3			X
15.	Risk mitigation	2			X
16.	Development process control	3			X
17.	Delivery process control	4	X		
18.	Quality control	5	X		
19.	Service-level agreements	3	X		
20.	Documentation	2			X
	Total		6	9	5

TABLE 6-4

Training Make-or-Buy Matrix

Software	Function	Class	Make or Buy	Assigned To
WCS	HR	Employee master maintenance	Buy	Gary, Trudy, Mike
WCS	HR	Employee payroll setup	Buy	Gary, Trudy, Mike
WCS	HR	Employee benefits setup	Buy	Gary, Trudy, Mike
WCS	System administration	WCS HR administration	Buy and customize	Gary, Kathy
KIS	E-mail	KIS e-mail	Buy and customize	Lauren, Kathy
KIS	Creator module	KIS databases	Buy	Lauren, Kathy

It was also decided that Jack would work with Dave and Shawn to customize and document the curriculum as needed for AWI. Dave and Shawn would also be responsible for monitoring the quality of the outsourced training. Because both of them have good credibility with AWI employees, their involvement with the training, even though it's outsourced, will make the training process smoother.

PLANNING THE SME AND TRAINER MIX

Mike and Bob worked with Gary and Lauren to select SMEs who would work well with both internal and external trainers. Richard decided that John, the WCS HR liaison, would act as the SME for the WCS HR training, and that Lauren would continue in her role as the KIS expert. John and Lauren will work with the training team to select vendors, check and modify the content, and monitor the quality of the material delivered. By having John and Lauren involved, the training team gains valuable expertise in areas that trainers may have limited knowledge. This helps keep vendor "hype" from getting the best of the training team. It also teaches the SMEs some valuable training skills that will be important in the postrollout support period.

Coming Up in Chapter 7

If you are going to buy training, how do you evaluate the courseware and vendors? Is there a selection process methodology? How do you write a request for proposal for training? What types of criteria should be set for evaluating proposals? How are sources selected for material? Books? How do you negotiate with a vendor for the best deal? All this and more, coming up in Chapter 7.

REFERENCES

Baty, C., & Vandyke, J. (1996, November). Outsourcing—From pain to gain. *Open Systems Review.* November, 54–55.

Earl, M. J. (1989). *Management strategies for information technology.* London: Prentice Hall.

Fox, Paul G. (1997). *Make or buy? How to decide.* Fox Performance. Website: www.foxperformance.com. Phone: (860) 870-4640.

Reid, Warren S. (1997). Outsourcing: The 20 steps to success. *Corporate Counsel's Guide to Outsourcing.* Chesterland, OH: Business Laws, Inc. Website: www.wsrcg.com. Phone: (818) 986-8842.

Walsh, K. (1997, May 6). Angst over IT outsourcing. *The Bulletin,* p. 14.

Zalusky, Jeff. (1994, April 4). Make or buy decision key to consultant staffing. *Accounting Today 8* (6).

Purchasing Training

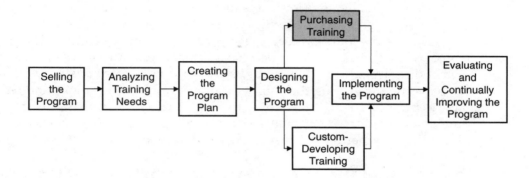

In This Chapter

OVERVIEW

Now that many organizations have reduced or eliminated their training departments, they're often interested in obtaining training expertise from the outside. Outsourcing training has many advantages, but there are some major problems that can occur, and you frequently hear horror stories about how it didn't work out. Many organizations have been burned by a consultant or training firm. The process of finding another vendor to provide training to organizations that have had problems is very difficult and expensive.

Purchasing training is similar to purchasing other products or services. The needs analysis (i.e., requirements) and designs are used to produce requests for information (RFIs) or requests for proposals (RFPs). The next step is finding vendors and then evaluating their courseware and the vendors themselves. Then it's time to get bids and negotiate for the best deal. Once the evaluation and/or negotiation is complete, the packages and vendors are selected. In addition, there may be supplemental materials that the vendor or buyer may supply, such as handout sources and books.

There are a lot of options when selecting training vendors. There are some national chains, some good local firms, and a number of one-person consulting firms. You want to find a trainer who meets your needs. For a larger company, having the ability to support multiple locations and being able to provide consistent training to large numbers of students are important considerations. For smaller companies, responsiveness to needs and the ability to schedule courses on demand will be considerations.

7.1   PREPARING A REQUEST FOR INFORMATION OR PROPOSAL

RFI versus RFP Overview

Depending on where you are in the training development process, either a request for information or a request for proposal is the first logical step in purchasing training. In situations where the process is just beginning, the first step in the vendor selection process is completing an RFI. An RFI solicits details about the kinds of training services currently offered. Once responses to an RFI are received, selected vendors might be invited to make formal presentations. In some instances, it may be appropriate for selected staff to tour vendor sites and meet with other vendor staff.

The RFI has two purposes: (1) to inform industry, potential users, and the public about the project and (2) to request information on industry products. The first section of the RFI is designed to do the project advertising. The remaining sections, asking the questions, are designed to determine the functionality of supplier products as they relate to the project. RFI responses are used as input to refine requirements for the RFP. Likewise, training content changes and opportunities identified by other than the training team's efforts will refine training requirements. Information received from suppliers during the RFI process will also be used as input to developing high-level estimates for implementation and ongoing costs.

An RFP is typically required for outsourcing training, regardless of whether or not an RFI was prepared in advance. If not done as part of an RFI process, selected vendors can be invited to make formal presentations to the staff after RFP responses are received. If the staff did not visit vendor sites during an RFI phase, they can visit during the RFP stage. References also need to be checked following the RFP process. The estimated time to complete the RFP phase is about 2 to 4 months, including time for reviewing responses, sponsoring vendor presentations, and visiting vendor sites.

It is very important to develop a rigorous request for proposal in a format that forces the responding vendor to answer questions in a way that will allow you to compare responses from multiple vendors. Ask vendors to simplify their answers to pricing so that you can really understand which services will be included and which will be extra. Note that pricing can take on many forms, and that different services may be priced differently or in alternative combinations to your advantage. Sometimes bundling training design and delivery services works to your advantage.

The timing of RFPs is also important to consider. RFP deadlines always precipitate a flurry of activity since the RFP must contain accurate descriptions of the requirements and constraints. Often, these issues require the attention of senior executives and are not dealt with until the deadline is close. It's important for you to get the RFP to vendors soon enough to allow them to provide you with good information. RFIs can be used as input, and these two steps are often tightly linked.

The RFI Process and Outline

The RFI process can be a good learning experience for both your organization and the vendors. You can get more information on the training you need, and the vendors can get better acquainted with your organization, the software (and the rollout), and your training requirements. The RFI process is designed to seek alternatives for putting the training infrastructure in place and to find the service and support for training now and in the future. The RFI leads to the definitive RFP distributed to training development and delivery providers. The purpose of the RFP will be to select one or more vendors.

A first step is to ask several vendors to come in for a vendor meeting. Explain what you envision, but also explain that you're not sure what you want. Ask vendors for ideas, suggestions, and possible solutions for your problem. Most vendors are willing to take a couple of hours to help you. Make it informal, and promise nothing. Be up front, open, and honest. Take time to read trade magazines, attend conferences, and learn as much as you can about things related to your project. Make sure the vendors understand that these sessions are strictly for information gathering and that no contracts will be let.

The RFI document can request detailed information, or it can be as simple as requesting brochures and glossy marketing literature. (Of course, you'll only be able to believe half of what you read in the marketing glossies.) A sample RFI outline is as follows:

1. Purpose of the RFI
2. Software and/or project background
3. Standards
4. Design specifications for training modules
5. Implementation schedule
6. Cost estimates
7. Customer list
8. Invited demonstrations
9. Instructions for submitting the information
10. Appendixes

This outline resembles the RFP outline, and that's intentional. There should be a smooth transition from the RFI to the RFP. The RFP is where things get "serious," and should be much more formal than an RFI, which is primarily an information-gathering tool.

The RFP Process and Outline

Developing a well-written RFP takes time and planning. The proposal format typically contains a technical details section and time and cost section. In the technical details section, the vendor should include time lines, projected required personnel, and schedules for completing the project. In the time and cost section, the vendor must specify the time and costs that will be required to complete the project. Vendors should include a short demo or direct you to an Internet site that demonstrates their production capabilities. The RFP should also include sections that reflect your desires and needs such as:

- Requests for references
- A submission deadline

- The person to whom the vendor should submit the proposal
- A contact for additional information or clarification
- The basis on which the contract will be awarded and the award date

Be sure to follow standard policies set forth by your organization. It's likely that those guidelines were created by attorneys who have your organization's best interests in mind. Like it or not, there are frequently lawsuits over bidding processes, even in the private sector. An RFP includes an introduction, administrative requirements, specific activities, the required submission format, project details, and the budget, if known. A sample outline and document are included in Appendix E and on McGraw-Hill's website at www.books.mcgraw-hill.com/training/download. The forms can then be opened, edited, and printed using Microsoft Word or other word processing software. It's extremely important for both legal and evaluation purposes to make sure that all vendors use this format.

Next, distribute the RFP to the vendors you qualified. Send out your RFP 8 to 10 weeks before your requested submission date. Writing a detailed proposal takes time; give potential vendors time to think about and respond to your request for proposals. Distribute the RFP to those vendors whom you have identified as being able to produce the materials that you need. Be sure to send your RFP only to organizations with whom you want to work. Be sure to make someone (the key contact, preferably) available to answer questions about what you want, possibly with the exception of financial queries.

Award the project on the date indicated. Being indecisive about awarding or starting a project makes you and your organization look unprofessional. Also, contrary to popular belief, you do *not* have to award the project to the lowest bidder. However, if the basis for the award is not lowest price, be sure to tell potential vendors on what basis you will award the project. Nothing upsets a vendor worse than to lose a contract if it is the lowest bidder. Suspicions soon circulate among vendors and your industry, and you will probably be ignored if you approach the vendor to submit a proposal for a future project.

Be sure to debrief bidders. Telling vendors that they did not get a proposal is never pleasant. Take time to talk with each vendor who submitted a proposal and give the individual vendors a critique of their proposal. Be empathetic, and be specific about why the vendors didn't win. If handled properly, this can be a great way to learn more about the vendors, and a great way for the vendors to learn about improving their responses. This will help the vendors to do a better job and to be more competitive next time when you ask them to respond to a future proposal.

Tips for Optimizing the RFI/RFP Process

The request for proposal process can be very expensive and time-consuming. The paper chase it represents is despised by vendor sales representatives, and both the time and cost involved have grown astronomically as organizations try to be more thorough *and* avoid litigation from the losers. The typical RFP is easily a hundred pages long, can cost up to $100,000 to produce, and generates a dozen or more boxes of paper from vendor responses. To save money, there are several steps organizations can follow to involve users more in the process and reduce the time and paper-handling costs of the traditional RFP.

Instead of sending out a dozen RFPs, narrow the field to the handful of vendors who specialize in your industry and who have a strong presence in your state. A simple request for information can gather this information early in the process and solicit reports from vendors to ensure that only really interested firms are considered. This will reduce the volume of proposals that you receive, and improve the likelihood of selecting an appropriate vendor anyway.

Also, instead of paying a consultant to draw up the "wish list" contained in most RFPs' feature checklists, work with the user areas to draw up a short list of the top 10 to 20 features that would make their departments more productive. Use these checklists to evaluate vendor demonstrations. A simple spreadsheet of scores can reveal more than the boxes of proposals that the typical RFP generates.

When making visits to potential vendors, avoid visiting their flagship customer sites, usually found in sunny locations, where vendors prefer to take prospective customers. Often, these showcase customers have a financial incentive to give demos. To both see a more realistic site and lower your travel cost, insist on visiting a customer about the same size as your company and in the same industry; this will not only cut down the airfare to fly to a dozen user sites, but also let users and evaluators check out how well the vendor provides support. Let your users determine if the training is useful, not how good the food is at the demos.

7.2 FINDING VENDORS

The two most obvious ways to find training vendors is word of mouth and Internet searches. Searching for specific vendors is easy on the web as well. If you know the business name of the vendor you are seeking, enter it into the address field on your web browser. Certainly the largest, and potentially the best quality, source of software training vendors is the Information Technology Training Association, or ITTA (www.itta.org). Your organization probably has a list of preferred vendors that it works with, which will make your life easier.

To find a training vendor for your software rollout, you can ask the software vendor. Most software vendors have partners for particular purposes. For example, an ERP vendor will likely have a database partner, hardware partner, training partner, and so on. The only potential problem is that the two vendors may have a vested interest in recommending each other, which may be independent of the training supplier's actual capability or quality. It's important to be aware of conflicts of interest.

Talk to other clients of the software company. Ask which vendor(s) they've used, and find out what their experiences have been, both good and bad. Make sure you ask about how the vendor handled specific training needs like the ones you have, and how the training vendor responded to customization requests. Ask about the trainer's personality, the quality of work products, timing and responsiveness to requests, and other matters of concern to your particular organization. Price is important, so ask about rates as well.

Try to find vendors that can perform program need analysis, design, media selection, custom training program development, execution, follow-up, and custom training program assessment services for almost any client. Sometimes a vendor's standard program core content can be modified to fit your organization's needs, saving the organization both time and money. When that isn't possible, a vendor should have sufficient training experience in many different environments and settings that allows the vendor to produce the program needed. The vendor should be able to "train the trainer" if your organization prefers to use in-house trainers to deliver the training developed by the vendor.

7.3   EVALUATING VENDORS AND COURSEWARE

Evaluating Vendors

Evaluating the vendors and their courseware is a long process. It may take up to 6 months, so allocate the time necessary and back-time the program plan if you must. The major question is: Which vendor under consideration poses the fewest risks to your budget and/or deadline? You know that you're probably going to be with the vendor for the term of the project, so which vendor leaves you feeling least exposed? Remember that no vendor can satisfy everyone's needs, because every client has different needs. Besides the courseware itself, the most important task is checking references and case studies. Ask for case studies of prior projects so you know the vendors are capable of doing yours, too. Always ask the vendors for any standardized methods they use. When you check references, ask specific questions like:

- Did this company hit your deadlines?
- Did the company stay within budget?
- How did it handle problems?
- Did it offer advice?
- Was the advice any good?
- Did you have as much faith in the company at the end of the project as you did at the beginning?

These questions are available for use as a checklist in Appendix F and on McGraw-Hill's website at www.books.mcgraw-hill.com/training/download. The forms can then be opened, edited, and printed using Microsoft Word or other word processing software. Besides these questions, there is a huge set of questions that can be asked of vendors. These other questions are designed to ensure that the vendor really knows the training area. Answering these questions requires the vendor to *do* something, not just send out pretty brochures. Some questions are:

- Does the vendor demonstrate originality or innovation?
- Does the vendor write influential papers or articles in relevant trade magazines?
- Is the vendor recognized as a leader in the field?
- Does the vendor demonstrate a readiness to customize his or her services to your needs?
- Is the vendor using the same person to market, sell, and deliver the service?
- Can the vendor provide references from delighted customers on successful projects (a minimum of 3)?
- Does the vendor honor commitments and display integrity?
- Does the vendor offer a reliable résumé for all project team members?
- Does the vendor fit into your organization or culture?
- Are the training results guaranteed by the vendor?

- Does the vendor inspire personal and professional acceptability?
- Does the vendor have the correct level of rapport and credibility for you to do business with him or her?

These questions and many more are available in a checklist located in Appendix F and on McGraw-Hill's website at www.books.mcgraw-hill. com/training/download. The forms can then be opened, edited, and printed using Microsoft Word or other word processing software.

Focus on the things you respect and want most in a vendor. Do you respond best to a vendor who wins awards and projects the highest professional image, but may cost more? Or do you feel more comfortable with a vendor who's willing to get dirty and participate actively in the training development process, which usually costs less? No vendor can do both interchangeably, of course. Whatever your values are, it's important that you can feel comfortable that your vendor believes in the same ones.

Evaluating Courseware

The style of the courseware, trainers, and vendor philosophy is also critical to the success of the training. Since most software training is competency-based, it's easy to make the courseware technically accurate, but very user-unfriendly. The course design (like that in Chapter 4) should state the objectives clearly in terms the student can understand. Good, structured training is developed by experienced, qualified trainers, and focuses on learning skills. Adults generally learn best in an atmosphere that is nonthreatening and supportive of experimentation and in which different learning styles are recognized. The approach that the training takes to the student is also important. The training should:

- Concentrate on teaching concepts and solid skills
- Have a uniform design and consistent format
- Be concise (no superfluous text)
- Use short sentences appropriate to the student level
- Use simple English and avoid unnecessary jargon
- Be technically accurate
- Be free of distracting errors (such as spelling errors)
- Be tested prior to release by independent trainers

These and many other characteristics are part of the Courseware Evaluation Form in Appendix G and on McGraw-Hill's website at www.books.mcgraw-hill.com/training/download. The forms can then be opened, edited, and printed using Microsoft Word or other word processing software. Please review this form for a comprehensive overview of what to look for in courseware. It's important that the training materials be easy to use. Nothing turns a student off faster than finding material that's hard to read, has numerous errors, or is written to the wrong level.

7.4 GETTING BIDS AND NEGOTIATING FOR THE BEST DEAL

After contacting the individual bidders initially, invite the bidders to a conference at your site and take each bidder separately on a tour of your site. Have top management and the training team meet with the vendor for at least 45 to 60 minutes during the tour to demonstrate the importance and visibility of the training project. This sets the tone of the relationship, and lets the vendor know how important the training is to the rollout and the organization. Negotiate the contract using your expert team and using predetermined target clauses and criteria to keep the vendor relationship on track.

The vendor's willingness to negotiate is a good indicator of how the relationship will flow later. The actual process of negotiating the contract and reaching agreement on difficult alternatives gives you an idea how the vendor will handle unanticipated problems. How each vendor handles the negotiations regarding the contract, and how willing each vendor is to listen to your story and needs and modify his or her approach, will indicate whether or not your relationship will be successful in the future.

The next and possibly most important step is lowering the project costs by negotiating with the vendors. Several simple principles can help save you money. The first is the simplest, but yet one that is easily tempted to overlook: use competition. Since the final approval of a contract is based on recommendations from the user departments and selection committee, the temptation is often to call the winning vendor and ask the vendor's salespeople to come work out a deal. The trick is to have the users select the best two finalist vendors with whom to conduct simultaneous negotiations.

Don't just look at the reduction from the list price or at the discount being offered, as some vendors have set their list prices extremely high to enable them to offer impressive discounts to unwary trainers. The only way you can tell if you are getting a reasonable deal is to compare the price of the two best vendors your selection committee picked, over the life of the contract, factoring in all costs. This avoids another vendor ploy of offering low initial costs and then nickel-and-diming you to death.

Due to the increasingly competitive nature of the training industry, vendors have begun shifting much of their revenue from products to their implementation services. It is possible for the fees for services to equal the license fees charged for materials. Such enormous sums are worthy of the same negotiating tactics mentioned above: (1) insist on a detailed work plan of who will be doing what and when, (2) get detailed monthly invoices for review of hours charged, and (3) negotiate the rate. Ask to see résumés, demand the right of refusal of rookie installers, and reserve the right to dispute any unwarranted charges. Additional tips include:

1. Use realistic numbers in your bidding documents. You're only setting yourself up for later problems with your training vendor(s) if you promise more dollars than you can deliver.

2. Know when to stop negotiating. You can push too far. Only win-win negotiations work. If the vendor ends up feeling beat up, it will come back to haunt you. Also, as you push prices lower, something has to suffer, and it's usually products and services that fail to meet expectations.

3. Bear in mind that negotiating contracts is not the time to be informal. Create a bidding process, even if it's a simple one, to show vendors that you're serious about giving them a fair evaluation.

4. Contracts are a must. Get it in writing. Assume nothing. Make sure all promises are documented.

5. Make sure your attorney reviews *every* document.

6. Keep in mind that commitment goes both ways. Be prepared to make a hard commitment to training volume. The more money you can guarantee vendors, the more they are willing to negotiate price.

7. Remember that change is a constant. Be sure to build into your contract a way to change terms and conditions as your needs change. Make sure your contract allows you to revisit courses, prices, etc., over time.

8. Try before you buy. Visit the vendor's facilities; don't just take a 1-hour tour or sit in a conference room for half a day listening to presentations. If you're buying instructor-led training, be sure to evaluate several full-day classes. If you're buying CBT or other

technology-based products, you have to evaluate several products in their entirety to get a good idea of quality.

9. Clearly spell out preservices and postservices. Make sure you actually get all the great presale and postsale services promised during the sales process.

10. Think like the vendor. What would you like to hear from a potential client that would motivate you to make the sale? A little empathy can help you to negotiate a better deal.

Never assume "We can't get that" or "They don't do that." Remember, your challenge in negotiations is to pay only for the value brought to the table by the vendor. You must know everything you can about the vendor, project, and pricing. If so, then you can approach negotiations with the mindset that the package price should be in direct proportion to the value that the vendor brings to the organization.

7.5   SELECTING PACKAGES AND VENDORS

Once you've evaluated the vendors and courseware, there are important selection issues to be discussed, including confidentiality, contract expectations, copyrights, and customization (more in Chapter 8). Trade secrets can't always be shared, even as part of the needs analysis. You must establish an appropriate level of trust with new suppliers, and make them work to achieve that trust. Additionally, certain types of company information can't be given to every vendor.

Make sure you communicate clearly in the RFP the roles and responsibilities of the vendor, and do this again during contract negotiations. Sometimes additional consultants are brought in after the "front end" of a project has been developed, resulting in the second consultant suggesting approaches that may contradict the original. It's important to create guidelines for internal and external training providers that include key contracting elements such as communication, needs analysis, priorities, and status updates.

It's not unusual to make mistakes when selecting training vendors. It's important to find vendors that have the skills and courage to challenge you. Evaluate professionalism, expertise, and the vendor's "new knowledge," views, or approaches that are not common to your organization. The main reason to hire outside firms is to have access to skills and experience not normally available to you. Insist on a customized approach to your needs (see Chapter 8). And avoid looking to one person to do it all.

The forms and the checklists in Sections 7.3 and 7.4 will give you a good idea of whom the best candidate is. Remember that cost isn't everything, and that you often get what you pay for. The vendor with the best qualifications is likely the best selection, regardless of cost. As mentioned above, it may be possible to use a very expensive vendor to lead the project and to use lower-cost contractors or subcontractors to actually do the bulk of the work.

7.6   SELECTING HANDOUT SOURCES

Although the training vendor you've chosen will (it is hoped!) have good handouts, you may want to consider additional information to help the users and the I/T staff learn more about the software. There are an infinite number of places to find information about most software packages. Depending on your need, you could choose from:

- The public library
- An academic library
- The Internet
- Business information centers
- Books
- Trade journals
- Anywhere else you know of which provides the type of information you need

It is often useful to start by browsing through relevant books and journals, or by surfing the Internet or skimming a CD-ROM. This should give you a better, broader understanding of what's available for your particular software, industry, audience, and training needs.

7.7   SELECTING BOOKS

Finding books is usually easy. Finding the right books can seem impossible. Textbooks are an important part of a variety of learning experiences for students. Textbooks give essential facts and concepts, provide sources of information, and serve as a written authority regarding a particular field or area of knowledge. Decisions regarding textbook selection are made in the context of the situation in which they will be used and are influenced by many factors.

The cost of the textbook and the overall budget (see Chapter 3) are other items that the training team must consider in the textbook selection process, while working with vendors. The question regarding the cost of the textbook is whether the price is reasonable in relation to the extent that it will be used in the classroom, for assignments, and as a study resource following completion of the course.

There are many features that an ideal textbook might contain. Probably the most important features are an adequate and balanced coverage of the content area as prescribed by the course description, a clear presentation and sequencing of ideas, and readable language suited to the reading level of the student who will be using it. When considering a potential textbook, some of the more important features to look for and examine are:

- Are a table of contents and divisions of each chapter listed under the chapter title?
- Does the author provide an outline of the book in the table of contents?
- Do topics correspond to objectives for the course?
- Are topics arranged in a logical sequence?
- Does the author give a good overview in the preface regarding where the book is going and the type of audience he or she is addressing?
- Do introductory statements or paragraphs begin each chapter or major section?
- Are there clear and well-marked divisions of content within chapters?
- Are there titles, headings, subheadings to help the student visualize the organization and relationship of content?
- Are there summary sections or paragraphs at the end of each major division or chapter?
- Are illustrations accurate, and are they properly captioned and placed near the related text?
- Are the illustrations clear and culturally relevant?
- Are there study questions or quizzes at the end of chapters?
- Does the author include discussion and review questions and/or examination items related to the content and concepts as presented in the chapter?
- Are there lists of related readings at the end of chapters and/or a comprehensive bibliography at the end of the book?

- Are there study aids? Do they help students generalize, apply, and/or evaluate content, stimulate critical thinking, or require problem-solving?
- Do appendixes, where applicable, contain additional helpful information closely related to the book's content?
- Is there an index at the end of the book? Is there a glossary of terms as used in the text?
- Does the author provide an index with keywords and important terms?

These features are part of the Book Evaluation Form in Appendix G and on McGraw-Hill's website at www.books.mcgraw-hill.com/training/download. The forms can then be opened, edited, and printed using Microsoft Word or other word processing software. Ideal textbooks that include all of the above features are, in most cases, not available. Therefore, you will need to evaluate the available books by such features as those listed above and select the book that comes nearest to meeting those criteria.

CASE: ACME WIDGETS—PURCHASING THE REQUIRED TRAINING MODULES

In Chapter 6, the training team, along with the users and rollout team, made the decision to outsource most, but not all, of the training for the WCS and KIS rollouts. Because of the rather short time frame, the team decided to skip the RFI and prepare an RFP. Bob, the I/T training manager, and Mike, the I/T training team lead, worked with Kathy, the training developer, to develop RFP criteria and format rules, which were then handed to Jack, the technical writer. Jack developed the RFP like the one in Appendix E, RFP Outline and Completed Sample.

Finding training vendors was done through both WCS and the ITTA. The team received an extensive list of vendors and narrowed it down to two key vendors, Trainers-R-Us (TRU) and IT Training Co. (ITTC), because of their knowledge of the software and comparative prices. Both vendors were compared using the checklist in Appendix F. TRU's score is shown in Table 7-1.

For the most part TRU has a good group of trainers. The only minor problem is that the trainers tend to concentrate on the training process itself, and less on selling management. ITTC is somewhat more of a recognized leader, though the company's prices are considerably higher. The major advantage that the ITTC trainers bring to the table is that they understand the importance of selling to management. ITTC's score is shown in Table 7-2.

The team found that ITTC scored a few points higher, but had higher prices and occasionally subcontracted work. While neither of these findings was necessarily a deal-breaker, the training team knew there were going to be some negotiations

TABLE 7-1

Item	Question	Point ✓
1.	Does the supplier demonstrate originality or innovation?	√
2.	Does the supplier write influential papers or articles in relevant trade magazines?	
3.	Is the supplier recognized as a leader in the field?	√
4.	Does the supplier demonstrate a readiness to customize his or her services to your needs?	√
5.	Is the supplier using the same person to market, sell, and deliver the service?	√
6.	Can the supplier provide customer references on successful projects (a minimum of 3)?	√
7.	Does the supplier honor commitments and display integrity?	√
8.	Does the supplier offer a reliable curriculum vitae for all project team members?	√
9.	Does the supplier fit into your organization or culture?	√
10.	Does the supplier guarantee the training results?	√
11.	Does the supplier inspire personal and professional acceptability?	√
12.	Does the supplier have good rapport with you and good credibility?	√
13.	Is the supplier ready with a risk assessment report, identifying any high-risk areas?	
14.	Does the supplier have training results on job performance changes from previous jobs?	√
15.	Does the supplier require active involvement from your training manager before, during, and after the training events?	√
16.	Does the supplier insist on getting support from management?	√
17.	Does the supplier demonstrate interest in seeing joint participation between the student and his or her manager before and after the training event?	√
18.	Does the supplier require that both student and manager identify job-improvement areas prior to the training event?	
19.	Does the supplier ask the student's manager to motivate the person enrolled?	
20.	Does the supplier plan that the training be followed by a learning-related project?	√
21.	Does the supplier commit to a follow-up evaluation process?	√
22.	Will the supplier present a report of training results?	√
23.	Does the supplier require feedback from the sponsor about the training?	√
	Total points for TRU	19

on quality assurance for the subcontractors and price. The team also asked TRU and ITTC to complete a risk assessment report since neither included it as a standard piece.

The courseware evaluations came out in a similar manner. Both vendors had good courseware, and in fact, a combination of the two would serve the needs of AWI perfectly. Since ITTC typically farmed out some of its work anyway, Bob and Mike asked the two vendors if they could work together to provide complete coverage of the rollouts. The two vendors agreed, and submitted a combination bid, which resembled the one shown in Table 7-3.

TABLE 7-2

Item	Question	Point ✓
1.	Does the supplier demonstrate originality or innovation?	√
2.	Does the supplier write influential papers or articles in relevant trade magazines?	√
3.	Is the supplier recognized as a leader in the field?	√
4.	Does the supplier demonstrate a readiness to customize his or her services to your needs?	√
5.	Is the supplier using the same person to market, sell, and deliver the service?	
6.	Can the supplier provide customer references on successful projects (a minimum of 3)?	√
7.	Does the supplier honor commitments and display integrity?	√
8.	Does the supplier offer a reliable curriculum vitae for all project team members?	√
9.	Does the supplier fit into your organization or culture?	√
10.	Does the supplier guarantee the training results?	√
11.	Does the supplier inspire personal and professional acceptability?	√
12.	Does the supplier have good rapport with you and good credibility?	√
13.	Is the supplier ready with a risk assessment report, identifying any high-risk areas?	
14.	Does the supplier have training results on job performance changes from previous jobs?	√
15.	Does the supplier require active involvement from your training manager before, during, and after the training events?	√
16.	Does the supplier insist on getting support from management?	√
17.	Does the supplier demonstrate interest in seeing joint participation between the student and his or her manager before and after the training event?	√
18.	Does the supplier require that both student and manager identify job-improvement areas prior to the training event?	√
19.	Does the supplier ask the student's manager to motivate the person enrolled?	√
20.	Does the supplier plan that the training be followed by a learning-related project?	√
21.	Does the supplier commit to a follow-up evaluation process?	√
22.	Will the supplier present a report of training results?	√
23.	Does the supplier require feedback from the sponsor about the training?	√
	Total points for ITTC	21

Because the budget was considerably smaller than Bob and Mike had envisioned (see Table 3-12), the team decided to accept the bid. However, AWI was still going to lose some productivity dollars based on salaries, and adding that number back in brought the total back up to approximately $6 million. This was still below the budget, and with a 15 percent change allowance built in, the project was well within the limit set by AWI management.

TABLE 7-3

Item	Cost
Labor	$2,500,000
Travel, lodging, meals	200,000
Facilities	400,000
Hardware	500,000
Software	400,000
Purchased instruction materials	300,000
Grand total	**$4,300,000**

Handout sources were selected from articles written about WCS and KIS. Most of the popular trade journals covered the software, from both an I/T perspective and a business view. The team decided to make copies of the articles as appropriate. There was also a website and discussion groups for the software, which would help users and I/T staff learn tips to make using the software easier.

There were lots of books on both software products. The team worked with the vendor to standardize on two easy-to-understand third-party books, one each for WCS and KIS. The evaluation for the WCS book is shown in Table 7-4.

After rating the book, the team discovered that they would need to supplement the book with the handouts. Even though there was limited review material, the training itself included a manual for each of the classes, supplementary material, and a vendor-oriented summary of the training. Each of the lessons supplied by the vendors would include a drill and test. These materials, combined with the third-party book, were seen by the team to be sufficient for the majority of students.

Coming Up in Chapter 8

Once you make the decision to purchase a specific vendor's package, you probably need to customize the packaged training to meet the needs of your organization. This includes refining the needs analysis to get the details, which leads to determining customization requirements and doing the gap analysis. Working with the vendor to meet your needs, you'll want to design the perfect solution.

TABLE 7-4

Item	Characteristic	Strength (1–5)
1.	Are a table of contents and divisions of each chapter listed under the chapter title?	4
2.	Does the author provide an outline of the book in the table of contents?	4
3.	Do topics correspond to objectives for the course?	3
4.	Is there adequate and balanced coverage of the content area as prescribed by the course description?	3
5.	Are topics arranged in a usable sequence?	5
6.	Can they be adapted without disrupting the usefulness of the book?	2
7.	Does the author give a good overview in the preface regarding where the book is going and the type of audience he or she is addressing?	4
8.	Do introductory statements or paragraphs begin each chapter or major section?	3
9.	Are there clear and well-marked divisions of content within chapters?	3
10.	Are there titles, headings, and subheadings to help the student visualize the organization and relationship of content?	4
11.	Are there summary sections or paragraphs at the end of each major division or chapter?	2
12.	Does the textbook contain readable language that is suitable for the reading level of the students who will be using it?	5
13.	Do students have a sufficient background to understand the author's material?	4
14.	Are illustrations accurate, and are they properly captioned and placed?	5
15.	Are the illustrations clear and culturally relevant?	5
16.	Are there study questions or quizzes at the end of chapters?	0
17.	Does the author include discussion and review questions and/or examination items related to the content and concepts as presented in the chapter?	0
18.	Are there lists of related readings at the end of chapters and/or a comprehensive bibliography at the end of the book?	3
19.	Are there study aids? Do they help students generalize, apply, and/or evaluate content, simulate critical thinking, or require problem solving?	2
20.	Do appendixes, where applicable, contain additional helpful information closely related to the book's content?	4
21.	Is there an index at the end of the book? Is there a glossary of terms as used in the text?	4
22.	Does the author provide an index with keywords and important terms?	4
	Total score	73

REFERENCES

Brookfield, Stephen. (1986). *Understanding and facilitating adult learning.* San Francisco: Jossey-Bass.

Fox, Paul G. (1997). *Make or buy? How to decide.* Fox Performance. Website: www.foxperformance.com. Phone: (860) 870-4640.

Hartley, James. (1994). *Designing instructional text,* (3d ed.). London: Konan Page.

Jonassen, D. H. (1982). *The technology of text.* Englewood Cliffs, NJ: Educational Technology Publications.

Merriam, Sharan, & Caffarella, Rosemary. (1991). *Learning in adulthood.* San Francisco: Jossey-Bass.

Reid, Warren S. (1997). *Outsourcing: The 20 steps to success. Corporate Counsel's Guide to Outsourcing.* Chesterland, OH: Business Laws, Inc. Website: www.wsrcg.com. Phone: (818) 986-8842.

Walsh, K. (1997, May 6). "Angst over IT Outsourcing," *The Bulletin,* p. 14.

White, R., & James, B. (1997). *Outsourcing manual.* Brookfield, VT: Ashgate Publishing Company.

CHAPTER 8

Customizing Packaged Training to Meet the Needs of Your Organization

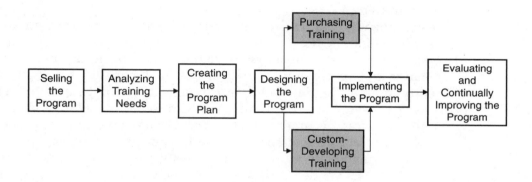

In This Chapter

OVERVIEW

Most organizations need training courses specifically tailored for their audience, and training vendors will typically develop a custom course curriculum. The organizations will work with you to create presentations and practice exercises for your software, based on the audience and needs analysis and designed to achieve the training objectives (see Chapter 5). The training team and vendors can then present the course to your trainees or teach it to your trainers to deliver themselves.

Customizing training plans gives you increased flexibility, and helps you meet the goals and/or objectives stated in the training plans. You can deliver the right mix of content to specific groups or individuals quickly and easily, and you can combine CBT-based courseware with instructor-led lectures, or other tools and techniques, for maximum effectiveness. Customization, although not cheap, can actually cut training costs. Customization makes it convenient for students to study the peculiar characteristics of the software as it relates to your organization. This capability decreases the cost of ownership and reduces the need to send students to specialized learning centers. It also increases student participation in training.

Customization also raises the strategic value of training to your organization. Training is important, but only the proper training raises the effectiveness and knowledge of your I/T and business staff. When your staff is more productive, your systems will be up and running more efficiently more of the time, and your organization will be able to focus on strategic issues rather than who did what to which system. Customized training is more attractive because it's fitted to your particular need and can be scheduled according to your project times.

Customizing a training program to meet your specific needs can be a complex task. The vendor and other consultants can assist customers by analyzing and defining their requirements. An effective training program should be more than a set of classes; it must have the ability to educate customers and entice them to learn. The vendor's team of creative, technical, and training professionals should help you communicate your message while helping you build your training program.

8.1   REFINING THE NEEDS ANALYSIS TO GET THE DETAILS

Chapter 2 walked you through the process of gathering and analyzing the training needs of the organization. In Chapter 4, you designed the course details based on the training needs of the organization. Now that the decision has been made to purchase at least some training, it's necessary to review the details required to make the training work with the chosen vendor. The original needs analysis documents must be refined, which means summarized enough to be useful, but detailed enough to guide you through the process of adapting the purchased training. A detailed course layout or syllabus must be started, although it won't be completed until after the gap analysis (see Sections 8.2 and 8.3).

Defining the Content and Objectives

Defining the content means first defining what skills you want the audience to master. Which of the skills to be taught are relatively generic? Generic skills are skills that people in your organization need that are not company-specific. For example, understanding basic e-mail is a generic skill most people need in today's workplace. Which of the skills to be taught are relatively unique? Unique skills are those specific to your company. This means that an off-the-shelf package won't capture your unique needs.

Complex skills are those that involve higher-order concepts (such as problem solving and decision making) or multistep processes. Skills that must be totally mastered fall into this category as well. If the skills needed are complex, people will need to be given specific, intermediate goals to get them to the final goal. Performance support systems and independent study work well when the skills to be taught are easily mastered.

The content and objectives must correspond. Specifying the objectives means describing the learner characteristics before instruction and the new capabilities afterward. A subject matter expert will also learn about instructional design. The product of this learning will be representations of the subject such as a content-to-objective listing for each course. Table 8-1 presents an example. This form is available for use in Appendix G or on McGraw-Hill's website at www.books.mcgraw-hill.com/training/download. The forms can then be opened, edited, and printed using Microsoft Word or other word processing software. This table builds on the products that were produced in the design phases. The end result is the completed instructional courseware for the customized purchased products.

This table also gets you started on listing learner activities. Remember that development begins with specifying the learning activities that will best assist in the learning process. To select the proper activities, you first have to know what the needs are. For more details, see Chapter 2.

Laying Out the Course Details

Once each of the objectives has been tied to a specific piece of content, the next step is to lay out all the course details. This is generally done by creating a syllabus. The syllabus provides basic, necessary information. You should include the dates, the course title, the number of sessions, and the meeting time and location. Indicate any course meetings that are not scheduled for the assigned room. List your name, phone number

TABLE 8-1

Item #	Course	Objective	Content
1.	HR basics	Enter a new employee's data in 10 minutes with <2 mistakes	Intro to policies for new employees on the new system
2.	HR basics	Enter a new employee's data in 10 minutes with <2 mistakes	Screen fields handling
3.	HR basics	Enter a new employee's data in 10 minutes with <2 mistakes	Screen PF keys overview
4.	HR basics	Enter a new employee's data in 10 minutes with <2 mistakes	Screen processing details
5.	HR basics	Enter a new employee's data in 10 minutes with <2 mistakes	Screen error handling

(and voice mail), e-mail address, and other contact information. A syllabus includes:

- Introductory information
- Prerequisites
- Course description and/or objectives
- Tentative schedule of assignments and activities
- Course requirements
- Testing, grading, and evaluation policies and procedures
- Attendance and participation policies

A sample of these details is created in the case study in this chapter. Also, be sure you include accessibility information so that students can find you if needed. If you are an internal trainer or SME, you'll want to be perceived as accessible; otherwise students won't be as receptive to your instruction.

It's very important to describe the prerequisites to the course. Help students realistically assess their readiness for the course by listing the knowledge, skills, or experience you expect them to already have or the courses they should have completed. Meet with the students and/or their managers ahead of time to ensure that they don't get frustrated or drag the rest of the group down.

Give an overview of the course's purpose. Provide an introduction to the subject matter and show how the course fits in the college or department curriculum. Explain what the course is about and why students must learn the material. State the general learning goals or objectives. What will students know or be able to do after completing this course?

Provide a course calendar or schedule. The schedule should include the sequence of course topics, the preparations or readings, and the assignments to be done in class. For outside work, estimate the required effort. Give students a sense of how much preparation and work the course will involve. How much time should they anticipate spending on reading assignments, problem sets, etc.? Include supplementary material to help students succeed in the course. Some ideas include:

- Helpful hints on how to study, take notes, or do well in class
- Glossary of technical terms used in the course
- References on specific topics for more in-depth exploration
- Supplemental readings
- Information on the availability of videotapes of lectures
- A list of websites, third-party books, and other helpful information

Provide space for the names, telephone numbers, and e-mail addresses of two or three classmates. Encourage students to identify people in class they can contact if they miss a session or need help after the class.

In Chapter 4, you created a course description form (Figure 4-6). This form can now be fleshed out in more detail to include the sections and items mentioned in this section. An example is presented in Figure 8-1.

This form is available for use in Appendix G or on McGraw-Hill's website at www.books.mcgraw-hill.com/training/download. The forms can then be opened, edited, and printed using Microsoft Word or other word processing software. It builds on the summary course description and adds detailed course information. It is likely that the evaluation section will change as the evaluation criteria evolve.

Analyzing Your Audience

An accurate analysis of the target users affects the design, method, and delivery of the training program. Audience analysis may well be the most critical of all activities. Regardless of the quality of the material, if the audience doesn't receive it, the training was useless. Part of this task was done in Chapter 2, using the Current Skills Assessment Form for Computer Skills. Besides the items on that survey, audience analysis may include:

- Reviewing each learner's general educational level, knowledge level specific to the content materials, and level of computer skills
- Identifying the learner's general approach to existing training to identify areas of success and avoid potential areas of fear or resistance

WCS HR Employee Master Screen Course Abbreviated Syllabus

Course Purpose

This course is designed to provide the student with the ability to enter a new employee record and fix any errors that occur during the entry. Should errors occur that are outside the scope of normal entry problems, the student will know when to call the help desk.

Prerequisite

None

Instructor

Shawn Jones is a professional trainer with 5 years of experience in WCS HR fundamentals.

Objectives

Upon the completion of this course, the student will be able to:

- Log on to the HR part of WCS
- Enter all new employee data in 5 to 10 minutes with two errors or less
- Save the data
- Create an e-mail list of the people who need to know about the new employee
- E-mail involved parties within 2 hours of data entry
- Find the source of any problems
- Solve the problems, if possible, without assistance
- Find the problem in the manual, if needed
- Call the help desk if the problem is complex or systematic

Course Approach

The student will be using a simulated WCS system for both parts of the class. The performance metrics will be based on the learning and data entry accuracy and speed. The student must meet the criteria specified in the objectives to receive the certificate of completion.

Course Schedule

The course will run in two parts: (1) data entry and error correction and (2) problem solving. Data entry training will take about 2 hours, and problem solving will take about 4 hours.

F I G U R E   8 - 1   (*Continued*)

WCS HR Employee Master Screen Course Abbreviated Syllabus

Course Policies

Because of the amount of work to be done in the classroom, class will start and end on time. Students are asked to comply with the break time limits to facilitate learning. Students should feel free to help each other, as we are all going to learn together.

Tentative Schedule of Assignments and Activities

Day 1:
   1. Log on to the HR part of WCS
   2. New employee data screen overview
   3. Field details
   4. Setting up the e-mail list
Day 2:
   1. Find the source of any problems
   2. Solve the problems, if possible, without assistance
   3. Find the problem in the manual, if needed
   4. Call the help desk if the problem is complex or systematic

Testing, Grading, and Evaluation Policies and Procedures

Students will be evaluated on their ability to complete the work. There will be a facilitated walk-through of each function first, with time for questions and help. After the facilitated walk-through, students will be expected to complete the assigned task independently.

- Determine an audience profile by which content, design, and delivery should follow, including suitable approaches for the projected training, methods of delivery, themes, and content tonality

In analyzing your audience, there are additional factors to consider, including audience size, skill levels, frame of reference, and attitudes. If you have a large number of trainees, you can justify the purchase of customizable or fully customized training. If a small number of people are to be trained, the development costs must be kept low. This can be done through standardized CBT or off-site classes.

Table 8-2 provides a summary of the detailed information gathered using the Current Skills Assessment Form for Computer Skills. The purpose of this form is to provide a simple, concise summary of the audience

TABLE 8-2

Audience Member	Department/Area	Software Functions/Modules	Skill Level (1=Beginner, 5=Expert)
Jane Spears	HR	Personnel	1
Gary Rondeau	MFG	Reporting	2
Carol Sivan	I/T	HR administration	4

that the "perfect solution" will need to accommodate. This form is available for use in Appendix G and on McGraw-Hill's website at www.books.mcgraw-hill.com/training/download. The forms can then be opened, edited, and printed using Microsoft Word or other word processing software. The skill rating is a summary of what the individual knows about various software modules. An individual could have some prior experience, or could have been involved in testing the software as it was configured. Thus, someone could be a 2 or 4 even prior to training.

8.2 DETERMINING CUSTOMIZATION REQUIRE-MENTS—DOING THE GAP ANALYSIS

To complete the training program design, the training development team must gain an understanding of the existing gap between the current training and the new courseware. A gap analysis is the activity in which the team looks for deficiencies between the required training and the courseware being implemented. As the training project team members gain a better understanding of how the courseware works, they should continue revisiting the documents to identify existing, critical training needs that cannot be supported by the new courseware's functionality. These missing functions must be documented as gaps and resolved prior to training program implementation.

    A gap analysis generally includes a review of existing documentation and brief interviews with users and I/T staff. The organization and the vendor can also gather a team of managers who have total knowledge of the existing training and subject matter, and then guide them through a comprehensive checklist. Also, using questionnaires, team members interview staff to begin baselining the existing training and software needs. In addition to pinpointing the gap in detail, this analysis yields information needed to produce the training manuals. The vendor should work with you to make the additions, changes, and improvements needed to close the gap.

Examining the Purchased Training Package

There are essentially two steps in the gap analysis process. The first is to compare the purchased training with the needs analysis and design documents. The second is to create the gap document that contains the customization specifications. A gap list should be considered a work in progress. Today's gaps may be resolved tomorrow. The gap analysis forms will be used to document gaps and identify possible solutions. Some questions that can be asked as part of the comparison are:

- If the purchased courseware is missing a feature, do you really need it?
- Can you change policies and/or procedures to accommodate the courseware as is?
- Could the courseware accommodate the gap?
- Is there a work-around for the gap?

To compare the purchased training, it's a good idea to "eyeball" the courseware in its generic form and then go into the specifics. The form in Table 8-3 is used for a summary view. This form is available for use in Appendix G and on McGraw-Hill's website at www.books.mcgraw-hill.com/training/download. The forms can then be opened, edited, and printed using Microsoft Word or other word processing software. Once the general summary is completed, the next step is to dig into the details. At the detailed level, the process is basically to compare the current courseware with the desired end state and then identify all high-level activities required to close the gap.

Four areas deserve attention:

- Identifying improvements that must be made to courseware components that the training requires
- Identifying areas where new functionality is strongly desired by users or I/T staff

TABLE 8-3

Item	AWI Course Module	Vendor Course Module	Goodness of Fit (1=Bad, 10=Perfect)
1.	Personnel	Employee master	8
2.	Reporting	Tax reporting	5
3.	HR administration	HR setup basics	7

- Identifying functionality that may not be delivered or that will have significantly changed
- Identifying tasks that must be completed to support the coexistence of the courseware with the original program plan and design

The form shown in Table 8-4 provides placeholders for filling in the details of the gaps between the purchased training or courseware and the needs and design. This form is available for use in Appendix G or on McGraw-Hill's website at www.books.mcgraw-hill.com/training/download. The forms can then be opened, edited, and printed using Microsoft Word or other word processing software. The form presented in Table 8-2 will probably be revised as a result of preparing Table 8-3. It is still often useful, however, to begin with a quick summary to get a general idea of "how big the breadbox is."

Within the areas specified in the two tables, the components of a project that are affected are activities, required human resources, and the training program deliverables produced. The form provided in Table 8-5 can be used to detail the activities required to close the gaps. This information can be added to the project plan for use in revising the effort and dollars needed to complete the training program design. This form is available for use in Appendix G or on McGraw-Hill's website at www.books.mcgraw-hill.com/training/download. The forms can then be opened, edited, and printed using Microsoft Word or other word processing software. It's important to remember to transfer all the information from this form to your project plan. Failure to do so generally results in blown budgets and time lines.

Creating the Gap Document

When you have all the information you need to modify the purchased training to fit the organization's needs, it must be packaged in a single,

TABLE 8-4

Gap	AWI Course Module	Vendor Course Module	Required Improvements	Required Additions	Potential Misses
1.	Personnel	Employee master	Modify order	Add three objectives	N/A
2.	Reporting	Tax reporting	Change CBT menu	Add report training	Nontax rpts.
3.	HR administration	HR setup basics	Adapt to AWI	Add AWI security	Student #'s

TABLE 8-5

Gap	Deliverables Affected	Modification Task	Assigned To	Assigned Date	Estimated Done Date	Completed Date
1.	Objectives	Change course	Shawn	3/3/2000	3/16/00	3/16/00
2.	Objs., content	Change curricula	Dave	3/3/2000	3/21/00	3/22/00
3.	Objectives	Change layout	Kathy	3/3/2000	3/17/00	3/21/00

easy-to-read and easy-to-use document. There will obviously be a great deal of information in this document, so a good outline or table of contents is critical to the document's usability. A sample outline follows.

I. Introduction
    a. Brief overview or review of the organization's training plan
    b. Brief overview or review of the vendor's training material
    c. Executive summary of the new time lines and costs
II. Course and audience summaries
III. Detailed gap analysis
    a. Goodness-of-fit matrix
    b. Gap analysis matrix
    c. Gap punch list
IV. New cost/benefit analysis
V. New time line
VI. Appendixes, if any

This outline can be tailored to fit your organization's needs and documentation requirements. The review of options and design of the adapted program should detail the implementation scope, cost, and benefit, as well as the adapted project plan. Overall, the document should provide a training blueprint for the future.

8.3 DESIGNING THE PERFECT SOLUTION

Designing the perfect solution may be done via courseware engineering, which is an emerging set of practices, tools, and methodologies that result from attempts to take an engineering approach to the production of courseware. The courseware engineering for gaps is divided into two tasks: defining the curriculum and defining (or refining) individual courses or gaps.

Once the gap analysis is completed, it's usually a good idea to work with the managers and systems staff to find out what skills and objectives are mission-critical versus nice to know or needed later. It's important that their expectations match the gaps and solutions identified. Check to see if the revised time frame and budget are feasible or unrealistic from the start. Check the time pressure, and check for flexibility to adapt the training schedule. Be willing to say no when you are asked to deliver the impossible. There will most likely be gaps that simply cannot be filled, so be sure to let management know ASAP.

Designing the Curriculum

There is no single perfect solution for courseware development that can be used in all circumstances of package customization. Most curriculum design solutions are set up for custom-developing training. Designing or redesigning the overall curriculum to handle the gaps can be done vis-à-vis Chapter 4, using the same techniques.

When developing the training material and media, ensure that they are synthesized into an integrated program. It should flow as naturally as possible, with each lesson block building the foundation for the next one. Provide variety that is conducive to learning. Break practice periods up with instructional periods, rather than having all the instruction in the beginning followed by nothing but practice.

Time will have to be considered when synthesizing the complete learning program. For example, if you have five 3-hour blocks of instruction, how do you break them down to run smoothly in two days? Which one gets chopped to 2 hours one day and 1 hour the next day? It might be better to break the most difficult one apart so the learners get a rest from complexity.

The last step is to validate the material by testing the program on a target population and then revising the program as needed. The heart of the systems approach to training is revising and validating the instructional material until the learners meet the planned learning objectives. Success or failure is not measured at a single point. Continue with the test process until the training is no longer needed or until the training courseware is the best piece of training material produced!

Designing Individual Courses

The new design must specify the objectives in educational terms and define the kinds of experiences to bring about the desired behavior. The training team must create an environment that is responsive to the behavior deemed important, and that creates an environment that allows the learner to be rewarded for behaving in accordance with various course objectives. Whether the learner is correct or incorrect, the student must know as soon as possible. For more information, see Chapter 4.

The training team must also create, purchase, or specify the instructional and support material that will provide the most effective learning stimulus. Care should be taken not to select materials just because they are available. For example, there are probably several hundred VCR instructional tapes floating around that were developed because a camera and VCR were readily available, not because it was the best way to teach. The purpose of this step is not to show your mastery of the latest technology, but to select media that will best magnify the learning process.

The media should be suited to the particular type of training. Time is also a critical factor. When and how many learners must be trained by a given time? Is there more than one group to be trained, and how closely will each group follow? Is there time to create the perfect media for the curriculum? Will more than one type of medium be used throughout the curriculum? Each of these questions may be answered differently for each organization.

As each question is answered, the syllabus and course layout may change. A strong course description early in the syllabus can often generate student interest by giving a stimulating overview of the course, including its content, its value, and the assumptions behind it. You will want to increase student enthusiasm and to emphasize the relevance and applicability of the course. You will also want the description to reflect your values and attitudes.

Course objectives or goals can sometimes be combined with the course description, depending on their complexity and the nature of the course and discipline. Course objectives, ideally characterized by action verbs, usually appear as a statement or an outline describing what students should be able to do at the end of the class. Clear objectives can foster a sense of partnership and an awareness that you and the students are working toward the same goals. Objectives provide a focus and a motivation for learning, and the syllabus must lay out in a simple order the objectives, content, and measurements.

8.4   WORKING WITH THE VENDOR TO MEET YOUR NEEDS

When you outsource some or all of a training development project, the process doesn't end with the selection of an external resource. It's important to establish a positive, ongoing relationship with the consultant or firm and manage it successfully. Be prepared to take some time to work closely with a vendor to develop a profile of organizational requirements and specifications. Vendors will provide documentation and some forms to be completed by the staff. The amount of effort required for starting up the services depends on the size of an organization and the scope of services that are needed from the vendor.

Building the Bridge from Your Organization to the Vendor

It's important to build a climate of trust in which both parties can share their feelings and observations. Be sure to openly discuss concerns as soon as they arise with everyone who should be involved. Discuss concerns about the quality and timeliness of the work immediately. Discuss the consulting relationship regularly, particularly what you and the vendor expect from each other and whether expectations are being met.

To facilitate this, establish a formal, written communication system to keep the work on track and be sure your objectives are met. On large projects, develop a detailed project plan and timetable. Require periodic status reports from the external resource, and hold face-to-face status update meetings. Involve the vendor in appropriate meetings. There is a tendency to treat contractors as outsiders and only talk to them on a "need-to-know" basis. In this case, the contractors are providing you with a critical path service for your software rollout. Blocking their access to important information, whether done intentionally or by accident, is a really bad idea. Watch for possible red flags such as missed deadlines, misunderstandings, complaints from others, or a change in attitude on the part of the vendor. Here are some key qualities to look for in a consultant:

- Is open and honest
- Is objective
- Is creative
- Offers fresh ideas
- Shows a willingness to confront new challenges
- Exercises good judgment
- Takes initiative
- Adheres to your standards or exceeds them
- Has patience

- Focuses on goals and on getting results
- Is energetic and enthusiastic
- Communicates effectively
- Works well with people in your organization
- Inspires your confidence

It's important to also find a consultant that adapts to change easily. This list is available as an evaluation form in Appendix G or on McGraw-Hill's website at www.books.mcgraw-hill.com/training/download. The forms can then be opened, edited, and printed using Microsoft Word or other word processing software.

Manage the vendor relationship. Instead of withdrawing from the outsourcing situation, the training and rollout staff need to embrace the new vendor relationship. Take responsibility for managing political situations and internal resources, even if it is not normally your role. This includes ensuring that subject matter experts cooperate fully with the vendor, and obtaining and maintaining support for the program from internal decision makers.

Give the process time to work: Once development and implementation begin, the process can take a year to complete. Understand that it takes time to overcome obstacles and to resolve problems that will inevitably occur when implementing an outsourcing program. Along those lines, keep a sense of humor—it almost goes without saying that a sense of humor will help anyone endure even the most troublesome times.

Focus on the long-term benefits and goals: It is easy to be overwhelmed by the enormous amount of details associated with planning and implementing an outsourcing program. In the midst of coping with daily challenges during the early stages of outsourcing, it is important to remain focused on the long-term benefits and goals that will be achieved as a result of outsourcing. Strive for a win-win relationship with vendors and consultants, and require them to do the same with you.

Controlling Consulting and Customization Costs

The first tip concerns how rarely organizations negotiate the fees vendors charge, even though they may even hire consultants to negotiate other vendor's fees. Market forces (and your organization is one) dictate what a year's worth of a vendor's customization services should cost, and the fees should be negotiated aggressively. Indeed, most consulting firms start with high bids as a contingency for just such negotiating situations, and only the unwise buyer ends up paying "list" prices. Organizations should consider negotiating the customization rates as warm-up for the main event of later negotiating the much larger vendor's fees for training materials and software.

Before the deal is struck with the consultants, begin to control their customization fees by insisting on a detailed work plan of exactly who will be doing what and when. Rather than just buying a finished package for a $100,000 fixed price, insist on seeing what specific deliverables the work effort will consist of and what level of consultant will be involved. Also, question the background and experience level of "IROCs" (idiots right out of college), who are often put on a project under the wing of senior consultants to learn the ropes.

Finally, there is increasing concern about consulting firms and the potential for conflicts of interest. Probably the biggest example of this is the growing tendency of software companies to partner with specific consulting firms. This means that ABC ERP Company has either a written or verbal agreement to add certain training vendors to its "preferred vendor" list. This typically raises prices and compromises quality. To avoid this problem, insist on screening potential consultants up front for any such arrangements they have with software vendors. This will save money on consulting fees, and prevent you from paying to improve the relationship between two external vendors.

CASE: ACME WIDGETS—CUSTOMIZING THE PURCHASED HR TRAINING

In Chapter 7, the training team, along with the users and rollout team, made the decision to outsource most, but not all, of the training for the WCS and KIS rollouts to a pair of vendors: Trainers-R-Us (TRU) and IT Training Co. (ITTC), because of their knowledge of the software and comparative prices. ITTC was to take the lead, and use TRU as a resource to do the bulk of the actual work. The next step is to customize the training to meet the unique requirements of AWI discovered during the needs analysis. The team took a look at the needs analysis and began to identify gaps between the training supplied by ITTC (from Chapter 7) and the original design as specified in Chapter 4. In addition, the material in Chapter 6, where the make-or-buy decision was made, is needed to proceed. Table 8-6 (old Table 6-4) was created to decide on the work needed to produce the two modules to be discussed in this section. This table is also useful in assigning work, as well as human resource allocation, for the revised program plan to completion.

REFINING THE NEEDS ANALYSIS

Kathy, the training developer, began outlining the detailed objectives and content for the WCS and KIS modules, working with Gary, the WCS software rollout team leader, and Lauren, the KIS software rollout team leader. Together they listed the

TABLE 8-6

Software	Function	Class	Make or Buy	Assigned To
WCS	System administration	WCSHR administration	Buy and customize	Gary, Kathy
KIS	E-mail	KIS e-mail	Buy and customize	Lauren, Kathy

objectives and the content that would help the students meet the objectives. Tables 8-7 and 8-8 present the results of that work.

The three team members then combined the content and objectives to create abbreviated syllabi for both courses (see Figures 8-2 and 8-3). It's important to note that these syllabi represent further development of the syllabi created earlier in Chapter 4. It's a bad idea to change directions or content requirements because of vendor products. The objectives and important concepts identified in Chapter 4 should be represented here; otherwise the organization doesn't get what it needs—only what the vendor can offer.

TABLE 8-7

Item	Course	Objective	Content
1.	HR administration	Set up a new user in not more than 5 minutes with no more than two mistakes	Check user's job title, employee number, and department
2.	HR administration	Set up a new user in not more than 5 minutes with no more than two mistakes	Using the information from Item 1, create the user ID
3.	HR administration	Set up a new user in not more than 5 minutes with no more than two mistakes	Set the password to PWD and set expiration to 1 day

TABLE 8-8

Item	Course	Objective	Content
1.	KIS e-mail basics	Create an e-mail group	Enter group name
2.	KIS e-mail basics	Create an e-mail group	Insert addresses
3.	KIS e-mail basics	Create an e-mail group	Send test message to group

FIGURE 8-2

WCS HR Administration Course Abbreviated Syllabus

Course Purpose

This course provides the student with the ability to create a new user and administer various HR system functions in WCS.

Prerequisites

WCS User Basics, WCS Power User course

Instructor

Gary is a SME with 10 years of experience in WCS HR administration. His trainer/assistant Dave Johnson is a professional trainer with 5 years of experience teaching WCS HR.

Objectives

Upon the completion of this course, the student will be able to:

- Set up a new user in not more than 5 minutes with no more than two mistakes
- E-mail the user to notify him of his new ID
- Reset passwords with a 1-day expiration
- Find the source of any problems
- Solve the problems, if possible, without assistance
- Find the problem in the manual, if needed
- Call WCS if the problem is complex or systematic

Course Approach

The student will be using a simulated WCS system for both parts of the class. The performance metrics will be based on the learning and data entry accuracy and speed. The student must meet the criteria specified in the objectives to receive the certificate of completion.

Course Schedule

The course will run in two parts, 1 day each:

Day 1: HR administration basics

Day 2: Advanced HR administration problem solving

FIGURE 8-2 (*Continued*)

WCS HR Administration Course Abbreviated Syllabus

Course Policies

Because of the amount of work to be done in the classroom, class will start and end on time. Students are asked to comply with the break time limits to facilitate learning. Students should feel free to help each other as we are all going to learn together.

Tentative Schedule of Assignments and Activities

Day 1:

1. Log on to the HR part of WCS

2. Create the security record for a new user

3. Set the ID and password

4. E-mail the user

Day 2:

1. Resetting passwords

2. Solving access problems

3. Finding the problem in the manual if needed

4. Calling the WCS help desk if the problem is complex or systematic

Testing, Grading, and Evaluation Policies and Procedures

Students will be evaluated on their ability to complete the work. There will be a facilitated walk-through of each function first, with time for questions and help. After the facilitated walk-through, students will be expected to complete their assigned tasks independently.

The syllabi in Figures 8-2 and 8-3 were written to address the needs identified in Chapter 2 and comply with the design created in Chapter 4. The courses are targeted at specific audiences, based on their needs. Only two AWI I/T staff members were identified as needing training for the WCS HR module, as presented in Table 8-9.

The audience for the KIS training was much larger than that for WCS since the functionality presented in the training was needed by a large group of employees.

FIGURE 8-3

KIS E-mail Basics Course Abbreviated Syllabus

Course Purpose

This course is designed to provide the student with the ability to create and send e-mails to individuals and groups.

Prerequisite

None

Instructor

Mike is a professional trainer with 5 years of experience in WCS HR fundamentals.

Objectives

Upon the completion of this course, the student will be able to:

- Log on to KIS
- Create, address, and send an e-mail
- Create a group list
- Use the group list to address and send an e-mail

Course Approach

The student will be using a simulated KIS system for both sessions of the class. The performance metrics will be based on the student's successful completion of the tasks.

Course Schedule

The course will run for about 4 hours, in one ½-day session.

Course Policies

Because of the amount of work to be done in the classroom, class will start and end on time. Students are asked to comply with the break time limits to facilitate learning.

Tentative Schedule of Assignments and Activities

1. Log on to KIS
2. Create, address, and send an e-mail
3. Create a group list
4. Use the group list to address and send an e-mail

FIGURE 8-3 (*Continued*)

KIS E-mail Basics Course Abbreviated Syllabus

Testing, Grading, and Evaluation Policies and Procedures

Students will be evaluated on their ability to complete the work. There will be a facilitated walk-through of each function first, with time for questions and help. After the facilitated walk-through, students will be expected to complete their assigned tasks independently.

TABLE 8-9

Audience Member	Department/Area	Software Functions/Modules	Skill Level (1=Beginner, 5=Expert)
Ron Lester	I/T	HR administration	2
Bruce Romano	I/T	HR administration	1

A decision was made to pilot the training first, with one to two members from each major department. This way, the training could be revised before rolling it out to the entire company, and the instructors would not be overwhelmed (see Table 8-10).

Each of the students in the class was given the basic e-mail training, although Ron and Bruce were exempted after evaluating their skills. It's generally a good idea to use pretests when possible, to make the training more efficient for the organization; otherwise, the staff may end up wasting time in mandatory training even though they know the material.

DOING THE GAP ANALYSIS

Once Kathy, Gary, and Lauren completed the detailed course descriptions, they and the rest of the team began the process of comparing the purchased training with the courseware requirements. They began with a summary-level view after walking through the vendor's video and CBT materials. Table 8-11 shows the results of the preliminary comparison.

The HR administration fit fairly well because AWI had planned to use the HR module as is with a few extra requirements. There wasn't really a need to create additional content because the purchased training met the needs of the "vanilla" software. The KIS e-mail basics, however, required considerable modifications because of AWI's environment. Table 8-12 shows the work needed. Note that the

TABLE 8-10

Audience Member	Department/Area	Software Functions/Modules	Skill Level (1=Beginner, 5=Expert)
Trudy Moen	HR	KIS e-mail basics	2
Steve Hanson	HR	KIS e-mail basics	2
Gary Squires	Accounting	KIS e-mail basics	1
Lynn Enzman	Accounting	KIS e-mail basics	1
Ron Lester	I/T	KIS e-mail basics	3
Bruce Romano	I/T	KIS e-mail basics	3
Tom Lee	Inventory	KIS e-mail basics	1
John Ramirez	Purchasing	KIS e-mail basics	1

TABLE 8-11

Item	AWI Course Module	Vendor Course Module	Goodness of Fit (1=Bad, 10=Perfect)
1.	HR administration	HR setup	8
2.	KIS e-mail basics	KIS basics part 1	5

changes to the KIS gap were more significant, thus requiring a longer time frame. This is why it's extremely important to retrofit the project time line in the program plan with the information gleaned from the gap analysis. Also, although the actual work was assigned to Kathy, she'll be getting help from both Lauren and Gary on her assignments. Gary will help modify the WCS HR, and Lauren will be primarily involved in helping Kathy and the vendors modify the KIS e-mail modules.

To smooth the process of bringing in consultants, Kathy worked with Mike to ensure that all the team members were kept actively informed of the progress. E-mails and meetings were kept brief and concise. Also, Kathy was designated as the "point person" for contact with the vendors. The major advantage of having such a point person is to provide a bridge between the vendors and the training department. That way, both vendors and team members can have someone to bridge the gap between organizational staff and outside vendors.

Coming Up in Chapter 9

You've analyzed the needs, planned and designed the program, and purchased and/or created a training solution for your organization. Now it's time to implement the program. Will the classes be on-site or off-site? How will you evaluate trainers? All these questions must be answered.

TABLE 8-12

Gap	Deliverables Affected	Modification Task	Assigned To	Assigned Date	Estimated Done Date	Completed Date
1.	Objectives	Add two objectives	Kathy	1/3/2000	2/11/00	2/9/00
2.	Objectives	Revise to fit AWI	Kathy	1/13/2000	2/21/00	2/26/00
2.	Content	Fit AWI architecture	Kathy	1/15/2000	3/17/00	3/21/00
2.	Screen order	Fit to AWI security	Kathy	1/15/2000	4/17/00	4/22/00

REFERENCES

Andrews, D. H., & Goodson, L. A. (1980). A comparative analysis of models of instructional design. *Journal of Instructional Development* 3(4).

Boyd, S. (1999). Course design strategies for coping with teaching at light speed. Susan Boyd Associates. Website: www.susan-boyd.com. Phone: (215) 886-2669.

Brookfield, Stephen. (1986). *Understanding and facilitating adult learning.* San Francisco: Jossey-Bass.

Gagné, R. M., & Medsker, K. L. (1985). *The conditions of learning* (4th ed). New York: Harcourt, Brace, Jovanovich.

Kolb, D. A. (1984). *Experiential learning: Experience as the source of learning and development.* Englewood Cliffs, NJ: Prentice Hall.

Leshin, C. B., Pollock, J., & Reigeluth, C. M. (1992). *Instructional design strategies and tactics.* Englewood Cliffs, NJ: Educational Technology Publications.

Posner, G. J., & Rudnitsky, A. N. (1986). *Course design: A guide to curriculum development for teachers* (3d ed.). New York: Longman.

Reid, Warren S. (1997). *Outsourcing: The 20 steps to success. Corporate counsel's guide to outsourcing.* Chesterland, OH: Business Laws Inc. Website: www.wsrcg.com. Phone: (818) 986-8842.

Sparkes, J. J. (1983). On choosing teaching methods to match educational aims. *Distance education—international perspectives* (pp. 251–256). In D. Sewart, D. Keegan, and B. Holmberg (eds.). New York: Croom Helm.

Walsh, K. (1997, May 6). Angst over IT outsourcing. *The Bulletin*, p. 14.

White, R., & James, B. (1997). *Outsourcing manual.* Brookfield, VT: Ashgate Publishing Company.

CHAPTER 9

Implementing the Training Program

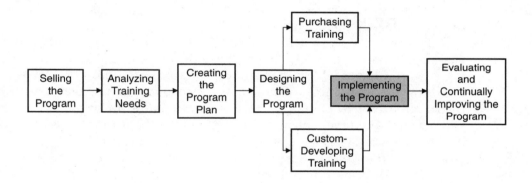

In This Chapter

OVERVIEW

Training is implemented properly by ensuring that the courseware, class setting, and staff are ready once the program begins. The learners must be scheduled and notified. The training staff may require training to perform their roles in the learning process. They must be given time to prepare and rehearse their instruction. A general rule of thumb is that every hour of training requires about 2 to 3 hours of preparation time.

This can vary with the difficulty of the subject and the trainer's experience with the subject. Implementation will proceed smoothly if you plan ahead for it. Implementation issues vary depending on whether people train independently or in a classroom on-site, or are sent to off-site classes.

For a successful implementation to occur, line managers must consider design and delivery of training as an essential part of their function. Managers and team leaders are responsible not only for their own development, but also for that of their team members and staff. Don't leave any employees out of the development activity, particularly if they'll need the information sooner or later anyway. Try to portion the training out as needed to avoid overwhelming employees.

The manner in which training is delivered varies widely, as discussed in Chapter 5. While instructor-led, small-group classroom training (with CBT) is the dominant (and preferred) method, videotapes and satellite broadcasts are not unusual, especially in some remote offices. Instructors tend to be drawn from a combination of organization and vendor staff. Some technical training may take the form of cross-training or retraining to develop or enhance new skills, and provide a backup in case of a staff absence. Most technical training also involves team building, shared leadership, change management, or quality improvement, all of which are designed to make the work force more productive and efficient.

9.1   ON-SITE OR OFF-SITE?

There are advantages and disadvantages to both on-site and off-site training. The obvious disadvantage to off-site training, if it's not local, is the expense. The main disadvantage of on-site training is the potential for distractions. When training is delivered in an on-site classroom, usually located where the trainee works, an instructor is provided to facilitate learning. On-site classroom training is usually scheduled at a specified time and location because of the need for instructional support. On-site classroom training is usually required when the skills to be taught are complex or must be completely mastered, as in the case of large software rollouts. If you will be operating on-site classes, it is important that a separate, self-contained space for instruction be used. It will be very difficult for trainees to pay attention if they are in a room with other activities. Finding space can be difficult for small and mid-sized companies.

On-Site Issues

Getting training sessions up and running is a complicated process. Organizations need to consider a number of issues when creating a learning environment on-site. These issues include:

- Ensuring that facilities are scheduled.
- Handling such logistics as location, media, and equipment.
- Making sure the network (if it's used) is available when needed. If you are delivering CBT over the Internet and it is not available at a certain time, you cannot deliver the training when needed.
- Making sure the training room cannot be accessed by unauthorized individuals.
- Moving personnel around to provide coverage for trainees when they are not at their jobs.
- Ensuring that the training facility is available.
- Taking into account the duration of lessons, tests, and sessions.
- Handling the logistical elements needed for scheduling and calculating training times. The training schedule should provide adequate breaks to allow for reflection and absorption.

Technical personnel must be available and responsible for implementing, operating, and maintaining the training environment. This is critical both for performance support systems and training instruction in on-site classes and for independent study. Technical personnel typically are organizational staff, because contractors usually don't have the in-depth knowledge required to maintain the environment.

Administrative personnel are also responsible for coordinating training activities. Technical personnel by themselves cannot ensure that the training will be successful within your organization. How the training is scheduled is equally important to its success. This is important in all cases and is critical for independent study and off-site classes. Good documentation will minimize the disruptive aspects of staff turnover, allowing new people to come up to speed quickly. It will also enable the organization to provide smooth maintenance and further development and revision of the training.

Off-Site Issues

If you are using an off-site training vendor, many of the implementation issues are the responsibility of the vendor. You are responsible for making sure your trainees have easy access to the off-site facility. You should schedule trainees' training times according to your organization's needs and policies and the trainees' own preferences. You may want to make travel arrangements for your trainees as well, unless the vendor is local or has access to local facilities. You need to decide whether you are going to have them train on their own time, pay them for the time they are in training, or choose some combination of these options.

9.2 TRACKING ATTENDANCE

Attendance tracking is an important part of training. By this point in the training program development process, target audiences have been identified, and it's essential that those targeted individuals attend the training. Preregistering employees via an intranet or groupware product is one way of helping to ensure attendance. Instructors can also improve attendance by giving rewards for perfect attendance. The other side, which is more negative, but sometimes necessary, is the reporting of absences, or extensive lost time on breaks, to the attendee's supervisor. This is rather punitive and should only be used as a last resort. The following sign-up sheet shown in Table 9-1 can be used by trainees to sign up for the class ahead of time, or can be used by trainers to record attendance. This sheet can also be used for breaks. It's important to note those students who leave for breaks and return either late or not at all. This form is available for use in Appendix G or on McGraw-Hill's website at www.books.mcgraw-hill.com/training/download. The forms can then be opened, edited, and printed using Microsoft Word or other word processing software. While it may seem silly to some people to track the tardiness of adults, trainers waste enormous amounts of time answering questions from late students that were already answered in the material covered. Sometimes trainers even charge some money for each minute students are late, and that can often add up fast.

Better performance is a direct result of better attendance, and building or buying a good tracking system can help. In course evaluation questionnaires, students can be asked to rate their own attendance. Then, the system can be used to compare the students' perception with reality. Course management software can track attendance and test scores for classroom training, seminars, etc. Good tracking systems make giving credit for scheduled and unscheduled training events easy. For CBT and other electronic training, information is recorded automatically. The software compiles all information to update students' progress, educational history, and reports. Other features may include the ability to:

TABLE 9-1

Name	Department	Time In	Time Out	Late? (Y/N)	Late By? (Minutes)
Jim Pappas	HR	8:30 a.m.	4:30 p.m.	N	0
Tommy Thomas	Accounting	8:35 a.m.	4:20 p.m.	Y	5
Chris Martin	Advertising	8:45 a.m.	4:10 p.m.	Y	15

- View students who have been assigned specific catalog items.
- Credit students for completing or attending assigned catalog items and class sessions.
- Credit students for completing or attending catalog items not previously assigned.
- Track assessment scores and completion dates on a per-student basis.
- Set recertification dates on a per-student basis.
- Quickly search for students by name and Social Security Number for recording individual students' activities.
- Filter catalog by user-defined parameters.

These types of software can be very helpful in managing training program implementation. They can be used to calculate ROI, track problem students, and help students with legitimate absences make up work.

It's also important to track attendance for each individual. An employee's attendance at training events can be tracked via the sign-up sheet presented in Table 9-1, as well as via the training log presented later in the book. Tracking individual attendance helps the manager understand any performance issues, measure ROI for training expenditures, and set up and administer performance appraisals. It's also useful for managers to gather feedback from instructors on the employee's behavior during training.

9.3   FINDING INTERNAL TRAINERS

Because of the vast amount of knowledge generated during the development of a software rollout training program, it's important to use some internal trainers in addition to training vendors. The last thing any organization needs is to have all of its training knowledge walk out the door after delivery. By pairing internal and external trainers on training development and delivery, the organization retains the knowledge generated during development, and picks up tips from professional trainers as well.

Internal trainers should be held to the same criteria and standards as external trainers. When you're looking for internal trainers, consider how well they understand your business. Have they been at the company long enough to understand your needs? While you wouldn't expect this from external trainers, internal staff should have the information needed, and can actually augment the external trainers. Also, consider their ability to support and advise you, as well as their ability to communicate with you honestly as peers. Internal trainers should also be able to:

- Analyze an audience.
- Organize ideas for impact.
- Design the most effective format.
- Plan content.
- Improve and modify purchased training.
- Edit for results.
- Structure sessions.
- Speak well.

Presenting to peers can be a bit intimidating, and it's important that trainers give a clear, simple presentation with confidence. They should also be able to choose the most appropriate words for the presentation from their vocabulary. They must know how to structure a presentation logically, so as to maximize impact, understanding, and retention. There will occasionally be side conversations, so the trainers must be able to control a group of people.

It is key to find internal trainers who strive to give the learners the best customer service possible. When running a class, the trainers have been entrusted with the students' time. The trainers should do their best to ensure that it is time well spent. That means that everything done should be designed to excite and delight, as well as educate, your customers. There's more to effective training than just giving knowledge. It doesn't matter what the subject matter is—you should be able to find ways of training that encourage the participants to actually want to learn, *and* to come back for more.

Those internal staff people with enough experience in the software and/or training can train someone who has less experience than they have. The quality of the training will depend on the skill and knowledge of the trainers, however. Ideally, training should be done by those who have many years of hands-on experience and have developed the skills needed to pass on their knowledge in an acceptable manner. While some may be well seasoned in the intricacies of the software, they may woefully lack the ability to successfully teach others what they know. Temperament, communication skills, ethics, and trust are just as important as intelligence, knowledge, and experience when choosing internal trainers.

The main problem with internal trainers is their ability to command the respect of their students, who may be peers or even superiors. Trainees often take more notice of external trainers because of their perceived objectivity, and student perceptions can be a major problem. Small organizations that have to work with funding constraints may find it useful to send internal staff to a training program and then have the newly trained staff train the remaining users.

9.4   DESIGNING TRAINER EVALUATIONS

Evaluating trainers is one of the most important tasks in a training program. If trainers aren't well perceived by students and aren't communicating the message properly, the entire training effort can fail. It's important to determine the characteristics most likely to make a trainer successful in your organization. Each organizational culture, and departmental culture within an organization, is slightly different, and trainers must be very flexible in their approach to delivery and coaching. You determine what is important to your organization.

Good trainers demonstrate a concern for the mechanics of training but also a concern for the participants. Trainers can demonstrate responsiveness by expressing interest in the individual learner, establishing a rapport with participants, and using relaxed mannerisms during training. Good trainers are receptive to comments and questions and are eager to promote discussions in class. Highly experienced trainers also know when it is important to generate discussion among students to help encourage collaborative learning. And they know when and how to appropriately end a discussion.

Great trainers also show an enthusiasm not only during the training event but prior to training and in most aspects of their work. They show optimism toward training projects. As well, they intentionally create an exciting, positive climate for the participants. Enthusiastic trainers also make sure they have a thorough knowledge of the training content prior to conducting the training. Trainers that are involved in the needs assessments and that prepare detailed lesson plans prior to training tend to be better prepared, more comfortable, and better able to be positive.

Good trainers also have a sense of humor. They should make the training fun for participants. The trainers may make fun of themselves during training, particularly during the all too frequent technical disasters. Good trainers incorporate humor in conjunction with personal, real-life stories and examples during training to relax the trainees and create an open environment.

Good trainers also establish a clear sense of direction during training to reduce participant anxiety. They take every participant question seriously and answer it thoroughly. The smart trainer also knows not to pretend to have answers to questions and to provide honest feedback on performance. Good instructors provide sincerity and honesty and can earn participants' trust easily.

Experienced trainers are comfortable recognizing the need to adjust, alter, or eliminate material during the training, based on the unique needs of the participants. They may eliminate less pertinent material to meet a time constraint. They can instantaneously adjust the content of instruction to accommodate participants' unique needs. They may also deviate from prescribed material, alter or eliminate less pertinent material, and explore new areas outside the canned course material to serve the needs of the participants and organization. Good trainers are not concerned with losing control of the classroom training. They can generate interesting discussion and then get back to the material easily.

Good trainers also know it's important to maintain a positive attitude and tolerate disruptions during training. Trainers should never become angry or frustrated during training and therefore lose their composure. Good trainers don't take participant criticism as a personal attack. Conflict resolution in a positive and professional manner is also important. Good trainers are willing and able to accommodate different learning styles.

More objectively, there are some specific competencies as outlined in the form in Table 9-2 that provide a basis for evaluating the trainer on the ability to deliver content and manage the classroom. This form is available for use in Appendix G and on McGraw-Hill's website at www.books.mcgraw-hill.com/training/download. The forms can then be opened, edited, and printed using Microsoft Word or other word processing software. This form can be used for almost any training situation, and can be customized as needed to provide a starting point for evaluating trainers.

TABLE 9-2

Trainer Name:			Date:			
Class Name:			Location:			

Item	The trainer	1=Strongly Disagree, 5=Strongly Agree				
1.	Sets goals and objectives for training	1	2	3	4	5
2.	Develops lesson plans	1	2	3	4	5
3.	Keeps current and up to date	1	2	3	4	5
4.	Conducts needs assessments	1	2	3	4	5
5.	Provides advice to students	1	2	3	4	5
6.	Designs instruction so it is easily understood	1	2	3	4	5
7.	Provides positive reinforcement	1	2	3	4	5
8.	Blends different training techniques	1	2	3	4	5
9.	Uses questioning to involve participants	1	2	3	4	5
10.	Facilitates group learning activities	1	2	3	4	5
11.	Clearly explains concepts	1	2	3	4	5
12.	Presents training in a logical sequence	1	2	3	4	5
13.	Recognizes and attends to individual differences	1	2	3	4	5
14.	Explains complex ideas so they are easily understood	1	2	3	4	5
15.	Evaluates effects and impact of training	1	2	3	4	5
16.	Is flexible and can guide the training as needed	1	2	3	4	5
17.	Is honest and open with participants	1	2	3	4	5
18.	Is sincere	1	2	3	4	5
19.	Manages the classroom in an orderly manner	1	2	3	4	5
20.	Is prompt	1	2	3	4	5
	Total points					

The organization should ensure that quality assurance mechanisms are in place for both trainers and the training program (see Chapter 12), so that all the education and training activities meet a required standard. This can be done through different ways of evaluating trainers and participants. The training department should devise various mechanisms as a matter of great importance, because ultimately the value of the training must be determined as a return on investment for the organization.

9.5   ONGOING TRAINING ISSUES

The two major issues that are ongoing in training programs are (1) maintaining the courseware and (2) monitoring and logging training on an ongoing basis. Both of these tasks are extremely important if the training program is to remain current and useful. Some other common issues are also faced by organizations as the training program settles into "maintenance mode."

When the training program was created, the link connecting training to career management may not have been made clear. Sometimes training programs, either short or long term, are just an alignment of figures or a show of training actions. It's very important to make sure that employees know how training will impact their careers, and that their progress through training is monitored.

Some general support tasks are required just to keep the program running from an administrative perspective. These tasks can be done by a support person or training coordinator. The person will need to keep up with news, mail, and requests, and will need to e-mail instructors to find out facility schedules for each course. The person must also post schedules for classes, and work with consultant supervisors so they can schedule consultants to assist with the classes. The coordinator may also need to verify that new hires have completed their paperwork and been registered for the appropriate classes. The coordinator will probably need to send e-mail to all participants, letting them know of any standard requirements and prerequisites. The support person will also answer requests and e-mail generated by students and instructors concerning accounts.

Maintaining Courseware

If the courseware is purchased and licensed, it's necessary to maintain the license currency. The training team keeps a record of the number of licenses per courseware module and the date maintenance begins, based on the vendor's notification of orders. The vendor typically bills the organization for the following year 60 days before annual coverage ends. Some vendors prorate maintenance expense and recharges to organizations, together with licensing fees if necessary. The training team should work with the vendor to ensure the best deal. Taking into consideration the availability of upgrades, updates, and maintenance releases, the vendor should issue a copy of the license to the organization.

Monitoring and Logging Training

All managers who have staff responsibility should monitor training as it occurs to ensure that the training is effective at meeting the identified needs. This training must be integrated with the employee performance appraisal. Managers are responsible for ensuring that the training identified for their staff is completed satisfactorily within the specified time frame. The training should be tracked on a form that captures the record of the employee's development. One example of a form that tracks training is given in Table 9-3. This form is available in Appendix G or on McGraw-Hill's website at www.books.mcgraw-hill.com/training/download. The forms can then be opened, edited, and printed using Microsoft Word or other word processing software.

It's also useful to purchase a curriculum management tool to track these details in an automated fashion. These tools provide comprehensive documentation of all employee education. They are usually integrated systems that automate the tracking and reporting functions in a training environment. Some features include:

- Curriculum management at an individual student level
- Ability to interface into and deliver any Windows-based training
- Ability to track, report, and test classroom and video-based training
- Reporting by location, department, course, and student
- Compliance reporting by location and department
- Certificate of completion by employee
- User-defined location and department parameters
- User-defined and modified site-specific information
- Access over local and wide area networks

TABLE 9-3

Name of Trainee:						
			No. of Hours			
Date	Location	Training Description	Off the Job	On the Job	Course ID	Comment

Many of these tools are powerful, easy-to-use databases with good reporting systems attached. Like any other software purchase, try to find one that has good references and that has been implemented in a wide variety of facilities nationwide. Training administration systems are now available that work on a client/server network, allowing multiple training administrators to access information as needed. Systems even allow staff members to view their personal educational histories and current assignments from any workstation, eliminating time-consuming calls received by your training or HR departments.

CASE: ACME WIDGETS—IMPLEMENTING THE TRAINING PROGRAM

The implementation of the program is one of the most important steps, so Mike, the I/T training team lead, wanted to make sure that the program was implemented in a way that added value to the learning experience, as well as to the students' careers. Together with the business users and Bob, the I/T training manager, Mike decided to bring the training on site. This decision was made for two reasons. The first reason was to provide the trainees with the most realistic environment possible, by training them on AWI's own systems. The second was to reduce costs.

The training for the more complex modules was set at a full day, with the basics being taught in the morning and the interfaces and error handling being taught in the afternoon. The simpler classes were scheduled for afternoon half days. The training team also knew to avoid Monday mornings and Friday afternoons, since few people are paying full attention to their work at those times.

Mike and Bob worked with the vendors to get the best trainers, and asked each trainer to interview extensively with the training team and end users. In addition, Mike specifically asked for work samples and references from similar clients. He and the team questioned them about their approach to problem students and cultural change and asked other rollout-related questions. They also asked the potential trainers how they determine or evaluate success (see Chapter 12). Finally, they asked the potential trainees what they thought it would take to be successful in AWI.

Finding internal trainers was actually very easy. Most of the top people had been hand-chosen by their department heads. The trainers chosen were told that they'd be provided with opportunities to enhance employee subject matter, presentation, and leadership skills. They would also gain recognition as a subject matter expert, have the chance to meet and work with others from around AWI, and increase their personal visibility in the organization. Training facilitators also received training in administration concepts and techniques and in interpersonal dynamics.

The trainer evaluations were designed in line with the culture of the organization and the role that training plays. Training is highly valued at AWI and has a long history there. Training for the software rollout, however, is new, not fully understood, and potentially underfunded. The trainer evaluations also took into account the mix of training needs for each department. The personalities of the individuals responsible for and involved in training, and their training background and experience, were also factored into the process. The form in Table 9-2 was also used for students to evaluate the trainers. Each major area was factored into the evaluation process using that form. It's important to note specific factors such as experience when setting expectations, so that those expectations are realistic.

Ongoing training and support issues were discussed with the "power user" for each department and the help desk. An important and ongoing training issue is to define ahead of time which types of training should follow help desk calls and which types of training can wait. This is critical, because trainees may find a need for advanced training just during the course of their regular work. If a particular person keeps calling the help desk with the same question, there's a good chance the training "didn't take." This may indicate a need for some additional training.

There was also a need for the training team to establish maintenance procedures for the courseware, both paper and automated. AWI purchased a system from one of the vendors that simplified the administration involved in maintaining automated courseware libraries and learner information management systems. The vendor provided AWI with software for learning plan development and tracking software. AWI's HR department now works with learners to ensure that their training records are updated centrally.

The training team would create and edit user accounts, and create and update individual learning plans from predefined curricula. They and the HR department would also be able to assign learning plans and curricula to users and groups of users, and view reports on course usage. The HR department would track progress on individual learning plans, and record, maintain, and view reports on assessments. The technical support staff were assigned the responsibilities of creating and editing user accounts on the system, and incorporating configuration information for courseware.

Coming Up in Chapter 10
Implementing the program doesn't mean much if nobody knows about it. Communicating information about the program, as well as tracking the attendance it draws, is very important. Also, setting up incentive programs to help motivate employees is important to maintaining their interest. Chapter 10 provides some tips on motivation and attendance.

REFERENCES

Carskadon, M. A., & Roth, T. (1991). Sleep restriction. In T. H. Monk (Ed.), *Sleep. sleepiness and performance: Human performance and cognition.* New York: John Wiley and Sons.

Laird, Dugan. (1985). *Approaches to training and development* (2d ed.). Reading, MA: Addison-Wesley.

Leshin, C. B., Pollock, J., & Reigeluth, C. M. (1992). *Instructional design strategies and tactics.* Englewood Cliffs, NJ: Educational Technology Publications.

McCord, B. (1976). Job instruction. In R. L. Craig & L. R. Bittel (Eds.) *Training and development handbook.* New York: McGraw-Hill.

McGehee, W., & Thayer, P. W. (1961). *Training in business and industry.* New York: John Wiley and Sons.

Communicating the Training Rollout to the Organization

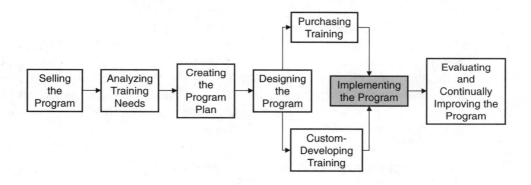

In This Chapter

10.1 Building enthusiasm and overcoming resistance to change

10.2 Giving employees incentives for training (or for demonstrating competency)

10.3 Holding employees accountable for training results

Case: Acme Widgets—Publishing and Releasing the Training Program

OVERVIEW

Training is critical to the success of a software rollout, and so is communicating information about the training to the organization. If you don't do it, or do it wrong, much of the effort, time, and money spent on the training program will be lost. There are many ways to let employees know about training, including e-mail, intranet, groupware, and paper newsletters.

Communicating the software rollout is only a first step. By becoming a member of an internal newsgroup you can pose questions to other staff about the software. By maintaining internal newsgroups open to all levels of employees about training, every area can see upcoming classes and other relevant tips and information. The marketing, engineering, accounting, personnel, and purchasing departments can all work together toward improving training, and pool their knowledge from the training for maximum impact. This helps improve productivity, ensuring that all the departments' needs are met through good communication. These discussions improve the sense of participation in the training process.

Groupware provides a central location for information about training, and with e-mail capabilities, allows you to point at the information location with a link. Products such as Lotus Notes provide groupware capabilities and some web capabilities as well. Groupware can also be used to create internal bulletin boards for class postings, establish a distribution platform for moving information from place to place, and support training functions in order to create a synergy between all departments and processes. Other products such as Novell's Groupwise provide library-type functions and document sharing functions as well. Paper newsletters, while old-fashioned, are still useful if done well.

10.1   BUILDING ENTHUSIASM AND OVERCOMING RESISTANCE TO CHANGE

Enthusiasm is infectious. Once a single employee gets excited about the training, others will follow, particularly if the right incentives are offered (see Section 10.3). Producing a supportive, enthusiastic environment is a task similar to selling the program to management, discussed in Chapter 1, only this time the program must be sold to the masses. The quality of energy that flows when people are working on something that they really care about is different from the quality of energy when people are doing something because they should, or because they are told to do so, even if they know it's "good" or "right." Culture is also very important. It's necessary to understand the "corporate culture" to be able to target communications effectively.

Building Momentum and Overcoming Inertia

Communication about the training program must be highly structured and directed. It's important to communicate clearly to your audience why you are sharing this information. Most employees just assume that they'll have to sit through some kind of training when new software is installed.

It is essential to understand what you want to achieve with your communication to know if you are succeeding. Do you wish that employees would understand how their daily work is connected to the company performance? Are you secretly hoping employees will appreciate the training that corporate officers are doing? Are you interested in teaching employees about how performance is tied to rewards? An honest appraisal of your objectives will enable you to set a course of action.

Enthusiasm is a means for group members to become actively involved in the training and perform functions at a higher level. The most important rule about maintaining your employees' enthusiasm for learning is to include them in the decision making and in the organizational processes. If they help create the training and believe in it, they'll help support it. Also, remember "WIIFM." Employees are likely to ask, "What's in it for me?" Why should your employees care about the training? Are you providing benefits and services they really want and need? Are you asking for their input? Are they part of the process?

Presenting the training program at an overview level to the bulk of the employees is important as well. The presentation should create enthusiasm about the training. Make sure that you are earnest about your subject. Enthusiasm is contagious, so utilize the persuasive power of earnestness to your benefit. When you walk before your audience to speak, do so with an air of anticipation. You are about to tell your listeners something worthwhile, and you should inform them of that clearly and unmistakably. Your actions will help you portray to your listeners that you have some information that they want to know.

Some instructors also conduct a brainstorming session about things that might be added to the course, place a suggestion box in the back of the room, or have students arrange study groups to help them learn collectively. The possibilities are endless. And it is never too soon for feedback. Besides brainstorming sessions, instructors might ask students to take a few minutes at the end of class to write their reactions to the first day of class. This not only provides early feedback but indicates an interest in learning from them. It can help in building a learning climate in which students assume more responsibility for, and feel more actively involved in, the learning that occurs in the classroom.

Managing Change

A new training program and new ways of working cannot simply be imposed on top of the existing bureaucracy. Changes in attitude, work roles, management techniques, and organizational structures are essential to creating and sustaining an environment that supports results-oriented training. Changes in organizational culture do not come quickly or easily. Unfortunately, all too often, little attention is given to managerial and employee training, to the exploration of alternative delivery systems, or to other organizational changes. Organizations can create an internal environment that supports results-oriented training. Critical success factors include:

- *Understanding the culture and disposition of your organization to gauge its readiness, or ability, to really use a good training program.* Factors to consider include the overall relationship between management and employees, as well as between management and its overseers. Is there a system in place that rewards risk taking? Are there adequate financial resources for the change?
- *Obtaining and maintaining visible commitment from top management, and building an awareness of the need for change throughout the organization.* If managers and employees fail to perceive and endorse a need for change, training will amount to little more than a paper exercise.
- *Developing a communications plan.* Over time, increase communication among all those involved in the training program, transferring ownership from an initial small group to all managers, employees, and stakeholders.
- *Addressing personnel issues.* Talk with employees to allay any fears about changing over to a new software system. Encourage their active participation in designing measures, and phase in the actual use of software in making budgetary and personnel decisions.
- *Establishing rules and guidelines.* While many organizations prefer to build interest and support informally, others opt to launch strategic planning and training activities with the support of senior managers and organizational influencers.
- *Adopting a supportive organizational structure and management style.* Moving from an authoritative to a more openly participative management style helps to reinforce a commitment to results.

Both good leadership and good management are essential to conducting a successful training program and implementing the changes that go with it. Good leadership is important to organizational change and growth. Change leaders recognize the need for training, create groups that can help introduce and implement the training, identify the obstacles to training, and devise change strategies that can lead to the realization of organizational goals and new organizational intelligence to support decision making.

Sometimes you only scratch the surface of what underlies the old feelings, concepts, ideas, etc. That's why it's important to listen at first—to get the *real* resistance on the table. The real resistance reasons will usually appear while we dust off what is on the top of it. Once you help employees get to the bottom of their resistance, your program can produce significant and lasting changes for the organization.

10.2   GIVING EMPLOYEES INCENTIVES FOR TRAINING (OR FOR DEMONSTRATING COMPETENCY)

Organizations can offer employees several types of incentives to entice them to participate in training. They can offer them financial incentives such as one-time bonuses or permanent pay raises. They can also offer promotions and other career enhancements as a way of creating demand for training. There is also the threat of job dislocation if an employee resists participation in training, though this should certainly be a last resort.

With national employment at an all-time low, market demand is so strong that retaining staff has become as problematic as hiring them. Salaries, bonuses, and other perks are soaring, and few organizations can match outside offers received by their staff. Organizations can, however, create a "retention-oriented" environment that encourages staff members to stay. One major part of a retention-oriented environment is training. Organizations must create and maintain an environment in which the staff are trained and developed in areas that interest the employees as well as benefit the organization. Management must understand what motivates the staff, how to implement programs that encourage productivity, and how to foster a desire in the employees to be part of the organization's team.

Performance Management Systems

Setting up incentive programs for training can be somewhat tricky. Typically, training incentive programs are part of a larger performance management system that focuses on individuals for the establishment of shared goals between management and employees about what is to be achieved. These incentive programs are also part of an approach to managing people that increases the probability of achieving job-related success. Developing and designing an organization's performance management system must be consistent with a pay-for-performance program designed to focus on specific criteria-based and measurable accountabilities. A good performance management system:

- Motivates employees toward achievement
- Links department objectives to organizational strategies
- Effectively links pay based on performance levels
- Is perceived by employees as fair
- Provides feedback to assist in employee development
- Is easily implemented and communicated

Performance management is the most personalized evaluation of an individual's "worth to the organization" and is the primary factor used in the determination of equitable pay distribution based on training completed and on productivity increases. The performance management program or system is a management tool to improve both individual performance and communication processes. The effective use of these programs has the greatest potential for bringing about and maintaining desired levels of performance and improvements in quality. Performance management systems combine training, total quality management objectives, customer service, and overall performance objectives into programs individually tailored to organizational needs.

Even though training may be organization-driven, it is possible for the more job-specific skills to be driven by the employee. As a general rule, employees and businesses that involve fast-changing technologies tend to be interested in training without the need for external incentives. Smaller enterprises often do not have the means to invest in and provide training, so sometimes employees must be "self-motivated." Employers are in a position to provide incentives for employees to develop skills through a pay system that rewards them for the acquisition of skills. Thus in the current decade employers have increasingly resorted to skill-based pay systems.

Incentive Programs

Motivating employees may well be the most difficult part of a manager's job. Motivation is hard to define, and often varies by individual, making incentive programs difficult to design and implement.

However, Jill Spiegel, founder and CEO of Minneapolis-based Goal Getters (www.speigelspeak.com), says there are two general rules for any incentive program. The first rule is to keep employees involved. When employees are involved in the design of an incentive program, the program tends to succeed more often than not. The second rule is that recognition often means more than money. This rule may seem contrary to the obvious, particularly given soaring salaries. However, as long as an employee is paid at or above his or her market value, recognition by peers and supervisors is likely to have a more lasting impact on an employee's attitude and productivity than a monetary reward.

The type and details of the program must fit the employee's needs and the organization's culture. There are four basic steps to implementing training incentive programs: identifying individual motivational factors, developing the performance criteria and reward system, implementing the program, and gathering feedback to continually improve the program. These steps can all be part of the training program itself.

Identifying individual training desires can be very difficult. Methods include surveys, interviews, organizational assessments, and observation. Ask employees what gets them excited, and have them rank their responses. According to Spiegel, past surveys have shown that personal development, a sense of control, and both recognition and monetary-based rewards are important. The fact that employees are involved in the program design is also an important factor, as it helps build enthusiasm.

In designing the program, always assume people will succeed, and offer them incentives that are linked to the training. Make sure that the incentives chosen are appropriate to the training. For example, if a clerical worker is moving to a technical role, be sure the pay matches the new role; otherwise that person will leave quickly when the first recruiter calls with a "great opportunity." Also, avoid programs that promote hypercompetition, and instead concentrate on those that promote teamwork.

The keys to implementing the program are to keep it positive and visible. Daily reminders such as posters and bulletin boards keep the program in the employee's mind and help the employee stay motivated. Make the program an important part of the organization by having a kickoff by executives, and publicizing it widely, including the results. If at all possible, do not change the rules midstream. There are few ways to demoralize employees faster than changing the rules, particularly if the changes make it harder to succeed or favor one individual or team.

Once the program is complete, hold follow-up sessions to find out what the staff learned about their own motivation and what they liked and disliked about the program. Management and/or program administrators should listen carefully and, if possible, implement the changes in the next round. If suggested changes aren't made, employees may feel ignored, and thus not participate fully next time.

Because motivation varies greatly by individual, there are risks associated with any incentive program. A nonmonetary reward that means much to one individual may mean nothing to another. Monetary programs are particularly hard to manage. Factors to consider when designing monetary reward systems include the measurement time frame, payout dates, and amounts. Establishing a measurement time frame means deciding how long the individual or team will be measured for the reward. Will they be evaluated monthly, quarterly, or annually? Payout dates are also an issue. Is the money paid out at the end of the measurement time, or is it delayed? A large mail-order company switched to an annual payout but left measurement on a quarterly basis. Because employees were used to being paid quarterly, they were not very happy with the payout-date change.

Determining payout amounts is probably the biggest issue. Many programs base the payout on a percentage of an employee's salary. The percentage and salary usually increase with rank in the organization. Because higher-level employees usually have higher payouts, some resentment may result among line employees. Keep in mind that most of the work is done by line workers and reward them appropriately.

10.3 HOLDING EMPLOYEES ACCOUNTABLE FOR TRAINING RESULTS

Managers often send an employee to classes, conferences, and seminars that cover subjects with which the employee will never be involved. Even if the employee is involved in a particular subject area, the specific skills acquired in classes sometimes go unused, and are not part of the employee's job description or included in the accountabilities section of a performance review. In one of my past positions, I once asked my manager to put an item in my performance review holding me accountable for the skills I had learned in a class. The manager said that he had never done that before and that it was not company policy to include training accountabilities in performance reviews! That certainly explains why I've seen so many people sleeping through training classes. If they're not going to be held responsible for the material, why bother?

If organizations are going to spend the time and money on training for their staff, the training should be timely, and employees should be held accountable for the knowledge, skills, and abilities (KSAs) acquired. One highly effective way to encourage accountability for training is to include a training plan in a performance appraisal (PA). In most PAs, there is a section called "plans for improvement"—this is the place to put future training objectives. If the PA is an annual event, set training opportunities on a quarterly basis. Trying to predict training necessities a year out is difficult given the pace of change in the software industry. Alternative training formats include computer-based training, self-study courses, or on-the-job training in a new business area or technology. Regardless of the format, try to include at least one new learning experience in each quarter of the yearly PA cycle, or set a goal of four for the year for each employee.

Set measurable objectives for each learning experience. Should the employees reduce their work defects? Should they require less assistance in their work? The answer to these questions is obviously yes. The more subtle question that's difficult to answer is, by how much? If quantitative measures are to be used, a performance baseline will need to be set prior to the training experience. The type of baseline and relative numbers depends on the task and current KSA level of the particular employee.

One of the advantages of aiming for quarterly training opportunities is the ability to target the training at a particular project on which the employee may be working. Training an employee in a skill that won't be used for 6 months is a waste of time and money. I've found that most people who do not immediately use new skills retain them for about 1 or 2 months. After that period of time, the employee must retake the course or reread the material. Either way, twice as much time as necessary is spent on one learning experience. To ensure that training is timely, use the department training plan (if there is one) and an employee's likely project involvement to drive training requirements. Once training is completed, the employee should write a summary of the course. This summary should address questions such as:

- What was the purpose or topic of the course?
- Were the course materials technically current?
- How did the technical course materials follow industry standards?
- Were the course materials (written or multimedia) clear and useful?
- Was the learning environment suitable to the course and conducive to learning?

- How effective was the instructor?
- What were the course's relative strengths and weaknesses?

This summary lets the manager know what and how much the employee learned, and helps management judge the course quality and potential to send other employees. Beware of critiques like, "The material was interesting...." If the employee writes in vague or brief sentences, the odds are that he or she slept or played through the course. Look for specific points, especially in the strengths and weaknesses section. Be sure to let the employee know that a summary will be expected after the course ends. This means the employee will be more likely to pay attention in class.

Beyond giving the employee an incentive to stay awake, a course summary can be used to judge the potential utility for other employees. A well-written summary can help management decide whether or not the course meets the expectations that were based on the course sales material. If the course is a good one, other employees can be sent. If not, then a potential waste of time and money can be avoided.

CASE: ACME WIDGETS—PUBLISHING AND RELEASING THE TRAINING PROGRAM

Connie, the CIO, Bob, the I/T training manager, and Mike, the I/T training team lead, sat down to discuss how they were going to communicate the training rollout to the rest of the organization. They had spent time working with Richard, the vice president of human resources, Trudy, the human resources training specialist, John, the WCS HR liaison, Gary, the WCS software rollout team leader, Lauren, the KIS software rollout team leader, and other key users. Now they have to communicate the program and its content to the rest of the organization. This is going to require contact with many more people, and it's important to maintain a positive image, even though the training will require people to take a considerable amount of time away from their current jobs.

To build enthusiasm and overcome resistance to change, the group members started by reaffirming management commitment from the top. They had meetings with key business leaders, including Dennis, the vice president of manufacturing, Diego, the vice president of sales and marketing, Jeff, the vice president of finance, and Sandra, the vice president of purchasing. Connie and Richard helped by building and maintaining rapport with their peers.

The group members decided to maximize their exposure through AWI's intranet, a newsletter, and e-mails sorted by department and training class. They used the audience analyses to decide who would get what information. The intranet link was prepared and opened to the entire company, though the class descriptions mentioned specific target audiences. However, because of AWI's open job application process, there is always the possibility that an inventory staff member might want to apply for an accounting job, so class enrollments were left somewhat open depending on space availability.

Newsletters and brochures were also prepared. The "Training for Success" newsletter was created as a collection of announcements and explanations that was sent on a weekly basis to a number of people in the internal or external audience. The brochures disseminated information and advertised the classes to build enthusiasm. As is consistent with best practices, the newsletter and brochure had a simple layout and design and contained short articles, art, graphics, visual information, and contact information. Because of the advanced nature of the software, AWI decided on a modern look since it would best relate the information to the target audience.

Attendance at the courses was first driven by the newsletter and other publicity. The training department decided to monitor the attendance to spot any initial trends, such as high absenteeism, overstaying breaks, etc. Because of the importance of tracking attendance, all students leaving or entering the class were required to use the form shown in Table 9-1 to ensure promptness for the beginning of class and after breaks. The instructors also provided incentives for prompt returns. In addition, AWI purchased an attendance tracking system that interfaced with the courseware management system. The program allows AWI to generate reports of attendance by class, so the instructor can see how much time each student has spent on various activities. It also allows AWI to compile statistics on usage by time of day, department, piece of equipment, etc., to improve administration and staffing of the training facility and to support requests for increased support.

The incentives for training were created to provide AWI's staff with the motivation to advance through the training modules in a logical manner that would help the staff enjoy their jobs more. AWI initiated several changes in the training system in an effort to provide the best balance between skill depth and breadth. Career plans now indicate whether a particular individual is eligible for advanced training in a particular area, or is eligible for training to gain additional proficiencies. Employees whose career plans target them for development advance through entry-level and proficiency skill blocks. Each of these blocks takes various times to complete, but there is the opportunity for salary increases more than once every year, which is a notable improvement. The expert-level course is available only in certain areas of the company and is limited to one person per area who is designated the power user in that area.

AWI implemented skill-based pay to provide training incentives. Skill blocks were designed, and a system of more pay for more knowledge was developed. The idea was attractive, and the pay-for-knowledge system encourages training, largely because there are opportunities to move to training positions. Bottlenecks in the training system are monitored to prevent problems with advancement in pay. Employees in each team are consulted to determine if modified skill blocks and compensation fit their particular area in consultation with the management committee.

Along with the pay incentive system, AWI is holding employees accountable for training results. The management has emphasized the need for individual responsibility. Employees must ensure that their training is proper, and consult with their manager to plan their training over each performance cycle (quarter and year). AWI recognizes that sometimes training must be tailored to meet the needs of different I/T and end-user groups. End users require training on standard applications to better utilize the rich functionality of these applications, and all departmental I/T professionals need regular exposure to new technologies and updates on state and departmental rules and procedures. The training team recommended that a varied set of instructional resources be provided to meet these different instructional needs. In addition, the training team recommended to management that program and division management be held accountable for training to assure this competency. This way, from senior management to each staff member, AWI collectively is responsible for maintaining a well-skilled employee base.

Coming Up in Chapter 11

Ever wondered how the best trainers do it? How do they keep trainees awake, alert, and hanging on every word? Should the classroom be warm or cold? Does speaking speed make a difference? Find out from some of the best trainers in the business.

REFERENCES

Argyris, C. (1992). *On organizational learning.* Cambridge, MA: Blackwell Publishers.

Laird, Dugan. (1985). *Approaches to training and development* (2d ed.). Reading, MA: Addison-Wesley.

Leshin, C. B., Pollock, J., & Reigeluth, C. M. (1992). *Instructional design strategies and tactics.* Englewood Cliffs, NJ: Educational Technology Publications.

Martel, L. (1986). *Mastering change: The key to business success.* New York: Simon and Schuster.

Senge, P. M. (1990). *The fifth discipline: The art & practice of the learning organization.* New York: Currency Doubleday.

Trepper, C. (1997, September). Employees should be held accountable for training. *Application development trends magazine.*

Trepper, C. (1997, September). Motivating for retention. *Application development trends magazine.*

Tips for the Trainer

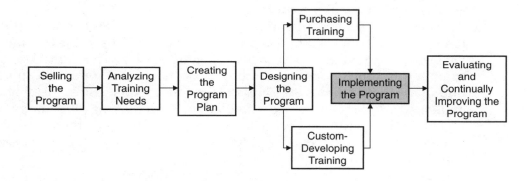

In This Chapter

OVERVIEW

It's incredibly important to make classes interesting and to use the right presentation media. The energy level of the class (also discussed in Chapters 9 and 10) can be greatly affected by how trainers handle the class. This was discussed somewhat in Chapter 6 regarding the use of professional trainers or subject matter experts. Training participants almost all have horror stories of instructors who droned on and on in a monotone voice, continually lulling them to sleep. Even in a software training class where participation is essentially mandatory, it's critical to keep the class moving and fun.

Trainers must know which essential elements are necessary to deliver informative and persuasive presentations, how to engage and interact with the audience, and how to give articulate impromptu responses to questions. Among the skills to be practiced are defining your objectives, reading your audience, structuring your ideas effectively, stressing main points convincingly, using verbal and visual aids to add impact, and projecting competence and confidence.

For many trainers, the idea of "entertaining" an audience is intimidating, even if they know the material well. Trainers must be able to analyze presentation topics, make opening and closing remarks, and smooth transitions from topic to topic. Also, nonverbal communication is important, and includes appropriate dress and mannerisms. Reading an audience includes connecting with the group, identifying allies, targeting potential "hecklers," and unifying a class, particularly if there are "dissenters" who aren't mentally prepared for the changes caused by software rollouts.

Delivery techniques must be structured to the unique needs of each class, and can be taught through mock one-on-one presentations, small-group meetings, and speeches before large groups of critics. Trainers must also possess a sense of humor, something that often cannot be taught. Things go wrong during training, and the trainer must never "let 'em see you sweat!" Remember that the two most important parts of your presentation are the first 30 and the last 15 seconds. Everything else is utterly forgettable if the presentation starts or ends badly. People make a credibility decision in the first 30 seconds.

Since many view employee training as a necessary evil and expense that must be tolerated, a program that keeps students interested and positive pays for itself and increases the bottom line. Such a program teaches new employees to "do it right the first time," by creating a positive, structured learning environment, thus minimizing downtime and data errors, while maximizing productivity and profits. A training program as recommended in this book ensures consistency of training and provides a means to objectively measure employee performance as training progresses.

Remember that simplicity is elegance. Too many training classes are too long, too slick, and too convoluted. I asked some class attendees how trainers could improve classes and make them more effective for participants. The response was overwhelming: Make the classes shorter and more pointed. The most memorable slides are the simplest. With high-tech training now being targeted at ever younger audiences, it's important to know that they are getting to the point and telling the truth in a straightforward way. Give them the information to do their job and send them on their way.

11.1   SETTING THE TONE THE FIRST DAY OF CLASS

The first day of class often produces a certain amount of anxiety in both new and experienced trainers. Because the first day of class is so vital in setting the tone for what is to come, it's important to think carefully about how to get the course established. Some things to consider include dressing appropriately, establishing rapport, setting clear expectations, and getting students motivated.

Making a Positive First Impression

Initial impressions tend to be lasting, and the way instructors choose to spend the first day of class will set the tone for the entire course. The first impression students have of instructors is their appearance. Many organizations have gone to a "business casual" dress code, which is often very vague. While there is no universal dress code, organizations may have explicit or implicit expectations of how instructors should dress when teaching. Casual clothing emphasizes accessibility to students, while suits emphasize professionalism. If new instructors lack confidence about their ability to command the attention of the class, professional dress may provide an ego-boost.

Instructors should also let students know what they want to be called. As with clothing, the less formal instructors are, the more accessible they will seem. However, a certain amount of formality can help keep students focused on the material that needs to be covered. At some time during the first class, instructors and students should take the opportunity to let each other know what they want to be called.

A light touch is important at the first class, and interjecting humor will help get things started. Instructors should be careful of jokes, cartoons, or comments that could be interpreted as politically incorrect. Here's where knowing your audience will help. Students who are offended even if the instructor did not intend to hurt anyone's feelings will most likely not feel free to voice their objections because of the power relationship in the classroom. It is very difficult to establish a positive relationship with students who feel that they are not welcome.

Before the class begins, instructors can help students to know that they are in the correct place by writing the name of the course on a whiteboard. Time before class might be spent by asking that students with problems come forward while the others are getting situated so that these individual issues can be cleared up. It is important to know in advance the organization's policy for approaching these issues. It is then important to go through the roster and note which students are present.

Instructors should spend some time introducing themselves. Students are interested in their instructors' personal and professional backgrounds and interests and wonder how they approach teaching. How much instructors care to reveal about themselves will depend on individual preferences and style; being personable will help to break down some of the forced formality that tends to hinder classroom communication. Students need to know that instructors want to be there teaching, that they care about the course, and that they will do their best to ensure that each individual makes the best possible progress.

Clarifying Expectations

After all the formalities, most instructors hand out a syllabus or course outline and go over it, clearly stating such matters as the frequency of breaks, grading criteria, required materials, and the nature of the assignments. It is also important to offer a summary of the goals for the course and to explain some of the background of the materials that the course will cover and its importance to the students. Time should be allocated for questions. Instructors should try to create an atmosphere where students feel comfortable asking questions. And questions should be answered as fully as possible.

When instructors know their students, they are able to tailor the course to incorporate relevant examples. Spending some time gathering student information will also help with learning students' names. There are a variety of methods to getting to know students. Have students talk about themselves for a couple of minutes to the rest of the group. This allows other students, as well as the instructor, to get to know class members. It is often helpful in promoting a sense of camaraderie and increasing rapport among students in the class, which facilitates class discussions in the long run.

Other instructors hand out index cards and ask the students to answer questions about themselves on the cards such as their telephone number, the reason they took the course, their expectations, and their worries about the new software. Review these cards later and use them to trigger discussions during the course as well as to help learn the students' names. In addition, instructors might ask students how they prefer to learn (reading, discussion, lecture, etc.) to assist in planning instructional strategies.

Creating Excitement

At least a few minutes of the first class should be reserved for generating some interest in the course material to avoid being consumed by administrative details. There are many ways to create excitement. Instructors might close the day with a burning question to be answered at the start of the next class. Some instructors show a short film or slides that introduce the subject area in a lighthearted manner. Another option is for instructors to ask students what they want the course to answer, and then explain at what point they can look forward to their interest area coming up for discussion.

Instructors can speak with excitement about a topic that always generates controversy, outline details of some upcoming activities, suggest how revealing a given assignment can be, or tell the students how much they will enjoy completing some of the assignments that are to follow. Some instructors conduct brainstorming sessions about the course, place a suggestion box in the back of the room, or have students arrange study groups to help them learn collectively. The possibilities are endless.

It is never too soon for feedback. Instructors can ask students at the end of class to write their reactions to the first day of class. This provides early feedback and indicates an interest in learning from them. It can help in building a learning climate in which students assume more responsibility for, and feel more actively involved in, the teaching and learning that occur in the classroom.

11.2   READING THE AUDIENCE—HOW DO YOU KEEP THEM AWAKE, ALERT, AND INTERESTED?

As I mentioned in the overview, getting and keeping the participants' attention is critical to the success of the class, and may be critical to the success of the trainee. If a participant misses some of your words, it may cause him or her to make critical errors operating the software. Unless the trainee is doing useless work, this can cause significant problems. To get some great tips from some great trainers, I talked to some well-known trainers and visited their websites:

- Paul Fox of Fox Performance (www.foxperformance.com)
- Susan Boyd of Susan Boyd Associates (www.susan-boyd.com)
- Sivasailam Thiagarajan of Workshops by Thiagi (www.thiagi.com)

These websites have lots of free stuff that includes tips, games, and other materials for trainers. In addition, Workshops by Thiagi also offers its GameLetter, which is a newsletter containing interesting tips, tools, and techniques for trainers. (See Section 11.4.)

Motivating Trainees

Motivating students or trainees to learn is one of the more difficult tasks for a trainer. While I mentioned earlier that financial and performance appraisal incentives can help students want to attend, keeping their attention and motivating them to really dig into the material with some enthusiasm are feats that take some creativity. Fox Performance lists some interesting approaches and tips for motivation including:

- Help people see how the material relates to their real world
- Remember that trainees want to know "WIIFM"—what's in it for me. Help them see the personal payoff and relate training to their concerns and construct it to solve their immediate problems
- Use interactive learning when possible, like paired discussions, small group and team activities
- Change delivery methods often and don't lecture for more than 10–15 minutes at a time
- Use real-life stories, demonstrations, and examples to make points
- Be an interesting presenter, and use voice inflection, pauses, facial expressions, and enthusiasm. Monotone, boring trainers make for sleepy trainees
- Stop often to solicit trainee concerns and questions
- Invite them to challenge points you've made to generate discussion about "will it work?"

Trainees who want to learn are more likely to take back the knowledge and skills needed to be successful. Sometimes more formal mechanisms are needed, such as these mentioned on the Susan Boyd website:

- Learner contracts and commitment statements—These tools help trainees determine what they really want to learn, and commit to doing well in the course.

- Job-related practice exercises—While this may sound like common sense, many software training modules (especially CBT) use preset cases that don't relate to the work environment. When they get back to their job, the software doesn't work exactly the way it did in class, confusing trainees.
- Team discussions on how to apply the training—This technique not only stimulates discussion, but also helps trainees build contacts to use when they need help back on the job after class.

Experienced trainers may already have a bag of tricks. If you're new to the training field, remember that it helps to think like the trainees. What do they need to do their job? One common mistake of new trainers is to gloss over topics that should be covered in detail. Remember that the trainees are beginners and may need some things spelled out in detail that seem simple to the trainer.

Dealing with Problem Situations

Every trainer experiences situations where students are either too loud or too quiet. Some students are difficult to work with, and others seem to have a more difficult time "getting it." Dealing with problems is what sets the good trainers apart. You can find standard tips and ideas for these situations on the Fox Performance website. People in training programs are under more pressure than ever before and can be more demanding, and even hostile. If they feel your program is not right, you'll have problems.

Someday you will find yourself facing an audience more inclined to jeer than cheer. These groups may contain people who are hostile to the ideas you are presenting or are angry at being required to attend. Some tips for handling a hostile group and ensuring the success of the class include:

- Know your audience.
- Gather intelligence about the audience in advance of the presentation or training program.
- Determine who has already spoken to them about the class.
- Know their various positions on the class.
- Know who the "troublemakers" and your "friends" are in the group.
- Find out the hot buttons of people in the group and why people may be opposed to the change.

Gathering intelligence will increase your confidence and help you design the training to be more successful with a particular audience.

Even more important than being prepared in front of a hostile audience is being credible. To be credible you must acquire three traits:

- *Expertise.* If you are considered an amateur in the field, there will be little respect for your opinions. Thoroughly research the subject so you can demonstrate you know at least as much as your audience does, preferably more.
- *Believability.* If you are perceived as glib, your message will probably be rejected.
- *Likability.* Even a hostile audience relates positively to friendly, sincere, and enthusiastic speakers who believe in what they are advocating, but respect other views and listen to them.

Credibility and rapport are closely linked, but credibility does not automatically build rapport. Rapport requires a chemistry between you and the class. If it's not there, you won't persuade many people to accept the training, no matter how impressive your credentials.

The natural tendency for anyone confronting a hostile audience is to limit exposure by arriving at the site just before the scheduled time and leaving immediately after. This is a mistake! Arriving early and staying after your presentation are wonderful opportunities to build rapport. Other benefits include:

- You can meet early arrivals and possibly discover some allies in the audience.
- Informal conversations help break the ice, and loosen up your vocal chords and nervous system. Give early arrivals the impression you are relaxed and approachable, not a remote official.
- Arriving early permits you to talk with those who are strongly opposed to your position. If you haven't met with them privately before the presentation, you can hear their concerns now. During your training session you can mention their name and their concerns. This will show you respect the opinions of others. You may even find the hard-liners become less critical.

No matter how heated the give-and-take may have been, you should stay to mingle with the audience afterward. They will form a more favorable impression of you even if you've been pelted with tough questions and objections. Those who speak and run are often considered weak or fearful.

Staying after also gives you a chance to reinforce key points made during your presentation.

There are specific delivery techniques that work well with hostile audiences. Statistics and facts, if not overdone, can add authenticity to your position. They offer proof that your point of view is the correct one. Repeat key points several times to add weight to your position. Use body language that makes you look confident and authoritative. Eye contact, facial expressions, and hand and arm position telegraph how you feel inside. Approach a hostile audience with a positive attitude. You may not be able to win everyone over, but some wins are better than none.

One interesting approach to coping with difficult learners is to make them own their success. If learners are invested in the training, and are willing to take responsibility for their success or failure in the course, they're more likely to participate actively. To facilitate the transfer of learning responsibility from trainer to trainee, the Susan Boyd website offers these 10 commandments for learners:

1. Thou shall review the course description prior to class and make sure it meets the prerequisites. Prior to class, review the course description, objectives and topics and see if you meet the prerequisites. Talk to others who have attended the course and see how they are using the skills.

2. Thou shall meet with thine manager before and after the course to discuss the training and how it can be applied. Meet with your manager before class to discuss how the course information can be applied to your job needs. Find out your manager's expectations. After the class, discuss the training with your manager and determine what support is needed for you to apply the skills.

3. Thou shall be responsible for thine own learning. As an adult, you are in charge of your learning, not the instructor. Take advantage of practice sessions and instructor's knowledge while in class.

4. Thou shalt participate and be an active learner. Learning is an active process! Ask questions, do the exercises, participate in the discussions, take notes, help other class members, etc.

5. Thou shall be willing to make mistakes and learn from them. Don't be embarrassed or frustrated when you make mistakes. Mistakes are learning opportunities for you, the instructor, and the rest of the class. You learn more when you correct mistakes than if everything goes perfectly.

6. Thou shall ask how the training can be applied to thine own job needs. Take skills learned and ask yourself and classmates, how to use or adapt this skill/technique to my job demands?

7. Honor the time schedule and be on time for class and after breaks. Time is money in a training class. If you are late, you are wasting your learning time and money, and the rest of the class's.

8. Thou shalt not whine or be negative. Whining doesn't make the software go faster or work better. Whining doesn't change corporate policies or procedures. It just wears down your energy, as well as that of the instructor and other learners. Don't feel compelled to kill the messenger. The instructors do not make the policies, they are there to help you develop new skills to do your job.

9. Thou shall give the instructor feedback throughout class if thou has concerns, issues, or questions. If you feel that the class is too slow/fast, or topics aren't pertinent, convey this to the instructor during a break. Don't keep this all to yourself or complain to your classmates. Most instructors will try to be flexible and see if they can address your concerns.

10. Thou shall take the time to complete the course evaluation and give honest, constructive feedback. Course evaluations are important to the instructor as well as to the managers in the training department. Take the time to give useful, pertinent feedback and offer suggestions, not just criticisms or smile sheets with no meaningful comments.

These 10 commandments imply that both the trainer and trainee are responsible for the success of the class. Particularly in a software rollout, it's critical that students participate actively, because they must understand how the software operates and what must be done to solve problems. Collaborative learning means that the trainer and trainee work as a team to meet the objectives of the course.

Another major problem is when someone constantly dominates discussions in class. The other participants hold back their ideas, and other class members get bored (which is appropriate, since the talker is usually a boor anyway). The website of Workshops by Thiagi offers some suggestions for dealing with participants who talk too much:

- Avoid discouraging the excessive talker. Instead, encourage the others to participate more.
- Go around the group, giving each participant a turn to talk.
- Divide into pairs for preliminary sharing of ideas, and ask each pair for a summary report.
- Impose air-time limits on participants. Give the participants each 30 seconds of talking time.
- Interrupt the person with a question directed to someone else.
- Acknowledge the comment and involve others.
- Before the meeting or during a break, enlist the help of the excessive talker in encouraging the silent participants to open up.
- At the start of the meeting, establish equal participation by all members as a team goal.

It's critical to ensure that all participants have the opportunity to ask, as well as answer, questions during class. A know-it-all keeps others from fully participating, which inhibits their learning. All the participants must share in the learning experience fully, not just one person.

Workshops by Thiagi also offers suggestions for when you desperately need to get the participants' attention in the middle of an activity. Usually the participants are so busy talking to each other, solving problems, making decisions, or working out strategies that they totally ignore you. You need to announce important rules or procedures, and you may be worried that people will miss your announcement and blame you later. In situations like this, you have to be assertive. One thing you can do is turn the lights off. Total darkness gets everyone's attention. Then turn the lights back on and make your announcement. Obviously, it will not work if daylight streams in through the windows.

Experiment with different noisemakers (gongs, xylophones, bells, chimes, buzzers, banging on the wall, drums, sirens, and screams). They work effectively, but some of them irritate the participants. A favorite noisemaker and attention-getter is the train whistle. It is a wooden whistle usually sold in craft shops and county fairs (or you can order it from Workshops by Thiagi). The sound is pleasant and nostalgic. It attracts participants' attention. At the beginning of a group activity, stress the importance of paying attention to announcements. Then, introduce the participants to the sound of the train whistle and ask them to please stop whatever they are doing and listen when they hear the whistle blow.

11.3 ACCOUNTING FOR INDIVIDUAL LEARNING STYLES

Learning style is often defined in terms of conditions, expectations, stimulus/reaction, distinctive behaviors, past experience, environment, and other characteristic patterns of processing information that have notable differences. It's important, however, to be cautious of an overemphasis on learning style differences which may lead to a new form of inaccurate labeling and stereotyping. Not only are there striking differences in the way people learn and process information, but there are significant differences in how learning styles are defined and measured.

Adults are motivated to learn by both external and internal factors. Wages, salaries, promotion, better working conditions, etc., are external factors for adults. More persistent motivators are internal ones, such as the need for self-esteem, broadened responsibilities, power, and achievement. There are general adult learning principles, as well as individual learning styles, that often must be addressed to maximize the impact of the training. In general, adult learning principles are accounted for in the initial design and development of training courses, and they should continue to be considered in the tailoring and delivery of training. These basic principles are:

- *Understanding.* Sufficient information should be provided so that participants understand the concepts and principles related to the topic at hand. This understanding must be demonstrated by meeting the objectives set forth in the course outline or syllabus.
- *Practice.* Participants must have the chance to practice the skills through interactive sessions.
- *Feedback.* Participants must have the opportunity to ask questions and receive feedback.
- *Application.* Since participants must persist in using new skills and knowledge back on the job, they should leave the course with a practical action plan. This is covered in Chapters 9 and 10.

These principles should be applied intelligently to the design and delivery of training. It's important to remember that adults are a diverse group, and individual learning styles significantly affect the approach used by trainers. Adults tend to be independent, learn for specific reasons, and question the value of some training. Table 11-1 lists some learning concepts and some approaches to addressing those concepts. Each of the concepts in the table can be applied to various types of learning experiences and styles. Learning can also be broken down into various sublevels of knowledge. Memorization, the acquisition of knowledge that can be retrained and/or utilized in practice, and learning as an interpretive process, aimed at understanding reality, are ways of applying adult learning principles and concepts.

The idea that differences in personality affect the way people learn is generally accepted. It is commonly invoked as the reason for people's different approaches to life and for the different ways in which people handle similar situations. Some fairly stable personality factors include intelligence, extroversion versus introversion, fear of failure, and creativity. Also important are memory, internalized rules, and previously learned skills. Finally, there are cognitive styles of visual versus verbal style, and comprehension style.

Individual learning styles may affect various factors in a training class. It's important to assess how various curriculum design methods, or combinations of methods, will cater to individual learning styles. Balancing learner needs against organizational needs is also important, though software packages may not be able to be tailored to every individual. During the

TABLE 11-1

Learning Concepts	Approach Ideas
Adults learn only when they are ready to learn and can see a reason for learning.	Motivate the trainees early. Explain what they will learn, how they will use the knowledge and skills, and why it is important to them.
Adults learn best by doing.	Try to hit the 30/70 goal in presenting training: 30% instruction, 70% trainee activity/involvement.
Adults organize information (content) internally based on how the information is used (context).	Stress how knowledge and skills will be used and deliver the content in its job context.
Learning is strengthened when students have positive experiences.	Give positive feedback. Praise and reinforce success (verbally in front of a group). Minimize criticism.
First impressions usually set the stage.	Present correct information the first time.
A vivid, dramatic, and exciting learning experience teaches more than a routine and dull experience.	Use training media that appeal to as many of the trainees' senses as possible (e.g., visual, auditory).
Things most often repeated are best remembered.	Plan for repetition of critical knowledge and skills.
All other things being equal, the things last learned are first remembered.	Repeat all critical knowledge and skills and summarize often: Important content should be reviewed often.

training, the learning style may change the effect of the presentation method on learners.

New technologies provide opportunities to introduce new ways for supporting individual learning styles for students, and create new issues for instruction. New computer-based training and rapid instructional systems design methods have not only changed the quality of training, but also changed the emphasis from accumulation of knowledge to new ways of communicating and assisting students to learn. Some of the shifts occurring in training as a result of new technologies include:

- Moving from classroom lectures to computer network access to educational resources
- Personalizing the learning experience using services on the Internet or within an intranet
- Helping students move from passive to active learning
- Emphasizing team learning and group discussion rather than individual learning
- Shifting from stable course content to fast-changing content presented in a wide range of formats

A major trend in technology-based learning has been distance education. The Internet supports distance learning by providing students with the ability to connect to educational resources when it is convenient for them, and allowing students to explore the educational resources in an order that suits their needs.

Each student has individual preferred patterns or methods for learning which need to be recognized and supported with the appropriate learning technologies. While there are many classifications of learning styles, there are some generally accepted categories, such as:

- *Visual or spatial.* The ability or preference to learn using graphical images and 3D models
- *Auditory.* The ability or preference to use sound to understand training material
- *Kinesthetic.* The ability or preference to learn by actually touching an object
- *Interpersonal.* The ability or preference to learn by discussing with others
- *Linguistic.* The ability or preference to learn by understanding words and language and by reading

You may hear people say, "I need to see the object." That indicates that they're visual learners. You may also find that others are more attuned to listening to an instructor and then doing. These kinds of learners are auditory learners. Others must actually be touching and using the computer or software and only learn by doing. These people are kinesthetic learners. While it's difficult to assess a trainee prior to a class, it's certainly reasonable to adapt to individual styles during a class.

11.4   INTERESTING IN-CLASS ACTIVITIES

Another way of keeping the trainee's attention is to provide interesting activities in class. While software training may not seem to provide opportunities for such activities, there are ways to use class time to make the training more fun. Lightening things up not only makes the class more enjoyable for both instructors and trainees, but also keeps the students engaged and interested.

Reinforcing Learning

Besides making the class more fun, in-class activities can be used to reinforce learning. It's particularly important in software training to make sure that drills don't become too boring. Otherwise, trainees "zone out" and don't concentrate on their work. This can cause problems later, when the trainees return to their jobs and don't remember everything. The Susan Boyd website offers some review activities that help reinforce and practice the skills learned:

- Independent practice exercises—These are exercises that are job focused and designed to allow the learner to use the skills and concepts presented in the preceding lesson. These exercises should be designed on two levels, with Part 1 covering the essential commands and features, and an optional Part 2 for additional concepts and practice. There should be a 15 minute timeframe for the exercise, and Part 1 should be able to be completed by all learners within this time limit. Faster learners will be able to also complete the optional Part 2 within the same amount of time. Learners should be encouraged to use all available resources such as the training manual, quick reference cards, on-line help, and user manual. After the exercise is completed, the trainer can involve the learners in a brief discussion regarding the major learning points.

- Walk-thru procedures—Another review technique is to ask volunteers to do a step by step walk-thru on how to complete a specific procedure or job task using the software. The volunteer can review this for the whole class, or you can set up partners and ask one partner to guide another through all the steps. Typically this takes less than 5 minutes per procedure or job task.

- Stump the class—Assign teams of 3–4 people per team and give each team 3 index cards. They are to write a review question and answer on each card that would test the class's knowledge of the topics covered so far. They have 10 minutes to review all their training materials and come up with the questions. The trainer collects the cards and tosses a ball randomly to ask a question. The person who catches the ball may answer the question, confer with the team, or toss the ball to someone else. Once the question has been answered correctly, the person who has the ball tosses it to someone else and the process continues until all the questions have been answered.

- Baseball review—This is a variation on the above stump the class activity. Divide the group into two teams, choose team names and give each team 20 index cards. The team members write a question and answer on each card to test the other team's knowledge of the material. Set up the bases in different corners of the room. There is a "pitching team" and an "answering and running" team. The pitching team asks questions. If the running team member correctly answers within the specified time limit, that runner advances one base, and continues to advance if the next person answers the next question correctly. If a team member misses a question, that's an out. Once there are three outs, the teams switch. At the end of game, the team with most "runs" wins.

- Help scavenger hunt—This review activity is designed to have the learners work in teams to answer a list of written questions that involve using the Help resources available. This would include the on-line help facility, user manual, and reference cards. This activity helps the learners become more independent by becoming familiar with the help resources. Assign a timeframe of 10–15 minutes for this activity.

- What have you learned so far—This activity is designed for teams to list all the skills, concepts and topics they have learned so far in the course. The team with the most items will win a small prize. The learners are encouraged to go back to their notes, training manual, user guide, reference cards, on-line help and also look at the software screens and menus to come up with their list. Give a 5–10 minute timeframe so they have to work quickly. Reward the winners.

- How can you apply this to your job—Periodically during a course, have each team list on an index card 3 ways they can apply a particular software feature or command to their job. Allow 5 minutes for this activity. Collect these and send an e-mail list after the course summarizing the important topics covered and how they can be used on the job.

- But, what I really want to know—Before teaching a new topic or concept, ask teams to write 3 questions they have about the topic. Then after the trainer has presented the topic, ask the teams to review their cards and see what questions are still unanswered. The trainer can decide if the questions can be addressed now or at a later time.

- Game show review—Using a format like Jeopardy or Concentration, create a game made up of questions that review a section of the course and have individuals or teams compete to answer the questions. There are several game show software programs that can be used to create the game electronically or they can be created using poster board.

All these activities provide opportunities for students to demonstrate what they've learned in a relaxed manner. When learners are stressed or tense, they tend to concentrate more on relieving the stress, and less on actually absorbing material. By keeping the class relaxed and moving, trainees will learn more effectively and efficiently and enjoy the class more.

Keeping Energy Levels Up

One way of keeping learners engaged is to play games that make them learn in a fun way. As noted earlier, Workshops by Thiagi publishes a GameLetter with various activities each month. One of the games available free on the website has some great applications for learning software. This game is called Third Degree. The game maximizes the learning from handouts and software instructions. Third Degree reinforces an exercise with an interesting combination of peer pressure and peer support.

Here's how it works. Distribute copies of the handout, or set of exercises, or questions about a part of the software and warn the players that they will be subjected to an inquisition on the content. At the start of the game, organize the players into groups of four to seven. Within each group, identify the first victim through some random means. For the next 2 minutes, the other players in the group will take on the role of inquisitioners and pile on various questions. The inquisitioners may refer to their handouts and notes, but the victim should not. The inquisitioners can fire questions as rapidly as they wish.

At the end of 2 minutes, stop the torture. Ask the current victim to select a new victim. Repeat the procedure for another 3 minutes. Continue the process until all players have had an opportunity to be the victim. To convert this activity into a game, use this scoring procedure: At the end of the last inquisition, ask each player to distribute 100 points among the other players on the basis of their relative performance. The players do this by writing the points on pieces of paper, folding them, and placing them in front of the appropriate person. Each player opens the pieces of paper and adds up the points. The player with the highest total wins the game.

Que Cards is another game that ensures that the participants read materials for details and recall these details later. Distribute the handouts, etc., and ask each participant to read the material and prepare 10 question cards based on its content. Each card should have a closed question on one side and the single correct answer on the other. Ask each group to mix up the question cards from its members and exchange the whole pile with another group.

After the exchange, ask the group to place the cards in the middle of the table, question side up. The first player reads the question on the top card, without removing it from the pile. Within 10 seconds, this player must give an answer. Any player may challenge by giving a different answer. If there is no challenge, the first player wins the card. If there is a challenge, the card is turned over to reveal the correct answer. Whoever gave the correct answer (the original player or the challenger) wins the card. If neither answer is correct, the card is buried in the middle of the pile for recycling.

It is now the turn of the next player to read the question on the next card and continue the game as before. The card pile may contain duplicate questions or questions that are similar to previous ones. This introduces an interesting element of chance to the game. This game can also be played in the same manner as Trivial Pursuit, using a board to advance player pieces during the course or course day. The game comes to an end when the group runs out of the question cards. (Alternatively, you can stop the game at the end of a prespecified period of time.) The player with the most cards wins the game.

There are endless variations of knowledge-based games that can contribute significantly to trainee class involvement and learning. The more learners smile, the more they learn, and the more effective they become back on the job. It's critical to avoid boredom, even though a software class may seem to be no more than drilling on the product's feature/function set.

11.5   THE BEST PRESENTATION METHODS AND MEDIA

Most people do not remember much of what they hear or see. Usually most presenters will be lucky if half of the audience can tell their friends what the presentation was about with any accuracy right after the show! So how can you get your audience to remember what you want them to? Your "tell 'em" slide will be the thing they remember first. Several days or weeks later they might also remember the logical organization of your ideas and points, but only if they can remember your main points. Give them reference materials for the rest of the material. This section provides some tips for setting up the presentation and choosing the right media.

Presentation Tips

When selecting content and creating the presentation, it's important to make sure the workshop progresses logically. The structure should allow for an appropriate balance between lecture and participant involvement. The exercises must be well thought out and able to be completed in the time allowed; otherwise participants will feel rushed and make unnecessary mistakes. The timing of each section should be appropriate to its importance and complexity. Some sections, such as troubleshooting ERP server errors, can be extra difficult and will require extra amounts of classroom and instructor time.

The pace must reflect the experience of the target audience. If the students represent a group of novice e-mail users, zipping through the material isn't going to let them build the confidence they need to be effective. The closing statement must tie together all elements of the workshop. Also, it's very important to make sure that additional resources are mentioned, so learners will have references when they go back to their new jobs.

The pace should be even, not too fast and not too slow. How much time do you have and how many words do you plan to say? Everyone wants to put as much as possible into the presentation. Unfortunately, most people put in too much and either end up sounding like motor mouths or run too long and are cut off when the next group starts coming into the room. If you have rehearsed well, you know how long your presentation will take, give or take 10 percent. You need to sound relaxed, smooth, and thoughtful. Your thoughts should progress logically and your slides should flow accordingly.

There are no fixed rules about how long each slide should be up. But if a slide is up less than 15 seconds or longer than 2 minutes, there should be a good reason. If you are spending several minutes on one slide, think about having several slides with smaller content. Some charts or graphs might take quite a while to present, so there are good reasons to leave a slide up for a while. Once you are done talking about a slide, lose it. Don't leave slides up that are not pressing on to the next point.

Presenting training to participants also involves "looking good" and appearing professional in your manner. Professionals know what the audience should do at the end of your presentation. Knowing the objectives is the key to developing an effective presentation. Visual aids are designed to reinforce the main points of your presentation. Without effective visuals, you are missing a key opportunity to communicate with your audience.

It is sometimes helpful if you have the time to rehearse in front of a live test audience. Eliminate your "tell 'em" and conclusion slides from the presentation and only show the body of the presentation. Then see what the test audience members found interesting, memorable, or confusing. Have them list what they thought was most important and find out if they got your message. Use this information to refine the material.

Don't try out new equipment 15 minutes before the presentation starts. And keep your presentation focused on the message—don't get carried away with special effects and razzle-dazzle. Real training is not sales vehicles or media events. Training is designed to convey important information, so don't make it too frivolous with mischievous little dancing icons and loud music.

Do not attempt to wing it. You need to know the training in order to keep to the point and not wander. You don't want to memorize your script either—otherwise why do it live at all? It would be pointless to gather everyone together and play a recording. You need to know the training well enough so that you will not have to pause to compose your thoughts. You want to present, not recite. Rehearsal is essential to gain the smoothness and comfort you will need to have the audience concentrate on the point you are making and not your nervousness or your ineptitude at operating the projector, laser pointer, computer, public address system, or even room lights.

Implicit in rehearsal is the assumption that you are well prepared and will not wait till the last minute to throw everything together. Few presentations are really ever "finished," and it's normal to put the finishing touches on your presentation right up to the last minute. But there's a huge difference between polishing up good training material and starting the creative process 2 days before class.

Presentation Materials

Creating the presentations is as important as creating the content. There are many considerations, including color, font, font size, etc. When you create a presentation using a new multimedia presentation program, you should look to the research to provide guidelines for using all the capabilities the program has to offer. The primary areas of concern are color, text, visuals, and slide effects.

With respect to color, the first principle is "do no harm." Color must work to enhance information absorption. Today's computers are capable of generating millions of colors. As a result, the designer can quickly overpower the viewer with palettes of unnecessary and confusing hues and values. The basic principles of graphic design are imperative when given the endless possibilities of color available with our current computers. Tips include:

- Limit the selection to two colors per screen.
- Make sure that text color provides high contrast to background color.
- Use solid-color background for screens, and avoid using textured or designed backgrounds.
- Use consistent colors for text and background throughout a presentation.
- Use color to direct the learner's attention.

When selecting text, the designer is confronted with many options, including font, size, color, placement, justification, case, spacing, and style.

Users prefer screens that use headings, directive cues, and spaced paragraphs to indicate the hierarchy of the content and to break the content into easily distinguished chunks of information. Designers should consider the content being delivered when deciding on the simplicity of the screen text format. Some general guidelines include:

- Use simple fonts.
- Be sure the size of type is 18 points at a minimum.
- Use 6 to 7 lines of text per screen.
- Present a single concept or topic per screen.
- Limit the number of colors you choose for your text.
- Left-justify the text.
- Use headings and subheadings to provide a hierarchy of the content.
- Use a combination of uppercase and lowercase; avoid the use of all uppercase.
- Use a minimum of 1 1/2 spaces between lines.

Visuals should be used only when they support the instructional content. Keep in mind that developmental level influences the learner's ability to utilize visuals effectively. In addition, the type of visual influences the appropriateness for a given content. Degree of realism is a consideration when using visuals to teach content. General tips include:

- Be sure visuals are directly related to the content of the text on the screen.
- Teach inexperienced learners about the visual that is being used so they understand the context in which the information is being presented.
- Discuss the content of the visual with the learners.
- Use visuals when the content is dependent on the detail in the supportive visual.
- Limit the number of visuals per screen.

Special effects should be minimized. Overuse directs the learners' attention away from the content and toward the special effect. Transitional time factors should be considered as another element in helping the learners keep focused. If the designer chooses slow transitions, there is a tendency on the part of the learners to lose interest and motivation. When using transitions and "builds," keep them consistent throughout the presentation. Try to:

- Minimize the use of special effects.
- Use consistent styles of builds and transitions throughout a presentation.
- Avoid builds that use overpowering effects such as flying or walking text.
- Avoid effects that are slow transitions from one screen to another.
- Avoid transitions that change the viewer's focus of attention such as checkerboard dissolves.

Bear in mind that individual taste will guide the trainer or training developer using these presentation programs, though there is existing research to provide guidelines. As these presentation programs proliferate, these will become the preferred method for presenting information. This is an area that is open to great discussion and debate!

Since "good taste" guides the screen design strategies, it is best to keep simplicity in mind when doing multimedia design. Just because one has the ability to produce special effects does not mean it is the most instructionally sound decision. Successful designs will be helpful, clear, and utilitarian. Ask not that students admire the display screens and all the functions depicted, but rather that students simply go ahead and learn effectively and efficiently.

CASE: ACME WIDGETS—MAKING THINGS FUN!

Shawn and Dave, the trainers, met with Kathy, the training developer, and Jack, the technical writer, to find ways to make the training more fun. They realized that simply sitting and slogging through weeks of software modules for WCS and KIS would not only be overwhelming in content, but also be boring. Shawn and Dave realized that their audience would be very diverse, and that learners would range from high school students working part time with AWI to the traditional corporate and business employees. They designed some games and learning activities to give the learners a chance to test their knowledge of the material along with their colleagues in a fun manner.

They knew that setting the tone the first day of each class was critical, so they decided to dress in business attire the first day and then business casual for the remainder of each class. Of course, the dress code would also be somewhat dictated by their audience. For the executive presentations, they would let Bob, the I/T training manager, and Mike, the I/T training team lead, tell them the best way to dress. They would also go over the class syllabus in detail, explaining each of the major sections.

During the first meeting, they would provide the students with ways to practice or review the material after class. The students received a list of concepts and terms that would serve as the core of the material. The students could use the list to organize the material and generate possible questions. The team created subsets of notes and readings organized around key concepts. Discussion questions were created from key concepts. Note cards and keyboard templates were created to aid the students' memory.

Because the training would be long, and because operating the software is so critical to AWI, the team decided to work together and make a list of tips on reading the audience and keeping them awake, alert, and interested in the class. The tips list would be reviewed before each class by the lead trainer and SME. They compiled the following list to help:

- They would speak slowly so the audience could understand the words and ideas.
- They would make sure they knew the material well, so they could make eye contact with the audience. Looking at the audience frequently helps keep everyone engaged and interested.
- They would test the material on others to get feedback about both the content and clarity of the material and the presentation.

The team also decided to scan the list of participants to get to know the audience ahead of time. Each trainer would visit the department to determine who the primary and secondary audiences were. The team would also try to learn what thinking processes the participants used and how much they already knew about the subject and software modules on which they were going to be trained. The team would also take readings of the audience periodically. If the members of the audience were looking at the trainer, were attentive, and smiling, and were taking notes, then the training would continue as is. If they were looking at their watches, yawning, or just nodding off, the trainer would announce a break or initiate an activity to get them back.

By visiting each department prior to classes, the team could also work toward accounting for individual learning styles. The team realized that effective learning is most likely to happen when the strengths and weaknesses of students are considered. It's also important to help individual students build on their strong points to learn the material in the way in which the student can relate and internalize the material for future use. Some of the factors the team considered were:

- Sensory preferences and cues such as auditory, visual, and kinesthetic
- Environmental factors such as preferences for sound or quiet, light needs (bright versus dim), temperature (cool or warm environment), and work area (crowded versus relaxed)
- Preferences for working alone or in a team

- Attitude issues including motivation (internal versus external), persistence, conformity, and structure

All these factors may have a significant effect on the efficacy of the learning environment, and how well the material is received. The team decided to require the trainees to arrive at 8:00 a.m., though the training wouldn't start until 8:30 a.m. for all-day and morning classes. This would allow the participants to get familiar with each other and set up their work areas in a comfortable manner.

Because the class Dave was teaching involved team administration of KIS resources, he decided to use a different activity to start the class. His goal was to have each participant learn enough about one other person to be able to introduce the person to the entire group. All participants got to hear about other participants from the perspective of a third party instead of from the persons themselves. He first allowed them to pair off the audience. The two members of the team then interviewed each other. Once that was done, each team took a turn introducing the other team member to the audience at large. Interviews were timed from 2 to 3 minutes. For those teams that were stuck for questions, Dave prepared questions ahead of time and provided general guidelines for the interview. He also made people pick someone to interview that they didn't know.

The training team also realized that a lecture-only format was likely to put trainees to sleep fast. Therefore, they chose a multimedia presentation method, using some computer screenshots, videos from the vendors, and some lecture. The idea was to keep the trainees engaged over the life of the class. Each concept introduction was approximately 25 minutes for the presentation and questions (if any) from the audience. For the presentation the team used a whiteboard, an overhead projector (OHP), and a Windows NT machine hooked up to a projector capable of display 800 × 600 pixels in thousands of washed-out colors.

The team developed a list of pointers for using the classroom resources that it would share with the rest of the trainers. Because of the large number of classes, there were going to be trainers and SMEs from various parts of the company, as well as from the vendors. Some of the tips included:

- Do not lean on the lectern for long periods. Trainees may wonder when you are going to fall over.
- Maintain eye contact.
- Use pastel backgrounds on overhead transparencies and slides since bright white light can be harsh on the eyes. This causes your learners to tire easily.
- Learn the name of each student as quickly as possible and use the learner's name in class.
- Tell the learners by what name and title you prefer to be called.
- Conduct a personal interview with all learners sometime during the class.
- Listen to comments and opinions. This may be valuable feedback for improving the class.

- Use familiar examples in presenting materials. If you teach rules, principles, definitions, and theorems, explicate these with concrete examples that the learners can understand.

- Be prepared to use an alternative approach if the current one isn't working. Let the individual learning styles, not lecture notes, determine the format of instruction.

These tips were shared with all the trainers and were given to the SMEs as well. Once the classes started, the trainers met once a week to discuss their successes and their opportunities for improvement. Bob and Mike also visited each trainer's classroom at least once per class to get a feel for the way things were going and the general comfort level of the trainers and trainees.

Coming Up in Chapter 12

How do you know if the training worked? How do you evaluate and measure an employee's learning? This is probably the most vexing phase of the training process, and yet tons of material have been written about it. Chapter 12 presents several measurement and evaluation processes and provides tips on setting up a continual improvement program.

REFERENCES

Boud, D., & Griffin, V. (Eds.). (1987). *Appreciating adults learning: From the learners perspective.* London: Kogan Page.

Boyd, Susan. (1999). Susan Boyd Associates. Website: www.susan-boyd.com. 270 Mather Rd., Jenkintown, PA 19046. Phone: (215) 886-2669.

Brookfield, Stephen. (1986). *Understanding and facilitating adult learning.* San Francisco: Jossey-Bass.

Brookfield, Stephen. (1990). *The skillful teacher.* San Francisco: Jossey-Bass.

Carey, L., & Dick, W. (1996). *The systematic design of instruction.* (4th ed.). New York: HarperCollins.

Fox, Paul. (1999). Fox Performance. Website: www.foxperformance.com. 904 Autumn Chase, Ellington, CT 06029. Phone: (860) 870-4640.

Gaines Robinson, Dana, & Robinson, James. (1989). *Training for impact.* San Francisco: Jossey-Bass.

Posner, G. J., & Rudnitsky, A. N. (1986). *Course design: A guide to curriculum development for teachers* (3d ed.). New York: Longman.

Rothwell, W. J., & Cookson, P. S. (1997). *Beyond instruction: Comprehensive program planning for business and education.* San Francisco, Jossey-Bass.

Wager, W. W., Gagne, R. M., & Briggs, L. J. (1992). *Principles of instructional design.* Fort Worth, TX: Harcourt, Brace, Jovanovich.

Workshops by Thiagi. (1999). www.thiagi.com. 4423 E. Trailridge Rd., Bloomington, IN 47408-9633. Phone: (812) 332-1478 or (800) 996-7725.

Measuring Training Success by Measuring On-the-Job Trainee Performance

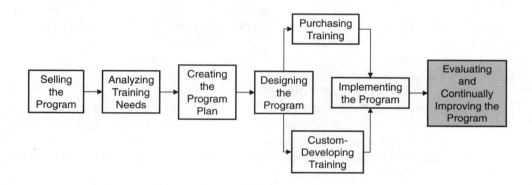

In This Chapter

12.1 How do I design and conduct effective evaluations and tests?

12.2 How do I measure the effects of training on employee performance?

12.3 How do I use course evaluations and test results to continually improve training?

Case: Acme Widgets—Evaluating the Training Program

OVERVIEW

Evaluation is often seen by trainers as a necessary evil to keep the money coming. Visions of difficult procedures, complex equations, and detailed analysis strike fear in the hearts of those thinking about evaluation. But evaluation is simply looking at the training and determining whether it is having an impact. Most evaluations are carried out to answer a few key questions to help get a clear picture of the work you are doing. Evaluation helps to answer questions like:

- Does the training achieve its objectives (for the course and program)?
- Did the training team develop and deliver the training according to plan?
- What could be done differently?
- What changes should be made?

These types of questions help you measure the results of your activities. Evaluations look to see if the training actually achieved its objectives as specified in the needs analysis (Chapter 1) and design (Chapter 4). Evaluations can also be carried out to look at how results are achieved. A process evaluation looks at the way the work was carried out and the operational aspects of your program.

There are many reasons for evaluating training, each requiring a different approach. If the purpose is to improve the instruction, you will likely use a formative evaluation. A formative evaluation is what the name implies—an evaluation that helps form or shape the course. If you are trying to assess the degree of demonstrated achievement, then you would do a summative evaluation. A summative evaluation is a more objective measurement designed to measure whether the learner "got it" and whether the course helped.

Evaluation helps training managers figure out how well the training is delivering the information needed by the organization. It can help identify and shed light on problems that prevent the training from achieving its objectives and point to ways these problems can be overcome. It can show where to improve training and provide ideas and information for planning future training. It also informs other groups (e.g., senior management) about what works and what doesn't work in the program. In essence, evaluation is important because if you don't evaluate the training, how will you know if it was successful?

To assess the value of training, the organization must find out if positive changes occurred and if the changes were due to training. In evaluating training programs, the organization must measure change in four categories, established by Dr. Donald Kirkpatrick in 1959: reaction, learning, behavior, and results. In the reaction category the trainers ask the participants how they felt about the training program. In the learning category the question is how well have the trainees learned what was taught. In the behavior category the results are monitored once the employee is back on the job. Finally the results category asks to what extent have cost-related training outcomes resulted from the training.

From a continual improvement perspective, evaluations should include determining which learning activities are working best and what parts of the training should be changed. It's also important to determine why parts of the training are not being used, relative to content and needs analysis. Training departments should also work with help desks to ensure that the training is being supported properly. Last, but certainly not least, ROI is critical in determining the benefits that result from the training.

The evaluation phase is actually ongoing throughout the entire process. It's performed during the analysis, design, development, and implementation phases. It is also performed after the learners return to their jobs. Its purpose is to document learner performance in a training course, as well as on the job. The goal is to fix problems and make the system better. Evaluation is the process of determining the value and effectiveness of a learning program. It uses assessment and validation tools to provide data for the evaluation. Assessment is the measurement of the practical results of the training in the work environment, while validation determines if the objectives of the training goal were met.

Training teams responsible for providing a concrete ROI for training programs must think like businesspeople and understand what drives the need for training (see Chapters 1 and 2). Training teams must respond by implementing solid, easy-to-understand measurement tools and by evaluating classes against various criteria. Three basic concepts include:

1. Evaluating customer satisfaction, which may include the trainee's manager, the department, and the organization as well as the trainee. Besides measuring effectiveness, we are measuring perception of quality, convenience, and value. This is important to attendance and funding.

2. Determining whether the training made a positive difference in the business. The training team must work with business managers to identify business problems at the beginning (see Chapters 1 to 4). By doing this, the trainers think of training as a problem-solving tool and not just a class.

3. Measuring the ROI for the training. Training teams must demonstrate the effects of the classes on the productivity of the organization. And it is no longer considered impossible to measure the ROI of training, so many organizations work with accountants to nail down the actual ROI.

Justifying investments in training is difficult, and so using meaningful methods of evaluation is important. Training teams must statistically and precisely justify the costs of the training program.

There is usually resistance to measuring training and the results or effects of training. There are many difficulties inherent in measuring job performance. First of all, most people don't react positively when hearing that their job performance will be measured. Measuring adults in job training seems to strike fear and loathing in their hearts. And admittedly, the nature of some jobs makes them difficult to measure. Office work is different from assembly-line work, and is less tangible and more service-oriented with fewer easily defined outcomes. Quality service is more difficult to measure than quality widgets.

12.1   HOW DO I DESIGN AND CONDUCT EFFECTIVE EVALUATIONS AND TESTS?

Designing and conducting course, trainer, and student evaluations is more art than science, though many articles, books, and papers on the subject have been published since the landmark research published by Dr. Kirkpatrick, as mentioned in the Overview. There are also hundreds of statistical methods that can be applied to the measurement, quality control, and continual improvement of training. The reality, though, is that most training programs only need a few of these measures to be effective, and it's really pretty easy to measure training if you consider that there are four basic steps to this process:

1. Deciding what you want to measure
2. Deciding on the type(s) of evaluation(s) to be used
3. Creating a course and/or trainer evaluation (this includes tests)
4. Administering and following up on course and trainer evaluations

These steps are easy to follow and execute. The really hard part is remembering to measure (and to instill in the organization the discipline to measure) and continually improve training programs. It's really easy to run the course, administer the evaluations, and then file the evaluations in a drawer somewhere for posterity. Following up with learners and using the evaluation results to revise, update, and improve the training is the hard part. This is where most organizations fail, and why most training becomes obsolete.

Never assume that knowledge and skills have been acquired. Verify that the training responds to a proven need that is met and achieved by the training process. Initially, students must be provided with measurement and feedback on acquisition of knowledge by using performance-oriented, competency-based testing of the new skill. Managers must have proof in the form of certified, numerically based scores that clearly illustrate the success or failure of the trainees.

Deciding What You Want to Measure

The key question to ask is: What do you want to measure? There are many potential answers to this question, but there are usually two general items to be measured: the instructor and the course. These items can be evaluated using four general types of measures. As mentioned earlier, Dr. Kirkpatrick created four general categories or levels of evaluation. The first level is reaction. Evaluation at this level measures how those who participate in the program react to it. This level is often measured with attitude questionnaires administered after the training classes are over. This level measures one thing: the learner's perception of (reaction to) the course. It does *not* measure the effectiveness of the course.

The second level is learning. This can be defined as the extent to which participants change attitudes, improve knowledge, and increase skill as a result of attending the program. This level addresses whether or not the participants learned anything. The learning evaluation requires posttesting to determine what skills were learned during the training and how well they were learned. The posttesting is only valid when combined with pretesting, so that you can differentiate between what the participants already knew prior to training and what they actually learned during the training program. It's important to remember that measurements in the second level might indicate that a program's instructional methods are effective or ineffective, but it will not prove if the newly acquired skills will be used in the working environment.

The third level is behavior. The level of behavior is defined as the extent to which a change in behavior has occurred because the participants attended the training program. This evaluation involves testing the students' capabilities to perform the skills learned on the job. Level 3 evaluations can be performed formally by using various types of productivity testing or reviewing performance appraisals posttraining, or they can be done informally by observing the worker. New learning is worthless unless the participants actually use the new skills, attitudes, or knowledge in their work activities.

The final level is defined as the results that occurred because the participants attended the program, such as the ability to apply learned skills to new and unfamiliar situations. It measures the training effectiveness by measuring what impact the training had and whether the benefits sold to management (see Chapter 1) were actually realized. These impacts can include changes in areas such as costs or revenues, efficiency, or morale. It's important to think beyond the impact on the learners who participated in the training program and ask what happens to the organization as a result of the training.

Within each of these levels you must determine what's important to the organization, and thus what students will be measured against. In Chapter 4, the objectives were determined based on the needs analysis and the software feature/function set being installed. Once the objectives are known and the metrics are determined, you must identify measures that determine whether objectives were achieved. It helps if you simply list each objective and follow it with a statement indicating the measurement, such as the time period specified or the number of errors tolerated while entering a new employee.

Deciding on the Type(s) of Evaluation(s) to Be Used

There are many different types of evaluations depending on the training or trainer being evaluated and the purpose of the evaluation. The two basic evaluation types are (as mentioned in the Overview) formative and summative. Formative evaluations improve the course or trainer being evaluated. Formative evaluations literally help form the training by examining the delivery of the program or technology, the quality of its implementation, and the assessment of the organizational context, personnel, procedures, inputs, etc. Summative evaluations examine the effects or outcomes of some object. Summative evaluations summarize training results by describing what happens subsequent to the delivery of the program or technology, such as measuring employee job performance.

Formative evaluation means evaluating the process of curriculum design and construction, the training deliverables, and the trainer. Formative evaluation takes place during the instruction. Here the reason for evaluation is not to grade the learner; it is to help both the learner and the trainer focus on the particular learning necessary for movement toward mastery. Since formative evaluation takes place during the formation stage, every effort should be made to use it to improve the process. This means that in formative evaluation, training departments must develop evidence that will be useful in the process and help improve the material over time.

The most important value of formative evaluation is the feedback provided to both the student in learning the subject matter and the trainer or developer for each unit of learning. Formative evaluation helps trainers improve their instruction. It's often useful for trainers to prepare an analysis of the errors students are making on each item in tests. That way the trainers can reconsider their instruction strategies while they and the students are dealing with the unit and learning outcomes. Formative evaluation can be used to make the process more effective before the summative evaluation.

The formative evaluation of materials while in development initially provides continual feedback to the designer on how the course can be improved. The summative evaluation is used at the end of each semester to determine the course's effectiveness in meeting the objectives. Formative evaluations include both expert evaluations of the course content during development and student evaluations at the midpoint and end of each course. Summative evaluation is based on student scores, student evaluations and feedback, and faculty feedback. At the midpoint and end of each course, students are given exams to measure learning.

Summative evaluation is a type of evaluation used at the end of a course or program for the purpose of grading, certification, evaluation of progress, or research on the effectiveness of a training program. The difference between formative and summative evaluations is that in a summative evaluation, the student, trainer, or curriculum is judged on accuracy, relevance, and/or effectiveness. The principal rule of summative evaluations is to look at content areas in terms of large categories of subject material. If you see the purpose of your summative evaluation as that of testing a few generalized objectives, you should decide which objectives you are going to sample, and then drill down through those objectives to get to the specific behavior being tested.

Summative evaluations have a variety of purposes, one of them simply to give grades and another to certify competence in a given area. As purpose varies, so will the procedures for developing and scoring the test. One popular summative evaluation method that is used to actually demonstrate learning is the pretest-posttest method. Students are pretested at the first class meeting to determine their current skills. That same test is used as a final exam to determine the actual increase in knowledge over the course of the class. The major issue with this method is that there is no way to verify that an improvement in test scores is actually the result of this course versus the student's memory of the pretest.

The most common type of summative evaluation is the use of tests to diagnose and evaluate. The diagnostic use is an evaluative use, but the purpose is to identify the cause of some problem or make some assessment of the individual's skills. These evaluations provide information regarding what and who need additional attention. Different criteria are used in the measurement of learning. The three most commonly used are accuracy, speed, and required effort of a response.

Most trainers evaluate on the basis of accuracy of response. This is evident by grading scales that indicate a grade based on the percentage (or number) of correct responses. However, speed of response is a major criterion when learning new software. It's very important that the students be able to do their jobs quickly, effectively, and efficiently when they complete the training.

Developing a Course and/or Trainer Evaluation

Once you know what you want to measure and what your goals are for the measurements (e.g., whether you're using the evaluation to revise the class or grade students), you can begin creating the evaluation. One factor to consider here is whether to use close-ended (e.g., yes/no), Likert scale (ranking 1–7), or open-ended (e.g, essay) questions. If the evaluation is a test or summative evaluation, you must decide whether to use objective questions, such as multiple choice or true/false, or essay questions. Each of these methods has its advantages and disadvantages. For both the course evaluation and test, essay questions provide more latitude for the students to express themselves. Objective answers or Likert scale answers are easier to measure, but restrict the student. Most evaluations use both open-ended and close-ended questions on both formative and summative evaluations.

Evaluations that measure reaction can combine both course and instructor evaluations. However, if the evaluations are combined on a single piece of paper or web form, be sure to separate the sections with the course and instructor evaluation questions so the student doesn't confuse the two. A sample combined form is presented in Figure 12-1. This form measures various factors regarding both the course and instructor, as well as the training program and facility in general. This form is available in its entirety in Appendix G, and can be used from McGraw-Hill's website at

FIGURE 12-1

Course: _____   Instructor: _____

Date: _____   Facility: _____

Training facility:

Effectiveness of the training site for comfort:
Excellent __ Good __ Fair __ Poor __ Unacceptable __ Not Applicable

Quality of the training equipment for efficiency:
Excellent __ Good __ Fair __ Poor __ Unacceptable __ Not Applicable

Level of error-free operation of the training equipment:
Excellent __ Good __ Fair __ Poor __ Unacceptable __ Not Applicable

Training:

Usefulness of curriculum:
Excellent __ Good __ Fair __ Poor __ Unacceptable __ Not Applicable

Relevance of curriculum:
Excellent __ Good __ Fair __ Poor __ Unacceptable __ Not Applicable

Ease of learning of curriculum:
Excellent __ Good __ Fair __ Poor __ Unacceptable __ Not Applicable

Instructor:

Instructor timeliness:
Excellent __ Good __ Fair __ Poor __ Unacceptable __ Not Applicable

Instructor subject knowledge:
Excellent __ Good __ Fair __ Poor __ Unacceptable __ Not Applicable

Instructor communication skills:
Excellent __ Good __ Fair __ Poor __ Unacceptable __ Not Applicable

Instructor training preparation:
Excellent __ Good __ Fair __ Poor __ Unacceptable __ Not **Applicable**

Additional Comments:

_____

www.books.mcgraw-hill.com/training/download. The forms can then be opened, edited, and printed using Microsoft Word or other word processing software. It's important to remember that this form should be tailored to match the needs of your organization. The questions presented in the evaluation should reflect the organization's needs and management's expectations of the training program.

Analyzing Evaluation Results

The evaluations must be administered and analyzed when the training is implemented. Using the evaluation, the next step is to begin collecting information about the measures you have identified as important. The information is then summarized and analyzed. Ongoing monitoring ensures that training is being evaluated on a continual basis. Monitoring means looking at training over time to determine whether it has been implemented as planned and is running smoothly.

The information is collected immediately after the conclusion of the training course (or at some other predetermined point). You are now in a position to analyze your information. It is at this stage that you turn the raw information into a format that will tell you if your project has been a success. This means analyzing your findings to identify any emerging trends or patterns such as:

- Patterns that emerge from each course or trainer evaluation. Are people generally giving the same responses to your questions?
- Patterns that show trends in certain evaluation items such as instructor friendliness.
- Patterns that show customer satisfaction (or not) with the program as a whole.

In arriving at your final evaluation, compare results to determine whether there have been any changes, and if so, whether these changes moved in a direction that satisfies your objectives. Your analysis should also note the extent of this change. In other words, if there is a change in the rating of the instructor's speaking speed, you should note how much change there actually was.

For each evaluation, determine if your measures are changing in the direction specified in your objectives. It may help to do this by constructing a table for each evaluation over time, which allows you to compare findings from each evaluation. This table will list your evaluation items, measurements for each test, and the direction of change (positive or negative) in each evaluation item. Once a table for each evaluation has been completed, combine the columns from each table to arrive at an overall conclusion on whether the program has reached its objectives. A sample table and resulting chart is shown in Table 12-1.

If you were trying to improve the training and the instructor, you'd look for upward (or positive) trends in the changes. Charting the important items can be a helpful method of visualizing the results over time. For example, the chart in Figure 12-2 shows a comparison of overall instructor ratings with ratings of the training itself. This chart shows that students perceive good improvement for the instructor over time, while the training course stays fairly constant. This is appropriate, because the training probably didn't change with each class. The instructor's delivery of the training, however, can and should improve with each class. It's necessary to know which measures are important and how significant the trends of those measures are to be able to judge how well the training is being delivered.

Developing a Test

Tests represent one particular measurement technique. A test is a set of questions or tasks, each of which has a correct answer or action, which trainees answer. Test questions differ from those used in measures of attitudes, interest, or preference or certain other aspects of training. The questions in tests of achievement or many tests of intelligence have answers that content experts can agree are correct; correctness is not determined by the particular values, preferences, or dislikes of a group of judges.

There are a number of standard tasks to be done in writing a test. It's important to create a test bank of questions. If you produce a sufficiently large number of questions, a virtually unlimited number of tests with an unlimited number of test questions can be generated. You must also decide on test formats—T/F, multiple choice, fill in the blank, and essay questions are the most common. The test should be randomized. A test

TABLE 12-1

Evaluation Item [Scale Is 1 (bad) to 5 (good)]	Average Rating 3/3	Average Rating 3/8	Change Direction	Change Magnitude
Instructor knowledge level	3.4	4.3	+	.9
Classroom temperature	4.1	3.9	−	−.2
Facility cleanliness	4.3	4.3	0	0

FIGURE 12-2

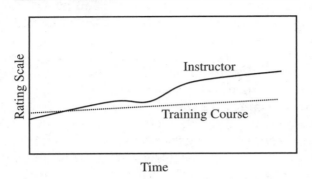

bank of questions can generate a number of randomly chosen questions in random order—no two tests should ever be the same. You must also establish grade scales.

There are common problems that trainers developing tests encounter. One of the biggest pitfalls is that test scores may not measure what you want them to. For example, if all the test items require students to simply repeat the drills from instruction (for software training), the test will not likely provide a measure of the students' ability to apply their knowledge or to solve problems. It's important to develop a test that has situations and problems that extend the students' knowledge of the software. You should make sure your instructional objectives (designed in Chapter 4) and the test items match.

Careful test planning allows you to prepare and assemble your test more effectively. Be sure to provide general directions for the test. Include how much time will be allowed for the test, how the items will be scored, and how to record answers. Set off the directions by appropriate spacing or by a different type style. Arrange items systematically. Group similar items (such as all multiple-choice items) together. Provide a clear set of directions for each new group of items.

Obtain feedback about the effectiveness of your test from other sources. For example, other trainers can provide valuable input on the importance or appropriate difficulty of items. Testing specialists can determine factors in the test format that might raise or lower student scores, and students can indicate whether the material was covered in class. It's useful to give a small random sample of the test to students to "prototype" the test and check its effectiveness. After administering the test, review statistical feedback about the quality of the test.

So how do you know when a test should be revised? Items that more than 90 percent of the students answered correctly may be too easy. Low item difficulty may suggest that the item contained clues to the answer. This could be caused by an incorrect answer key or by a poorly worded question. A low percentage of students answering an item may indicate students ran out of time during the test or they were unsure of the answer and didn't want to guess. Items that fewer than 30 percent of the students answered correctly may be too difficult. A large number of difficult items may suggest the need for a revision.

You should also do a statistical analysis of the questions using tables and charts, as you did with the evaluation. It's important to know how the class as a whole scored on the test. An analysis plots the scores from highest to lowest and indicates the number of students taking the test and the number of students receiving each score. You should also determine how the typical or average student scored on the test. An analysis calculates the class mean or average. A low class average may indicate the test was too difficult, while a high class average may indicate the test was too easy.

Many other calculations can be done including how far apart the scores were spread and how consistent the test was with various classes. These calculations are explained in some of the references at the end of this chapter. Also, the various points in this section are summarized in a checklist for use in Appendix F and on McGraw-Hill's website at www.books.mcgraw-hill.com/training/download. The forms can then be opened, edited, and printed using Microsoft Word or other word processing software. A sample test is also presented in the case study, which is also available in Appendix G and on McGraw-Hill's website.

Tips for Administering and Following Up on Course and Trainer Evaluations and Tests

It's important to measure program effectiveness on an ongoing basis, as this forms the foundation for continual improvement (see Section 12.3). A workshop evaluation form, which is distributed to each participant after each class, asks about the presentation of material, the skills of the presenter, the organization and content of the class, classroom facilities, etc. It should also ask about other training that students might want. Instructors must set the stage for a high return rate by assuring all participants that the evaluations will be the basis for improving the workshop for future participants.

Course evaluations must be administered in a way that makes students feel comfortable with the process. Obviously, this means anonymity for students and the freedom to write comments outside of the numeric rating scales. The more comfortable the students feel with the evaluation process, the more honest they're likely to be, which means better information for improving the training. However, the instructors must be open to criticism. If the instructors won't or can't change based on the feedback, the evaluations are pointless, and students will quickly stop completing them.

Relying exclusively on workshop evaluations may not accurately tell how effectively the classes give people the skills they need, so you may want to do a follow-up survey with participants. The survey should be published, and copies of both the workshop evaluation form and the follow-up telephone survey should be available upon request. Personal follow-up can help produce the best positive image possible for a training department.

Preventative medicine is also helpful. Consider the amount of time that will be allowed to complete the test. In test design there are "speed" tests and "power" tests. Speed tests would have instructions such as, "You are not expected to finish, but finish as many as you can," while power tests would say, "You have as much time as you wish to answer the questions." Due to class schedules, time does become a factor in giving tests. If you have a 60-minute class period, you should construct the test on that basis. It is recognized that some students work faster than others. You should allow time for the average student to complete the test, and it is advisable to provide some extra time for the slower-responding student (e.g., make the test a 45-minute test for a 60-minute class period).

It is important to monitor the success of the training, to actively solicit user input, and to actively listen to what your users have to say about the training. Training departments must be very aware of the real needs of the organization since superfluous training wastes money, and training that was neglected costs the organization real dollars.

12.2 HOW DO I MEASURE THE EFFECTS OF TRAINING ON EMPLOYEE PERFORMANCE?

The effects of training on job performance must be measured. Clear, consistent, and visible involvement by senior managers is a necessary part of successful performance measurement and management systems. Senior management should be actively involved in both the creation and implementation of its organization's performance management systems. This provides employees with backing, and also helps keep management apprised of the training department's effect on the organization beyond just the software rollout.

A conceptual framework is needed for the performance measurement and management system. Every organization needs a clear and cohesive performance measurement framework that is understood by all levels of the organization and that supports objectives and the collection of results. Benchmarking should use a balanced set of measures to align them with the overall organizational goals and objectives. It's critical to have a standardized and easy-to-understand structure that indicates how the process works and a clear list of expected outcomes for each organizational level and employee.

Performance measurement systems must provide information that managers can use for decision making. Performance measures should be focused on both the employee and strategic organizational goals and objectives, and should provide timely, relevant, and concise information for use by managers to assess the employee's progress toward achieving predetermined goals. Try not to collect data simply because the data were available to be collected or because having large amounts of data looks good. Instead, organizations should choose performance measures that can help describe employee and organizational performance, direction, and accomplishments, and then use these to improve employee performance, and ultimately products and services for customers.

Compensation, rewards, and recognition should be linked to performance measurements. Successful organizations link performance evaluations and rewards to specific measures of success and tie financial and nonfinancial incentives directly to performance. A good link sends a clear message to the organization and its employees about what's important. The most successful performance measurement systems are not torture devices, but learning systems that help the organization identify what works for each employee. Ideally, performance measurement systems should be a tool that lets the organization track the progress and direction of employees toward goals and objectives. Posttraining measures include:

- Productivity as measured by throughput (e.g., the number of customer orders processed per hour)
- Error rates (e.g., mistakes per order)
- Overall employee satisfaction
- Organizational performance (e.g., profitability or cost containment)

All these measures and others can be affected by training. It's important to note, however, that not all measures are training-related. As an example, there are arguments both for and against training affecting organizational morale. On one hand, employees who don't know their job duties or how to operate the software can get frustrated. On the other hand, if employees are disgruntled to begin with, or dislike their supervisor, training is unlikely to make a difference.

Setting a Baseline

Once an organization has decided on its employee performance measures, the next step in the process is to determine a baseline for each of the measures selected. Once data are collected for the first time on a measurement, the organization has the baseline data it needs to measure trends against the original information. Determining appropriate goals for each measure after the baseline data are collected can be accomplished in several ways.

A common practice is to set goals that will force the employees to stretch themselves and exceed their past performance. By benchmarking measures, an organization can validate the fact that the goals are still attainable. For example, a goal of zero defects on orders entered is an admirable goal for any organization. However, if average industry standards are 5 percent, a goal of zero defects may not be realistically attainable. Setting a goal no one can meet can easily demotivate employees by giving them an essentially impossible target. To communicate, it is important to provide information on performance goals and results to employees in the form of intranets, newsletters, and bulletin board displays. This increases the employees' understanding of the organization's mission and goals, which helps them buy in.

An important aspect of performance measurement is its iterative quality. Organizations should continually assess whether their current measures are sufficient or excessive, are proving to be useful in managing the business and employees, and are driving the employee and organization to the right result. This review lets the organization make sure that it is maintaining the right measures. When measures become obsolete, they should be discarded and replaced with something else. Many organizations find that they begin with too few or too many measures and need to adjust the number, type, and specific measures tracked for each employee.

Performance analysis also lets organizations change the priority of specific measures over time. Some performance goals, for instance, are intended to influence behavior and should be switched to a "maintenance mode" once targets are achieved. Some other goals may change due to the nature of the business, market conditions, or regulatory requirements. A best practice is to regularly develop employee change teams to look at the measures and determine whether adjustments are necessary.

Continuous and regular review of measures as they relate to the corresponding goals and the employee's and organization's strategic plan is key to success in performance measurement. It not only helps in deciding the right things to measure, but provides needed information to assess progress toward reaching goals of all levels within the organization. Performance measurement has no purpose if data are not used to improve employee and organizational performance.

Because there are so many factors new to employees during a software rollout, it is often difficult to get a good baseline established. Generally speaking, however, a baseline can be developed by looking at the objectives specified in the evaluation or test measures (see Chapter 4). For example, if the average data entry person should be able to complete five orders per hour after training on the new software, then that can serve as the baseline. The key is to evaluate employee performance against the baseline early after training and make adjustments based on the facts that come to light during the initial posttraining period.

Measuring Performance after Training

Like evaluating training, measuring the effects of training on employee performance involves deciding what to measure in a job. You can usually measure behavior and results. It takes less time to develop performance standards based on results, but some aspects of the work can't be measured in any way except behaviorally. To get the best of both worlds, begin by measuring results and only measure behavior when you have to. Most people try to identify the results of a position by listing its responsibilities and asking what product each activity generates. This process can take several hours and usually ends up with a very long list of results. A faster and better method involves identifying your customers and what you provide to them. This produces a list of key performance indicators (KPIs).

There are two kinds of KPIs, numeric and descriptive. Your objective for KPIs should be verifiability. It's important to use measures that can be verified for whether a standard was met, exceeded, or not met. Numeric measures are easily verified, so they meet the criteria. Quantifying a result can be difficult, but, ultimately, all results are measured in time and dollars.

Identifying measures for a given result can be easy. There are four general measures you can use as a starting point.

In general, any result can be evaluated against quantity, quality, cost, or timeliness (or some combination of the four). When you have difficulty identifying a measure, you can begin by trying to fit the measure into one of those four categories. The next step is to identify a specific measure for each task or behavior. If you can measure the result with numbers, write down the units you would count or for which you would track the percentage (e.g., error rates). If you can't measure an aspect of the result with numbers (such as the quality of widgets produced), you'll need to describe the performance by identifying a factor against which the measure can be judged.

For example, customer relation skills (for a customer-response software rollout) might be difficult to measure directly, but complaint calls and market share are two factors that might indicate employee performance. Creating an operational definition for each measure is critical, and you must ensure that these measures are understood by everyone in the organization. A typical definition includes a specific goal or objective as well as the data requirements. The measurement approach should also include the population the metric will include, the frequency of measurement, and the data source.

Remember that, in general, a good measure is accepted by and meaningful to the customer and tells how well goals and objectives are being met. The goal should also be simple, understandable, logical, and repeatable. For measurement purposes, the goal must also show a trend and should be clearly defined. A measure should also be timely and sensitive to organizational and employee-related changes. Above all, however, a good measure drives appropriate action.

Several characteristics are associated with the implementation of a successful performance measurement (PM) system. A good PM system comprises a balanced set of a limited, vital few measures. It should also produce timely and useful reports at a reasonable cost. If the system is automated (such as a control panel), it should be able to display available information that is shared, understood, and used by an organization. Organizations can also create an inventory of common measures that cross business units. A popular approach today is to develop an economic value-added index to measure financial performance. An effective performance measurement system serves, but not drives, the business. The primary purpose of measuring performance is to develop, deliver, and improve on world-class products and services, not to audit or find fault.

An organization also needs to establish who is responsible for performance measurements. This may be HR, the training department, or the functional area, but someone must be responsible for getting the information needed and for reporting it in a timely manner. Others need to be responsible for the actual outcomes on the measurements. Some organizations have team-level measurement experts who are responsible for helping team members understand the significance of the performance data collected and who guide the team in using data at weekly goal meetings.

Through a variety of techniques, a goal owner establishes goal targets. This ensures a high degree of integrity in the process and the people involved. Lately, the mainstream media and other employee unions and organizations have been asking for organizations to formally link executive compensation to organizational performance, as well as judge individual performance by the achievement of strategic objectives. It's important that both employees and management be held to high standards; otherwise employees may not buy in to the process.

It's essential to develop standardized evaluation forms for performance management. The purpose of a performance management form is to specify goals and targets agreed to by the supervisor or manager and the employee for the employee to achieve within a specified time frame. A good form also ensures that the employee knows what is expected and what will form the basis for the evaluation. A performance plan may also increase understanding of the organization's goals and how individual performance contributes to achievement of those goals.

A performance plan must have specific time frames and measurable objectives. It will form the basis of the performance review and should clearly define performance expectations. The goals must be consistent with the current job, or the new job as it relates to the software rollout. Each objective must be observable in order to be evaluated. The objectives must be specific and defined in precise language and leave no doubt about what is expected. It's important that the plan be specified in quantifiable terms that are meaningful and leave no doubt when the goal has been achieved.

It's vital to note that organizations are dynamic. The plan must take into account the idea that changes may be made during the period of planning. Goals should be reviewed and updated periodically. A sample form is shown in Figure 12-3, which takes baseline skills developed in class and measures the employee against those baseline skills over a period of time. This form is available for use in Appendix G and on McGraw-Hill's website at www.books.mcgraw-hill.com/training/download. The forms can then be opened, edited, and printed using Microsoft Word or other word processing software. Note that this form is only a plan. It doesn't indicate how the employees did, just what they are supposed to do.

The purpose of a performance review is to evaluate employee performance against the goals and targets set out in the performance plan. It also provides the supervisor or manager and employee with useful feedback regarding expectations that will enhance the working relationship. A good review can also identify discrepancies in expected and actual level of competence in job functions of the employee. With regard to training, it will provide the organization with data on employee performance to be used for training and development needs and pay for performance.

Most review processes have a regular time frame for the formal review to be completed at the end of a quarter or year. Ongoing reviews are done at predefined times (e.g., 3 months). Special reviews are done as required, e.g., to adjust for contingencies, to address performance problems, etc. The supervisor and/or training team compare the individual's actual performance against targets forecasted as part of job requirements and training goals. They rate the competence of an employee per goal or target. The review should also identify strengths and/or deficiencies in performance. The process must also allow employees the opportunity to

---

FIGURE 12-3

PERFORMANCE PLAN FOR: James Woods   **POSITION:** Accounting Clerk II

DATE OF PLAN: 1/1/2000   **PERIOD ENDING:** 3/31/2000

Objectives	Target time frames	Change allowances
Enter all accounting transactions with two or fewer errors	Should be at accuracy rate by 3/31/2000	Software changes during evaluation period may cause objective change
Complete accounting by EOM	End of each month	Absences, other unforeseen incidents
Learn and cross-train to other functions as contingency	3/31/2000	If job descriptions change or a reorganization occurs this may change

Signatures:

_____   _____   _____   _____

Employee   Date   Supervisor   Date

complete a self-review. A sample form is shown in Figure 12-4. This form is available for use in Appendix G and on McGraw-Hill's website at www.books.mcgraw-hill.com/training/download. The forms can then be opened, edited, and printed using Microsoft Word or other word processing software. Note that this form indicates how the employee did against the plan that was established earlier.

FIGURE 1 2 - 4

PERFORMANCE PLAN FOR: James Woods   **POSITION:** Accounting Clerk II
DATE OF REVIEW: 1/1/2000   **PERIOD ENDING:** 3/31/2000

Objectives	Target	Result	Comments
Enter all accounting transactions with two or fewer errors	Should be at accuracy rate by 3/31/2000	EXCEPTIONAL	Software changed during the period, but James succeeded
Complete accounting by EOM	End of each month	FULLY COMPETENT	Absences, other unforeseen incidents caused delays
Learn and cross-train to other functions as contingency	3/31/2000	INCOMPLETE	If job descriptions change or a reorganization occurs, this may change

Signatures:

_____ _____   _____ _____
Employee   Date   Supervisor   Date

PERFORMANCE RATING KEY:

EXCEPTIONAL

Significantly exceeded all goals and values of performance.

SUPERIOR

Consistently met and frequently exceeded goals and values of performance.

FULLY COMPETENT

Met overall goals and values of performance—100%.

DEVELOPMENTAL/NEEDS IMPROVEMENT

Met some goals; with further development likely to meet overall values of performance.

UNSATISFACTORY

Did not meet goals, values of performance; requires significant overall improvement to achieve goals.

INCOMPLETE

Through no fault of the employee, the goal or objective could not be achieve.

Performance reviews can be used to monitor the results of training. If a large number of employees could not meet the goals set as a baseline during training, then it's possible that their independence was never established. That is, the trainees can do the tasks with an instructor present, but not on their own. It's important to review groups of employee performance reviews over time posttraining. Also, the training department should work with the HR department to ensure that performance reviews measure whether the objectives of the training were achieved. Training departments should be intimately involved in the design and use of performance reviews.

12.3   HOW DO I USE COURSE EVALUATIONS AND TESTS TO CONTINUALLY IMPROVE TRAINING?

To continually improve training, organizations must continually evaluate current and future training requirements and classes. It's also important to utilize fiscal resources to optimize the training delivered. Ongoing improvement requires a continual feedback loop to provide the training department with the information needed to revise training. This means gathering large amounts of data about employee and organizational performance, storing the data, and analyzing them for trends and problems.

Performance measures must be timely, easy to implement, and clearly defined. Speed is essential in both data collection and distribution. Best practices dictate that organizations try to collect data as work is done rather than through separate collection and maintenance tasks. A simple and clear approach should be used, measures should be user-friendly, and the data collection effort should not be too difficult. Standard data definitions help business units in an organization use and understand the analysis of the performance data. A clear data collection plan helps streamline the data collection process. Here are some simple steps:

1. Identify the data to be collected, the employees from whom the data will come, and the length of time over which to collect the data.
2. Identify the reports to be used, the reporting frequency, the type of comparison to be made, and the calculation methodology.
3. Identify the characteristics of the data to be collected.
4. If the performance measure is new, try to identify existing data sources or create new sources. All data sources need to be credible and cost-effective.

Resources must be allocated for the data collection effort. This includes the person responsible for collecting and reporting the data. Management must identify who will ensure that the data collected are reliable, timely, and accurate, and that the process is confidential. In addition, the training or HR resources allocated must describe the way the data will be collected and the summarization methods.

Most organizations use information systems to support data collection and reporting. They use both automated and manual requests for periodic updates. Organizations should try to automate when possible to reduce the burden of data collection on employees and managers. They should also centralize their databases, create an on-line data entry system, make sure it is flexible enough to respond to improvements and changes, and make it user-friendly.

Analyzing Performance Data

Many approaches can be used to analyze and validate performance data, including operations research, statistical analysis, quality control, and activity-based costing. An organization and its business units that use advanced statistical techniques to analyze data tend to do better than those that don't. The best organizations often apply expertise in advanced technical methods to improve performance at a lower level of the organization so as to effect results at a higher level. An analyst needs to be able to explain to senior leadership how the measures were obtained and what the measures mean. The training team then reviews results versus expectations and makes corrections (see the next section).

A very useful method for measuring performance is statistical process control (SPC), a scientific method of analyzing data and using the analysis to solve practical problems. The most common statistical tool in SPC is the control chart, which is used to detect differences in variation among numerical results obtained. Numbers always contain variation. There is variation in the way the numbers are generated, collected, and analyzed, as well as variation in the measurement process itself. The control chart filters out routine variation so that exceptional values can be revealed.

Graphic presentation of key information is a critical element of the analysis and review process. People tend to relate better to charts to identify meaningful trends. Best practices dictate that the organizations analyze data at least annually against intended targets and look for trends. Based on these trends, the training team can take appropriate action as required. In an effort to relate employee progress to training without sharing inside information, some organizations visually indicate targets without using actual data. Some organizations color-code their charts, e.g., green for good, red for bad, and yellow for caution.

Using Course Evaluations and Employee Performance to Revise Training

Performance information must be formally reviewed and acted upon to improve or simplify training. Most training organizations incorporate a review of performance measurements into their planning process in order to provide feedback for adjusting future training plans and resources and for confirming or modifying performance plans or targets. Organizations also use performance information to perform benchmarking and comparative analysis with best-in-class organizations and to identify opportunities for training. The best organizations base rewards and recognition on results.

Training departments use performance information for continual improvement. A popular continual improvement model is the three-step approach: plan, do, evaluate. The *plan* is what is expected to happen for any selected action. The *do* is the execution of what was planned; often, this is in the form of a pilot test. The *evaluate* compares the results of what actually happened with the expected results. The results of the evaluation are fed back into the plan step for the next round. If the analysis holds true, then execution can be standardized. The process for taking action varies, but generally includes the following steps: Understand the results, establish and clarify priorities, generate recommendations, develop action plans, implement action plans, and monitor progress.

Continual improvement also means using data to determine gaps between goals and reality. Performance results can be used to determine gaps between specific training objectives and actual achievement. The root causes of these gaps are analyzed, and training is developed and implemented. The continual improvement process can also be used to address student criticism. If a training department focuses on measuring complaints, it can improve the training product. Performance data can also improve the training process, including trainee selection, training development and delivery, and training and student evaluation.

Training process improvement measures may also actually be used to adjust goals. In most cases, if performance goals are not met, corrective action is implemented. Conversely, if goals are exceeded, the bar is reset to establish stretch goals. One way of adjusting goals and the approach to their achievement is to combine resources and adjust the goals as part of the organization's strategic plan. Organizations must recognize and understand that variation occurs in many selected measures, and that there are both normal and special causes for such variations.

Specific metrics that are continually monitored are generally established as prescribed in Section 12.1. Prior to training, it's useful to measure the number of people who say they need training (this information is gathered during the needs assessment process) versus the number of people who sign up for it. After training has occurred, you can measure the number of people who attend the session, customer satisfaction (attendees), and student satisfaction at the end of training. It's also useful to measure the willingness of the students to try to use the skill or knowledge at the end of training to see if you've gotten them past the "fear factor" of new software.

It's also critically important to measure on-the-job behavior and performance changes continually over time. This includes individuals who report that they changed their behavior or used the skill or knowledge on the job after the training. Also included are individuals whose managers report that they changed their behavior. You must also survey trainees whose managers report that their actual job performance changed as a result of their training.

Some other measures include management knowledge and satisfaction with the training program and the number of referrals to the training program by those who have previously attended the training. Departmentally, it's potentially useful to monitor the additional number of people who were trained (cross-trained) by those who have previously attended the training. Finally the popularity of the program compared with other voluntary training programs is important for attendance.

CASE: ACME WIDGETS—EVALUATING THE TRAINING PROGRAM

Because the WCS and KIS implementations represent a significant monetary and labor commitment for AWI, Bob, the I/T training manager, and Mike, the I/T training team lead, decided to set up evaluations for the course, trainer, and student. The evaluation for the course and trainer is contained in Appendix G and on McGraw-Hill's website at www.books.mcgraw-hill.com/training/download. The forms can then be opened, edited, and printed using Microsoft Word or other word processing software. The formative evaluation consisted of a review of the course materials by Gary, the WCS software rollout team leader. (*Note:* For the purposes of this example, the HR personnel course is used.) The test for the HR personnel course is based on the objectives specified for the course:

- Set up a new employee in not more than 15 minutes with no more than two mistakes.
- E-mail the employee and the employee's manager to notify them of the new employee ID.
- Find the source of any problems.
- Solve the problems if possible without assistance.
- Find the problem in the manual if needed.
- Call the help desk if the problem is complex or systematic.

These objectives will be measured in the test. Because setting up a new employee is a critical function, Kathy, the training developer, recommended that a written test be given, as well as a task-based test, to complete the objectives.

The written portion of the test was formed by taking the material that relates to the objectives from the WCS manual. The discrete tasks from the manual were combined into a process, and then test questions were generated. Because the order of tasks is critical in an employee setup, list questions (i.e., numbering a list) were used, as well as multiple choice. Two sample test questions are as follows:

1. The configuration table that is modified for a new employee is:
   a. employee_rec_1
   b. employee_pay_1
   c. personnel_req_3
   d. none of the above

2. Number the following tasks in the order they must be completed.
   _____Initialize the employee record.
   _____Create a new employee number.
   _____Enter a SSN or tax ID.
   _____Transfer the automatic application from the application database.
   _____E-mail the manager.

These test questions and others were used to measure the degree to which students had picked up the information taught. Since the purpose of this class is to actually learn to do something, there were also task questions such as the following:

3. Please enter the employee information from record 2 on your employee list sheet and save the record. You will have 15 minutes to complete this task. The instructor will check the database and verify that all data have been entered correctly.

The task questions were measured using both manual and automated means. The testing software that accompanied WCS produced a report that provided a summary of the student's performance. A sample of the report is shown in Table 12-2.

TABLE 12-2

Name: Trudy Moen		**Department:** HR	
Course: Personnel basics		**Date:** April 22, 2000	
Test: 1		**Score:** 9 of 10, or 90%	
Test Item	**Student Answer/Time**	**Correct Answer/Time**	**Correct?**
1.	Tom Sned	Tom Sned	√
2.	5 minutes/SSN	10 minutes/SSN	X
3.	Address1	Address1	√
4.	A	A	√
5.	D	D	√
6.	F	F	√
7.	1	1	√
8.	3	3	√
9.	2	2	√
10.	5	5	√
Total			9

This report is an automated version of a scoresheet. Most computer-based training has some type of automated scoring, though it may often cost extra in addition to the CBT courseware.

The tests were administered at the end of each unit of the course. The course and trainer evaluations were administered confidentially by having the trainer(s) leave the room while the students completed the survey. A student was asked to collect the surveys and place them in an envelope. The envelope was sealed, so that the trainer(s) couldn't see the individual surveys until after the students left. The team compiled and graphed the surveys to determine which courses the students felt were working well and which needed improvement. The survey results for the HR classes are summarized in Table 12-3.

From the table, it is obvious there aren't any major problems with any of the courses. However, Kathy and Mike decided it would be useful to examine the courses where the trainer or course is rated a "5." While a rating of 5 is certainly not bad, it does indicate room for improvement.

To develop an assessment of the impact of the training on the employee's performance, Mike and Kathy realized that they needed to expand their view of the evaluations. They met with Shawn and Dave, the trainers, Richard, the vice president of human resources, and Trudy, the human resources training specialist, to develop work performance plans and reviews that were specific to the training material delivered. To do that, they developed an on-line KIS form for instructors and managers to complete as employees returned from training and began their new jobs. A sample is shown in Table 12-4.

TABLE 12-3

Item	Course	Course Average (1=Bad, 7=Good)	Trainer Average (1=Bad, 7=Good)
1.	HR administration	4	5
2.	Personnel basics	6	6
3.	Payroll basics	5	7
4.	Benefits basics	5	5

TABLE 12-4

Employee: Trudy Moen   **Department:** HR
Job/Position: HR Specialist   **Rating Date:** 3/19/2000
Class(es): Personnel Basics   **Class Date(s):** 1/5/2000

Item	Course	Objective	Class Performance (1=Bad, 7=Good)	OTJ Performance (1=Bad, 7=Good)
1.	Personnel basics	Set up new employee in less than 15 min. with less than two mistakes	6	6
2.	Personnel basics	E-mail the employee and manager with the employee ID	5	5
3.	Personnel basics	Find the source of any problems	5	7
4.	Personnel basics	Solve the problems if possible without assistance	4	7
5.	Personnel basics	Find the problem in the manual if needed	6	6
6.	Personnel basics	Call the help desk if the problem is complex or systematic	7	7

The form in Table 12-4 was specifically designed to compare the performance of the employee in class with the employee's performance on the job posttraining. The class date and training date allow the training team and the employee's supervisor to see how the employee's skills grow or fade as the training is left further behind. While the rating was at a high level, Mike talked with the various functional managers, and they agreed that the objectives were specific enough to compensate for the rating scale being more general. *Note:* This form is available for use in its entirety in Appendix G or on McGraw-Hill's website at www.books.mcgraw-hill.com/training/download. The forms can then be opened, edited, and printed using Microsoft Word or other word processing software.

To complete the loop and incorporate feedback from the classes (and test scores), the training team developed two additional forms. The first (Table 12-5) schedule reviews each course and ensures that scheduled reviews are completed each quarter. This is very important, because if feedback gathered isn't used, the courses become obsolete, and trainees aren't willing to attend.

Notice in the table that all the reviews are scheduled in April. After each quarter of teaching (in this case, January–March), the course ratings and test scores are reviewed to check the quality of the course. The next review date would be July, then October, then January, etc., on a rolling cycle. *Note:* This form is available for use in its entirety in Appendix G or on McGraw-Hill's website at www.books.mcgraw-hill.com/training/download. The forms can then be opened, edited, and printed using Microsoft Word or other word processing software.

The form used to perform the review is shown in Figure 12-5. For each of the evaluation types (course, trainer, and test) there are sections to capture the score and modifications made. This log is critical, because if the instructional changes aren't tracked, there can be no measurable improvement. Even if improvements are made that cause better test scores, there's no way to know what caused the improvement if the course changes aren't correlated with the score changes.

The form in Figure 12-5 is important because it captures the trend in the test scores and evaluations. *Note:* This form is available for use in its entirety in Appendix G or on McGraw-Hill's website at www.books.mcgraw-hill.com/training/download. The forms can then be opened, edited, and printed using Microsoft Word or other word processing software. The information in this form can also be graphed if needed to check trends over time. Monitoring and graphing evaluation and test scores can show how modifications affect perceptions of the course and trainer. For example, if the course was lengthened by 1 hour and the test scores improved, this might indicate that the additional material

TABLE 12-5

Item	Class	Development Complete Date	Last Taught Date	Scheduled Review Date	Review Team Members
1.	HR admin	1/3/2000	3/15/2000	4/15/2000	Mike, Kathy, Gary
2.	Personnel basics	1/3/2000	02/26/2000	4/10/2000	Trudy, Kathy, Shawn
3.	Payroll basics	1/3/2000	3/15/2000	4/15/2000	Trudy, Kathy, Shawn
4.	Benefits basics	1/3/2000	3/15/2000	4/15/2000	Trudy, Kathy, Dave

FIGURE 12-5

Class: Personnel Basics   **Last Review Date:** N/A (First Quarter)
Course Evaluation
  Average: 5.2
Trainer Evaluation
  Average: 6.1
Test Average: 82%

Course Modified By: Kathy
Course Modifications:

1. Changed CBT system to increase complexity of employee record.
2. Improved backgrounds of entry screens by changing color to blue.

Trainer: Dave
Trainer Improvement Instruction:

Dave viewed a video of his instruction to help him slow down his speech.

Test Modified By:
Test Modifications:
Corrected typo on item 20, had two choice "A"s.

improved the test score. On the other hand, if the trainer was changed in a particular course and the test scores improved, but no actual changes were made to the material, that might indicate that the original trainer was performing subpar.

Coming Up in Chapter 13

There are some I/T-specific training issues to consider when creating a training program. Technology changes so fast that tailoring the training program for technical staff often means creating training that can be modified quickly to meet new demands. It's also important to teach I/T staff to be trainers and coaches and to provide specific training for the help desk. If continual improvement is the goal, the Software Engineering Institute's Personal Software Process Program is useful.

REFERENCES

Alliger, G. M., & Janak, E. A. (1989). Kirkpatrick's levels of training criteria: Thirty years later. *Personnel Psychology 42,* 331–342.

Alreck, P., & Settle, R. (1995). *The survey research handbook.* Chicago, Irwin.

Basarab, D., & Root, D. (1992). *Training evaluation process: A practical approach to evaluating corporate training programs.* Chicago: Kluwer Publishing.

Eble, K. E. (1976). *The craft of teaching.* San Francisco: Jossey-Bass.

Kane, J. S. (1976). The evaluation of organizational training programs. *Journal of European Training, 5*(6), 289–338.

Kelley, A. I., Orgel, K. F., & Baier, D. M. (1984). Evaluation: The bottom line is closer than you think. *Training & Development Journal 38,*(8), 32–37.

Kirkpatrick, D. (1998). *Another look at evaluating training programs.* Alexandria, VA: ASTD Publications.

Kirkpatrick, D. (1994). *Evaluating training programs: The four levels.* San Francisco: Berrett-Koehler.

Laird, Dugan. (1985). *Approaches to training and development* (2d ed.). Reading, MA: Addison-Wesley.

Leshin, C. B., Pollock, J., & Reigeluth, C. M. (1992). *Instructional design strategies and tactics.* Englewood Cliffs, NJ: Educational Technology Publications.

Merwin, S. (1992). *Evaluation: 10 significant ways to measure and improve training impact.* Minneapolis, MN: Lakewood Publishing.

Phillips, J. (1991). *Handbook of training evaluation and measurement methods,* (2d ed.) Houston, TX: Gulf Publishing Company.

Rae, L. (1993). *Evaluating trainer effectiveness.* Chicago: Irwin.

Senge L. R. (1990). *The fifth discipline: The art & practice of the learning organization.* New York: Currency Doubleday.

Swanson, R., & Gradous, D. (1995). *Forecasting the financial benefit of human resource development.* San Francisco, Jossey-Bass.

Training the I/T Staff

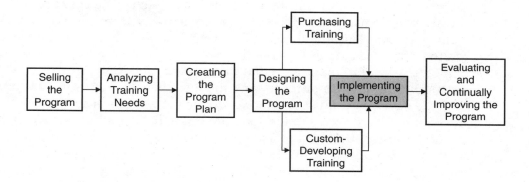

In This Chapter

OVERVIEW

The I/T staff are really the backbone of any software rollout. They are ultimately responsible for knowing all the parts and tasks needed to complete the rollout project, including the training. The goal of training the I/T staff is to help them learn to use the system with confidence and to adjust to the technological change without fear. They must also be able to grow in their jobs with the comfort of skills well learned. Ultimately, the training department should help the organization improve productivity and profits through quality I/T training and system documentation. The pace of change is extremely rapid in I/T and sometimes makes developing training for I/T like shooting at a moving target.

It's important to use plain language to describe in terms suitable for all staff how to operate and get the information they need from the new software. Even the I/T staff can be overwhelmed with new acronyms (aka TLAs, or three-letter acronyms). Using plain language, common sense, and humor, the training department should work with SMEs to teach the staff how to get the most from their use of their system. The training department should ensure that the I/T staff come away from training sessions calm and confident that they are in control and that they have the tools to do their daily tasks and to serve the users.

It's helpful to make sure that the I/T staff obtain the software before attending training. In order to gain the most benefit from software training, the developers must have access to the software in their daily work. If they do not have access to the software immediately after (and preferably before) training, they will quickly lose the ability to apply their new skills to the job. Studies show that exploring the material before attending a class can help reinforce learning and build better job skills. Preclass learning can make the developers more familiar with the material and eliminate the confusion that occurs in a classroom.

The developers should be encouraged to get a feeling for the way the software works. They should look at the menu or command structure, the basic features of the product, etc. Software manufacturers often provide demonstrations or tutorials that may be very helpful. You could also get someone who knows the software to show the developers a few samples of what the software can do prior to training. The developers should also have a feeling for the basic vocabulary or main ideas. For example, SAP has its own vocabulary and acronyms, including LIS (logistics information system) and ABAP (SAP's proprietary programming language). By knowing the vocabulary, significant time can be saved by allowing instructors to concentrate on the technical details.

The developers should learn exactly how they will use the training on the job. If the training team knows the specific ways that training will be applied to the jobs, the training will be far more helpful. The trainers and developers can seek input from supervisors about what will be expected of the developers after training and with the new knowledge. The developers should think of specific problems they may encounter or questions they have, so the training can be applied to their needs.

To get the most job benefit out of their new skills, the developers will need time to practice applying them. This should occur at least a day or two per week, soon after training. During this time, the developers can continue to explore the software and practice what will be most beneficial to their jobs. I recommend that before the developers attend training, they schedule practice time after the training event(s). Posttraining practice can also be done in teams. Test or development environments should be set up for the developers to use as practice areas. Timing the training is also important, as has been mentioned throughout this book. Try to schedule developer training about 1 to 3 weeks before it will be needed.

13.1   I/T-SPECIFIC TRAINING ISSUES

While the training issues mentioned so far in this book apply to all areas of an organization, a few of the issues involved in a software rollout are specific to I/T. The two most notable ones are the large number of pieces that I/T staff are responsible for and the rapid pace of change which includes updates to the software that must be installed. The I/T staff must build the I/T infrastructure, and develop and manage electronic data interchange with other organizations using the new software. They will also need to plan and integrate multivendor open systems technologies with the software being rolled out. Additionally, they will need to work with all the users and other technical people, and so it becomes clear that there is certainly a need to make I/T staff as effective as possible on the new system.

Setting Up I/T for Training

It's important to select and acquire infrastructure software to facilitate technical training early, since I/T staff will be leaders on the rollout. Training departments should also make an appropriate suite of training options available to I/T managers and technical support staff. Within the rollout project, the organization should establish a centrally provided staff that focus on technical training issues and provide leadership on software rollout training issues. This staff can be administered from the training department or I/T.

Developers and project managers must both acquire more expertise in how to manage the new technology and the impact of the associated change. Top management must be involved in and educated on key rollout issues. When a rollout starts, there are usually too many desktop computers assigned to an individual tech support person. As the organization moves into more high-end applications and newer equipment, the demand for technical support will increase.

The training department should provide a single point of contact to coordinate I/T training concerns. Ongoing professional training needs to be provided to all I/T personnel. The computer industry is moving at a fast pace, and technical and programming personnel must be given the opportunity and initiative to keep pace with these changes; otherwise there will be insufficient support for the rollout. Certification in key skill areas should be supported, particularly in the software being rolled out. The organization should also encourage professional certification or advanced training or education.

Organizations must also examine salaries paid to I/T staff and whether the organization offers sufficient compensation to attract and retain staff. ERP software expertise, in particular, is valued highly, and it's easy to lose skilled workers. There must be periodic skills assessment of specific I/T staff and a comparison of those assessments with the expected need for specific types of skills. This will drive both recruiting and training plans.

Dealing with I/T Staff Difficulties

I/T staff seem to attach very little importance to training, and trainers often feel stumped because they need to move ahead with design. However, trainers can offer to help by analyzing business processes, providing insight into instructional design issues. Trainers should also make it clear that training is a key component for successfully introducing new software, and have training placed on the agenda of regular work planning meetings. Integrate training into the project work plan.

It's also important to use a system such as needs analysis, design, development, validations, evaluation, and implementation. The I/T staff understand a systematic approach to working. Explain the process to them and look for ways to integrate it with the software development process. Move forward from phase to phase as planned. Explain the instructional design process to everyone who will listen.

Capture and explain roles, relationships, and high-level layout issues in a clearly written document. Consult with stakeholders on the format of training materials, prepare an explanatory document, finalize the guidelines, and stick to them. Remember management is responsible for training, and so keep management engaged throughout the process. For example, when writing a training development update, include other material written from a management perspective.

Identify reasons for resistance and deal with them in the training. In the training materials, explain very clearly the advantages of software functionality and how it will benefit the I/T staff. At the beginning of a course have participants identify their concerns; then you can address them throughout the course. Teach people how to use the software to do their job. Explain all the software bells and whistles. Use flowcharts to explain how the new software fits into the business process. Also, learn to use the new software. The I/T staff respect trainers who know what they're teaching. When teaching the software, identify issues a new learner will face and address them in instructional materials.

Keeping Current

Staying up to date on software releases is very difficult. Software vendors constantly send updates, which may require small or enormous amounts of time to implement. When a technical training program is created, it will be obsolete almost immediately after the rollout. It's not that training departments won't have done their job; it's just that the technology is constantly changing.

There are several approaches to keeping developers and managers current on new technology. An annual "boot camp" can be held for each new release to assure a minimum level of familiarity with the technology. All staff will be expected to have this basic knowledge. The technology staff can set up an "expert support crew" to provide basic training and help for all developers. This crew may consist of various I/T staff who become the "first line" of experts.

Based on the results of the needs assessment survey, the technology staff can recruit specific experts in each area (DBAs, hardware, etc.) for intensive training. In-house workshops, project groups, and informal meetings will provide the opportunity for developers to develop and share ideas on integrating the new technology and releases into the organization. The trained experts or core team will then recruit the next level of trainees. (An annual update to the TNA can assist them.) Their training will consist of more intensive in-class support with a focus on integrating the new technology into their daily work and work teams.

The organization should also provide developers with the opportunity to develop advanced skills in one or two areas of their choice. This will make them the "resident expert" of that technology or aspect of technology in their area and a source of information for the rest of the staff. On an ongoing basis, new releases should be communicated via informal meetings, bulletin boards and/or a website, e-mail, and demonstration-type activities. In addition, developers should have the option of applying for advanced training and new positions as they progress in their knowledge. The organization should encourage attendance at conferences and other public and private forums to facilitate education.

13.2   TAILORING THE TRAINING PROGRAM FOR TECHNICAL STAFF

Training departments may need to get I/T to assist in tailoring a training program that will address the separate or joint needs of the technical staff and the organization as a whole. This effort should improve those individual or group skills required to foster technical proficiency, cooperativeness, and productive relationships on a continuing basis. Hands-on workshops help assist the parties in better understanding the dynamics of interpersonal relationships and applying technical skills for the project and ongoing maintenance.

Both vendors and consultants can help organizations with convenient access to a full range of cost-effective, on-site training programs and services. Training departments may need to work with software vendors and consultants to develop a customized training package specifically for your organization. The I/T staff must be involved in choosing the content, time, and format to meet your I/T organization's special needs.

It's important to concentrate on developing the specific technical competencies for the I/T staff. Technical competencies may require a limited transfer of knowledge, a smaller number of transferable skills, and yet a higher level of complexity when targeting the learning at the specific area of I/T (e.g., DBAs, system programmers, etc.). Since I/T staff generally see their role as existing within a specific skill set, it's important to provide the technicians with the big picture, but keep them interested enough to learn their own required skills well.

Upon completing the training and entering the new or changed job, the trainees need to draw heavily on their independent capability. While the trainees might be expected to display at least technical competence in relation to problems that are likely to be familiar, the context of the problems faced is temporarily unfamiliar. To ensure that the trainees can solve the problems, they must receive the same level of support and guidance received during similar simulated problems previously faced within a learning context. Thus, it's critical to develop technical SMEs to be available for help.

Adding Technical Detail to the Training

To add technical detail to the training materials for I/T staff, the steps followed are similar to those described in Chapter 8, Section 8.1. First, the technical knowledge requirements must be analyzed. Next, the specific objectives and content required to meet the objectives are identified. The course details and syllabus are created, and the course is delivered. The "gotcha" here is that many pieces are involved in system implementation, and the lines between those pieces are rarely black and white. It's important to create some kind of "overall architecture diagram" to help I/T staff understand how the pieces fit together, and their specific role on the project.

The purpose of creating an architecture diagram is to develop a baseline view of the organization's businesses and systems as they currently exist, and to gather information about future directions. The overall goal of the architecting effort is to establish an improved architecture that will meet today's needs and be flexible enough to handle future requirements. This allows the organization's I/T staff to learn their functions more effectively and efficiently, and improve customer-related functions such that I/T provides the organization with a significant competitive advantage in its target markets.

Benefits from an architecture diagram include an agreement on training content, uniform application development, better training materials, and standard technologies. A time savings of 25 to 50 percent can be achieved in the needs analysis and design phases since the deliverables can be developed and maintained over time, as the architecture evolves with the organization. For more information see the Zachman Information System Architecture Framework at www.zifa.com.

Because the smooth operation of the software is critical to the organization, it's important to determine the priority of the material to be presented. Most software rollout training has the potential to become information overload for the trainee. When setting up the training, try to include enough material to fill out the available time and to have some extra material in reserve. Try to be flexible, too, in case there are any unforeseen developments. Prioritize the content of the training activity in terms of the subjects, topics, and issues that must, should, and could be covered. Things that must be covered will usually constitute the main learning points, and it's essential to cover these if objectives are to be met.

Technical training courses include all classroom, laboratory, computer-based training, and individualized instruction activities that are designed to provide a structured and formal learning environment for technical training. Technical training courses must support the competencies documented in the technical base qualification standards created by the organization and needed for the software. The architecture diagram will provide the training team with the information needed to drill down through the software to find the required details.

For example, if the user setup function of a groupware package is to be covered in the training, there's more to the course than just the procedure. The technician must be able to troubleshoot any problems that occur. That means being able to look beyond the software process and menu options to the underlying operating system, and possibly even the hardware. It may be that the users couldn't be set up because they were short of disk space. Figure 13-1 presents the many layers that are present in the average computer architecture. As is obvious from looking at the figure, there are lots of pieces to troubleshoot, even for a simple problem! It's important to incorporate all the necessary pieces in the training.

The best way to obtain the necessary information is to work with technical SMEs from either your organization or the vendor. It may be possible to construct a matrix that would present the possible hardware and software problems for each task. For example, during user setup for groupware, the matrix might look like Table 13-1. This matrix is available for use in Appendix G and on McGraw-Hill's website at www.books.mcgraw-hill.com/training/download. The forms can then be opened, edited, and printed using Microsoft Word or other word processing software. Each trainer will want to modify this matrix to meet his or her needs.

FIGURE 13-1

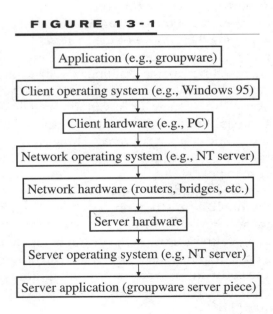

TABLE 13-1

Item	Task	Hardware Variables	Software Variables
1.	User setup	Disk space, network traffic	Valid user license
2.	E-mail setup	Network traffic, server error	User exists on server
3.	Server bounce	Disk space	Operating system status

Creating Train-the-Trainer Courses

Strengthening the training capabilities of technical staff is often cited as a primary goal of organization management. Training is now widely recognized as the fundamental link between old conventions and the adoption of new approaches. It is generally recognized that the future must hold more training for technical staff, for both cost and relevance reasons. Often, however, those who are assigned the task of developing training programs have not had the formal training or experience needed to be effective trainers. As mentioned throughout this book, there are key characteristics of trainers that cannot be ignored if trainers are to be effective, regardless of their background.

It's important to provide trainers-to-be with practical training techniques for those individuals whose primary job responsibility is the development of people. Instructional materials should enhance the training skills of novice and seasoned trainers alike, by providing proven instructional design and presentation methodologies. Train-the-trainer courses for technicians should be designed to provide actual processes and tools to increase training effectiveness, bring training issues into focus, and provide concrete steps for immediate implementation of training technologies.

Technical trainers may have lots of expertise, but it's also important to design training information for maximum impact. Technical trainers must learn how to construct training for maximum effect, building interest and enthusiasm that carries their message from beginning to end. They must present techniques that transfer information from trainer to trainee in an interesting, creative manner, using books, stories, transitions, and other proven methods.

At a high level, technical staff must at least learn about adult learning techniques, the process of learning, and the way it should be approached. They must also learn about beliefs and values, and what is important to them about training and why they do it. Technical staff must certainly learn the basics and the levels of training needs analysis and the essential elements of designing training for maximum results. They will eventually also need to know about developing a training style to suit them. It will probably be easy to help them understand how to make training interactive to promote learning, particularly if it involves CBT. Finally, they must learn the basics of the four types of evaluation and how to evaluate training.

13.3 TEACHING I/T STAFF TO BE TRAINERS AND COACHES

In a generic sense, teaching an I/T person to become a trainer requires the same skills as needed to teach any other person. However, it can be difficult for a technical person to make the transition from a subject matter expert to a trainer. It's important to raise the awareness of SMEs about the business benefits that training can provide. Convincing the SMEs that by training others, they will be able to impact their organizations is critical, and will be the basis of discussion with the technicians to convince them to help the training effort. A way to achieve that is to present real-life examples, giving them concrete cases of the use of training in the main business areas, and to show them how the main business activities will become more effective, and ultimately make their lives easier because they'll have less support issues. Skills that should be emphasized include:

- Identifying the learning needs of individuals and groups
- Planning to meet the learning needs of individuals and groups
- Delivering training to individuals and groups
- Reviewing and supporting progress toward learning objectives
- Assessing competence
- Evaluating program effectiveness
- Identifying further learning needs

While these skills are certainly teachable, it's critical to begin teaching those skills early in the project, so SMEs are capable and ready to go when needed. For more information, see Chapter 6.

I/T staff must possess or learn all the skills required for in-house and contract trainers (see Chapter 9). They must also possess excellent interpersonal and leadership skills, because users will look to them to lead the way using the new software when it's rolled out. I/T staff must also know how to deal with upset customers, and have good overall management skills, because they are going to be very busy supporting users when the rollout is complete. Some of the general skill areas include:

- *Organizing and planning.* Can the employees establish goals and procedures, set priorities, and schedule activities to keep their workload flowing smoothly?
- *Decisiveness.* Do the employees take the initiative, give opinions effectively, make timely decisions, defend those decisions, and take appropriate risks to achieve results?
- *Interpersonal relations.* Trainers meet a wide variety of people in different positions in an average workday. Can the new trainer interact with them, develop rapport, elicit their ideas, and present feedback effectively?
- *Flexibility.* Nothing stays the same in I/T, and none of us adapts to change at the same pace or in the same way. Can the staff generate new perspectives and options, reorder priorities, revise their goals, and take adaptive action?
- *Presentation skills.* Can the members of the I/T staff speak effectively to present a well-structured message? Do they use their voices and appropriate nonverbal cues to achieve audience rapport?
- *Written communication.* Is their writing effective? Does it win the reader's attention? Does it have a clear focus with the necessary details?

These are just some of the generic skills needed. The transition from "techie" to trainer can be difficult, but the right training and incentives can provide I/T staff with an entirely new set of very useful skills.

Interpersonal skills are fundamental to training in today's changing workplace. By providing I/T staff with the understanding of their own motivation and perspectives and that of the people around them, they can learn how to build productive and cooperative relationships within a training environment. It's important to teach I/T staff persuasive skills that enhance the interpersonal abilities of supervisors, managers, and development staff by engaging them in a variety of realistic scenarios that test and develop their awareness and competency in interacting with people of different styles.

Effective leadership in training both other I/T staff and business users is the key to increased productivity, high levels of worker morale, and continuing employee development. Training for I/T staff must include helping them understand how the program helps construction managers and supervisors meet their responsibilities as leaders. A good I/T training program should not only provide technical training, but create an understanding of primary and secondary leadership styles and provide skills to assess employees in terms of competency and job commitment.

More and more, I/T staff see themselves in the role of service providers, serving others either outside the organization or within. Regardless of where their customers are, the delivery of services and information depends on the ability to respond to needs or expectations. When these are not met, the service providers must be able to deal effectively with the customer's reaction and their own. I/T staff must be provided with interpersonal and self-management skills to help face problem situations with customers. A customer service orientation is very important when software is rolled out to help comfort users in their new environment.

I/T staff must be taught that when the people receiving the training get off track, the staff must avoid closing down too quickly on a solution—strive to dig deeper into how the other person thinks by probing with further open questions. Also, technical people should be taught to acknowledge any insights gained and good points made, and to ask what the participants will do differently the next time a problem is encountered. Above all, it's important to remember to strive to maintain and enhance the participants' self-esteem, but to keep working until they understand what to do differently the next time a problem or situation is encountered. A good coach:

- Encourages others to think for themselves
- Teaches them to fish (which feeds them for a lifetime), rather than feeding them fish, which only feeds them for a day
- Does not operate with the technical expert hat on
- Asks questions that lead others to the solution, rather than simply telling them the answer
- Helps people solve their own problems, rather than doing it for them
- The toughest challenge of all—resists offering the answers

Technical people can be sent to training or coaching classes to learn these skills. Almost certainly, classes are offered by local universities and consulting companies, though universities are likely to be much less expensive than the consulting companies.

13.4 CERTIFICATIONS FOR APPLICATIONS

In Chapter 4, I discussed creating internal certification programs. Internal programs are usually developed along the lines of programs offered by companies such as Microsoft, Novell, SAP, Oracle, Lotus, and others. External certification is offered by the manufacturer of the product. When manufacturers provide for certification, they are telling you that if you hire persons who have demonstrated knowledge of the product by passing a certification test, you are hiring persons who the manufacturer believes can properly use the product. Certification programs are offered by many software companies, including Microsoft, Lotus, SAP, Oracle, and Peoplesoft.

Organizations must also consider that a certified person had the discipline to invest the time, effort, and money to become certified. Those are important traits to look for in an employee. Certification testing can be used as an inexpensive screening tool. Suppose you're looking for someone proficient in Microsoft Word and Excel. How do you know just how much the candidate really knows about these products? Ask for an MS Office certificate. Training and certification can also be used as an award and incentive. Most employees respond very well to incentive programs based on increasing their own skill set. This usually turns out to be a win-win for the employee and the organization.

Individual technicians gain valuable benefits from becoming certified, including recognized proof of professional achievement. Certification validates that the developer or manager has reached a level of competence commonly accepted and valued by the industry and the manufacturer. Also, many employers give preference in hiring certified applicants. Some employers may require certification as a condition of employment. They view certification as proof that a new hire knows the procedures and technologies required to be a successful developer. Certification can be a plus when an employer awards job advancements and promotions.

Microsoft Office

Microsoft Office is probably the most widely used software package in the world. It's a comprehensive office "suite" that provides tools for word processing, spreadsheets, databases, and presentations. As explained in Chapter 15, the basic components are:

- Word 97/2000
- Excel
- PowerPoint
- Access

The Microsoft Office User Specialist program includes both proficient and expert levels for each of these tools. The performance competencies for each of these levels reflect a difference in the ability of the trainee to use the product effectively at various levels. As organizations standardize on desktop products, there continues to be a wide range of how the application is used in different jobs or offices. The certification levels are skill designations that are distinct for training, placement, and compensation. For more information, check out http://www.mous.net.

Microsoft Certified Professional Programs

If organizations want to ensure that their developers and administrators know the Microsoft technical product line, they may want those developers and administrators to get certified through the Microsoft Certified Professional (MCP) Program. It's certainly one of the best ways to show employers, clients, and colleagues that I/T staff have the knowledge and skills required. It proves that they're experts who have what it takes to meet the industry's demands. There are eight MCP certifications:

- Microsoft Certified Systems Engineer + Internet
- Microsoft Certified Systems Engineer
- Microsoft Certified Database Administrator
- Microsoft Certified Solution Developer
- Microsoft Certified Professional + Site Building
- Microsoft Certified Professional + Internet
- Microsoft Certified Professional
- Microsoft Certified Trainer

Most Microsoft certification exams can be applied toward more than one certification track. With planning, organizations can help their staff earn certifications as they work toward meeting both their career goals and the needs of the organization. Certified Technical Education Centers, or CTECs, can be found in most large and medium-sized cities, but the Microsoft website also lists locations for CTECs and testing sites for certification. One particularly helpful section of Microsoft's website that's somewhat hard to find is http://www.microsoft.com/train_cert/cert/?MSCOMTB=ICP_Certification. This area is a good starting point for deciding on the certification and for moving around the training sections in general.

Lotus Notes

Lotus Education offers Certified Lotus Specialist (CLS) certification. Certification as a CLS demonstrates specialized technical product knowledge at a base level for Lotus Domino and/or Notes. Certification ensures that the trainee demonstrates competence in supporting and developing Lotus products and applications. The CLS program requirement is successful completion on any one of the CLS exams, including the four core Lotus Notes certification examinations:

- Notes Application Development I
- Notes Application Development II
- Notes System Administration I
- Notes System Administration II

Visit Lotus Education at www.lotus.com for more information on the CLS certification, including benefits, preparation guides, and places where you can take the exams. Lotus Education's comprehensive certification program offers exam guides, training, and assessment tools.

SAP

SAP AG offers a number of certifications, ranging from the very technical to more business process-oriented certifications. Participants can obtain certification as SAP R/3 technical consultants for the Basis module in R/3. This certification applies to a specific R/3 release and to the combination of operating system and database tested. There are no eligibility requirements for certification. Certification candidates should, however, have the know-how that can be obtained in corresponding courses in the SAP training program and in preparatory courses given by partners for the operating system and database concerned. Partner certificates are not, however, required for admission to the certification test. The same type of training and certification is also available for SAP R/3 application consultants.

In addition, the TeamSAP Partner Academy is a rather unique partnership program between SAP and its training partners. It is an international institute of higher education in SAP applications and one of the most comprehensive training academies in the business software industry. The academy ensures consistent quality of SAP support worldwide. Each academy location offers the same core curriculum of high-level training courses, supplemented and expanded by courses tailored to specific local needs and business practices. For more information, check out http://sapnet.sap.com.

Oracle

The Oracle Certified Professional (OCP) Program certifies professionals who can deliver increased productivity and reduced operating costs using Oracle packaged solutions. It also helps managers identify proven performers who can fill key positions and enhance an organization's information management capabilities. The Oracle Certified Professional Program can provide developers with a distinct advantage in an intensely competitive marketplace.

The OCP Program is part of a continuing commitment to provide top-quality resources for technical professionals who want to become Oracle specialists in specific job roles. Delivered in conjunction with Sylvan Prometric, an industry leader in professional testing, Oracle certification tests are scenario-based. This is one of the most effective ways to assess hands-on competence and time-critical problem-solving skills.

The applications track includes the applications implementation process. The applications implementation team brings together a diverse group of I/T professionals and functional users. This certification will get them working effectively together, following a step-by-step implementation methodology. After building an understanding of Oracle application information flows, common modules, interfaces, and multiorganization considerations, applications implementation team members focus on data conversion issues as they learn how to integrate and extend application product families. For more information, check out Chapter 19 or www.oracle.com.

13.5   A NOTE ON THE SOFTWARE ENGINEERING INSTITUTE'S PERSONAL SOFTWARE PROCESS PROGRAM

The Software Engineering Institute (SEI) has an excellent resource for helping I/T staff get better at what they do. The SEI's Capability Maturity Model (CMM) has become the de facto standard for measuring software quality with an engineering-style discipline. What's not as well known is the SEI's Personal Software Process (PSP) Program. It's important to realize that each I/T staffer must contribute to the quality of the software developed. An organization can adopt the CMM to improve its software development process, but unless individual I/T staffers improve their own efforts, the CMM is essentially useless.

The PSP is a new SEI technology that brings engineering-style discipline to the practices of individual I/T staff, improving quality and reducing project times. PSP makes I/T staff aware of the way they do their work and their individual performance. They learn to set personal goals for improvement, measure and analyze their work, and adjust their approach to meet measurable objectives. In this way, I/T staff develop the ability to predict their performance and manage the quality of the work they produce. It is a strategy for professional self-development and enhanced productivity. For more information on the SEI PSP, see http://www.sei.cmu.edu/activities/psp/.

CASE: ACME WIDGETS—GETTING THE I/T STAFF UP AND RUNNING

To ensure that Acme Widget's I/T staff remained ahead of the curve during the training and rollout of the WCS and KIS systems, the training department worked with Gary, the WCS software rollout team leader, and Lauren, the KIS software rollout team leader, to gather the requirements for the I/T training. The rollout and training team worked together to establish a series of course needs that formed the essential I/T curriculum. This was published jointly, and all requirements for training were then referred to the training team to create the courses. The training team retained control of the training requirements, thereby ensuring quality, service, and cost-effectiveness.

The training team created an integrated set of modules united by a core curriculum, which provided a smooth, easy-to-use set of training materials to avoid some common software training issues. The training team decided to provide the resources and capabilities to support such activities as KIS and WCS certification. To do that, the training team created a number of strategic partnerships with WCS Software and Knowledge International, the maker of KIS. The team found local training partners and found some extra resources at a local university. The traditional client-supplier relationship model gave way to new and improved ways of working with the WCS and KIS vendors. With all such business partnerships, the benefits sought by the organization were to:

- Reduce the "organizational distance" between the partnering organizations.
- Enable the client partner to focus its scarce resources on core competencies, safe in the knowledge that the critical support functions were effectively and efficiently being managed and resourced, while training was occurring.
- Create a client-supplier relationship that best distributes the risks and benefits associated with the training activities and overall program.
- Provide trainers and trainees with the ideal environment in which to learn and grow.

These focus points provided a guide when the training team needed to select partners. By including many organizational units, the training team was able to support the I/T staff more completely during their training.

Focusing on the customer made the training team aware that the result that the I/T staff desired from their training was an improvement in the ability of staff to use the software tools for work-related tasks. These included preparing and delivering presentations, writing reports, and analyzing budgets. The training team began to understand that there would be a benefit from offering an integrated training solution for users and I/T staff, designed to ensure staff are equipped with the software and personal skills to make effective use of the software. The training team built the skills and competencies to enable WCS to deliver "task-based" training programs that focus on the business use of technology where appropriate.

It was very difficult in the beginning to make time for training programmers who were already working on the project, and still have time to complete the existing workload. One way management decided to overcome this obstacle was by allowing 3 hours per day on each employee's schedule for existing work and allocating the other 4 hours to training activities. Even with staff meetings and other time spent away from work, this still gave everyone time to spend on existing work and training. Each AWI I/T manager also developed a schedule where the additional resource hours were captured.

Because WCS and KIS were both running on similar hardware and software platforms, the training team was able work with the I/T staff to develop a comprehensive list of additional training, outside of the software itself. This enabled the I/T staff to receive training that met the depth and breadth needs of their problem-solving skills. Table 13-2, a modified version of Table 13-1, depicts the way that depth was added to the course/task matrix.

With the customized training, AWI's training staff were able implement the tools necessary to deliver training to the staff and began seeing a return on the investment in just a few days. Tailoring training and deliverables to meet the needs of a unique environment will usually provide you with a proven road map for success.

Because the I/T staff were going to be intimately involved and helping with the training, it was vital to teach the I/T staff to be trainers and coaches. The training

TABLE 13-2

Item	Task	Hardware Classes	Software Classes
1.	User setup	Network setup	Configuration management
2.	WCS backup	Managing tape devices	FastBack basics
3.	Server cleanup	Disk management	WCS operations

team helped the I/T staff to understand some of the basic principles of training. The training team helped the I/T staff ensure that every participant had a computer. The training team also taught the I/T SMEs that training doesn't end with the class—that it is ongoing and continual—so that the training team had to provide follow-up and technical support to class participants.

The I/T staff made sure they included curriculum integration and practical applications in every technology class. They also made sure that the participants trained on the type of machine the participants would be using on the job. The training team also provided extra tips, such as:

- Provide an environment that is physically comfortable, with breaks and snacks as appropriate, and with a balance of hands-on and lecture presentation.
- Determine a realistic time line for instruction. Adjust pacing as you go, so that participants don't become confused and frustrated.
- Encourage support groups for users so that they become self-sufficient posttraining.

The training team asked the SMEs to coteach with the trainers, providing some transition time for the SMEs to learn good training techniques. The training team included and built upon commonly recommended instructional strategies such as cooperative learning, so the I/T staff could learn training techniques, while the training team learned the software. The training team also had participants evaluate professional development sessions, the team adjusted the instruction accordingly. The I/T staff learned to plan for technical support, and to establish a clear procedure for identifying, reporting, and solving repair problems. This smoothed the installation and implementation of WCS and KIS.

Coming Up in Chapter 14

Suppose that you already have the software rolled out, and need to develop a training program. What steps are different? How do you measure the needs based on job performance versus the software needs analysis performed in Chapter 2? Once the software is rolled out and changes are made, everyone must be kept current, and so ongoing training is vital as well. These matters are addressed in Chapter 14.

REFERENCES

Carey, L., & Dick, W. (1996). *The systematic design of instruction* (4th ed.). New York: HarperCollins.

Gaines Robinson, Dana, & Robinson, James. (1989). *Training for impact.* San Francisco: Jossey-Bass.

Lotus products are ©1999 Lotus/IBM Corp. All rights reserved.

Masie, Elliot. (1999). The MASIE Center, 10 Railroad Place, Saratoga Springs, NY 12866. Website: info@masie.com http://www.masie.com. Phone: (518) 587-3522.

Microsoft products are ©1999 Microsoft Corp. All rights reserved.

Oracle products are ©1999 Oracle Corp. All rights reserved.

Peoplesoft products are ©1999 Peoplesoft Corp. All rights reserved.

PSP and Personal Software Process are service marks of Carnegie Mellon University.

Rothwell, W. J., & Cookson, P. S. (1997). *Beyond instruction: Comprehensive program planning for business and education.* San Francisco: Jossey-Bass.

SAP products are ©1999 SAP AG. All rights reserved. "SAP" is a registered trademark of SAP Aktiengesellschaft, Systems, Applications and Products in Data Processing. Neurottstrasse 16, 69190 Walldorf, Germany. The publisher gratefully acknowledges SAP's kind permission to use its trademark in this publication. SAP AG is not the publisher of this book and is not responsible for it under any aspect of press law.

The Software Engineering Institute. (1999). Pittsburgh, PA: Carnegie Mellon University. Website: www.sei.cmu.edu.

Wager, W. W., Gagne, R. M., & Briggs, L. J. (1992). *Principles of instructional design.* Fort Worth, TX: Harcourt, Brace, Jovanovich.

Training Issues After a Software Rollout

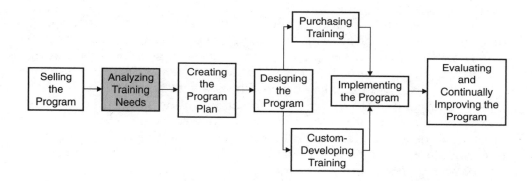

In This Chapter

14.1 Defining the key training areas

14.2 Finding opportunities for employee performance improvement

14.3 Tailoring a program for your installation

14.4 Developing advanced training programs

14.5 Keeping training current with new software releases

Case: Acme Widgets—Handling the postimplementation environment

OVERVIEW

As has been discussed throughout this book, training is not always at the top of the corporate priority list. Often training is developed casually as the software is rolled out. Once the rollout is complete, training needs are often discovered, particularly if no formal training development process was followed during the rollout. There are some steps that are different, and there's more of an emphasis on solving employee performance problems than in a normal, structured approach that would have (and should have!) paralleled the rollout. While the steps involved in developing training postimplementation aren't entirely different from a normal approach, there are certain issues that must be addressed.

Often, a limited training program is developed for sometimes mysterious reasons during software rollouts. The basic elements may be included during the rollout, with no eye on the future. Management sometimes only sees the basic reasons, which include teaching new skills to recent or current employees, retraining employees in skill areas they may have lost or not used in many years, or keeping employees abreast of changes in technology and design, etc.

As mentioned in Chapter 2, the first step in the training process is to determine the need for training. A thorough needs analysis should be performed on the organization, sorted by employee and position. In assessing the organization's needs, it is necessary to look at the organization as a whole. What are its strengths and weaknesses, and how does it compare with its competition? In determining the organization's overall needs, it is necessary to look at both short- and long-term needs. For example, if more hires are to occur, or I/T staff will be rolling off the project upon completion, now is the time to start developing training so that the new people will be able to hit the ground running.

One method already mentioned of assessing the general training needs and attitude of staff is to conduct interviews and questionnaires completed by management and staff. This will help determine more specifically what and where training is needed. A thorough analysis must be done on each need in the organization to determine not only the duties and responsibilities of the positions, but also the needed skills a person must have to successfully do the job. As mentioned in Chapter 2, this includes:

- The activities people in each position do in relation to information or other people
- The procedures and techniques they use
- The equipment, tools, etc., they need
- The products or services that result from their effort
- The skills, traits, and attributes required of the person in the position

Finally, a needs analysis must be done to determine what skills each person has or lacks. This will help determine what training they may need to better perform their job, what position they can move into next, and how they could grow in the future. The TNA should be done during the rollout, but not all organizations have the foresight to allow training teams to perform such detailed analysis.

Few organizations have a well-established training department. Most simply take advantage of isolated seminars, and often only certain people attend these programs. Training is frequently considered the responsibility of the individual, who is expected to plan, schedule, and finance his or her own program. As a result, most organizations are not adequately prepared to respond to the need for new services or to meet the challenge of an enormous software installation. The training team must help the organization understand that regular training will result in a more productive and profitable organization.

Sometimes, postimplementation training can be started by having a group of trusted employees establish an educational planning group or staff development task force composed of individuals representing all staff levels and chaired by a principal. This group should be charged with working with the training department, developing and managing the training program, researching training options and techniques, and preparing specific programs. It's obviously also important to establish a training budget as part of the annual budgeting process conducted by the organization.

Also, even if a training program is in existence, it's critical to review the performance of the training program. At least once a year, the entire program should be reviewed for its effectiveness, cost, and impact on morale and productivity. The budget must be evaluated for its short- and long-term cost-effectiveness. Software changes often, and software training materials must be kept current. The easiest way to do this is to work with the software vendor and get on the vendor's mailing or e-mail list for updates.

14.1   DEFINING THE KEY TRAINING AREAS

As mentioned in Chapter 2, there are two sides of a training need that must be examined to define the key training areas. The first is the software itself, and the second is the employee. It's important to create an integrated model for defining required knowledge, skills, and abilities to successfully perform job tasks. These definitions should be easily accessible and understood by users and are used by the trainers as the template for development. This model can be created by examining the software as it's installed and by using standard instructional design methods and techniques.

Defining the Feature/Function Set

The software structure and feature/function set are used by the training team as a model for defining training requirements. The feature/function set provides an integrated framework to define the knowledge, skills, and abilities required to perform any individual job task. The training team must also develop implementation plans for training and support to ensure responsiveness to requirements. As an integral component of this process, the training team works together with the users and I/T staff to identify and prioritize new or unmet training requirements. During this process, the appropriate trainers are made aware of these requirements so they can adjust their plans as needed.

Taking the correct steps and ensuring that each part of the training development process is completed will produce a high-quality training management system. The quality of the management system will be reflected by the quality of the training programs and resource materials. It will also be proven by increased productivity and reduced quality problems.

Management must endorse the training development process and provide funding for postimplementation training. This is probably a step that was skipped in the beginning. To overcome previous objections, the training manager should arrange a steering committee consisting of all affected parties, including workers and management. Under the training manager, the steering committee should establish a purpose, achievable goals, responsibility for tasks, a budget, and a timetable for completion.

The training manager must also establish a training team to meet the needs of the program. The team should set up and maintain a schedule of training courses. The training coordinator establishes a method for maintaining data and records relating to the training system The training manager, along with line managers, must assess the function of training and the effect on employee performance and product quality. This training review regularly indicates progress, results, and other information to the steering committee.

Due to limitations in budget and staffing resources, the training team must establish priorities for potential training topics so that resources can be directed to those areas where the need is greatest, that is, where the impact on operational proficiency with the software would be the greatest by not providing training. The team defines a training need for any skill or knowledge set as the gap between current skills or knowledge and the operational proficiency standard for that skill or knowledge set.

Assessing Software Training Needs

When software is already installed, a needs assessment typically addresses two types of need, felt needs and assessed needs. Felt needs are those that the workers identify for themselves. For example, workers will probably feel that they require more training in the use of the software if they didn't receive any prior to installation. Assessed needs are those that managers or assessors determine are required by workers. As indicated in Chapter 2, the assessment process should be performed in four basic steps:

1. Identify and assess the desired state.
2. Identify and assess the current state.
3. Assess the gap between the two states.
4. Identify objectives to bridge the gap.

However, when the software is already installed, and you identify and assess the desired state, you are laying out the basic components of the knowledge that the workers should have and not the ideal situation for operation. Since you already know that the ideal won't happen, the difference between the two states is the information that must be addressed through training. And this gap must be addressed realistically, which may be a quick fix to begin to at least get the workers on track.

When needs assessments and training are developed postimplementation, it's important to keep things simple so that they move quickly. The first step is to determine what the purpose of the needs assessment is and how you will apply the results. You will have to decide if the results will be used to create new training, determine content of a proposed program, modify existing training, or just serve as a reporting tool for a program justification. It's possible that the reason formal training was never created in the first place was because management didn't think it was necessary.

Once you know the purpose, establish the scope and methods to be used for assessment. Determine how many people to assess, how you can contact these people, and what are the most efficient methods for gathering the most accurate results. Then, determine whose needs are going to be assessed. Choose the methods for assessment. The methods chosen should be techniques that will provide the most reliable and valid results without taking excessive time. You may use different methods, including questionnaires, surveys, and interviews. You can use templates that have been developed for these purposes or develop your own instruments. You may want to consult with assessment experts for help as well.

As mentioned, it's useful to pilot assessment tools before you apply them. Use a small group of people to determine if the methods will gather information accurately and reliably. This step can help avoid a waste of time and energy. Once you have the information, classify, analyze, and interpret it. Find trends in the responses that can guide you in establishing objectives. If the responses are numerous enough in one area, certain topics or training deficiencies need to be addressed. From these results, you determine which deficiencies can be addressed through training. Prioritize the needs and determine what type of program is required to address those needs. Then, translate the needs into objectives.

The HR management team must assist the training team in the training planning process by handling HR issues, such as identifying personnel needs and defining other training needs based on requests or employee complaints. Often, employees who receive no training or the wrong training will ask HR for help, or HR becomes involved because of poor performance reviews. HR consults strategically with the training team and business units, but also is involved with working out the nuts and bolts of putting people where they need to be, with the necessary skills and training.

14.2   FINDING OPPORTUNITIES FOR EMPLOYEE PERFORMANCE IMPROVEMENT

When training programs are established before software is installed, it's difficult to find opportunities to measure employee performance, since there is no baseline because the employees have never used the software. If a training program is developed after implementation, it's important to examine employee performance to help set the objectives and to drive the needs analysis process, mentioned in Section 14.1. The objectives of an employee performance management system are to:

- Provide an accurate and objective method for evaluating employees.
- Improve work performance and encourage growth and development of employees.
- Support the accomplishment of organizational goals as stated for the rollout project.
- Provide documentation to support salary adjustments, promotions, etc.

Employees should be rated using standard levels of performance, and should be evaluated on designated performance characteristics to be rated either acceptable or unacceptable. Performance appraisal training should periodically be made available to employees. New employees, or those new to the rollout, should be briefed on the performance appraisal system during orientation.

Success Factors

The key to creating a successful performance-based employee performance management process lies in the organization's ability to generate "buy-in" at senior levels for a new way of looking at training. The organization should also use work performance evaluations to establish training goals. The training team helps the organization build support for this kind of change. The team must utilize organization development techniques to assure commitment, implementation, and follow-through. It's also important to incorporate the latest technologies to make the process easy to understand and use, and most importantly, accessible.

Involving the software users in the process will gain support for training they help create. The challenge is to change the common opinion that performance management systems are meaningless, waste time, and don't make a difference. The training team can show the parties approaches to performance measurement, as well as provide significant help for users struggling with software they're not sure how to use. The training team should use experts and consultants to help guide them through the best-practices choices, helping them customize the training program and the approach to creating the program.

As the training is designed, underlying assumptions about the meaning of tasks, the preferred approach to performing those tasks, and the priority of training for each task should be documented. The parties review the latest priorities and measurements, and use the performance management process as an opportunity to identify and clarify the objectives of the training program. The training team works with management to assure that a balance between business objectives and personal and team development is struck.

Coaching and skill- or task-based training are critical to support a successful performance management process, which feeds the training needs analysis. The training team provides training for supervisors and managers to evaluate the training needs of employees effectively. There are some performance issues helped by training, and others that training won't help. Managers and employees both must understand how to differentiate between the two. The training team, managers, and employees can use the forms in Chapter 12 to measure and improve the performance of employees through training.

To use performance improvement to drive training needs, there are some specific steps you can take that are similar to a standard needs analysis but focus more on people and their needs, and less on the software. First, define the current gaps and opportunities that exist. Some symptoms of training needs include:

- People complain of "information overload."
- Work quality is substandard for previously exemplary employees.
- People feel that information in training manuals, policies, or employee communications is confusing or not credible.
- There are few standards for "exemplary" performance and analyzing of the costs for not achieving exemplary performance for specific jobs.

It's important to get the support of at least three internal peers and managers. You'll also need other employees to add perspectives and endorsement. You need at least one unbiased and well-credentialed expert to echo your views, because internal sources are often seen as not being objective.

Be sure to thoroughly evaluate the return on investment of the program. It's likely that no concrete ROI could be shown for training preimplementation, and that's why it never happened. Create "grassroots" enthusiasm for a new way of training. Study outside sources and accurately reflect how you stand with respect to benchmark departments or professionals outside your own organization. Get the buy-in of at least one top executive, and let that executive help you develop and time your resource requests.

Prioritizing Training Needs

It's also useful to create some kind of survey and/or tracking form. This form should be a living document that captures the frequency and severity of help requests on various parts of the software. It's possible that certain parts of the software are simple enough to learn OTJ, whereas others are extremely difficult. The training department should work with the help desk, and create a form to help prioritize training development (see Table 14-1). This kind of form is available for use in Appendix G or on McGraw-Hill's website at www.books.mcgraw-hill.com/training/download. The forms can then be opened, edited, and printed using Microsoft Word or other word processing software.

TABLE 14-1

Item	Priority	Software Module	Software Feature/Function	Requests	Usage Difficulty
1.	1	Purchasing	Create P.O.	15	Very hard
2.	2	Inventory	Create new item	8	Somewhat hard
3.	2	Logistics	Release backorder	4	Somewhat hard

Use the priorities described in the form to work out the implications for human resources. Time targets must be set and costs estimated to cover the top priorities first. The approach must send people to one- or two-day "quick-hit" courses first, and evaluate the effectiveness. Once the pilot is complete, formal in-house training on the software begins.

If the organization has an "antiwhining" culture, where employees tend not to complain, a survey can be used to gather information on current training needs. The survey should determine which training topics receive top priority and which training delivery methods are needed. Also, the survey will help determine how often training must be conducted, and will give you an idea of expected training expenditures and whether training dollars will increase or decrease over time.

Training delivery methods vary widely, as mentioned in this book, but the majority of employees tend to desire the traditional teaching methods such as classroom programs conducted on-site and vendor seminars as the primary media for employee training. Distance learning methods such as video and web-based DL can also help. In a situation where the software is up and running, but the users aren't, the best time to train is now.

14.3 TAILORING A PROGRAM FOR YOUR INSTALLATION

It is highly likely that the software being rolled out had to be modified significantly to fit your installation. Thus, it's probable that training continued to evolve over the course of the rollout and couldn't be completed in time for go-live. In this case you have two options: (1) create and/or modify training yourself or (2) use a vendor. The major advantages of tailoring the program yourself are the lower cost and the increased likelihood that you'll get exactly what you want or need. The disadvantage is the need for human resources, because some organizations don't have the staff to create formal training programs.

Most vendors offer organizations convenient access to a full range of on-site training programs and services. They can also often deliver existing courses, seminars, and workshops or develop a customized training package specifically for your organization. Some vendors provide consultation, instructors, assessment, and client-centered customer service. You choose the content, the time, and the format to meet your company's special needs. The vendors can usually have a member of their professional staff come to meet with you, at your convenience, to explore the details of tailoring a training program to your needs.

Either way, customized training means that the training developer must tailor the curriculum to match your organization's requirements precisely. This is particularly important when the software is already installed but not being used to its fullest potential. This way you ensure that new staff are trained to the standards of your environment. For instance, trainees can learn required file naming procedures as well as other business and technology conventions. Customized training is almost always required for organizations that standardize on a particular ERP package, which often dictates practices and procedures.

Fitting the Pieces Together

To meet the needs of installed software systems, you must apply a broader view to understand the complexity of making the people and software system(s) fit together. We have to take into account the ways in which a system is being used, the changes in the hardware and software, and the degree to which a system provides means for adapting procedures to the current business. To develop the training requires an understanding of the new software and application of the software. In this situation the training team can't influence the human factors design. Thus, training development in this situation is more reactive.

The phenomenon of training development postrollout is not unusual. However, it indicates that training development, where the training team can influence the rollout, is only possible to a limited extent. Individual variances and preferences require that a certain degree of flexibility and adaptability be an inherent property of all training. However, with the software installed, concerns for security, integrity, reliability, and transparency will always triumph. The dilemma of stability versus adaptability poses several questions within the design and delivery of training, including:

- To what degree have the users been asked to adapt to specific situations?
- What specific qualifications are needed to operate a system?
- What are the technical prerequisites (for both the system and the training)?
- Where do we draw the line between setting up training formally and getting it done quickly?

The training team must tackle such questions from various angles and perspectives in order to obtain a balanced view of organizational settings in which the problem of customizing or tailoring training must be done postrollout. In addition to discussing specific practical approaches, the training team may want to consult with experts to discuss theoretical frameworks designed for this situation.

The effective use of common generic training for software like word processing, spreadsheets, database management, etc., requires that the users engage in de facto customization processes. This training is not supported by training specialists, and users miss features that are somewhat "hidden" but valuable. It's important for trainers to get involved early, and help assess users' strengths and weaknesses, which provide the foundation for customization strategies in which users play an active role. The process involves a great deal of collaboration in the context of actual work situations. These activities can be done using the techniques recommended for the participative development of training specified in this book.

Customization Issues

Most of the discussions about customization focus on enabling users to adapt tools to particular needs through explicit acts of reshaping. However, some software, like office suites, require end users to engage in explicit programminglike operations in order to modify the system. This means that users will need to learn the intricacies of the software's configuration features. Usage-based training means tailoring the training to the way a particular user or group of users operate the software. This implicit customization could be expressed in several ways—e.g., highlighting the most frequently used menu options or displaying interactional history excerpts relating to a particular software option throughout the training.

It's important for trainers to help users with little tips and memory tricks. This information might be useful in recalling what one did last time when invoking an infrequently used function, in finding others who had made similar attempts, or in locating someone who had offered assistance with this function. Identifying patterns of repetitive operations (and hence potential opportunities for creating shortcuts) or common breakdown situations in need of repair could also be integrated into the training.

Gathering usage information through unobtrusive recording of usage behavior raises concerns about its possible abuse. The most obvious is that it becomes the basis for evaluating user performance by supervisors. Information generated in this way belongs to the individual and the training developer concerned and should not be communicated without informed consent. If users do not trust that appropriate safeguards are in place, it is likely the effect would be just the opposite of that.

There are some major workplace politics involved in the postimplementation customization of training. If the training was never developed prior to the rollout, there are going to be some seriously disgruntled workers, who usually make bad students. Sometimes, users must make the software changes directly. However, while the development process may be quite different, the outcome is very similar in significant respects. In essence, job skills must be closely associated with and tailored to the worker.

14.4   DEVELOPING ADVANCED TRAINING PROGRAMS

The purpose of an advanced training program is to provide "power training" to both users and I/T staff seeking to become master users or software engineers. As defined by some vendors, master user-I/T staff members are those who have completed an advanced certification program designed to prepare them to be collaborative leaders and mentors. Therefore, the foundation and implementation of all advanced training activities are focused on the knowledge and skills needed to understand more than just the use of the software. The advanced trainee must accumulate enough knowledge to enable one to become a collaborative leader and mentor for meeting the needs of students, other staff, and managers.

Program Design Elements

As mentioned throughout this book, the universal elements of curriculum design are the objectives, the subject matter, the learning activities, and the evaluation methods. In particular, the evaluation methods appraise the degree and level of accomplishment of the stated objectives. In advanced training programs, evaluation is particularly important because the power users and I/T experts must know the products well enough to teach others. Objective evaluations must be created to truly measure learning for these advanced trainees. (See Chapter 12.)

Advanced curricula as frames ensure that the organization's mission, purpose, and staff competencies are provided in a logical scope, sequential, and measurable manner culminating into an identified product or outcome. This is important, because the advanced trainees will be viewed as leaders in their respective areas. Included in the framework is a core of courses and competencies, specialized emphasis (marketing, accounting, etc.), and electives (a chance to study and experience areas outside a specific field) that culminate in certification. This activity allows students to demonstrate performance of the noted competencies through an individualized and creative process.

Advancements in instructional technology (e.g., web-based DL) provide the opportunity to develop globally deployable affordable training that allows the student to be monitored, enables the training program to adapt to the performance of the individual, and makes for consistency in training materials. Training needs required to meet this goal include the development of advanced training interfaces and advances in distributed training technologies. It's critical to understand that advanced training does not have to include advanced instructional technologies. Basic CBT or classroom training can be used to teach advanced concepts. Of course, if the technology itself is highly evolved (e.g., rolling out an expert system), using advanced training methods enhances the learning experience.

Implementing Advanced Training

Advanced training courses focus on partnering with learners, rather than lecturing. It's important to establish common standards and develop a service and support infrastructure capable of responding more rapidly to learner needs when training is complete. Most advanced learners are going to be leaders who will need quick access to answers back on the job. Developing advanced training means enhancing the functionality of existing training, adding new training, and creating programs that help personnel drive higher levels of product quality, significantly reduce time to market, and improve customer satisfaction.

Advanced training programs are typically topic-specific, can be covered in an 8-hour day, and are designed to expose the user to techniques and processes for further development of core software skills. Advanced programs are only offered to persons who have completed an introductory training program or have verifiable previous experience. In advanced training, trainers typically do not review or go over materials in detail. The assumption is that most folks will have at least skimmed the materials before the course. Students use the booklets as a framework that allows trainers to present current examples and ideas while maintaining a structure to the course and identifying future references.

Advanced trainers must understand the implications of training and provide "how-to" knowledge of the software. Advanced courses are different from basics courses in that peers provide examples of their own uses and experiences with technology and tell how technology solves specific problems. It's important for both learners and trainers to provide demonstrations of successful techniques and provide teaching opportunities on a trial, short-term basis for power users who will be expected to teach others.

As mentioned in Chapter 4, a certificate program may be more relevant than even an advanced degree and it's less costly, faster to complete, and more focused. Certificate program courses are usually presented by practicing professionals and emphasize real-world skills you can immediately apply in the workplace. A certificate program presents concentrated specialized study that complements and expands the learner's existing knowledge and skills. As participants in one or more certificate programs, staff can meet others to create a support network that can be tapped when help is needed after training.

In addition to formal professional development, vendors and consultants can be called upon to lend assistance to the training program where there is relevant expertise. For example, if there are local experts with knowledge in the use of specific software, then those individuals can help training personnel increase their comfort level. It will also be necessary for the staff to be able to create basic program guides for advanced learners.

Training needs will differ based on the specific software module and/or feature/function. However, limited funding may hinder the ability of all to receive as rich a training program as may be desired. Prioritization is therefore necessary. Together, the team will need to make training decisions that best meet the objectives of the technology plan, the needs of the students, and the expectations of the organizations. As with any training program, feedback is both a critical component of evaluation and a tool for adjustment. The training programs put in place for the business and I/T staff should foster feedback to ensure continual improvement over time.

14.5   KEEPING TRAINING CURRENT WITH NEW SOFTWARE RELEASES

With the incredible pace of change in I/T, it's easy to fall behind the technological times with regard to both software and training. If the last upgrade to your training was more than a month ago, you probably have. Staying current is next to impossible, but it's important not to let technology pass you by or you'll be faced with a huge catch-up task down the road. It's almost always easier and less costly to make small changes frequently to training than to redo materials en masse at a later date. The challenge is to maintain training materials and balance the cost of continual improvements by constantly expanding the associated benefits.

Why Stay Current?

Training departments may be asked why they need to maintain a complete staff once the training is implemented. After all, if the training area is working properly and meeting your needs, why make the investment? The obvious reason is that the training must be kept in sync with the software release. However, there are benefits to be gained by taking advantage of newer training technologies, even for the same release of the software. If you're locked into older technology, you may be missing out on things that could be a benefit to your organization, such as CBT or web-based training.

As the utilization and integration of technology into the workplace continue to progress at a breakneck pace, the need for employees to stay current and be expert with their new tools becomes the differentiating factor by which some companies succeed and others fail. While increasing the budget for technology training is important, the company's investment is not realized unless it is accompanied by the maintenance of those training materials necessary to allow employees to take advantage of the capabilities of their new tools. Keeping training materials up to date allows companies to maximize their return on their training investments.

At some point the software's creator will abandon any software package in favor of the "next silver bullet." Continuing to support older software is a cost burden that most vendors don't want to shoulder. What this means to your business is that at some point you will be out there, all alone, with an outdated release of some ERP or other large software package. The media are flooded with commands to upgrade dutifully at regular intervals, but this creates a dilemma that confounds many business users when it comes to software. In this case training materials can literally save the organization.

It's critical for organizations to create a process to facilitate rapid response to new or changing training priorities within any fiscal year. When software changes unexpectedly, or the scope of a new release is larger than anticipated, training teams should identify requirements that cannot be met due to resource limitations or additions to training priorities, and raise the issues to senior management. The training team should communicate with software and training vendors, as well as the rollout teams, to discuss any revisions to requirements that arise during the year. It is the team's responsibility to identify any recommended adjustments to training materials for consideration by senior management. The team also notifies senior management if the workload for developing new training exceeds the capacity of the trainers to perform such development.

As releases and software evolve, the training department must establish an effective evaluation process to ensure that staff are reaping the intended benefits of training and that the training is as current as the software. Trainers should involve staff supervisors in assessing the impact of training on job performance and in providing feedback to the team. Training developers are responsible for producing an end-of-training critique to allow trainees and their supervisors to assess the impact of the training. Management is responsible for assessing whether the training had the desired effect on job performance. Management also coordinates with the staff to address training needs and to ensure that any remaining training deficiencies due to software changes are brought to the attention of the team.

An easy way to ensure that communication is ongoing among all organizational players is to designate a point person for each major software package in the organization. This person is then responsible for ensuring that all materials stay current. The point person is also responsible for obtaining or creating the resources needed to keep training up to date. A frequent complaint among many employees is that they do not have adequate or current training to do their jobs. One major cause has to do with the rapid growth of a business. While growth is good for most organizations, employees must be kept current on the organization's technology. This is the responsibility of the training team.

Keeping Documentation Current

The deliverable most likely to be remembered by trainees is the documentation they take with them, or the materials the training department keeps on hand for help. Good training documentation is absolutely critical to the ongoing success of the organization. Documentation should be task-based, concise, and driven by business processes, and it should provide management information as a by-product. Documentation must also be created and maintained efficiently. This requires structured and automated authoring environments for writers who understand how to write for specific audiences.

Documentation processes have remained largely unchanged in the past. They are expensive and inefficient and in many cases ineffective as well. Good documentation can cut training costs and deliver tremendous benefits. However, to achieve this, training management must actively drive change. The distinction between training content and delivery is often misunderstood. Training content should be created with the organization's standard software, and stored in standard paper and on-line formats. Training delivery, as discussed in Chapter 5, can take many forms.

Organizations make extremely inefficient and expensive use of documentation. All repetitive or complex material should be automated. Automation saves time, ensures consistent output, frees people to focus on content, and guarantees problem-free translation of documents into any on-line format. The problem with on-line material is that most organizational staff have no training at all in business writing for on-line delivery. Also, decision makers must understand that you cannot document everything. Unnecessarily large documentation sets are intimidating, difficult to navigate, and expensive to maintain. The goal should be to maintain a high-quality minimum.

With respect to I/T training, it is important to document all aspects of the system, both the technical specifications of the hardware and software components and the administrative uses of the full system in the normal course of agency business. Full technical documentation of system components, application software, and operating systems is essential to facilitate long-term access to records stored on electronic imaging media. This particular type of documentation is typically the responsibility of the I/T department, but training and technical writing staff may want to get involved to ensure the quality and applicability of the documentation.

Training documentation for systems software and application programs should indicate version numbers and implementation dates for all software upgrades. If application software was developed on a customized basis, flowcharts, source code, and other training documentation should be included. In cases where the developer or seller of the system retains ownership, organizations should require the seller to supply a copy of the system documentation and any relevant training material in case the vendor fails.

Application-specific operational procedures should also be documented. Scanning, data entry, and quality control procedures must be fully documented for each application. Written instructions should be prepared for users, and the instructions should indicate the details necessary to complete the work. Any problems encountered from the use of the system, along with the measures used to solve those problems, should be recorded as training material.

CASE: ACME WIDGETS—HANDLING THE POSTIMPLEMENTATION ENVIRONMENT

The Widget Control System and the Knowledge Information System were both heavily modified during development, and even somewhat after rollout. Bob, the I/T training manager, and Mike, the I/T training team lead, both knew that there would be some surprises in the postimplementation world. So they had Kathy, the training developer, and Jack, the technical writer, check the installation and go-live checklists for potential postimplementation training projects. What they found was a combination of some features that were unaccounted for in the training already developed, and a few new needs that weren't caught because of last-minute changes in the software's configuration.

To complete the reassessment, Kathy worked with Gary, the WCS software roll-out team leader, and Lauren, the KIS software rollout team leader, to determine the changes that were needed. Jack reviewed the technical documentation, and checked with the software vendors for upcoming releases. As with the original needs analysis process, HR assisted the training team with the replanning process, employee satisfaction surveys, and other HR issues, such as identifying needs.

The training team was determined to find more opportunities for employee performance improvement through enhanced training. The team members convinced Richard, the vice president of human resources, and Trudy, the human resources training specialist, to work with them and create a multiperspective feedback system that would be used as part of a review. It meant managers would evaluate an employee's strengths and weaknesses in terms of training opportunities using standard review forms. The process would focus on helping the individual develop, and the data would be clearly communicated to the individual and managers. The skill model was based on clear, specific behaviors and skills that can be improved, and the skills reviewed are relevant to job success and linked to organizational goals.

As the software implementation continued, Shawn and Dave, the trainers, got involved to customize the training as needed. Their prework activity began with surveys of the organization, the in-house training sponsor, and the workshop participants concerning course-related issues, including prior experiences with the subject matter. Participants were also asked to provide information on actual work problems and current work processes so the training team could provide specific help for problems. The results of these profiles helped the sponsor, Kathy, and Jack tailor the courses to the company's environment and gauge the participants' skill level against the objectives.

Many users needed to update their training after the rollout for updates. Once the implementation was complete and the software frozen, users wanted to see if they were using the software effectively. The advanced working sessions focused on how the various tools in WCS and KIS can be used. The power-user training taught many new concepts and skills for the first time, and reviewed some basics.

Several classes were developed for the experienced I/T staff as an in-depth exploration of the technical aspects of WCS and KIS. Training included systems administration, as well as integration with other systems. At the completion of the training the students had a solid understanding of the "tool set" and could use that understanding to problem-solve product development issues within their organization, as well as customize the system to meet the specific needs of AWI.

The training team knew it had to keep the documentation current as the software evolved over the next 3 to 6 months postimplementation. Jack took on the leadership role because he was knowledgeable about the training issues and was enthusiastic about its potential benefits to the organization. He was careful to solicit cooperation from workgroups within the rollout and business community and made sure he continued to communicate the project's successes to ensure ongoing support.

The End of Part One

This chapter concludes Part One of this book. But don't despair—Part Two provides some examples and specifics of key training points for some of the hottest applications. This includes MS Windows and Office, Lotus Notes, SAP, and Oracle Applications. So keep reading. There's more "good stuff" to come!

REFERENCES

Carey, L., & Dick, W. (1996). *The systematic design of instruction.* (4th ed.). New York: HarperCollins.

Diamond, R. (1991). *Designing and improving courses and curricula in higher education.* San Francisco: Jossey-Bass.

Fuller, J., Fuller, J., & Farrington, J. (1999). *From training to performance improvement.* San Diego, CA: Pfeiffer & Co.

Gaines Robinson, Dana, & Robinson, James. (1989). *Training for impact.* San Francisco: Jossey-Bass.

Kirkpatrick, Donald L. (1996). *Evaluating training programs: The four levels.* San Francisco: Berrett-Koehler.

Leshin, C. B., Pollock, J., & Reigeluth, C. M. (1992). *Instructional design strategies and tactics.* Englewood Cliffs, NJ: Educational Technology Publications.

Posner, G. J., & Rudnitsky, A. N. (1986). *Course design: A guide to curriculum development for teachers* (3d ed.). New York: Longman.

Rothwell, W. J., & Cookson, P. S. (1997). *Beyond instruction: Comprehensive program planning for business and education.* San Francisco: Jossey-Bass.

Wager, W. W., Gagne, R. M., & Briggs, L. J. (1992). *Principles of instructional design.* Fort Worth, TX: Harcourt, Brace, Jovanovich.

PART TWO

Application-Specific Training Issues

MS Office Training

In This Chapter

OVERVIEW

Microsoft Office is probably the best known office suite. In various configurations, MS Office may contain word processing (MS Word), spreadsheet (Excel), presentation graphics (PowerPoint), database (Access), publishing (Publisher/PhotoDraw), web publishing (FrontPage), and scheduling/calendaring/mail software (Outlook). The various combinations are based on needs (normal versus power user), price (!), organization size, and other software available. For example, if you are using Lotus Notes e-mail and scheduling, you would not need MS Outlook. This chapter presents information about creating and implementing training for an MS Office rollout.

15.1 KEY TRAINING POINTS

MS Office has become an extremely integrated package. In fact, the manual for Office is more a "how to use Office" than a reference guide on each product. Most training classes will be segmented by product, although there is certainly the opportunity to discuss other products while teaching a class. Each product is discussed independently, and there is a short concluding section on tying things together.

MS Word

The key training points for MS Word that will be of interest to most people are the general features, such as creating a document and adding special effects (bold, underline, etc.). At a minimum, training should include teaching students to:

- Understand the MS Word screen and know how to move through the screens.
- Know how to investigate new things using MS Word's Help functions.
- Know how to create, format, save, and print a document.
- Use spell checking, grammar checking, and the thesaurus.
- Be able to use MS Word's editing features and document styles.
- Know how to move text within a document or between documents.
- Understand and use tables and columns.
- Be able to create document headers and footers.
- Use special effects.
- Use document sharing and editing features.

These features are also common to other applications, and a basic introduction to these will assist the student in learning other MS Office products.

Excel

The value of Microsoft Excel lies in its ability to create and manipulate spreadsheets. Users often use Excel for budgets, pro formas, and financial tracking. The Excel document is called a worksheet, and a workbook can be made up of many worksheets. Data stored in the workbook can be easily used to create charts for illustrations in other documents. Information can be saved and imported into other programs such as Microsoft Word. Students at a minimum should learn to:

- Know the basic function of the Excel program and the various parts of the screen.
- Create new worksheets by entering text, values, and formulas.
- Format cells and worksheets to improve their functionality and appearance.
- Know where to look for further help.

Excel can be a very complex program, with lots of capabilities. It's important to start out slowly, and then move students gradually through the program's capabilities. It's also useful to work with the students to teach them things they'll use in their everyday work.

PowerPoint

PowerPoint can be a very effective tool for making presentations. PowerPoint can be used to make three different kinds of presentations:

- *Overhead slides.* The slides can be used with an overhead projector, but are limited to the printer you use. You can also save your document on a disk and take it to a printing center if you want overheads.
- *Slide presentations.* Any copy center can convert PowerPoint presentations to 35-mm slides.
- *On-line slide shows.* If you have access to a portable computer and a "hotplate" projection device, this is by far the most effective use of PowerPoint because it's possible to add movement and even sound to your presentation.

There are also numerous books on presentation tips, as well as information in Chapter 13. More books and links are presented in Section 15.5.

Access

Microsoft Access is a relational database that can be used by itself or as a database that custom programs can access for information. Access integrates with other Microsoft products to allow quick and easy manipulation of data. Access runs on the Windows 95/98/2000 and NT platforms but can also share information over networks and the Internet. It is also scalable, meaning that it can grows when your data grow. Access comes in various configurations, including single and multiuser.

MS Access is essentially made up of tables, forms, queries, reports, and macros (also Visual Basic modules). Because database design can get very complicated very fast, try to keep Access training to the basics that a user would need, unless the user is an I/T person. All these features make up a fairly sophisticated, but easy-to-use, product that can be installed on a desktop. However, it's important to set user expectations when designing MS Access training. For more complicated applications, the user should consult the I/T department.

Outlook

Microsoft Outlook manages e-mail, calendars, contacts, tasks and to-do lists, and documents or files on the hard drive. Outlook has e-mail, phone support, and group scheduling capabilities. Outlook also helps users share information by means of public folders, forms, and Internet connectivity. Outlook also allows users to create and view information using a consistent interface. Outlook lets users arrange information any way they want to see it. Users can apply any of Outlook's standard five views to information, or they can customize a view using the Field Chooser and Group by Box features. Basic training should include the menu structure, toolbar, and use of the e-mail/address book features.

Microsoft FrontPage

Microsoft FrontPage 98 is a tool used to create and manage Internet or intranet sites without programming (but you can program if you want). Features let you create professional websites without programming. Create WYSIWYG frames pages, and draw HTML tables in the WYSIWYG FrontPage Editor. Site management tools let you build and maintain websites. There is automatic hyperlink maintenance, and collaboration features let you work with others on your website. Since creating and maintaining websites within an organization is usually a complex process, there really aren't any specific "basics" that can be taught. Following is a brief summary of the three primary components.

The three components are FrontPage Explorer for managing your webs, Personal Web Server to expedite working off your own hard drive, and FrontPage Editor, a powerful WYSISWG HTML editor. You can also download a free fourth component, the FrontPage Publisher, which makes it easy to update your site on a non-FrontPage server.

FrontPage Explorer gives you two views. Outline View shows you how the files in your web relate to each other hierarchically. Document View gives you a document-centric view of your web. It shows which files link to a particular document and to which links that document points.

Microsoft PhotoDraw

Specifically designed for business users, PhotoDraw 2000 is a graphics program. PhotoDraw provides illustration, photo editing, and text tools in one integrated product. Smart image correction tools ensure that you create professional-looking graphics easily without having any design or graphics experience. PhotoDraw includes professionally designed templates, preset defaults, and automatic correction features. It provides 20,000 pieces of clip art, photos, and backgrounds. It also supplies 300 professionally designed business templates for everything from business logos and flyers to web buttons.

With PhotoDraw you can customize standard clip art and photos and draw, paint, edit photos, and manipulate clip art and text within a single program. You can use the image touch-up for image and color correction. It includes automatic corrections for red eye, dust and scratch removal, and despeckle. Also, 50 special effects can be applied to text, clip art, photos, and other graphics. With the visual preview you can sample effects before applying them.

Microsoft Publisher

MS Publisher works similar to Word in that it provides a word processing interface for creating simple publications. Utilizing Publisher enables users to reduce the time required in designing and creating a publication. It also allows users to customize publications in unique and creative ways. This product is also useful when used in conjunction with other Office products because you can take advantage of the strengths of each product and then combine the material created in Publisher.

Like most products, these features have layers of complexity. It's important to tailor training to fit the needs of the specific class or group of users. Microsoft is also introducing Publisher 98, Deluxe Edition, which includes Publisher 98 and an image-editing program, Microsoft Picture It! Publisher Deluxe provides tools to create and edit images and drag and drop them into your Publisher 98 publications. This feature allows it to work with PhotoDraw.

Bringing These Tools Together in Training

Microsoft Office 2000 is fairly new, and while most people are using Office 97, there is a benefit to moving to 2000 if organizations really want to combine the tool set. Office 2000 extends desktop productivity by bringing the entire Office set of tools together using a common interface, and giving users new ways to use the web to share information and collaborate on projects. It also provides analysis tools within each product. All Office applications have:

- A consistent look and feel
- Familiar toolbar functionality
- Common commands and functions

This is important, because it enables users to move from one tool to another easily, and trainers to cover products at an increasing pace once users understand the basic toolbars, help, etc. Some possible ideas for combining tools in a comprehensive training class include:

- Creating a document using Word, PowerPoint, and PhotoDraw for graphics, using Excel for a financial model, and then publishing it using Publisher
- Creating a presentation and inserting spreadsheet data and photos
- Using MS Access to create a report, and then enhancing and publishing the report using various tools

As noted in Sections 15.4 and 15.5, there are lots of resources for coming up with ideas for exercises. The key, though, is to ensure that the training meets the needs of the organization and its staff.

15.2 POTENTIAL PROBLEMS

The sheer complexity of MS Office is enough to overwhelm anyone. There are so many problems, and there aren't many good manuals. Third-party books are probably the best way to go, and there are thousands available. There are also some potential training problems for each product. Users can quickly build an Access application that they cannot maintain. Often, this responsibility gets shifted to I/T, and the user gradually becomes less happy and more disconnected.

Migration compatibility between Office versions is probably the greatest area of concern for organizations moving to a new version of desktop productivity applications. Unfortunately, new features that greatly enhance software often require changes to the file format. For example, additions such as Microsoft Excel PivotTable dynamic views, Visual Basic for Applications, an object model, and support for shared code such as for the new OfficeArt have all required changes to the file formats.

In a mixed environment of Microsoft Office users, sharing files can be problematic, as can training from one version to another. Administrators don't want to expend the effort and cost of installing converters for older versions of software, and users of the new version don't want to give up new features in order to save in older formats. Migration to new versions of Microsoft Office can be smoothed using tools, since users working with different versions of Office will not have problems sharing files. There are no costs associated with this solution, which can be downloaded free of charge from www.microsoft.com.

15.3 HOW TO CUSTOMIZE TRAINING FOR YOUR ORGANIZATION

Trainers should provide custom training on MS Office to suit the needs of the particular organization. Training groups or vendors can usually create classes and courseware centered on interactive learning and practical skills. Most Office training vendors offer a variety of flexible delivery methods and customize the course topics to your specific business functions.

Providing customized applications training geared specifically to the needs of your company and staff is important to ensure maximum productivity quickly. In some cases, external vendors can customize training to suit your needs if generic training is insufficient. Training can be at your site for your convenience or be arranged off-site to get away from the office. Whether developed in house or via a vendor, you can customize training sessions to review only those tools you want to learn.

Some important points to consider when customizing Office training are standard templates, network file locations, and database security. Most organizations have standard templates for memos, form letters, proposals, etc. It's important to include these in the training so that users don't unwittingly violate organizational policy. Users should be made aware of network directories, and how to set those locations as defaults in Office products.

If trainees are to create new standards, be sure to teach them the skills to do so. After taking the course, the user should be able to use and create forms, use and create reports, customize forms and reports, and print forms and reports. While printing may seem trivial, each printer configuration is slightly different and affects the margins and appearance of forms and reports. Each organization may have different printers or printer models, and training must be customized to account for these.

15.4   OFF-THE-SHELF TRAINING VENDORS

Literally thousands of vendors offer MS Office training. There are several ways to find vendors. Word of mouth is probably the best way. As mentioned in Chapter 7, checking vendor references will get you the most information the fastest. Beyond word of mouth, the Microsoft Certified Technical Education Center program is the next best way to find training vendors (http://www.microsoft.com/train_cert/programs/prog_ctec.htm). After that, searching the Internet and yellow pages are the two least desirable ways to find vendors. The URL for the Microsoft training provider page is http://www.microsoft.com/isapi/referral/training.asp.

To find a training vendor by zip code, use:

> http://www.microsoft.com/isapi/referral/postalcode.asp?q01=3&r01=355

A short list of 10 large international and national providers in alphabetical order are:

Catapult
3830 Monte Villa Parkway
Bothell, WA 98021-6942
(800) CATAPULT
http://www.pbt.com

CBT Systems
900 Chesapeake Drive
Redwood City, CA 94063
(888) 395-0014
http://www.cbtsys.com

CompUSA
420 Fifth Avenue
New York, NY 10018
(800) 872-4680
http://www.compusa.com

ExecuTrain Corporation
4800 North Point Parkway
Alpharetta, GA 30022
(800) 535-9479
http//www.executrain.com

Infotec
3100 South Harbor Boulevard, Suite 100
Santa Ana, CA 92704
(800) 700-8724
http://www.infotec.com

NCS—Virtual University Enterprises, Suite 300
11000 Prairie Lakes Driven
Eden Prairie, MS 55344-3857
(612) 995-8800
http://www.vue.com

New Horizons Computer Learning Centers, Inc.
1231 East Dyer Road, Suite 110
Santa Ana, CA 92705-5643
(714) 432-7600
http://www.newhorizons.com

Software Architects, Inc.
120 North LaSalle Street, Suite 1030
Chicago, IL 60602
(708) 876-8100
http://www.sarktss.com

Software Spectrum, Inc.
2140 Merritt Drive
Garland, TX 75041
(800) 624-2033
http://www.softwarespectrum.com

Sylvan Prometric
1000 Lancaster Street
Baltimore, MD 21202
(410) 843-8000
http://www.prometric.com

15.5 RECOMMENDED TRAINING RESOURCES, BOOKS, AND WEBSITES

Microsoft

Besides the companies listed in Section 15.4, there are thousands of websites and books written for Microsoft Office. One good place to start is the Microsoft Office User Specialist program resources network, located at http://www.mous.net/. This is a Microsoft website that provides links worldwide to Microsoft Office User Specialist (MOUS) websites and vendors. One of the largest publishers of MS Office training materials is MS Press, located at http://mspress.microsoft.com/office2000/books/. To receive updates for MS Office, go to http://officeupdate.microsoft.com/default.htm.

Third-Party Books and Publishers

Several thousand books about MS Office exist. The easiest way to find them is to do subject searches at publishers' websites. Most third-party publishers now allow you to view and order via the web. While there are hundreds of small publishers, this list includes 10 of the largest, in no particular order. The websites listed are current as of this writing.

McGraw-Hill
http://www.bookstore.mcgraw-hill.com
Addison Wesley Longman
http://www.awl.com
Amazon.com
http://www.amazon.com
Barnes and Noble
http://www.barnesandnoble.com
Que Publishing
http://www.mcp.com/publishers/que
Sybex Books
http://www.sybex.com
IDG Worldwide
http://www.idg.com
Prentice Hall
http://www.phptr.com
DDC Publishing, Inc.
http://www.ddcpub.com/
Prima Publishing
http://www.primapublishing.com

To find Microsoft Office resources on the web, you can use any of the major search engines to locate newsgroups, bulletin boards, and other resources, as well as vendors.

Windows 98/NT/2000 Training

In This Chapter

OVERVIEW

Microsoft Windows has several versions. The newest versions include Windows 98, NT, and 2000, which combines both. In various configurations, MS Office may contain word processing (MS Word), spreadsheet (Excel), presentation graphics (PowerPoint), database (Access), publishing (Publisher/PhotoDraw), web publishing (FrontPage), and scheduling/calendaring/mail software (Outlook). The various combinations are based on needs (normal versus power user), price (!), organization size, and other software available. For example, if you are using Lotus Notes e-mail and scheduling, you would not need MS Outlook. This chapter presents information needed for you to create and implement training for an MS Office rollout.

16.1 KEY TRAINING POINTS

Windows 98/NT/2000 constitute the current family of MS Windows operating system products. Though there are certainly desktops with Windows 3.x still running, this chapter focuses on the latest three releases, 98/NT/2000. Because of the enormous number of variables in an operating system, it's impossible to list all the details that would make up a comprehensive training program. However, I've listed the general categories of information that users and developers need to know about Windows 98/NT/2000, and that should be incorporated in a training program:

- Taking advantage of new features in a Windows release
- Planning an effective implementation of a Windows release
- Upgrading and migrating your Windows NT/9x network and effectively integrating a Windows release with down-level operating systems
- Creating step-by-step instructions for using a Windows release
- Installing and configuring a Windows release
- Administering and managing a Windows release
- Optimization
- Security
- Troubleshooters
- Using administrative tools and utilities, and finding the tools that Microsoft moves and renames in each release
- Control panel
- Server setup wizard
- Command line
- Scripting
- Resource kit tools
- Third-party utilities
- What a Windows release means for your network
- Hardware considerations
- Selecting the best deployment options

- When it's best to upgrade from one Windows release to another and when it's best to start over
- Multibooting
- Performing a standard installation from the Windows release CD-ROM
- Performing over-the-network and remote installations
- Automating deployment of a Windows release with scripts and SMS technology
- Plug-n-Play and Device Manager for hardware installation and driver management
- Adding hardware not detected during installation of a Windows release
- Monitoring and reallocating hardware resources
- Working with adaptive menus
- Redesigned dialog boxes, the places bar, and AutoComplete
- Using Windows Installer to deploy applications
- Repairing and troubleshooting applications automatically
- Handling recovery from application errors with Dr. Watson
- Troubleshooting network connectivity problems
- Administering an Active Directory enterprise network
- Managing user, group, and computer accounts
- Implementing a distributed file system
- Configuring and managing disks, partitions, and file systems with the disk management snap-in
- Windows file system features: disk quotas, EFS, compression, defragmentation
- Optimizing a Windows release
- Troubleshooting a Windows release
- Backing up and restoring in a Windows release
- Automatic System Recovery

Within each of these areas, there are many details. With respect to Windows 2000 specifically, Microsoft is setting up a training program via software vendors and the MSDN (Microsoft Developers Network, http://msdn.microsoft.com/). As of this writing, the Microsoft training initiative for Windows 2000 was scheduled to start in summer 1999, and was to include the following courses:

- Accelerated Training for Updating Support Skills and Designing a Directory Services Infrastructure for Microsoft Windows 2000
- Designing a Microsoft Windows 2000 Networking Services Infrastructure
- Designing a Change and Configuration Management Infrastructure for Microsoft Windows 2000
- Installing and Configuring Microsoft Windows 2000 as a File and Print Server
- Deploying Microsoft Windows 2000 Professional

For more information on class registration information and MS CTECs, check out the Microsoft Training and Certification website at http://www.microsoft.com/train_cert/.

16.2 POTENTIAL PROBLEMS

Any training requires careful planning and preparation. However, training on Windows releases can be especially problematic both because of the amount of change required from people and because of the compatibility issues from release to release. The training should be designed to achieve full transfer of information with the minimum of upheaval. The training should be set up in dual tracks (I/T and business staff) and should be easy to use so both users and I/T staff can learn to take advantage of all the features of Windows. To maximize effectiveness of Windows training and avoid transition problems, there should be three areas of competency:

- Windows general skills (mouse, icons, menus, etc.)
- Use and administration of local and network versions
- Application software

Familiarity with at least Windows 3.1 is often assumed, but not all users (I/T or business) are truly proficient in the use of Windows. Staff must be both familiar and confident with at least the basics, or they will be lost in the new releases and new applications. The training plan should account for various backgrounds and skill levels.

There is a wide range of training available in basic Windows 95 and NT, including courses aimed at the beginner level. Windows training may take different forms, including formal classes and self-paced computer-based training. It's important to classify training into beginner, intermediate, and advanced, as mentioned in Chapter 4.

In most instances, people hired by an organization come in with lower or different computer skills than they will need in their jobs. When new employees enter the organization and are familiar with a different version of Windows, it may take them a while to get up to speed. Many organizations are finding it is more effective to quickly upgrade new employees' computer skills at the beginning of their employment. The training team is in an ideal position to assist in identifying what skills are needed and help individuals develop those skills quickly.

16.3   HOW TO CUSTOMIZE TRAINING FOR YOUR ORGANIZATION

Many organizations have specific needs or uses for Windows, depending on the transaction processing or office-related tasks. As mentioned in Chapter 8, when training people, it is often desirable to modify course materials to include or focus on these specifics. Not only does this benefit the current group being trained, but also it facilitates training future groups and new hires. This is especially important for Windows, because there are several ways to do everything. The problem of the fastest learners having many pieces but not all of the puzzle can make training interesting. A training team should develop both the training process and the course materials to support a Windows training program on a broad range of skills.

Another step that's important is scheduling a reinforcement development session 1 to 3 weeks after the training. The individuals in each class are encouraged to identify and collect actual items from their daily work that they would like to cover during the review session. This session is really for practice or real-world usage, away from the desk and protected from interruptions. Training personnel are present both to facilitate and answer questions one-on-one and to gain overall feedback on how the class may be tailored to be more efficient or more effective for the next group.

Because Windows is used by home users also, there are solutions that can range from a laptop take-home program, to a practice room in the building that is accessible during the evening and weekend hours, to facilities in the community such as the public library or school that have computers that can be used for practice. Other options include software discounted purchase programs, use-and-return software programs (depending on licensing), and staffed user sessions at your training facility. It's also useful to have practice exercises that home users can do in the evening if they wish.

Since there are multiple versions of Windows, including Windows CE, it's important to recognize certification programs as a means of customizing Windows training. As mentioned in Chapter 4, it's possible to utilize either in-house (Chapter 4) or vendor-based certifications (Chapter 13). Each certification program can be customized to meet the needs of the Windows release in house. For example, Microsoft Press offers a comprehensive line of just-in-time learning solutions to help you work with each Windows 2000 component.

Another way to customize Windows training is to work with Microsoft Certified Technical Education Centers. CTECs are technical training organizations that deliver systems, support, and developer instruction on Microsoft products and technologies in a variety of flexible formats to organizations. There are usually CTECs in most large cities, and these organizations can help you do some customization. If your organization decides to certify I/T staff through MCSE or MCP training, there is a major benefit that can help you customize both technical and nontechnical Windows training. The MSDN Online Certified Membership helps you tap into technical resources, connect to the MCP community, and gain access to resources and services. See the MSDN website for a list of certified member benefits. Other resources include MS TechNet (http://www.microsoft.com/technet/) and discussion forums and newsgroups.

16.4 OFF-THE-SHELF TRAINING VENDORS

There are as many vendors that offer Windows training as offer MS Office training. As with any training, word of mouth is probably the best way to find vendors. As mentioned in Chapter 7, checking vendor references will get you the most information the fastest. Beyond word of mouth, the Microsoft Certified Technical Education Center program is the next best way to find training vendors (http://www.microsoft.com/train_cert/programs/prog_ctec.htm). After that, searching the Internet and yellow pages are the two least desirable ways to find vendors. The URL for the Microsoft training provider page is http://www.microsoft.com/isapi/referral/training.asp.

To find a training vendor by zip code, use:

http://www.microsoft.com/isapi/referral/postalcode.asp?q01=3&r01=355

A short list of 10 large international national providers in alphabetical order are:

Catapult
3830 Monte Villa Parkway
Bothell, WA 98021-6942
(800) CATAPULT
http://www.pbt.com

CBT Systems
900 Chesapeake Drive
Redwood City, CA 94063
(888) 395-0014
http://www.cbtsys.com

CompUSA
420 Fifth Avenue
New York, NY 10018
(800) 872-4680
http://www.compusa.com

ExecuTrain Corporation
4800 North Point Parkway
Alpharetta, GA 30022
(800) 535-9479
http//www.executrain.com

Infotec
3100 South Harbor Boulevard, Suite 100
Santa Ana, CA 92704
(800) 700-8724
http://www.infotec.com

NCS—Virtual University Enterprises, Suite 300
11000 Prairie Lakes Drive
Eden Prairie, MS 55344-3857
(612) 995-8800
http://www.vue.com

New Horizons Computer Learning Centers, Inc.
1231 East Dyer Road, Suite 110
Santa Ana, CA 92705-5643
(714) 432-7600
http://www.newhorizons.com

Software Architects, Inc.
120 North LaSalle Street, Suite 1030
Chicago, IL 60602
(708) 876-8100
http://www.sarktss.com

Software Spectrum, Inc.
2140 Merritt Drive
Garland, TX 75041
(800) 624-2033
http://www.softwarespectrum.com

Sylvan Prometric
1000 Lancaster Street
Baltimore, MD 21202
(410) 843-8000

http://www.prometric.com

16.5 RECOMMENDED TRAINING RESOURCES, BOOKS, AND WEBSITES

Microsoft

Besides the companies listed in Section 16.4, there are thousands of websites and books written about Microsoft Windows. One good place to start is the Microsoft Windows Home Page, located at http://www.microsoft.com/windows/default.asp. This is a Microsoft website that provides links worldwide to Microsoft Windows training websites and vendors.

One of the largest publishers of MS Windows training materials is MS Press, located at http://mspress.microsoft.com/office2000/books/. For specific resources for Windows training, try http://www.microsoft.com/windows/professional/training/default.asp. There is also a list of related sites at http://www.microsoft.com/windows/professional/sites/default.asp.

Third-Party Books/Publishers

Several thousand books about MS Windows exist. The easiest way to find them is to do subject searches at publishers' websites. Most third-party publishers now allow you to view and order via the web. While there are hundreds of small publishers, this list includes 10 of the largest, in no particular order. The websites listed are current as of this writing.

McGraw-Hill
http://www.bookstore.mcgraw-hill.com

Addison Wesley Longman
http://www.awl.com

Amazon.com
http://www.amazon.com

Barnes and Noble
http://www.barnesandnoble.com

Que Publishing
http://www.mcp.com/publishers/que

Sybex Books
http://www.sybex.com

IDG Worldwide
http://www.idg.com

Prentice Hall
http://www.phptr.com

DDC Publishing, Inc.
http://www.ddcpub.com/

Prima Publishing
http://www.primapublishing.com

To find Microsoft Windows resources on the web, you can use any of the major search engines to locate newsgroups, bulletin boards, and other resources, as well as vendors.

CHAPTER 17

Lotus Notes Training: A Case Study and Lessons Learned*

In This Chapter

OVERVIEW

Lotus Notes has the world's largest installed base for a groupware product. The base features of the Notes client, which sits on the desktop, include database handling (authoring, editing, sharing), e-mail, calendaring, and

---

*Lotus Notes is a registered trademark and Domino is a trademark of Lotus Development Corporation.

to-do lists. The Notes client is connected to the Domino server, which links all the Notes clients together. The newest version of Notes (R5) includes web services in Lotus's next generation of Internet products. This includes the Notes integrated Internet client; Domino server platform for messaging, collaboration, and Internet and intranet applications; and Domino Designer, a web and intranet application development tool.

Groupware training often involves changing the mindset of employees. Rarely is an employee's first instinct to pass on information—usually the employee files it for his or her own future use. Because of this consistent educational strategy, objectives and training content across the entire organization are critical in Notes training. It's also important to provide flexible delivery options to support various learning styles, experience levels, budgets, etc. With Notes and Domino, education goes beyond enabling users around specific tasks, to understanding how Notes and Domino can change the way they work.

Training for groupware systems involves using technology that supports a group's communication and decision-making processes. Since the system replaces whiteboards and bulletin boards, participants can enter brainstorming ideas, make comments, organize ideas and concepts, make evaluations, and vote anonymously. The strength of groupware is information sharing, and thus groupware training must often go beyond the technology to the concept of information sharing. Participants must be interested in and encouraged to use Notes to share and gather information.

Notes training can cover a broad spectrum of users. From end users and administrators to developers and webmasters, there are dozens of combinations of skill sets that can be created or enhanced, based on the organization's needs. Some possible courses include Java and Javascript integration, server clustering, and web-enabled Notes applications. There are also Lotus authorized courses, including Domino Web Development, Advanced LotusScript, and Domino Messaging Administration. Not all of the technical and/or administration skills belong to just I/T. Power users may also want to get involved at a departmental level to administer certain databases unique to their workgroup.

17.1   KEY TRAINING POINTS

Most users can learn Lotus Notes basics in a 1-day course. The product is fairly intuitive, and users can learn the basic skills needed to use Notes as an environment for sharing and creating information easily. In an extra day, students can learn more ways of searching for, editing, and navigating information. Overall, good topics for a beginner class include:

- Applying basic Notes principles
- Opening and navigating within a database
- Opening and working within a document
- Formatting text in a document
- Navigating and organizing the workspace
- Using Notes Help
- Using and navigating views
- Using and creating folders
- Performing a simple database search
- Choosing letterhead design
- Creating folders
- Linking and embedding information
- Formatting documents and text
- Searching databases for information
- Replicating databases for local and remote use
- Using Notes mail to communicate with other users and send information (optional)
- Customizing the Notes workspace
- Moving documents between folders
- Creating links
- Using named styles to format documents
- Locally securing replicated databases
- Using the calendar and to-do views
- Adding entries to the calendar
- Managing calendar entries
- Creating and assigning tasks
- Managing tasks
- Understanding group scheduling
- Inviting others to a meeting
- Responding to invitations
- Managing responses

These tasks use a broad range of Notes features and provide the user with a good exposure to the basics of Notes.

There are also extended features for power users and I/T staff that must work "under the covers" with Notes. A power user course would use the basics training to provide a foundation for skills such as:

- Customizing database views
- Customizing database forms
- Creating views
- Creating actions and agents
- Creating new databases
- Creating and embedding objects
- Creating tables, hot spots, and text styles
- Creating new databases from templates
- Creating personalized stationery in mail

Of course, for the top end, developers and I/T staff in general will need a more in-depth understanding of the way Notes works and how to administer and develop Notes applications. Also, it's important for developers to understand how Notes interacts with web-based applications via Domino. There are two categories of technical skills: system administration and application development. A sample list of topics for technical staff in these two categories might include:

- LotusScript for R5
- Application development in R5
- Developing interactive web applications
- Notes system administration
- Domino messaging administration
- Domino web development
- Domino web administration
- Domino applications administration
- Developing Domino agents
- Developing Dynamic web pages
- Transitioning a Domino infrastructure to R5
- Planning a Domino infrastructure
- Implementing a Domino infrastructure
- Domino designer fundamentals
- Working in Domino databases
- Help Desk Support for Notes

- Deploying Domino applications
- Administering and maintaining Domino users
- Domino performance tuning
- Domino security
- Using JavaScript in Domino applications
- Using LotusScript in Domino applications

With the use of these skills, there are some general advanced topics that can be covered which round out the technical skill set. Some of these topics include:

- Designing and implementing efficient retrieval mechanisms for data from Notes databases
- Getting data from external data sources
- Taking advantage of form events to control user interaction and make it more effective
- Developing more efficient forms by using Notes document and data architectures
- Managing related documents in the same database using profiles
- Managing related documents across multiple databases

Other technical skills also are involved with Lotus Notes "internals." For more information on technical topics and certifications, check out http://www.lotus.com/home.nsf/tabs/education.

17.2   POTENTIAL PROBLEMS

As mentioned, groupware implementations require users to change more than technology. Users must learn to share information. Teams must learn to organize their information into forms usable by other team members. Group interaction style is hard to identify before implementation, whereas individual characteristics are often possible to determine before an implementation is done. This can significantly affect the perception of the new software and resistance to implementation. New groups change quickly during the group formation process, which affects training.

When prototypes are created during training, some users may want to take those prototypes and use them for real-world tasks. This is usually not possible, and modifying prototypes can be technically difficult because of the added complexity of groupware over single-user software. In software for large organizations, testing new prototypes can be difficult or impossible because of the disruption caused by introducing new versions into an organization. For example, if a team member goes to training to learn a new release of Notes and wants to incorporate those features in the current databases and documents, other team members may have to learn those new features in on-the-job training.

Another major problem is when the perceived benefit of using group-ware for any particular individual is less than the cost of adopting it. Even when groups benefit, individuals may not see the benefit they get by using it. For example, if all the members of the group enter all their appoint-ments into a calendar system, then everyone has the benefit of being able to schedule around other people's meetings. However, if it's difficult to enter meetings, then individuals may simply view other people's meetings and not enter their own schedule. It's important for the groupware train-ers to find a way to make sure the application is perceived as useful for individuals even outside the context of full group adoption.

Using groupware means some information must be shared, but there is often a concern about other information remaining private. Users must feel that critical information is secure even against aggressive attempts to obtain the information. In many situations, users may want to be anony-mous, and anonymity can be important in encouraging participation in discussions. Users must also realize, though, that the more information that is shared, the more easily solutions can be found.

17.3 HOW TO CUSTOMIZE TRAINING FOR YOUR ORGANIZATION

Like most training programs, Lotus Notes training can be customized to meet the needs of a particular organization. Customization can include custom outlines; instructor and reference materials; tailored course mate-rial that includes selected topics with customer-specific instructions and graphics; and fully customized courseware, usually developed for cus-tom applications. Customization can range from fairly simple to com-plex, and in most circumstances it is recommended that instructional designers and curriculum developers play some role in the design and development process. The development of training must parallel the roll-out, as mentioned throughout this book. Customization services are pro-vided by Lotus/IBM, Lotus/IBM business partners, and, in the case of technology-based training, third-party multimedia developers and train-ing companies.

Lotus Training Customization Products and Services

Lotus Professional Services, through its education group, provides worldwide delivery of education and training solutions that enable clients and customers to implement Lotus technology. An important focus for Lotus is providing customers with training designed to help users learn. Lotus Professional Services offerings provide training solutions with development, delivery, and reinforcement options. Lotus also provides customized, task-based instruction to meet your training needs, from Domino system administration and application development to end-user topics.

Instructor-led courses are available directly from Lotus Professional Services, from a Lotus Authorized Education Center (LAEC), or from a Lotus Education Academic Partner (LEAP). Check the worldwide schedule for course descriptions and a complete schedule of authorized courses offered at LAEC and Lotus locations. Lotus offers a range of custom instructor-led training curriculum development capabilities for organizations to provide training on specific best practices or mission-critical applications. For more information, contact your local education office, or check out http://www.lotus.com/home.nsf/tabs/education.

There are also a number of "turnkey packages" produced by Lotus that organizations can purchase as needed. Domino/Notes Documentation Packages and Lotus reference manuals can now be purchased through the Education Store. Previously only available with the software and with technical courseware kits, Lotus documentation is now available in document sets. See http://www.lotus.com/home.nsf/tabs/education.

IBM Redbooks are technical "cookbooks" that help you and your users understand and install products and integrate them into real-life systems. They are real-world technical information written by professionals from the field on the products. See all Lotus Redbook titles for ordering at www.lotus.com/redbook.

Lotus offers a list of published books about Lotus products in association with Amazon.com. Current offerings include books about cc:Mail, LotusScript, Notes/Domino, and SmartSuite. To view a list of suggested titles and to purchase directly from Amazon.com, visit the Education Store at http://www.lotus.com/home.nsf/tabs/education.

The LearningSpace family is a combination of software and services for the creation and delivery of on-line training and education. Lotus Professional Services offers courses on the cutting edge of technical learning in an on-line, instructor-facilitated class forum in LearningSpace. For detailed product information on LearningSpace, visit the web at www.lotus.com/learningspace.

There are also computer-based training courses, developed by CBT Systems, for end users, application development, and systems administration. CBT Systems and Lotus have a cooperative development partnership providing interactive computer-based training for the users of Lotus products. For more information on CBT Systems' complete Lotus curricula, visit the web at www.cbtsys.com.

QuickCards for Lotus Notes, developed by Lotus partner Usability Sciences, is a just-in-time training support tool that addresses over 150 tasks via on-screen, step-by-step, text-based instructions, as well as ScreenCam movie tutorials. QuickCards for Lotus Notes are offered for on-line order, as well as for download for a try-and-buy 15-day trial period. For more information, visit the ScreenCam website at www.lotus.com/screencam.

Lotus Training Customization Approach

Whether a customer is interested in individual offerings, a complete education program, or a combined training and service solution, Lotus offers customers a range of products and services that support different learning models, and that can be positioned for a customer depending on buying behavior, education requirements, and timing. Lotus can also develop and deliver education solutions based on the Learning Performance Model (LPM) from the Lotus Professional Services education group. For customers, training solutions developed and delivered in the context of the LPM ensure that employees meet the objectives set forth in the training and help users realize the value of Lotus technology. The LPM addresses the entire life cycle of training development, and combines a collection of education offerings that range from competency assessment, program design and development, to delivery, certification, and performance improvement (see Figure 17-1).

The Lotus training development methodology is similar to the ISD model presented in this book. The first step is to analyze a customer's educational requirements and provide the guidance to develop the appropriate education program. Lotus assesses the business objectives, I/T strategy, training culture, political and behavioral issues, obstacles, and basic departmental needs. Then it identifies and recommends an education strategy based on that analyses. This is similar to the needs analysis described in Chapter 2.

The next step, program design and development, is typically driven by the results of the competency assessment. Lotus defines, sources, and

FIGURE 17-1

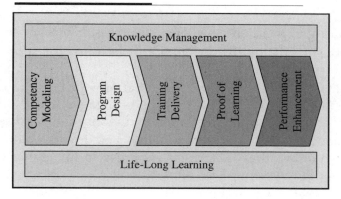

develops the required training content (standard, tailored, or custom) in the appropriate delivery format, develops an implementation plan, and addresses all the ancillary issues affecting an education program. For more information, see Chapter 4.

The third step, delivery of Lotus's educational offerings, has traditionally been focused primarily on technical and end-user instructor-led training. Tailored solutions are the rule and not the exception. Lotus has a portfolio of delivery options that support a broad spectrum of education strategies and solutions, including classroom, CBT, and distance learning, as previously mentioned.

The next step is to provide proof of learning or certification. Lotus offers a certification program in support of technical competency around Lotus Notes and Domino. Lotus offers two types of certification. Certified Lotus Specialist (CLS) measures the skills needed by professionals developing and administering Internet- and intranet-based solutions around Lotus products. Certified Lotus Professional (CLP) represents a high level of technical knowledge by job function. Lotus Professional Services provides Proof of Learning service for end-user qualification (leveraging previous competency assessments, if applicable) and assessment that confirm relevant Notes skills aligned with business-based performance requirements.

The last step, performance enhancement, is roughly equal to the continual improvement process described in Chapter 12. Performance enhancement involves educational offerings integrated with, or driving, other professional services, enabling existing Lotus customers to begin exploiting the full potential of their Lotus investment. An enhancement program may address one or many of the following:

- Ensuring a consistent level of skills across an enterprise
- Establishment and documentation of best practices and internal mentoring programs
- Facilitation and learning support that provides posttraining reinforcement via EPSS or on-site experts engaged in one-on-one contact, TeamRoom implementation and monitoring, and support
- Expanding basic messaging capabilities to broader Notes skills to build a foundation of technical expertise as an organization prepares to implement Notes applications
- Skills-based R5 migration

In addition to these tasks, it's important to continue educating executives, line or business managers, I/T personnel, and internal consultants on the potential of Notes within their organization.

In-House Developed versus Outsourced Training

If your organization hires Notes experts, or sends user and/or I/T staff to train-the-trainer classes, it's possible to provide rollout training in house. Classes are available via Lotus train-the-trainer programs. As mentioned in Chapter 5, there are a number of implementation and delivery methods, and Lotus supports most of them for train the trainer, including:

- Instructor-led training (classroom and/or facilitated CBT)
- Distributed learning via LearningSpace
- CBTs for technical and end-user audiences
- Self-paced training

Once the knowledge is acquired by your in-house trainers, they can develop classes customized to your organization. In this case, however, your in-house experts must continue to stay current on new versions, releases, patches, etc.

If a customer lacks internal resources to develop and deliver an education solution, Lotus/IBM and/or its business partners can deliver a turnkey program. It's important to note that instructor-led technical training for systems administrators and application developers would normally be provided by Lotus or a business partner. It would be fairly difficult for any single in-house resource to have the depth of knowledge necessary to create complex technical training.

17.4   BUYING TRAINING FROM IBM VERSUS THIRD-PARTY TRAINING VENDORS

Training from Lotus and IBM and their authorized training centers has numerous benefits over unauthorized training vendors, and in fact most large enterprise education solutions involve a partnership between Lotus/IBM and members of its education business partner network. Authorized training partners tend to have better educational professionals and facilities available worldwide for training and for customers with specific education strategies and programs.

Authorized training partners generally have access to a bigger array of educational services, content, tools, and resources for all audiences. Authorized training partners also have access to integrated offerings with Lotus/IBM's broader services, including consulting and support. Authorized partners can provide multiple delivery options, native and local trainers, and translated course material. In addition, content and processes across multiple delivery methods enable uniform competencies across geographies and product divisions, which may be important to distributed enterprises.

Also, while nonauthorized training providers may have developers and SMEs on staff, authorized training partners are more likely to have Notes knowledge and experience with messaging, migrations, and broader Notes solutions, as well as direct access to product development. In general, the closer a Notes training vendor is to Lotus, the better the training and consulting support are likely to be.

Many vendors offer Lotus Notes training. As with any training, word of mouth is probably the best way to find vendors. As mentioned in Chapter 7, checking vendor references from other customers will get you the most information the fastest. Beyond word of mouth, the Lotus Authorized Education Center Program is the only resource for Lotus-authorized training partners.

The LAEC program is a broad-based alliance of training organizations. LAECs are fully qualified and authorized sites that work closely with Lotus through the Lotus Business Partner program. They offer training at all levels for Lotus Notes and Domino. These training centers provide programs for customers, from the end user through the advanced student.

LAECs are required to have Certified Lotus Instructors (CLIs) on staff. These instructors not only have achieved Certified Lotus Professional status, but also have demonstrated their instruction skills to Lotus. Students receive a comprehensive study kit with valuable reference materials and a certificate upon completion. An LAEC's partnership with Lotus ensures it is always the first to get the latest information and support, especially on the newest products.

All exams for Lotus's certification programs are administered by two independent testing vendors. CATGlobal is currently rolling out select centers worldwide. To register on-line or to obtain more information, visit the CATGlobal website. Sylvan Prometric Testing Centers are located worldwide. In North America, register for an exam on-line, or call (800) 74-LOTUS [(800) 745-6887)]. Outside North America, consult the list of Sylvan Prometric Regional Service Centers. For a complete list of authorized education partners worldwide, check out http://www.lotus.com/home.nsf/tabs/education.

17.5 RECOMMENDED TRAINING RESOURCES, BOOKS, AND WEBSITES

Third-Party Books and Publishers

Several thousand books about Lotus Notes exist. The easiest way to find them is to do subject searches at publishers' websites. Most third-party publishers now allow you to view and order via the web. While there are hundreds of small publishers, this list includes 10 of the largest, in no particular order. The websites listed are current as of this writing.

McGraw-Hill
http://www.bookstore.mcgraw-hill.com

Addison Wesley Longman
http://www.awl.com

Amazon.com
http://www.amazon.com

Barnes and Noble
http://www.barnesandnoble.com

Que Publishing
http://www.mcp.com/publishers/que

Sybex Books
http://www.sybex.com

IDG Worldwide
http://www.idg.com

Prentice Hall
http://www.phptr.com

Macmillan/Sams Publishing
http://www.macmillan.com

Manning
http://www.manning.com

To find Lotus Notes resources on the web, you can use any of the major search engines to locate newsgroups, bulletin boards, and other resources, as well as vendors such as CBT Systems at http://www.cbtsys.com.

17.6   CASE STUDY

The Challenge

How do you go about training thousands of users, speaking different languages and spread across the globe, on Lotus Notes? That was the challenge that faced the project leader of Worldwide Notes Training, a major pharmaceutical firm, in May 1997. This research-based pharmaceutical corporation, with over $8 billion a year in sales, was deploying Lotus Notes across its global operations. With over 30,000 users working in 100+ locations, the company felt it could benefit from a Notes-based, corporatewide messaging system and tools for team collaboration. Notes would be used to improve employee communications, automate business practices, and help teams collaborate on projects. However, users first had to learn how to use the features of their new software environment. Management therefore needed a method for making sure that all employees were trained on Notes and could use it effectively. However, it was the nature of the company's far-flung operations that made training these remote Notes users such a challenge.

Part of the problem centered on the users themselves. With different skill sets, different job responsibilities, and different learning styles, it was difficult to come up with a "one size fits all" approach to Notes training. Executives needed to learn different Notes skills than their administrative assistants, for example, and had less time to dedicate to classroom sessions. A flexible approach to delivering Notes training, and one that could be customized to meet the preferences of various audiences, was needed. Other challenges included how to budget for and track the costs of a global training rollout, how to maintain internal customer satisfaction with the training solution, and how to manage the project logistics.

The Solution

After a review of several vendors' proposals, the company turned to Lotus as its Notes training provider. Lotus was able to provide what the company needed: Lotus-certified Notes instructors and training materials at a reasonable cost; the willingness to proactively work with the company as a partner; and the resources required to manage a multisite, corporatewide training rollout. Lotus ensured that employees received training options from a single source, and Lotus-produced student kit materials ensured each end user received consistent reference tools on the Notes products. Lotus also provided:

- A variety of instructor-led classroom formats, including one-on-one executive tutoring sessions and auditorium-style training sessions for end users
- Computer-based training tools and customized reference cards that could be used as study materials back at the office
- Fixed prices for global on-site training
- A dedicated account manager to work issues and manage activities
- An innovative voucher program and Notes database that allowed company management to monitor training expenses, track the delivery of classes in remote regions, and streamline payment cycles
- Training delivered in six languages (English, German, French, Spanish, Italian, and Chinese)

The Results

By working with Lotus, all employees received comprehensive training on their Notes environment in a cost-effective, timely fashion. Student evaluations and internal audits performed by company management demonstrated end-users' satisfaction with their Notes training experiences. The company's I/T leader of messaging states, "We have done training the right way by using Lotus Education." The company's project leader of Worldwide Notes Training agrees, "By taking the time to really understand the challenges we faced, Lotus Education was able to work with us as a partner, helping us overcome problems and ensuring our success."

SAP Training

In This Chapter

OVERVIEW

SAP is one of the world's largest ERP products. At the core of SAP R/3 are programs for accounting and controlling, production and materials management, quality management and plant maintenance, sales and distribution, human resources management, and project management.

Developing training for SAP can be a huge undertaking, and as mentioned throughout this book, organizations often don't want to spend the money to develop training or send people to training because the organizations typically look only at the current, measurable bottom line. Implementing SAP changes how people normally do their jobs, and an SAP implementation won't work if the employees aren't trained properly. Because of the enormous changes that occur with ERP implementations, there are two key tasks: to equip users with the KSAs needed to use SAP and to make sure that the users understand the goals of the project.

Official R/3 solution providers usually offer turnkey training packages for SAP R/3 implementation teams and end users as well as SAP R/3 classes for consultants. Full training materials are provided with courses. After the classes are finished, trainees can continue to consolidate their education by connecting to SAP's SAPNet system detailed in Section 18.6. Most trainers provide a range of SAP training, including accounts and finance, BASIS, ABAP, and other functional modules.

SAP is a very big integrated business software application. Lots of functionality, fully integrated application modules, multiple currency capability, and operational integrity make R/3 a huge effort for trainers and training developers. The same discipline used in designing and implementing SAP software should be applied to R/3 training. The courseware should be designed as educational building blocks, and offer the knowledge and skills that participants need to work efficiently with SAP R/3.

18.1   KEY TRAINING POINTS

SAP is an enormous software package with thousands of pieces. Most users take months or even years to get up to speed on the big picture, but it's important to provide some kind of foundation via the basic business model. Most SAP training programs are broken down into:

- Accounting and controlling
- Production and materials management
- Quality management
- Plant maintenance
- Sales and distribution
- Human resources management
- Project management
- Technical support and application development in SAP ABAP/4 Development Workbench

Accounting and Controlling

SAP's suite of integrated financial application components encompasses all aspects of financial accounting, investment management, controlling, treasury management, and enterprise controlling. Accounting transactions reflect all activities in an organization, so it's critical to train the right people properly on this part of SAP. At a somewhat detailed level, training for this area might include:

- Master data
- General ledger
- Accounts receivable
- Accounts payable
- Fixed assets
- Cost element accounting/cost center accounting
- Internal orders
- Profitability analysis
- Configuration and organization in financial accounting
- Executive information system (EIS)
- Integration
- Financial and management accounting and reporting
- Cost management and controlling
- Special ledger (FI-SL)

Organizationwide control of financial information is essential to business management. Users must be given the ability to track financial accounting data. The financial accounting component complies with international accounting standards such as GAAP and IAS. If your organization operates transnationally, you will need to incorporate differences based on culture and business unit.

Production and Materials Management

Depending on your method of production, you have the choice of using production order processing, repetitive manufacturing, or KANBAN production control. SAP also provides various inventor accounting and management methods, including JIT, FIFO, LIFO, etc. A sample curriculum might include topics such as:

- Material master
- PP master data
- Sales and operations planning
- Demand management and MRP
- Capacity planning
- Product costing
- Repetitive manufacturing
- Logistics information system (LIS)
- Production planning
- Production orders
- Inventory management
- Invoice verification
- Purchasing optimization
- Configuration and organization in manufacturing
- Configuration and organization in materials management

These functions combined provide the functionality to manage the production process from raw material orders through planning through completed goods.

The production order is primarily a tool for discrete, job-shop production. It provides status management functions and controlling per order. Repetitive manufacturing is designed for manufacturers of products that are typically produced repetitively on a particular production line over a long period. Capacity planning is integrated with production order processing as well as with repetitive manufacturing.

SAP's materials management application contains the functions to run requirements planning, purchasing, inventory management, warehouse management, and invoice verification. All functions are integrated with each other and with other functions in SAP R/3. The system passes purchase requisitions directly to purchasing, where they are converted into purchase orders. You can send purchase orders or forecast delivery schedules to the vendors either on paper or electronically.

Quality Management and Plant Maintenance

In SAP, an inspection is documented by an inspection lot and the corresponding inspection results. Materials can be maintained in batches on the basis of certain quality characteristics. You can use the batch characteristics defined in quality management (QM) as a means of searching for batches in a delivery. When you record inspection results, you have several options:

- Record the results directly in SAP R/3.
- Transfer results by linking test or measurement equipment to SAP.
- Transmit inspection specifications to a subsystem via a standard interface and retrieve the inspection results using the same interface.

The functions for statistical process control (SPC) provide a means of monitoring, controlling, and improving the processes. The SAP R/3 system supports the use of quality control charts for this purpose.

Plant maintenance supports various options for structuring technical systems with its object, type, and function-related views, and enables flexible navigation. Data concerning the planning, processing, and history of maintenance tasks are documented in the system and comply with business verification requirements. You can use the catalog system to define causes, activities, and maintenance tasks. All maintenance tasks, such as inspection, servicing, and repair activities, are saved in a historical database.

Sales and Distribution

The sales and distribution (SD) component provides tools to manage information on sales leads, sales calls, inquiries, quotations, marketing campaigns, competitors, and their products. Sales and marketing personnel can access the data to perform sales activities or carry out direct mailings. You can use SD to identify new sources of business as well. A sample of topics could be:

- Organizational structures
- Master data in SD processing
- Sales
- Pricing
- Shipping
- Billing
- Credit management
- Sales information system
- Integration with other applications
- Special business transactions
- Delivery processing

- Special features of LIS in SD
- Foreign trade

While this list may look small, the details behind an SD implementation are numerous and complex. In fact, in some organizations, this may well be the largest piece of an SAP rollout.

Pricing is carried out in the sales order. To determine relevant predefined prices, surcharges, and discounts, the system works from price lists and customer agreements, or it determines an amount according to the product, product group, or product cost. The system also carries out a credit limit check, checking against credit, financial, and sales data to verify the credit limits. The availability check is run in connection with the materials management production planning applications, and verifies that you have sufficient quantities for the requested delivery date to satisfy a sales order.

Shipping management offers functions for managing picking, packing, and loading tasks, and monitoring delivery deadlines. The system provides a list of all sales orders due for delivery, and gives you the option of delivering the order completely or partially, individually or collectively. The transportation module offers functions for transportation planning and processing, as well as functions for monitoring and controlling. You can also select forwarding agents and track shipments.

Human Resources Management

SAP HR offers payroll and time management capabilities, standard language, and currency and regulatory requirements for more than 30 countries. SAP HR includes employee self-service, manager's desktop, and SAP Accelerated HR. SAP Accelerated HR allows organizations to implement SAP through preconfigured settings, data transfer utilities, end-user training materials, and documentation. A sample set of SAP HR courses might include:

- Master data
- Time recording
- Gross payroll accounting
- Net payroll accounting
- Recruitment
- Organizational management
- Personnel development
- Training and events management
- Compliance reporting

There is a slight complication in HR training. The SAP HR solution is assisted by a set of solutions provided by complementary software partners, which means that you may need to get help from outside your SAP team to complete the SAP HR training.

Project Management

The SAP R/3 Project System permits you to link between project management and information processing. The functions available in the SAP R/3 system provide support that meets the requirements typical of projects. Training on the Project System may include areas such as:

- Investment management
- Marketing
- Software and consulting services
- Research and development
- Maintenance tasks and shutdown planning
- Plant engineering and construction
- Complex make-to-order production

You can use the Project System's graphical interface to create work breakdown structures. Integration with other modules in the SAP R/3 System enables you, for example, to plan resources in cooperation with purchasing, inventory management, etc. SAP Business Workflow is used to improve communications within large projects.

Throughout project processing, the system lets you tailor the layout and degree of detail of reports to suit your requirements. Listings and graphical analyses supply the information you need on budget, planned and actual costs, revenues, commitments, payments received and made, schedules, and resources. Standard interfaces provide the two-way communications base required for further planning and calculations in additional systems and at the local level.

Technical Support and Application Development in SAP ABAP/4 Development Workbench

Most technical curricula provide overviews of SAP R/3, the architecture, and the basic technology. This training must be customized to fit the technical details of the organization, including:

- Client and server operating systems
- Network operating systems
- Hardware (client, server, network, mobile)
- Application development processes, methods, and techniques
- Program promotion procedures
- Testing procedures

Each of these items can be a course or even a curriculum unto itself. It's important also to provide a technical overview of the organization's environment, so that technical staff aren't overwhelmed or don't get lost in the details of their own piece of the world.

The ABAP Workbench is the development tool used for writing programs in the R/3 System. Programs are developed in ABAP to bring exchange data with other systems, to modify and/or create reports, and to write on-line transaction program extensions (aka user exits). A good ABAP curriculum would include a course that teaches the fundamentals of the ABAP language and ways to work effectively with the tools. Because of the need to occasionally update the R/3 release installed, programmers must know how to implement enhancements and modifications to the R/3 System without modifying original R/3 objects, and they must know the best procedures for carrying out modifications. It's also important for technical staff to have a more advanced view of the ABAP dictionary and its facilities. Basis training would include operating system, hardware, and network support.

18.2 POTENTIAL PROBLEMS

As mentioned, SAP is a big piece of software. The sheer size and complexity of the package are going to make training development a major project. There are two sides to this issue. The first is the number of people the product will touch, and the second is the number of parts of the product. The training must include coverage of a number of issues related to achieving a successful implementation and functioning of SAP. The training must deliver information and share experiences, and address key considerations from both a resource and technical viewpoint. Key issues include:

- Support issues and resource requirements related to implementing SAP training
- Course design or redesign considerations when integrating SAP modules into a class

- Maintenance issues related to implementing SAP training
- Economics of implementing SAP training
- SAP instructor training issues
- Vendor and industry involvement and support with programs that include SAP courses

These issues are really only a starting point. There are likely to be other people and technology issues that will arise depending on the particular organization. Other common problems include:

- A short time frame prior to rollout to train all your employees
- Not enough instructors or classrooms
- The need to create customized documentation from scratch (lots of work!)
- A shortage of employees

CBT can help you rapidly deploy interactive learning methods for users and profiles throughout the entire organization, regardless of geographical location or connectivity issues. While CBT is not a panacea, it is possible to reach more people more quickly than traditional classroom training.

Another problem is training warehouse and plant employees in production and inventory control. The training for these activities is likely to involve a large number of people, because it may require training shop floor and part-time employees. Because of this factor, training in these areas will require extra planning. In addition, the education levels of these employees may vary widely. Employee handbooks and other job aids should be developed, and should offer plenty of practice time in the sandbox.

The training team must cope with SAP's thousands of parts, and one way to do this is to use SAP-compliant to-be process maps. Whether you are implementing the one module or multiple modules, you can ensure consistency and integration across projects by using SAP's business process maps as a checklist for developing training modules. The approach to designing training for SAP must include a flexible, integrated solution for skills transfer.

Although organizations are licensed to customize all SAP workshops for internal use, they sometimes do not have the internal expertise to do so. Also, some members do not have in-house training resources to actually deliver their training. Through the SAP business partner program, certified SAP partners can provide trainers for in-house training and can offer assistance in customizing training.

18.3   HOW TO CUSTOMIZE TRAINING FOR YOUR ORGANIZATION

SAP product knowledge is critical, and the approach used to training is important. End-user and technical staff training and system documentation are all vital to achieve complete success. The training team must provide your organization and its end users with the knowledge and tools needed to achieve the highest return on your technology investment. They must customize the training to fit the needs of your project and adjust to meet new requirements as your organization evolves.

Like most training programs, SAP training can be customized to meet the needs of particular organizations. The training team can perform education and training as standard workshops, as custom-tailored courses, or on original SAP materials. Ideally the training team should perform the training with your system and office environment, but can provide training rooms and equipment as well for simulations. The training team must customize training for not only your end users, but also SAP project teams and consultants. Some customized elements should include:

- SAP-Applications, all modules (including special modules like TR, SM, and PM)
- SAP workflow management for your organization's needs
- Delta training for SAP R/3 releases
- Administration of your specific SAP information database for SAP's training material
- Concepts for your end-user training, project team training, and consultant training
- Development of customer-specific course material

One place to look for training materials, particularly as a starting point for customization, is the SAP Academy Partner program. Vendors in the program have several years of experience in SAP R/3 training and education. These vendors can help you deliver SAP training to customers and users.

Trainers on SAP must have excellent technical skills based on project experience throughout the entire life cycle of an SAP implementation. They must also know the critical success factors for education of SAP project teams and end users for your specific installation. This provides them with expert knowledge in the education of consultants and the performance of customizing courses. SAP has established a consultant certification program that some trainers may want to consider.

The training team must offer customized overviews of the SAP system and modules to assist managers and workers in understanding the exact nature of SAP. Instructor-led overviews give an overview of the SAP software, including the purpose and functionality of the main SAP modules. Integration of these modules and how they will affect the organization's business processes must also be covered. Users of SAP must gain an understanding of how SAP impacts the entire system.

18.4   BUYING TRAINING FROM SAP VERSUS THIRD-PARTY TRAINING VENDORS

Training from SAP and their partners has numerous benefits over unauthorized training vendors, and in fact most large enterprise education solutions involve a partnership between SAP and members of its education and business partner network. The key partnership is TeamSAP.

TeamSAP partners work in cooperation with SAP to deliver business solutions and assist customers in reaching their goals. For every SAP solution, these partnerships combine resources, products, services, emerging technologies, and industry requirements. SAP partners are chosen and certified based on their expertise in hardware, complementary software, industry and business practices, information technology, and implementation support.

There are various types of TeamSAP Partners. Consulting partners combine information technology and business skills to support R/3 projects. SAP groups consulting partners in two categories based on business scope: global and technology partners. Global consulting partners have multinational and multi-industry SAP consulting capabilities. They constitute the largest consultancies with worldwide representation. National consulting partners provide SAP consulting throughout one particular country.

Technology partners are companies producing hardware, operating systems, and network and/or database solutions with a signed TeamSAP agreement. This agreement implies a certification process to ensure support, cooperation, and adequate skill levels. There are some VARs addressing the small and medium-sized enterprise markets locally with R/3-based solutions and services. They have signed a cooperation agreement with SAP. Complementary software partners are companies that develop add-on software solutions following the interface definitions of SAP and that have signed a cooperation agreement.

18.5 WHAT YOU CAN OR MUST DELIVER IN HOUSE

Anything that involves the organization's specific business processes must be customized as mentioned above. Basis training will also need to be heavily customized, since the technical environment is unique to each organization. Some of the items you will need to develop in house or customize heavily are:

- Change management procedures
- Process scope statements. Includes the "as-is" process chains, functions, processes, and tasks included in the scope and also those specifically excluded
- SAP functional scope statements. The R/3 functionality to be implemented
- Technical enhancement scope statements. Defining custom development or modifications or existing system reengineering requirements
- Organizational scope statements. Business unit/divisional scope, geographical scope, and job scope
- I/T infrastructure scope statements. The hardware, systems software, and communication scope for the development, test, training, production, and other environments
- Interface scope statements. The expected interfaces to and from the SAP system
- Data conversion scope statements. The data conversion efforts necessary to create the opening data for the new system
- Reports and forms scope statements. Any exceptional reporting and form-generation requirements

All this information will vary from organization to organization. Of course, the associated deliverables, such as interfaces, report formats, and infrastructure components, must be customized and installed to on-site specifications.

18.6 RECOMMENDED TRAINING RESOURCES, BOOKS, AND WEBSITES

There are many associations of SAP users and business partners, some sanctioned by SAP, some not. Either way, there are probably SAP user groups in your area. Listed here are some of the better known groups that can provide help in developing a quality SAP training program.

SAPNet

SAPNet (http://sapnet.sap.com) is SAP's main medium for information and communication between SAP and its customers and partners. SAPNet contains (nearly) everything you've ever wanted to know about SAP, its products and processes, and its partners and solutions. You will also find daily news, upcoming events, and much more. In the self-service area you can order brochures, call up certain services immediately, register for training courses, etc. SAPNet is being continually enhanced, making communication with SAP even easier and more fun to do. And your opinion counts. SAPNet is only accessible for SAP customers and partners who have a valid Online Service System user ID and password.

SAPAssist.com, http://www.sapassist.com/

This site is formatted as a portal, and looks like Yahoo! It has lists of and links to books, complementary software, consulting firms, hardware providers, SAP info and news, peer publishing, recruitment professionals, technical documents, partners, and training specialists.

SAP Fan Club, http://www.sapfans.com/

Believe it or not, there is actually an SAP fan club. The website is a loose collection of user forums, chat rooms, news and event listings, books, articles, and even CBT resources. It also has a repository of information and books on programming, implementation, and training. There are links to articles and research from various on-line publications and analyst groups as well.

SAP Technical Journal Online, http://www.saptechjournal.com

The entire first and second issues of the *SAP Technical Journal Online* are now available on this site, including the popular columns "BAPI Developer," "Dr. ABAP," "R/3 Administrator," and "User Group." The journal has added more feature articles and a "Reader Mail" column to its lineup. Make sure to check the Message Board, where you can post questions and share information with other SAP developers.

Third-Party Books and Publishers

Many books about SAP exist. The easiest way to find them is to do subject searches at publishers' websites. Most third-party publishers now allow you to view and order via the web. While there are hundreds of small publishers, this list includes 10 of the largest, in no particular order. The websites listed are current as of this writing.

McGraw-Hill
http://www.bookstore.mcgraw-hill.com

Addison Wesley Longman
http://www.awl.com

Amazon.com
http://www.amazon.com

Barnes and Noble
http://www.barnesandnoble.com

Que Publishing
http://www.mcp.com/publishers/que

Sybex Books
http://www.sybex.com

IDG Worldwide
http://www.idg.com

Prentice Hall
http://www.phptr.com

Macmillan/Sams Publishing
http://www.macmillan.com

Prima Publishing
http://www.primapublishing.com

One of the better books on SAP training is called the *SAP Documentation and Training Development Guide* by Kathryn E. Park. It's published by Bobkat Enterprises (ISBN 0965662128) and can be ordered at Amazon or Barnes and Noble on-line. In addition to her book, Park offers an estimating tool that allows a company to plug in the number of scripts and transactions being developed for a project and calculate the number of writers, editors, and project leaders required to develop documentation. Park's book and estimator software can be ordered using the toll-free number (888) BOBKAT3.

To find SAP resources on the web, you can use any of the major search engines to locate newsgroups, bulletin boards, and other resources, as well as vendors such as the Big Five consulting firms and others, whose web-sites include:

Andersen Consulting
http://www.andersenconsulting.com
KPMG Peat Marwick
http://www.kpmg.com
Price Waterhouse Coopers
http://www.pwcglobal.com
Ernst & Young
http://www.ey.com
Deloitte & Touche
http://www.deloitte.com
Booze Allen Hamilton
http://www.bah.com
EDS
http://www.eds.com

Many small and midsized firms work with SAP and other packaged software solutions. These firms can be found through the yellow pages, web searches, on-line directories, or SAP's website.

Oracle Applications Training*

In This Chapter

OVERVIEW

Oracle Applications is an Internet-enabled suite of more than 45 software modules for customer relationship management, manufacturing, supply chain management, financials, projects, and human resources. Oracle's strategy to develop and market products specific to selected vertical

---

*Certain portions of copyrighted Oracle Corporation documentation have been reproduced herein with the permission of Oracle Corporation.

markets is grounded in its applications. The applications can be customized for various industries, including:

- Automotive
- Aviation, aerospace, and defense
- Communications
- Consumer packaged goods
- Energy
- Financial services
- Health care
- Government and utilities
- Technology-based companies

The applications are customized to the industries mentioned by targeting specific concepts such as internal processes, supply chain and customer relationship management, decision support, global business practices, and I/T infrastructure support.

Oracle offers a wide variety of education services and educational consulting, in addition to the normal classes on applications. Various delivery methods are offered, including:

- Seminars
- The Oracle Channel
- On-site training
- Role-based Oracle applications training
- Custom training services

Seminars are short, self-contained training events that bring you up to date. There are two types of seminars. Strategic seminars enable decision makers to hear from Oracle and industry specialists about the use of existing and emergent technologies and future trends in the I/T industry. Technical seminars enable developers to explore a specialist topic in more depth or pick up the latest features of a new Oracle software release. Seminar titles change regularly to keep pace with new technology and releases.

The Oracle Channel is a television channel that delivers interactive training. The Oracle Channel combines satellite broadcasts with personal communication devices, allowing instantaneous interactivity between students and the instructor using voice and data. The Oracle Channel has already trained hundreds of Oracle staff. This service is now available to customers.

Oracle role-based training makes application users more effective in performing their jobs by focusing on the specific tasks and responsibilities of their roles, as defined by the organization. Custom exercises can be developed using your own data, policies, and procedures to create a productionlike environment. This type of class is particularly useful for technical staff who will be involved in administering and maintaining the applications.

Oracle courses are standard offerings designed to provide the most complete coverage possible. However, one size does not fit all, and about 30 percent of the courses Oracle runs are tailored to client requirements by selecting and combining topics to match client needs. Dedicated courses can be run at your site or Oracle's.

19.1 KEY TRAINING POINTS

Because of the number of modules in the Oracle applications suite, the training development effort is sizable. One advantage of the Oracle applications suite, however, is its modularity. Each application can be implemented either piecemeal or as part of a whole, integrated solution.

Supply Chain and Manufacturing

The supply chain part of the application is broken into a number of key product types, including sales and delivery, planning, vendor and trading partner management, purchasing, engineering workflow, and simulation. Manufacturing is broken into materials, production, cost, and quality management. The key training points are:

- Sales order management
- Global capable-to-promise
- Supply chain planning
- Supply base management
- Trading partner collaboration
- Enterprise procurement optimization
- New product engineering
- Planning and simulation
- Materials management
- Production
- Cost management
- Quality management

These functions work together as a single, integrated business management system to support the extended enterprise, from initial prospect contact to final product delivery to postsales service and support. The training should focus on facilitating the process, as well as the specific features.

Financials

As with most financial packages, Oracle's is broken into planning, analysis, consolidation, expenditure management, billing and collections, cash management, and asset management. The key training points are:

- Financial planning
- Financial analysis
- Financial consolidation
- Expenditure management
- Billing and cash collection
- Cash management
- Asset management

The training should tie together these pieces and address the areas facing most financial organizations today: implementing effective global financial management, lowering administrative costs, closing the books faster, improving cash management, and making better decisions.

Strategic Enterprise Management

Oracle strategic enterprise management (SEM) addresses value-based management conflicts by prioritizing decisions in the context of overall organizational goals, focusing the enterprise on value creation and shareholder return. SEM is an enterprisewide solution and a complementary addition to ERP systems. Oracle SEM provides a platform on which executives can coordinate the strategic planning process in the context of capital market fluctuations and competitive movements. The planning process defines corporate goals and objectives. Financial and nonfinancial internal and external key performance indicators (KPIs) that reflect the strategic plan of the enterprise are then identified. These help executives monitor the enterprise's progress toward achieving these goals and objectives. For more information on training for this product/concept, see http://www.oracle.com/applications/html/sem.html.

Human Resources

Oracle HRMS provides the ability to manage recruitment, staffing, training, compensation, benefits, and planning. Each module is part of a suite. The key training points are:

- Staffing
- Employee development
- Position management
- Total compensation
- Self-service features
- Payroll and retropay
- Time collection

This application should be fairly easy for most HR people to learn, as it uses well-known concepts. Oracle HRMS applications can also be integrated with Oracle's other offerings.

Customer Relationship Management

Customer relationship management (CRM) is hot these days, and Oracle uses a set of applications to help organizations market their products and services, tailor contracts, and provide access to customer history. A training developer should understand that Oracle divides its offerings into marketing, sales, service, call center, e-commerce, and mobile access. The Marketing product suite includes:

- Oracle Marketing
- Oracle iMarketing
- Oracle Marketing for Communications
- Oracle TeleBusiness for Financial Services
- Oracle TeleBusiness for Telco/Utilities

Some of these products are also included in other applications of the CRM concept as you will notice.

Oracle Sales automates the entire sales cycle, from opportunity management and pipeline analysis to forecast and order management. The Sales product suite includes:

- Oracle iStore
- Oracle TeleSales

- Oracle Field Sales
- Oracle Field Sales/Palm Devices
- Oracle Sales Compensation
- Oracle TeleBusiness for Financial Services
- Oracle TeleBusiness for Telco/Utilities

Notice that the telebusiness offerings are common to several applications.

Oracle Service is a suite of applications designed for end-to-end service delivery and customer care, including support, field service, and depot repair businesses. They can be deployed across the web, call center, and mobile field channels. The Service product suite includes:

- Oracle Service
- Oracle Web Customer
- Oracle Contracts
- Oracle Customer Care
- Oracle Mobile Field Service
- Oracle Maintenance, Repair, and Overhaul
- Oracle Service for Communication
- Oracle TeleBusiness for Financial Services
- Oracle TeleBusiness for Telco/Utilities

The Oracle Call Center and Telephony Suite supports the operation of inbound, outbound, and blended call centers. Oracle's Call Center is a single-source solution that is integrated with the business applications in CRM as well as ERP applications. The Oracle Call Center technology can be combined with applications. The Call Center product suite includes:

- Oracle TeleSales
- Oracle Telephony Manager
- Oracle Customer Care
- Oracle OpenTel
- Oracle Call Center
- Oracle Campaign Plus
- Oracle Predictive
- Oracle Fulfillment
- Oracle IVR Integrator
- Oracle Insight

- Oracle Call Blending
- Oracle TeleBusiness for Financial Services
- Oracle TeleBusiness for Telco/Utilities

Oracle offers an e-commerce suite, which addresses customer relationship management from lead generation, to unassisted sales, to aftermarket customer service. Oracle's e-commerce applications enable businesses to sell products and services, and provide customer care. The e-commerce suite includes:

- Oracle iMarketing
- Oracle iStore
- Oracle iBill and Pay
- Oracle iPayment
- Oracle Web Customers

Oracle delivers tools that can improve a field representative's ability to achieve customer satisfaction while selling or servicing products. Oracle's applications for mobile devices give field representatives the technology they need to exchange information with the office, enabling them to spend more time taking care of prospects and customers. The mobile access suite includes:

- Oracle Field Sales
- Oracle Field Sales/Palm Devices
- Oracle Mobile Field Service

Because of the integration of these suites, and because various pieces are used in multiple applications, training on these suites can be somewhat easier. Once employees are trained on Oracle TeleBusiness for Telco/Utilities, for example, they can transition into other functional areas easily.

19.2 POTENTIAL PROBLEMS

The size, complexity, and number of applications are going to make training development a major project. Training, in particular, is a key issue for companies implementing Oracle Applications, especially if the user interfaces are unfamiliar (e.g., Oracle forms versus standard Windows formats). Training issues are obvious during the kind of rapid ERP implementation that Oracle often advocates. There may be a 2- or 3-week period for training the project team, many of whom will be users. But this may be no more than adequate for the members of the project team, who in turn are expected to train coworkers.

Database administrators and other development staff may assume they know the applications because they know the Oracle database, but this is not necessarily true. You will still have a lot of tweaking to do to increase the performance of the system, and techies should understand the performance impact of the applications on a standard Oracle database setup.

Also, whether you're implementing the applications in a single site or going worldwide across multiple sites, training must be consistent. Some organizations that already have Oracle databases in place may assume they can roll out enterprisewide easily. The challenges of global implementation are unique, with more operational and geographical considerations. Characteristics include longer implementation life cycles, currency factors, language translation, and thousands of end users and support staff. It's important for training team members to help set realistic expectations.

The training program's complexity is the result of all the separate pieces of information being available, such as current manufacturing capacity, parts availability, inventory levels at all locations, distribution capabilities, and current and forecasted product demand. This level of complexity can be overwhelming for employees, and yet is a requirement for competitive success in many industries.

With respect to Oracle Projects, project management experts have long discussed establishing central project offices that oversee the management of all projects across the enterprise. The implementation of Oracle Projects may set some unrealistic expectations. The project office may suddenly be expected to analyze the impact of project management on the enterprise, and provide an analysis of return on project management investment. Barriers to success include the remote, distributed nature of project teams and the multiple islands of information containing project data.

19.3 HOW TO CUSTOMIZE TRAINING FOR YOUR ORGANIZATION

Organizations often think they "know" Oracle because they possess the database. However, they fail to realize that the applications will probably be customized as much as the database. End-user and technical staff training and system documentation, which are often lacking or nonexistent in the database world, are vital to achieve success when implementing the applications. It is essential to customize the training to fit the needs of your project and adjust to meet new requirements as your organization evolves. Trainers must understand that every organization has a unique set of I/T and business training requirements.

Like most training programs, Oracle training can be customized to meet the needs of particular organizations. An analysis and the results of competency assessments will provide details on requirements for customization (see Chapter 2). The training team can perform education and training as standard workshops, as custom-tailored courses, or through the Oracle Education group and its partners. The training team must customize training for end users, project teams, DBAs, and consultants.

Oracle's self-service information systems offer a particular customization challenge. If employees with questions are able to click directly to centrally maintained answers, there is going to be a need to train employees on more than just their specific function. For example, if a warehouse employee wants to check his or her own withholding, that employee must know how to access payroll screens. Obviously, the warehouse employee won't need the level of detailed training that the payroll clerk will, so that means that a payroll course will need to be customized for two different audiences.

If you're using vendors to customize Oracle training, remember that the high cost of customization and support of custom training must be taken into account. Most users try to use standard packages to the greatest extent possible. Vendors are certainly aware of customization problems as well. Also, some vendors may only have partial packages and are looking for someone to help them complete the development effort. Asking questions, rather than explaining your specific situation, allows the vendor to offer suggestions and demonstrate methods of operation that you may not have thought of.

Also, try to work with as many people as possible, including DBAs and DBA consultants from vendors. The more exposure key individuals have before a system is purchased, the less confusion there will be during the installation, and the more they will be able to help with training. Even though Oracle has business partners with lots of experience, vendors should not be asked to rush their responses unless there is good cause. One to two months, with iterative question and answer sessions, for a detailed response for an Oracle application training program complex system is not unreasonable.

Getting help from Oracle and Oracle educational consultants can help you match the training to the functionality of Oracle Applications for your business. They may also be able to suggest strategies for implementing off-the-shelf or tailored training. Working with Oracle Education will provide an implementation partner that can deliver a solution that you can either use or purchase and customize. There are also consulting service providers who have specialized practices in advanced technology and vertical industries with focused expertise to deliver targeted business solutions.

19.4 BUYING TRAINING FROM ORACLE VERSUS THIRD-PARTY TRAINING VENDORS

Training from Oracle and its authorized training centers has numerous benefits over unauthorized training vendors, and in fact most large enterprise education solutions involve a partnership between Oracle and members of its education and business partner network. Oracle Education can orchestrate a range of organizational learning services and training products to create a custom solution that will help your workgroup, department, or global enterprise achieve the results you envision.

Oracle Education can deliver the depth and breadth of resources you need for most application implementation projects. The learning solution it designs integrates the components being installed with the training needed to provide users with expert knowledge. Oracle Education can also bundle individual services and training methods. Oracle Education's Performance Consulting group works with management staff to organize and clarify the new roles of individuals as part of a comprehensive change management plan.

Oracle uses an ISD-like systematic approach to design a plan that fits Oracle's services to your project. Oracle usually starts to develop a detailed understanding of your needs. A proposal is then prepared which recommends a solution that maps to your goals. Oracle also provides training consultants to work closely with you to implement your plan. Oracle Education also has a system whereby it measures results and fine-tunes your plan.

The Oracle Education group also offers personalized professional development paths. This includes job role–focused training. Users or technical staffers can start at the beginning of their path and work their way to expertise. The professional development path system includes a variety of different training methods—and learners can combine related courses in different training methods. Oracle Education has identified two key milestones in the professional development path system. Learners first establish their competence by becoming an Oracle Certified Professional (OCP).

They then continue to build their skill set to the expert level of an Oracle Master.

There are four basic training methods. It's hard to beat the classroom for maximum-intensity, hands-on learning in a minimum amount of time, as mentioned elsewhere in this book. Oracle also offers CBT interactive courseware that can cut training time and costs by up to 50 percent. CD-ROM and Internet-delivered courses provide just-in-time training on Oracle products. Oracle Education Seminars are grouped together in 2- to 4-day seminar tracks to keep Oracle users and techies up to date. Certification and Master programs are also available.

There are, however, two advantages to using third-party training vendors, even if not certified by Oracle. The first is cost. Often third-party vendors will be 50 to 75 percent less expensive than Oracle. However, consider carefully the quality of the training. An ERP implementation should not be crushed by "cheap training." The other advantage is that customized training can be structured to leverage the extensive real-world experiences and skills of consultants to enable clients to maximize the productivity of end users and technical staff before, during, and after an Oracle Applications implementation.

Consultants can often provide an independent service that can be combined with their implementation services or can be utilized to provide the best training for all Oracle products at a lower cost. They will likely create their own training materials and customize them to the precise processes and transactions that are required. This helps clients to channel the exact focused training to their staff. A good consultant provides training on all Oracle products. Oracle Applications training should be based upon the actual processes and data relevant for each client.

19.5   WHAT YOU CAN OR MUST DELIVER IN HOUSE

Anything that involves the organization's specific business processes must be customized, as mentioned above. Also, the installation of the supporting Oracle database must be customized to meet the needs of the particular organization's hardware and software. The training department must put together a team of documentation and training specialists that will work with functional business process teams to develop custom training materials and classroom instruction to support the implementation.

It's important to understand how the Oracle implementation will affect the organization. An implementation impact statement must be developed in house, though consultants can certainly be involved. Modular documentation and training for each business process and the supporting Oracle application will usually be heavily customized or developed in house. Other potentially proprietary training includes functional task-based training so that students can focus on only the material that is needed for their job and so that training time can be accelerated.

Databases like Oracle change frequently, and it's important to establish the issues and trends in technology and training required within an organization. Training that will keep business and technical staff up to date with the changing technology of the organization should be developed in house, particularly with respect to an ERP system. The training team should provide strategies and techniques that include personal training and corporate training standards for Oracle applications and/or databases.

Obviously, any top-secret or highly proprietary technology that will be used with the Oracle applications, or that will feed or be fed by Oracle, should be developed in house. Because Oracle applications can use the same Oracle databases as other applications in an organization, there's often the temptation to interface many systems with the new applications. This works, provided that technical staff are trained on the interfaces and data communication methods needed to facilitate this data sharing.

19.6   RECOMMENDED TRAINING RESOURCES, BOOKS, AND WEBSITES

There are many associations of Oracle users and business partners, some sanctioned by Oracle, some not. There are certainly Oracle user groups in your area. Listed here are some of the better known groups and websites that can provide help in acquiring and developing the knowledge needed to produce a quality Oracle training program.

Oracle Education Partner Program

Oracle Education partners can be found by going to http://education.oracle.com/wizard/maps/. This site provides a tool to find partners in your state. Oracle Approved Education Centers deliver Oracle's most popular classes to Oracle customers using Oracle Education courseware. Partners provide the classroom facilities and the instructors, while Oracle provides Oracle software, courseware, product support, marketing, and the student registration system.

Oracle Education reviews all Oracle Education Center applicants. Appointment is based on a number of factors, including, but not limited to, applicant facility, instructor and education sales capabilities, projected growth of Oracle software and education sold in the area, proximity to Oracle direct training facilities, and location of other Oracle Approved Education Centers.

Self Supported Rental facilities offer Oracle's most popular classes to Oracle customers. Partners provide the classroom facilities and technical support, and Oracle provides the instructors, Oracle software, courseware, marketing, and student registration. Oracle Education reviews all Oracle Self Supported Rental applicants based on facility and technical qualifications, as well as location. Other Oracle partners can be found at http://www.oracle.com/partners/index.html.

Oracle Technet, http://technet.oracle.com/

This site is run by Oracle, and has free downloads, news from Oracle and its partners, and links to other parts of the Oracle website. It also has conference announcements relevant to Oracle.

Oracleassist.com, http://www.oracleassist.com/

This site is formatted as a portal, and looks like Yahoo!. It has lists of and links to books, complementary software, consulting firms, hardware providers, Oracle info and news, peer publishing, recruitment professionals, technical document, partners, and training specialists.

Oracle Fan Club, http://www.oraclefans.com/

Believe it or not, there is actually an Oracle fan club. The website is a loose collection of user forums, chat rooms, news and event listings, books, articles, and even CBT resources. It also has a repository of information and books on programming, implementation, and training. There are links to articles and research from various on-line publications and analyst groups as well.

Third-Party Books and Publishers

Many books about Oracle Applications exist. The easiest way to find them is to do subject searches at publishers' websites. Most third-party publishers now allow you to view and order via the web. While there are hundreds of small publishers, this list includes 10 of the largest, in no particular order. The websites listed are current as of this writing.

McGraw-Hill
http://www.bookstore.mcgraw-hill.com

Addison Wesley Longman
http://www.awl.com

Amazon.com
http://www.amazon.com

Barnes and Noble
http://www.barnesandnoble.com

Que Publishing
http://www.mcp.com/publishers/que

O'Reilly Publishing
http://oracle.oreilly.com/

IDG Worldwide
http://www.idg.com

Prentice Hall
http://www.phptr.com

Macmillan/Sams Publishing
http://www.macmillan.com

Oracle Press
http://www.oraclepress.com

To find Oracle resources on the web, you can use any of the major search engines to locate newsgroups, bulletin boards, and other resources, as well as vendors such as the Big Five consulting firms and others, whose websites include:

Andersen Consulting
http://www.andersenconsulting.com

KPMG Peat Marwick
http://www.kpmg.com

Price Waterhouse Coopers
http://www.pwcglobal.com

Ernst & Young
http://www.ey.com

Deloitte & Touche
http://www.deloitte.com

Booze Allen Hamilton
http://www.bah.com

EDS
http://www.eds.com

Many small and midsized firms work with Oracle and other packaged software solutions. These firms can be found through the yellow pages, web searches, on-line directories, or Oracle's website.

PART THREE

Appendixes

Rapid Development for Small Projects

Not all training projects involve large companies and big software packages. Some training projects may involve organizations of 5 to 100 people, or departments within organizations. Smaller projects are often treated as work that needs to be done by the end of the month. This appendix shows how to apply basic ISD techniques to managing, understanding, and coordinating small projects. At the same time, the techniques are fully compatible with methods for larger projects. It's important to follow a solid, structured training methodology if you want to produce a good-quality training program that can be accurately measured and continually improved.

While managing large projects calls for significant structure to formalize communication and decision making, small-project management requires a simplified tracking and review process to assure that projects don't fall through the cracks. This appendix uses a set of basic management elements that allow the amount of structure in the development process to be adjusted according to a small project's particular needs. Selectively applying this approach to small projects results in reduced cycle time and greater customer satisfaction.

SMALL-PROJECT STEPS AND DELIVERABLES

You can apply the activities described in Part One of this book, including analyzing the needs or opportunity, setting objectives, and defining requirements for an acceptable solution. Plan small projects by prioritizing multiple current projects for their urgency and importance and by tailoring the templates to create a work plan at the appropriate level of detail. Table A-1 provides an overview of a shortened life cycle and the minimum deliverables that should be produced. The templates are contained in Appendix G and on McGraw-Hill's website at www.books.mcgraw-hill.com/training/download. The forms can then be opened, edited, and printed using Microsoft Word or other word processing software. The set of tasks in the table can be completed within a few weeks or a few months, depending on the size and complexity of the effort. Be sure to schedule small projects realistically using methods that work best for single-person and several-person staffing.

Selling the program in a small company or for a small project is usually pretty easy because of the lower cost. It's still useful, however, to create a presentation of what you'll be doing, just to let management know that company money isn't being wasted. Also, by going through the formal sales process, people in the organization will become aware of the project. This is helpful because resources on small projects are usually limited, and the more people are willing to help, the easier the project will be.

Analyzing training needs is also simpler for small projects, as is analyzing the audience. In some cases, the trainer, training developer, and user may even be the same person. The key advantage to creating at least some formal documentation is that when a key training person leaves, the training program doesn't leave with that person. In addition, a needs analysis provides the opportunity to formalize training materials for new employees.

Creating the program plan can be done somewhat more informally on a smaller project. However, it's still a good idea to plan the work required to make sure that you have a handle on what needs to be done, how long it will take, and how much it will cost. Because budgets tend to be tighter on smaller projects, planning the training effort is just as important as it is on larger projects. Costing should be done carefully to prevent overruns.

Designing the program and custom-developing training can be done almost simultaneously, particularly if these tasks are coordinated with a vendor. As each part is designed, the content and class materials can be created. Often, smaller departments or organizations will purchase training because they don't have the resources (human or financial) to custom-

TABLE A-1

Phase	Steps	Minimum Deliverables
Selling the program	Convincing management of the need for a formal program	PowerPoint sales presentation template
Analyzing training needs	Discovering software training needs Finding out who needs what training Estimate effort	Feature/function matrixes Audience assessment forms Class needs estimate form
Creating the program plan	Determining dates and time lines Budgeting Project plan (abbreviated)	Estimating guidelines and form Budget spreadsheet Microsoft Project
Designing the program and custom-developing training	Determining courses Determining course objectives Creating syllabi Creating course content	Completed needs analysis data Needs-to-objectives matrixes Syllabus templates Slides and manuals
Purchasing training	Finding vendors Evaluating vendors and courseware Negotiating for the best deal Selecting handouts and books	Vendor and courseware evaluation forms and checklists Book evaluation form
Implementing the program	Tracking attendance Evaluating trainers and courses Measuring training effectiveness	Attendance form Evaluation templates Performance review templates
Evaluating and continually improving the program	Analyzing course results and employee performance Updating training	Performance review templates Course review forms Course update logs and templates

develop a complete program. If a vendor is used for most or all of a program, the vendor and courseware evaluation steps become extremely important. The forms and checklists specified in Table A-1 can help prevent vendor hype from fooling you.

Implementing a small program is often done through individual coaching. A trainer or SME acting as a trainer sits down next to the person using the system and walks the person through the process. This works well because of the personal attention received by the trainee. However, if the SME or trainer leaves, all of the knowledge goes too. That's why it's important to create formal training documents. In this situation, it's also especially important to do a thorough audience analysis. If the trainer doesn't know the person well, friction can result because of the close contact.

Evaluating and continually improving the program are steps often forgotten on small projects, and in small and medium-sized organizations. However, these steps are just as important on a small project as a large one. Training manuals in small organizations are often out of date because the person charged with maintaining them either left or switched jobs. The documentation must be kept current to be effective.

Evaluating small training projects actually can be harder than large projects, because the personalities of the trainer and trainee come into play into this step. If a trainer has been working closely with a trainee over a long period of time, judging performance can be tough from both sides. Neither wants to hurt the other's feelings, so the evaluations just get tossed aside. In this case, the trainee can be asked to evaluate the material, and, it is hoped, keep the trainer out of it. It is useful to have the trainer evaluate the course by looking at how the material helped or hindered the participant, without looking closely at the participant. It's very difficult to operate this way, but it's one way to avoid conflict.

Be sure to discuss with the rest of the organization both the challenge of coordinating the efforts of others and the benefits of teamwork. Describe to management the activities of the design and implementation phases and the benefits of formalizing those phases to help management understand why it's better to not fly by the seat of your pants even on small projects. Apply minimum-effort project tracking methods and assess project status. Small projects can easily get away from people, because what appears to be a small amount of work can quickly swell to a major effort.

SMALL-PROJECT ISSUES

The biggest issues with small projects are the "why not just do it?" syndrome and scope creep. It's important on a small project to at least size the project and plan the first phase, so that the trainer doesn't get overwhelmed. The trainer should make a first "guesstimate" at the effort required, and state the problem clearly. This in turn will help define the scope and objectives. It's also important to define requirements for an acceptable solution so that the effort isn't wasted.

It's possible that the small project may actually be multiple projects fit together. In this case, the trainer must establish priority over multiple concurrent projects, and make sure that the priorities assigned reflect those of the organization. It's also useful to make specialized activity lists for unique projects, so when those projects are done again, there's already a timesaving starting point in place. For a small project, often project management tools are overkill. In this case, scheduling methods such as calendar scheduling with a product like Microsoft Outlook are helpful.

Training Team Job Descriptions

This appendix provides sample descriptions of jobs that normally exist within a training department. The descriptions can be altered to fit the organization's needs and the specific skill sets required. As mentioned in Chapter 12, it's important to develop employee measurements based on specific job descriptions, and this includes the training department. Be sure to adapt these descriptions to the performance appraisal in place in your organization.

Position Title: <u>Training Manager</u>   Company: <u>Acme Widgets Inc.</u>
Location: <u>Minnesota</u>   Department: <u>Information Technology</u>
Incumbent: <u>TBD</u>   Reports To: <u>CIO</u>

Basic Functions:

- Provides senior management with the knowledge of the capabilities that the training personnel should, or could, render the organization.
- Identifies the minimum skills that training personnel should possess.
- Identifies the minimum areas in which performance standards should be developed.
- Plans, organizes, staffs, directs, and controls the activities of a training and development unit to meet the organizational and training goals of the department.

Staff:

Employees supervised: 3–10

Principal Accountabilities:

- Formulates training policy.
- Establishes measurable objectives for the unit.
- Prepares a training budget.
- Prepares a training and development plan that identifies and schedules what training and development will occur, explains why it will be conducted, specifies in what sequence, states the cost, and outlines the expected results.
- Allocates resources to implement the training plan.
- Manages the implementation of the training plan.
- Recruits, interviews, and selects personnel.
- Assesses development needs of staff, and provides them with appropriate growth opportunities.
- Assigns projects and tasks indicating who, what, when, where, why; provides recognition, rewards, and discipline; establishes standards of performance for subordinates.

<u>Nature and Scope:</u>

- This position reports to the CIO.
- The incumbent works with I/T application development and operations management and staff on the definition and publication of relevant documentation and training materials.

Position Title: <u>Training Specialist</u>   Company: <u>Acme Widgets Inc.</u>
Location: <u>Minnesota</u>   Department: <u>Information Technology</u>
Incumbent: <u>TBD</u>   Reports To: <u>Training Project Leader</u>

<u>Basic Functions:</u>

Works with the training team to monitor training materials for compliance with HR and government requirements.

<u>Staff:</u>

Employees supervised: 0

<u>Principal Accountabilities:</u>

- Participates in the creation of training materials.
- Checks training materials for problems relating to compliance with EEO and other government regulations related to human resource management.
- Works with other departments to determine the HR impact of training materials and programs.

<u>Nature and Scope:</u>

- This position reports to a training project leader.
- The incumbent works with application development and operations management and staff on the definition and publication of relevant documentation and training materials.
- The incumbent will work with managers, developers, and business partners to ensure the readability and compliance of all documentation.
- The incumbent will work with human resources to ensure that all materials comply with HR policies and best practices.

Position Title: <u>Technical Writer</u>   Company: <u>Acme Widgets Inc.</u>
Location: <u>Minnesota</u>   Department: <u>Information Technology</u>
Incumbent: <u>TBD</u>   Reports To: <u>Training Project Leader</u>

<u>Basic Functions:</u>

Develops/maintains systems, methodology, process/project management, and training materials.

<u>Staff:</u>

Employees supervised: 0

<u>Principal Accountabilities:</u>

- Writes, edits, and updates training documentation.
- Designs documentation layouts and templates.
- Assists the training developers in preparing and maintaining training documents.
- Assists the trainer in preparing and maintaining training materials.
- Designs, writes, and edits technical training publications including:
    - End-user documentation for publication
    - End-user and development/support reference
    - Product support literature for corporate programs and processes to specified format
- Maintains integrity of electronic and paper files and source data packages.

<u>Nature and Scope:</u>

- This position reports to the training project leader.
- The incumbent works with application development and operations management and staff on the definition and publication of relevant documentation.
- The incumbent will maintain a standard, centralized set of documents and templates.
- The incumbent will work with managers, developers, and business partners to ensure the readability and ease of use for all documentation.

Position Title: <u>Training Developer</u>   Company: <u>Acme Widgets Inc.</u>
Location: <u>Minnesota</u>   Department: <u>Information Systems</u>
Incumbent: <u>TBD</u>   Reports To: <u>Training Project Leader</u>

Basic Function:

Develops and executes the I/T training plan based on past, present, and forecasted training needs.

Staff:

Employees supervised: 0

Principal Accountabilities:

- Develops, administers, and maintains effective I/T training programs, methods, and materials.
- Recommends and supervises developed and contracted training resources. Assures that the contracted resources possess the necessary KSAs to perform the necessary functions.
- Monitors, supports, and improves all software tools associated with training.
- Works with the ERP and I/T managers and staff to ensure that I/T personnel are optimally trained on established software standards and processes.

Nature and Scope:

- This position reports to the training project leader.
- The incumbent works with application development and operations management and staff to determine I/T training needs; develops plans to meet those needs; and coordinates the development/purchase, delivery, and evaluation of the training.
- The incumbent coordinates training with HR to ensure that training is planned, delivered, and evaluated in a manner consistent with personnel policies.
- Because the incumbent works with all levels of I/T management to plan and implement training programs, strong interpersonal skills are necessary.

- The incumbent should have the following knowledge, skills, and experience:
  - Training planning and portfolio management
  - Systems training development, delivery, and evaluation
  - Training development methods
  - Human resource issues associated with training

Position Title: <u>Trainer</u>   Company: <u>Acme Widgets Inc.</u>
Location: <u>Minnesota</u>   Department: <u>Information Systems</u>
Incumbent: <u>TBD</u>   Reports To: <u>Training Project Leader</u>

<u>Basic Function:</u>

Delivers training.

<u>Staff:</u>

Employees supervised: 0

<u>Principal Accountabilities:</u>

- Works with training developers to create I/T training programs, methods, and materials.
- Recommends and supervises developed and contracted training resources.
- Uses, supports, and improves all software tools associated with training.
- Listens to participants and brings back feedback.

<u>Nature and Scope:</u>

- This position reports to the training project leader.
- The incumbent works with application development and operations management and staff to optimize I/T training and coordinates the delivery of the training.
- The incumbent coordinates training with HR to ensure that training is delivered in a manner consistent with personnel policies.
- Because the incumbent works with all levels of I/T management to implement training programs, strong interpersonal skills are necessary.
- The incumbent should have the following knowledge, skills, and experience:
    - Training planning and portfolio management
    - Systems training development, delivery, and evaluation
    - Training development methods
    - Human resource issues associated with training

Sample Training Sales Presentation

This appendix presents a sample presentation for selling a training program. As mentioned in Chapter 1, the key is to stress the benefits of spending the time and resources (both financial and human) to create a cohesive, effective program. If this doesn't work the first time, there's always Chapter 14, where you learn how to fix things that should have been done earlier, when the software was being selected and installed. These slides can be downloaded from www.books.mcgraw-hill.com/training/download.

Trepper Widgets Training Program Plan—Agenda

- Project overview.
- Why must we do this?
- Project phases and deliverables.
- Project staff plan.
- Project time line and budget.
- How will we know we succeeded?
- Benefits.

5/23/99   WCS/KIS Training Program   1

Training Program Plan Overview

- Widget Control System (WCS).
- Knowledge Information System (KIS).
- 2 *huge* paradigm shifts for AWI.
- Training will integrate both products.
- Training will provide hands-on experience.
- Follows a standard, proven methodology.
- Adds real value and cuts costs.

5/23/99   WCS/KIS Training Program   2

Training Program Plan—Why

- WCS and KIS are too big to learn OJT.
- Good training can increase productivity.
- Without a training program, there is a risk of incorrect use causing bad data.
- Incrementally, training is small $$$$.
- An integrated program is more valuable long term than lots of disjointed pieces.

5/23/99   WCS/KIS Training Program   3

Training Program Plan Project Phases and Deliverables

Phase	Deliverable	Responsibility
Analysis	Needs analysis, surveys, workflows, software use cases	Training, Systems Development
Detail Project Plan	Design and delivery plan based on needs, budget, timeline	Training, Senior Management
Design	Training materials, scope, and sequence documents measurements	Training, Systems Development
Determine Training Source	RFI/P, vendor selection, if internal — project plan for remaining phases	Training, Senior Management
Implementation	Training classes, hardware/software installations, ongoing support process	Training, Systems Development
Evaluation	Summative and formative evaluation, effectiveness measurements, productivity/P&L impact statement	Training, Systems Development, Users, Senior Management.

5/23/99   WCS/KIS Training Program   4

Training Program Plan Project Staff Plan

Title	Responsibilities	Deliverables
Training team lead	Sell, manage, and coordinate the training program	Project plan, executive summary, status reports, presentations
Training developer	Perform needs analysis, design training program, work with technical writers to produce materials	Training materials, evaluation plan and materials, feedback forms
HR training specialist	Monitor the training program for regulatory compliance, participate in training and evaluation designs	Regulatory compliance statements, HR follow-up plans, employee development impact statements
Trainer	Deliver the training effectively	Usability and participant feedback on training materials
Technical writer	Create and maintain training documentation and other materials	Training manuals, documentation updates, project document library

5/23/99   WCS/KIS Training Program   5

Training Program Plan Project Time Line and Budget

Phase	Staff Costs	Material Costs	Elapsed Time
Analysis	$75,000	$10,000	46 Weeks
Detail Project Plan	$10,000	$25,000	1 Week
Design	$350,000	$150,000	68 Weeks
Set Training Source	$10,000	$10,000	35 Weeks
Implementation	$200,000	$150,000	Ongoing
Education	$10,000	$10,000	Ongoing

5/23/99   WCS/KIS Training Program   6

Training Program Plan Measuring Success

- Formative evaluations help provide continual improvement guidance.
- Summative evaluations indicate learning.
- Expert content evaluations can ensure that the right knowledge is transferred.
- Productivity/cost measurements.
- P&L impact studies.

5/23/99   WCS/KIS Training Program   7

Training Program Plan—Benefits

- More productive staff.
- Fewer mistakes in processing.
- Lower costs.
- Shorter learning curve for new employees.
- Employees learn new skills.
- More effective, efficient use of software.
- Better use of I/T improves competitiveness.

5/23/99   WCS/KIS Training Program   8

Training Program Plan—Issues

- Organizational involvement
  —Users will help determine their needs by completing surveys.
  —Training staff will develop approach and format for materials.
  —Systems development staff will help create and approve content.

5/23/99   WCS/KIS Training Program   9

Training Program Plan—Issues

- Ownership
  —Content will be jointly owned by users, developers, and training staff.
  —Content will be maintained by training.
  —Format will be maintained by training.
  —Communication will involve all parties, with public management commitment.

5/23/99   WCS/KIS Training Program   10

Training Program Plan—Issues

- Complexity
  —Multiple tracks will be developed to provide more targeted, effective training.
  —Overviews of each track will be available to aid in course selection by participants.
  —Some content will be purchased for speed.
  —Training staff must increase to operate this curriculum effectively.

5/23/99   WCS/KIS Training Program   11

Training Program Plan—Conclusion

- We need six to eight training people to do this right.
- We need access to others on a timely basis.
- We must work with other areas to succeed.
- We need management backing.
- We must get started soon!

5/23/99   WCS/KIS Training Program   12

Sample Training Program Plan Outline

This appendix contains a sample and completed training program plan. This is by no means intended to be comprehensive, but should be used as a guide to determine what information should be included in such a plan. Each organization's management will almost certainly want different pieces or sections, and this document can be adapted to any training project as needed.

Program Purpose

This section details the purpose of the program, which can be the problem to be solved or business opportunity to be exploited. This section can also contain a "goal," or an unmeasurable "know it when I see it" type of statement.

Program Background

What happened before this program? What were the forces that drove the program into being? How was training handled up until now?

Program Scope/Exclusions

This section *must* outline the software that will be covered, and what will not be covered. Often, saying what won't be done is as important as saying what will.

Organizational Units Involved/Impacted

This program will impact many user and I/T areas. Specify what areas are and are not part of the rollout. This will often lead back to some selling work, particularly if a department that was to be excluded now wants to be part of the program.

Goals and Objectives

The overall goals of this program are generally not measurable. The objectives, however, *must* be stated clearly and must be measurable. There is often some confusion between a goal and an objective. An objective is always measurable; a goal may or may not be measurable.

Expected Benefits

This section should be about both tangible and intangible benefits.

Issues/Constraints

Are there any time or budget constraints? Is the proper technology available to do the job? What about the human resources needed to complete the program?

Critical Success Factors

This is a list of items that must be present to ensure the success of this program.

Risks

What happens if this program fails? What happens if the critical path or other resources aren't available when needed? What if some assumptions turn out to be incorrect?

Program Approach and Deliverables

The phases as specified in Appendix F (in the estimating guide) can be inserted here (without dates), and the deliverables grid can be inserted as well.

Management Approach

Time and Status Reporting

Weekly program and team status and time reporting requirements should be specified here and will likely include accomplishments and main efforts for the week, plans for the coming week, and any issues, concerns, or problems that arise.

Meetings

Team meetings for all staff and consultants directly involved in the program should be inserted here. These should be regular meetings. Other meetings to communicate with management or key end users will be set up on an as-needed basis.

Change Management Process

Any significant changes to estimates, schedule, or scope (e.g., additional tasks, expanded complexity, increased learning curve) will be documented (description of change, why it is required, impact), then discussed with the team for approval before proceeding. A form should be developed by the team for this use.

Acceptance/Sign-off Process

Major deliverables should be reviewed for completeness, compliance with standards, and accurate content prior to sign-off. At a minimum, the following people involved in this process will be:
(names here)

PROGRAM ORGANIZATION SECTION

Training lead   ?????
Business lead   ?????
Rollout lead   ?????
Consultants   ?????

Preliminary Program Schedule and Budget

This section contains the phase grid with dates and dollars.

Signatures

_____

Training Manager

_____

Business Manager(s)

_____

Rollout Manager(s)

WCS/KIS Training Program Plan Outline
Revision Date: January 27, 2000

Program Purpose

The purpose of this project is to develop a training program for the rollout of the Widget Control System (WCS) and Knowledge Information System (KIS) software packages. This program will serve both I/T and business users, through a combination of classes that address varying skill levels and needs. The program will be strong enough to support current activity, but flexible enough to change with future needs. The program will serve as a model for future training design.

Program Background

This program was initiated by I/T and business users, as well as the training department. It's important to note that training for previous software rollouts was developed "on the fly" and really didn't follow any specific, structured methodology. By following the industry standard ISD methodology, this program will be stronger and more precise and will serve the users better than past efforts.

Program Scope/Exclusions

This program covers only those software functions to be installed at AWI. This particular program will be developed to fit future efforts at AWI, and will develop and set documentation standards.

Organizational Units Involved/Impacted

This program will impact many user and I/T areas. The areas of I/T that will be impacted include systems development, operations, technical support, and the help desk. Business areas include manufacturing, purchasing, HR, sales, and finance and accounting.

Goals and Objectives

The overall goal of this program is to develop a training program that will enable AWI employees to use the new software (WCS and KIS) in ways that will greatly enhance their productivity. The measurable objectives are:

- Complete the training program by 6/1/2000.
- Deliver classes to all affected staff within 60 days of installation.

- Stay within budget.
- Have a complaint rate of less than 3 percent.
- Have median instructor ratings of at least 5 on a 7-point Likert scale.
- Have median class ratings of at least 5.4 on a 7-point Likert scale.

These objectives will be measured for each class taught and for the program as a whole.

Expected Benefits

Without this training, employees are unlikely to use the software properly or in a manner that at least maintains their current level of productivity. Thus, this training program must be completed to have users be most effective with the new software packages.

Because of the nature and complexity of the WCS and KIS, it is estimated that the class taught in this program will save users up to 80 percent of the time they would spend learning the software OJT, and reduce help desk calls by 70 percent. The intangible benefits are lower levels of frustration, more effective production support, and better employee morale.

Issues/Constraints

As with any large project, the major constraints involve time, money, and human resources. Because of the small size of the core training team, other I/T and business staff must be matrixed in to complete the work. It is possible that deadlines will be missed if more training developers aren't hired.

Critical Success Factors

1. Select the best models for the classes.
2. Develop relationships with business partners.
3. Manage the budget closely.
4. Assign training development responsibilities to the best qualified team member.
5. Involve the training department personnel as well as external expertise in critical decisions.
6. Satisfy departmental needs in a specific business area.

7. Be large enough to be meaningful to a wide/critical audience.

8. Provide added business value.

9. Understand both limitations and capability for growth.

Risks

The major risks to this program involve missing deadlines or misidentifying needs. Misidentifying needs is likely to result in training that "doesn't answer the question." The TNA must be complete, and double-checked throughout the program development period. In addition, the training staff must stay close to the rollout team to make sure that the program follows the software correctly. Some strategies for mitigating the known risks include:

- Being very familiar with the goals of the project, or the specific focus they are involved with
- Being familiar with the general risks that are outlined in this risk plan
- Periodically considering the impact of any events and developments that may impact the cost, effort, product functionality, product quality, and schedule
- Screening the project opportunity and requirements to ensure that they are aligned with the corporation's business objectives
- Performing a high-level cost/benefit analysis to determine the risk relative to the potential gain and the opportunities for reward
- Reviewing the solution and assessing its technical feasibility, based on current technology
- Identifying initial business and technical risks
- Developing a high-level risk response strategy to reduce the impact of potential risks
- Promptly reporting any identified risk to the program lead

These strategies should result in a lower risk of failure for the program.

Management Approach

Time and Status Reporting

Weekly program and team status and time reporting requirements should be specified here and will likely include accomplishments and main efforts for the week, plans for the coming week, and any issues, concerns, or problems that arise.

<u>Meetings</u>

Team meetings for all staff and consultants directly involved in the program should be inserted here. These should be regular meetings. Other meetings to communicate with management or key end users will be set up on an as-needed basis.

<u>Change Management Process</u>

Any significant changes to estimates, schedule, or scope (e.g., additional tasks, expanded complexity, increased learning curve) will be documented (description of change, why it is required, impact), then discussed with the team for approval before proceeding. A form should be developed by the team for this use.

<u>Acceptance/Sign-off Process</u>

Major deliverables should be reviewed for completeness, compliance with standards, and accurate content prior to sign-off. At a minimum, the following people involved in this process will be:

- Richard, vice president of human resources
- Dennis, vice president of manufacturing
- Diego, vice president of sales
- Jeff, vice president of finance
- Sandra, vice president of purchasing
- Gary, WCS software rollout team leader
- Lauren, KIS software rollout team leader
- Bob, I/T training manager
- Connie, CIO

These signatures together will constitute approval of a completed milestone or deliverable.

Program Organization Section

The following people are involved in actually developing and delivering the program. It's important that the roles be clear to ensure the team operates at peak efficiency on this project.

- Connie, CIO
- Bob, I/T training manager
- Mike, I/T training team lead
- Shawn and Dave, trainers
- Kathy, training developer
- Jack, technical writer
- Trudy, human resources training specialist
- Gary, WCS software rollout team leader
- Lauren, KIS software rollout team leader

The training team must work closely with the rollout team and representatives from key user areas to ensure that the program meets the needs of the software rollout.

Program Approach and Deliverables

Item	Task	Deliverable(s)	Who	Done ✓
1.	Identify critical path activities	CPM, Gantt, or other chart	Training team, rollout team, users	✓
2.	Identify critical path players	Personnel, roles, and responsibilities form	Training team, rollout team, users	✓
3.	Document drop-dead date ranges	Copy of project plan obtained from rollout team (to be used in planning and design phases)	Training team, rollout team	✓
4.	Estimate the remaining activity hours and costs	Activity-based cost worksheet and program plan	Training team, rollout team, users	✓
5.	Factor in the elapsed time ranges	Activity-based cost worksheet and program plan	Training team, rollout team, users	✓
6.	Estimate hardware/ software costs	Activity-based cost worksheet	Training team, rollout team, users	✓
7.	Calculate the total budget	Activity-based cost worksheet	Training team, rollout team, users	✓
8.	Generate alternatives	Potential solution set	Training team, rollout team, users	✓
9.	Communicate the program plan to partners	Completed program plan document	Training team, rollout team, users	✓
10.	Gain management approval	Management sign-off	Management	✓

Preliminary Program Schedule and Budget

	Task group	Task	Days	Est. Start	Est. Done
1.	**Design**	Develop objectives	125	1/12/2000	2/28/2000
2.		Develop metrics	25	1/12/2000	2/28/2000
3.		Select/sequence content	15	3/2/2000	3/17/2000
4.		Create groups/tracks	5	2/28/2000	3/2/2000
5.	**Choose delivery options**	Investigate options	20	3/3/2000	3/28/2000
6.		Decide delivery method(s)	5	3/29/2000	3/28/2000
7.	**Make-or-buy decision**	Capability assessment	10	1/12/2000	2/28/2000
8.		Decide on trainer versus SME	10	3/2/2000	3/18/2000
9.	**Purchasing training**	Decide what you need	25	4/5/2000	5/14/2000
10.		Find vendors	10	5/15/2000	5/28/2000
11.		Evaluate courseware	20	5/25/2000	6/14/2000
12.		Select packages/vendors	5	6/5/2000	6/20/2000
13.		Select handout sources	20	6/5/2000	7/14/2000
14.		Select book(s)	10	6/5/2000	7/14/2000
15.		Get bids and negotiate	10	6/5/2000	7/14/2000
16.	**Customizing training**	Refine the needs analysis	30	7/5/2000	8/14/2000
17.		Do gap analysis	15	8/5/2000	8/24/2000
18.		Design perfect solutions	10	8/24/2000	9/14/2000
19.		Work with vendors	30	Ongoing	Ongoing
20.	**Implementation**	Get the best trainers	5	8/5/2000	8/14/2000
21.		Find internal trainers	10	8/5/2000	9/1/2000
22.		Design trainer evaluations	15	7/5/2000	8/14/2000
23.		Install CBT software	20	9/10/2000	10/11/2000
24.		Assign support tasks	5	10/11/2000	10/15/2000
25.	**Rollout communication**	Build enthusiasm	25	Ongoing	Ongoing
26.		Track attendance	—	6/1/2000	Ongoing
27.		Develop incentives	10	4/8/2000	4/21/2000
28.	**Creating evaluations**	Design evaluations	20	3/15/2000	4/15/2000
29.		Conduct evaluations	—	6/1/2000	Ongoing
30.		Continual improvement	—	6/1/2000	Ongoing

Task	Labor Type	Hours	Cost/Hour	Total Cost
Develop objectives	Training developer	250	110	27,500
Develop metrics	Training developer	200	110	22,000
Select/sequence content	Trainer/developer	50	220	11,000
Create groups/tracks	Trainer/developer	50	220	11,000
Investigate options	Manager, developer	80	300	24,000
Decide delivery method(s)	Manager, developer	80	300	24,000
Capability assessment	Manager, developer	120	300	36,000
Decide on trainer versus SME	Manager, developer	40	300	12,000
Decide what you need	Developer/trainer	120	300	36,000
Find vendors	Developer/trainer	40	220	8,800
Evaluate courseware	Developer/trainer	80	220	17,600
Select packages/vendors	Training team	120	300	36,000
Select handout sources	Developer/trainer	120	220	26,400
Select book(s)	Developer/trainer	120	220	26,400
Get bids and negotiate	Manager	120	300	36,000
Refine the needs analysis	Manager, developer, trainer	200	300	60,000
Do gap analysis	Manager, developer, trainer	150	300	45,000
Design perfect solutions	Manager, developer, trainer	150	300	45,000
Get the best trainers	Manager, developer	40	300	12,000
Find internal trainers	Manager, developer, trainer	80	300	24,000
Design trainer evaluations	Manager, developer	80	300	24,000
Install CBT software	Developer	120	110	13,200
Assign support tasks	Manager	20	80	1,600
Develop incentives	Manager	80	80	6,400
Design evaluations	Manager, developer, trainer	120	300	36,000
Conduct evaluations	Manager, developer, trainer	120	300	36,000
Continual improvement	Training team	1200	300	360,000
Grand total		**3,950**		**$1,017,900**

Item	Cost
Labor	$1,017,900
Travel, lodging, meals	2,050,000
Facilities	800,000
Hardware	500,000
Software	400,000
Purchased instruction materials	300,000
Salary/lost job time	2,300,000
Grand total	**$7,367,900**

Signatures

Richard, vice president of human resources

Dennis, vice president of manufacturing

Diego, vice president of sales

Jeff, vice president of finance

Sandra, vice president of purchasing

Gary, WCS software rollout team leader

Lauren, KIS software rollout team leader

Bob, I/T training manager

Connie, CIO

RFP Outline and Completed Sample

This appendix contains a sample RFP outline and document. The document can be modified to fit the needs of a particular organization, but the core components should be included. Be sure to review this document and other external communications with your legal department prior to release. The completed document is tied to the case study in Chapter 7.

RFP Working Outline

1. Introduction to the requirements, the rollout project, and the organization
2. Administrative requirements
    2.1. Vendor instructions
    2.2. RFP conditions
3. Activities that will occur after the RFP is issued
    3.1. Vendor questions and organization replies
    3.2. Vendor conferences
    3.3. Review of RFP responses
    3.4. Evaluation of proposals
    3.5. Implement necessary agreements
    3.6. Notification of awards
4. Proposal format
    4.1. Vendor proposal format and content requirements
    4.2. Pagination, font size, etc. (may be ADA required)
5. Any pertinent definitions
6. Project details and training requirements from the needs analysis and/or design
    6.1. General requirements
    6.2. Needs analysis results
    6.3. Curriculum layout
    6.4. Proposed delivery methods
    6.5. Audience analysis
    6.6. Software requirements
    6.7. Organization particulars
7. Proposed budget (and schedule)
8. Appendixes

This sample may be used to prepare an RFP similar to the one that begins on the following page. This format can be easily altered to meet the needs of your organization. It can be downloaded from www.books.mcgraw-hill.com/training/download.

Acme Widgets Inc.
Request for Proposal
Training on WCS ERP Software and KIS Groupware
Prepared by: Jack
Revision Date: March 13, 2000

1. Introduction to the requirements, the rollout project, and the organization

Acme Widgets Inc. (AWI) recently purchased the Widget Control System (WCS) ERP package for client/server architectures. This package will automate Acme Widgets' major business systems. Some business functions are currently running on legacy mainframe systems, and other business functions are performed manually. The WCS will automate all business functions into a single, integrated system that will provide the company with a significant competitive edge. The major functions to be automated are purchasing, manufacturing, sales, finance and accounting, and human resources. Personnel in I/T and business areas must be trained on each area in the new WCS ERP system. At the same time, to facilitate productivity and information sharing among all employees, both technical and nontechnical, AWI is installing a new knowledge-sharing system called KIS (Knowledge and Information Sharing).

The transition from both the old legacy systems and manual processing will involve many changes, and corporate management must be convinced that an integrated training program will be needed to address the needs of various types of I/T staff and levels of end users. Some I/T staff are primarily hardware-oriented, and will need training on WCS and KIS hardware requirements, while others are primarily concerned with the software and will need training on the customization of both. Business users have skill sets ranging from personal computer (PC) novice to expert/power system user.

Acme Widgets' corporate management is not convinced that a formal training program is needed. Most of the executives feel that the staff should be able to learn the two software products from the systems development team or through manuals and on-line help screens. Besides, some of the executives argue that a formal training program for both pieces of software would be too expensive. The chief information officer (CIO) and head of information technology (I/T) for Acme Widgets, Connie, believes that a formal training program is the only way that the I/T staff will be able to install and operate WCS effectively, and that the users will need heavy training for such a major change in the way they do their work. The vice president of human resources, Richard, also thinks that a formal program is necessary for end users, but is unsure of how to sell it. Connie and Richard have asked Bob to put together a presentation to sell the program and then have Mike manage the development and implementation efforts.

2. Administrative requirements

You must provide a printed response with your original signature at the bottom. Your responses may include samples of your training design. You may alter and expand upon the basic training design contained on the diskette; however, any work done for the purpose of responding to this RFP is not billable to AWI if your firm is not selected for this project. If you would like to reserve the option to charge for work done in responding to this RFP in the event your firm is selected, you should separately include in your RFP response the proposed total charge for such preselection work (you should not submit a statement or invoice at such time) along with a detailed description of the work done, hours billed, expenses incurred, etc. Preference will be given to firms that include prototypes of the training design as a demonstration of their ability and an example of their understanding of the project.

It is very important from a legal perspective for the bidding process to be fair and impartial. Therefore, this section sets forth the conditions under which this process will take place. Vendors must abide by these requirements or be disqualified from the bidding.

2.1. Vendor instructions

- All replies must be in by May 19. *NO EXCEPTIONS!*
- The rules as indicated by federal, state, and applicable local laws must be obeyed. Any infractions, small or otherwise, will be grounds for disqualification.
- The rules contained herein are binding upon all participants, so please read them carefully.
- All proposals must meet format requirements for AWI to be able to compare them properly.

2.2. RFP conditions

- This RFP is not an obligation by AWI to commit to any work by any vendor.
- AWI will pay no monies during the course of this process.
- Vendors attempting to "end-run" the process will be disqualified from this and any other work with AWI for a period not less than 1 calendar year from the RFP date.

3. Activities that will occur after the RFP is issued

This section details the steps to be taken and the process for Q&A, as well as the review process.

3.1. Vendor questions and organization replies

Vendors may contact AWI only through the appointed representative. Any other contact is strictly prohibited during this process.

3.2. Vendor conferences

At some point, selected vendors may be asked to meet with AWI officials to clarify certain items.

3.3. Review of RFP responses

The responses will be reviewed after May 19 under strictly confidential conditions.

3.4. Evaluation of proposals

The proposals will be evaluated in the following steps:

Step 1: Proposals will be reviewed by the Purchasing Services Section for compliance with requirements. Those that comply will go on to Step 2.

Step 2: Proposals will be reviewed and evaluated by the Evaluation Committee. There will be three parts to the evaluation:

- Technical
- Management
- Financial

The Committee will complete the technical and management portions of the evaluation before addressing the financial evaluation. The Evaluation Committee may comprise staff from the training team, outside consultants, and staff from other departments. AWI may invite staff from other public agencies to assist the Evaluation Committee. The Committee may create subcommittees or working groups to perform portions of the evaluation.

Step 3: The Evaluation Committee will prepare and present a report to the Executive Committee. The report will consist of the scoring for each proposal, a ranking of proposals, and a recommendation.

Step 4: The Executive Committee will review the report and proposals as it deems appropriate, request additional information or analyses from the Evaluation Committee if it desires, and select the successful Proposer. The Executive Committee may disqualify any proposal or reject all proposals.

Step 5: AWI will initiate contract negotiations with the successful Proposer. The draft contract terms will be available by request, and will be the basis for such negotiations. If during contract negotiations and/or during the term of the Agreement, the successful Proposer finds that the requirements can be met and the work completed in a more advantageous way to AWI, the successful Proposer shall notify AWI in writing of such finding. AWI may incorporate such changes into the Agreement.

If AWI determines in the course of negotiations that a satisfactory contract cannot be executed in a timely fashion, AWI may reject the successful Proposer and either terminate the procurement process or initiate negotiations with other Proposers in the order of their relative ranking.

A scoring matrix will be constructed before the due date for proposals. This will be based on the general evaluation criteria and weights described herein, but will be much more detailed. The items of evaluation will correspond to the individual specifications and requirements of the RFP. The items will not be given equal weight. Rather, each of the items of evaluation will be assigned a weight reflecting its relative importance to AWI.

For each evaluation item, each proposal judged to fulfill the requirements will be given the full score. Proposals that partially meet the requirement will be given a partial score. Responses to items will be evaluated relative to each other, as well as on how well they meet the needs of AWI. During the evaluation process, Proposers may be contacted to clarify various elements of their proposals. Such contacts will be made only by AWI and will occur only when AWI deems it appropriate to the evaluation process.

Upon completion of this process, a formal evaluation of the proposals will take place. A weighted score in each of the areas will be given to each proposal by each member of the Evaluation Committee. The proposal award recommendation will be for the proposal with the highest overall score.

3.5. Implement necessary agreements

The contracts will be negotiated, constructed, and signed according to applicable laws.

3.6. Notification of awards

The award will be announced on November 1. Once the award is complete, AWI may disclose the following information in postaward debriefings to other offerors:

- The overall evaluated cost or price and technical rating of the successful offeror
- The overall ranking of all offerors, when any ranking was developed by the agency during source selection
- A summary of the rationale for award
- An outline of the content of the training to be delivered by the successful offeror
- Other information as may be seen to benefit AWI

Please read this information carefully, as you will be bound by it once you enter the bidding process. *Note:* Your attorney should always be involved in this process.

4. Proposal format

The proposal must be signed by an official authorized to bind your organization and must stipulate that it is predicated on all the terms and conditions of this RFP. Your proposal shall be submitted in the number of copies, to the addresses, and marked as indicated in the item entitled "Packaging and Delivery of Proposal" found in the "Specific RFP Instructions and Provisions" of an RFP. Proposals will be typewritten, paginated, and reproduced on letter-size paper, and will be legible in all required copies.

4.1. Vendor proposal format and content requirements

To expedite the proposal evaluation, all documents required for responding to the RFP should be placed in the following order:

  a. Proposal Cover Sheet
     Include RFP number, title, name of organization, name of principal investigator, names of other key personnel, name of any subcontractor(s) and their proposed principal investigator(s), and names of any collaborators or consultants, and indicate whether the proposal is an original or a copy.
  b. Proposal
     Format and organization of the technical proposal must follow the Table of Contents identified below, and must include the information requested in the Technical Proposal Instructions and as otherwise specified in the RFP references.
  c. Business Proposal
     The business proposal must consist of a cover page, a table of contents, and the information requested in the Business Proposal Instructions and as otherwise specified in the RFP references.

4.2. Pagination, font size, etc. (may be ADA required)

- The proposals will be in Times New Roman 12-point font.
- The proposals will be typed or computer-printed, single-sided, black on white paper.
- The proposals will be bound in a notebook or similar container. No loose pages are permitted.

5. Definitions

- *Discussions* are negotiations that occur after the establishment of the competitive range that may, at the contract point of contact discretion, result in the offeror being allowed to revise its proposal.
- *In writing* or *written* means any worded or numbered expression that can be read, reproduced, and later communicated, and includes electronically transmitted information.
- *Proposal modification* is a change made to a proposal before the solicitation's closing date and time, or made in response to an amendment, or made to correct a mistake before award.
- *Proposal revision* is a change to a proposal made after the solicitation closing date, at the request of or as allowed by a Contracting Officer as the result of negotiations.
- *Time,* if stated as a number of days, is calculated using calendar days, unless otherwise specified, and will include Saturdays, Sundays, and legal holidays. However, if the last day falls on a Saturday, Sunday, or legal holiday, then the period shall include the next working day.

6. Project details and training requirements from the needs analysis and/or design

This section contains excerpts from the needs analysis and design process required for vendors to respond. The amount of detail contained in this section meets AWI's proprietary information agreement, and is disclosed for the bidding process only.

6.1. General requirements

The WCS software for which training is required is structured according to the following diagram:

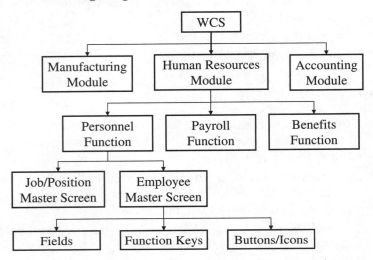

6.2. Needs analysis results

The matrixes depicting the details of the training requirements (from Chapter 2) are placed here.

Item	Job/Position	Function	Screen	Module	Business Task
1.	HR recruiter	Enter new employee	HRM01	HR	Hire employee
2.	Payroll manager	Change employee pay	HRP02	HR	Raise/lower pay
3.	BPA clerk	Select employee benefits	HRB03	HR	Benefits selection

Item	Software Module	Software Function	Screen	Job	Org. Unit	Est. Classes	Est. Hours
1.	HR	Enter new employee	HRM01	HR recruiter	HR	2	6
2.	HR	Change employee pay	HRP02	Payroll manager	HR	2	12
3.	HR	Select employee benefits	HRB03	BPA clerk	HR	2	8

Item	Software Module	Software Function	Screen	Person(s)	Org. Unit	Est. Classes	Est. Hours
1.	HR	Enter new employee	HRM01	Trudy	HR	1	3
2.	HR	Change employee pay	HRP02	Jane	HR	2	12
3.	HR	Select employee benefits	HRB03	Marsha	HR	1	4

6.3. Curriculum layout

AWI has two tracks, one for WCS and the other for KIS. The WCS track diagram is shown below.

6.4. Proposed delivery methods

A short discussion of the methods investigated are included to give the vendor an idea of our perspective. Some of the options discussed are:

- Self-study or classroom
- Computer- or web-based training options

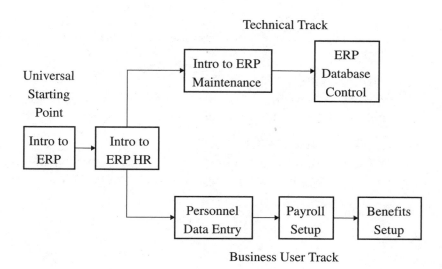

- Facilitated computer-based training (FCBT)
- Live distance learning options
- Combining methods for maximum effectiveness and efficiency

The proposed methods by class are:

Class	Audience	Factors	Delivery Method(s)
Employee master maintenance	I/T and business users	Beginner class Interaction needed Ease of use important	Classroom or facilitated CBT
Employee payroll setup	I/T and business users	Slightly advanced material Interaction needed Critical business function	Facilitated CBT
Employee benefits setup	I/T and business users	Beginner class Interaction needed Ease of use important	Classroom or facilitated CBT
WCS HR administration	I/T staff only	Advanced material Sophisticated audience Need to keep current	Web-based DL or self-study web-based CBT

Vendors should feel free to change this as needed.

6.5. Audience analysis

The audience will range from beginners to technical I/T staff, depending on the class.

6.6. Software requirements

Any CBT software must be thin-client and/or web-based (intranet or extranet), and must run on either Windows 95/98/NT or HP-UX.

6.7. Organization particulars

Many organization units are involved, including purchasing, manufacturing, sales, finance and accounting, and human resources.

7. Proposed budget (and schedule)

The proposed budget is set forth in the following table:

Item	Cost
Labor	$2,500,000
Travel, lodging, meals	1,200,000
Facilities	400,000
Hardware	500,000
Software	400,000
Purchased instruction materials	300,000
Salary/lost job time	2,500,000
Grand total	**$7,800,000**

A sample of the course development schedule is as follows:

Item	Software Module	Software Function	Screen	Est. Start Date	Est. Finish Date
1.	Purchasing	Update widget description	WMD01	1/15/2000	2/15/2000
2.	Accounting	Enter new G/L acct.	ARM01	1/15/2000	3/2/2000
3.	Manufacturing	Let down	MSH03	2/17/2000	3/17/2000
4.	HR	Enter new candidate	HRA02	1/15/2000	2/15/2000

8. Appendixes

Extra matrixes, reference information, fax and e-mail addresses, etc.

Training Program Process Checklists

This section presents a series of checklists that can be used to guide the training development process. Each checklist and the estimating guide help the training developer to avoid forgetting any major piece of the process. The forms are referred to throughout the book and are used within the case study in each chapter.

Training Needs Analysis Process/Deliverables Checklist

Item	Task	Deliverable(s)	Who	Done ✓
1.	Document the overall needs.	Feature/function hierarchy diagram and descriptions	Training team, rollout team	
2.	Document the business tasks accomplished for each feature/function.	Feature/function to business task matrix	Training team, rollout team, users	
3.	Document timing.	Copy of project plan obtained from rollout team (to be used in planning and design phases)	Training team, rollout team	
4.	Document new knowledge/skill requirements.	*New* job analysis and skills requirements statement/matrix	Training team, rollout team, users	
5.	Define *who* will do *what* in the new world.	Staff to feature/function and business task matrix	Training team, rollout team, users	
6.	Document current audience KSAEs.	Current skills audit	Training team, users	
7.	Analyze the gap in competencies between current and required skills.	Gap analysis document	Training team, users	
8.	Present new business tasks and job design to management.	Management approval of Item 4	Training team leader/manager	

Program Plan Development Process/Deliverables Checklist

Item	Task	Deliverable(s)	Who	Done ✓
1.	Identify critical path activities	CPM, Gantt, or other chart	Training team, rollout team, users	
2.	Identify critical path players	Personnel, roles, and responsibilities form	Training team, rollout team, users	
3.	Document drop-dead date ranges	Copy of project plan obtained from rollout team (to be used in planning and design phases)	Training team, rollout team	
4.	Estimate the remaining activity hours and costs	Activity-based cost worksheet and program plan	Training team, rollout team, users	
5.	Factor in the elapsed time ranges	Activity-based cost worksheet and program plan	Training team, rollout team, users	
6.	Estimate hardware/software costs	Activity-based cost worksheet	Training team, rollout team, users	
7.	Calculate the total budget	Activity-based cost worksheet	Training team, rollout team, users	
8.	Generate alternatives	Potential solution set	Training team, rollout team, users	
9.	Communicate the program plan to partners	Completed program plan document	Training team, rollout team, users	
10.	Gain management approval	Management sign-off	Management	

Program Plan Development Question/Answer Checklist

Item	Question	Answer	Who	Done ✓
1.	How long will the project take?		Training team, rollout team, users	
2.	What are the critical tasks that must be completed?		Training team, rollout team, users	
3.	What are the dependencies between the tasks?		Training team, rollout team, users	
4.	How long will each task take?		Training team, rollout team, users	
5.	When must each task start and end?		Training team, rollout team, users	
6.	Who will be responsible for each task?		Training team, rollout team, users	
7.	What resources will be required to complete each task?		Training team, rollout team, users	
8.	How will delayed tasks affect the project?		Training team, rollout team, users	
9.	What is the impact of a modification to the project scope?		Training team, rollout team, users	
10.	What is the cost of the project and the cost of each task?		Training team, rollout team, users	
11.	Is the project on schedule?		Training team, rollout team, users	
12.	How can slippage problems be corrected?		Training team, rollout team, users	
13.	What is the project's cost at any point in time?		Training team, rollout team, users	
14.	What is the best way to speed up the project?		Training team, rollout team, users	

Training Program Plan Estimating Guide

Task group	Task	% total task group	Average time/unit
Design	Develop objectives	30	1–2 days/class
	Develop metrics	40	2–5 days/class
	Select/sequence content	20	1–2 days/class
	Create groups/tracks	10	1–2 days/program
Choose delivery options	Investigate options	80	5–10 days/program
	Decide delivery method(s)	20	~2 days/program
Make-or-buy decision	Capability assessment	80	1 day/class
	Decide on trainer versus SME	20	1 day/class
Purchasing training	Decide what you need	15	1–2 days/class
	Find vendors	15	~1 day/class
	Evaluate courseware	40	5–7 days/package
	Select packages/vendors	5	2 days/package
	Select handout sources	5	2 days/class
	Select book(s)	10	2–4 days/class
	Get bids and negotiate	10	2–4 days/class
Customizing training	Refine the needs analysis	25	1–2 weeks/program
	Do gap analysis	25	2 weeks/program
	Design perfect solutions	25	2 weeks/program
	Work with vendors	25	2–3 weeks/program
Implementation	Get the best trainers	10	1–3 days/class
	Find internal trainers	15	1–3 days/class
	Design trainer evaluations	20	2–4 days/class
	Install CBT software	40	2–3 weeks/program
	Assign support tasks	15	Ongoing
Rollout communication	Build enthusiasm	50	Duration of program
	Track attendance	30	Delivery time
	Develop incentives	20	2–3 weeks/program
Creating evaluations	Design evaluations	70	2–3 weeks/program
	Conduct evaluations	20	Ongoing
	Continual improvement	10	Ongoing

Training Budget Question/Answer Checklist

Item	Question	Answer	Who	Done ✓
1.	Is there a clear overall cost?		Training team, rollout team, users	
2.	Is there a breakdown of what is included in the cost (analysis, development, delivery, etc.)?		Training team, management	
3.	Is there information about any additional training costs (time, salaries, travel, materials)?		Training team, management	
4.	Is there information regarding the cost to customize the program to the business needs?		Training team	
5.	Is there an outline of the cost of any finances involved (such as premises, travel, accommodation, etc.)?		Training team, management	
6.	Is there a cost measure of the training results in past similar programs?		Training team, software vendor	
7.	Is there an estimate of the cost per student per day?		Training team, management	
8.	Have all corporate policies been complied with?		Training team, management	
9.	Is there financial justification of the program?		Training team, management	
10.	Have maintenance costs been estimated on a yearly basis and included in the overall project cost?		Training team	

Training Program Design Question/Answer Checklist

Item	Question	Answer	Who	Done ✓
1.	Is the purpose of the training documented?		Training team, rollout team, users	
2.	Do the objectives match requirements gathered during the needs analysis?		Training team, rollout team, users	
3.	Is there a balance ensuring a diversity of learning activity types (exercises, case studies, opportunities for skills practice) to support adult learning?		Training team, rollout team, users	
4.	Have all delivery systems, appropriate for the objectives, been considered and the one(s) selected clearly documented?		Training team	
5.	Does the selection of learning methods and materials support the module objectives?		Training team	
6.	Has the team checked that content matches critical job performance requirements?		Training team, rollout team, users	
7.	Does the content include a description of the expertise level of the training event (basic, medium, advanced)?		Training team	
8.	Has the team determined objectives at the module level (knowledge, skills, and attitude) that support the overall training objectives?		Training team	
9.	Has the team discussed the length of each event and of the overall program?		Training team, management	
10.	Has the team created quality training documentation and detailed learning exercise descriptions?		Training team	

Training Certification Program Process Checklist

Item	Task	Answer	Who	Done ✓
1.	Use the objectives, along with the metrics for each objective, to create a test bank of items.		Training team, rollout team, users	
2.	Determine which test items can be answered in written form and which test items can be answered by performing a task.		Training team, rollout team	
3.	Determine which test items can be used for each type of student (e.g., I/T versus business user).		Training team, rollout team, users	
4.	Classify the test items by difficulty and type (e.g., finance versus sales and distribution).		Training team	
5.	Group the test items into logical units for a test or part of a test (see Section 4.4).		Training team	
6.	Group the units and/or tests into tracks and certificates (e.g., finance versus sales and distribution).		Training team, rollout team, users	
7.	Determine the pass/fail criteria or score. This will obviously depend on the level of criticality of the task or training need or objective.		Training team, management	
8.	Determine test and/or program administration guidelines.		Training team, management	
9.	Develop incentives that will encourage employees to participate. Maybe even more importantly, develop incentives for management to give employees the time to participate.		Training team, management	
10.	Use some kind of test bank software or database to manage test items and results.		Training team	

Training Incentive Question List

Item	Question	Answer	Who	Done ✓
1.	Is the task seen to be worthwhile?		Training team, management	
2.	Do the employees believe they can perform the task?		Training team, rollout team, users	
3.	Is there incentive for performing well?		Training team, rollout team, users	
4.	Do the incentives really matter to the participants?		Training team, rollout team, users	
5.	Is the incentive contingent upon good performance?		Training team, rollout team, users	
6.	Do the participants know the link between incentive and performance?		Training team, management	
7.	Are incentives scheduled to prevent discouragement?		Training team, management	
8.	Are all available incentives being used?		Training team, rollout team, users	
9.	Do the participants find the work interesting?		Training team, rollout team, users	
10.	Are there inner satisfactions for good performance?		Training team, rollout team, users	
11.	If incentives are mixed, is the balance positive?		Training team, rollout team, users	
12.	Is "punishment for good performance" prevented?		Training team, rollout team, users	
13.	Is "reward for poor performance" prevented?		Training team, rollout team, users	
14.	Is there peer pressure for good performance?		Training team, rollout team, users	
15.	Is task unpleasantness or stress within acceptable levels?		Training team, rollout team, users	
16.	Does poor performance draw attention?		Training team, management	

Training Vendor Question List

Item	Question	Point ✓
1.	Does the vendor demonstrate originality or innovation?	
2.	Does the vendor write influential papers or articles in relevant trade magazines?	
3.	Is the vendor recognized as a leader in the field?	
4.	Does the vendor demonstrate a readiness to customize his or her services to your needs?	
5.	Is the vendor using the same person to market, sell, and deliver the service?	
6.	Can the vendor provide customer references on successful projects (a minimum of three)?	
7.	Does the vendor honor commitments and display integrity?	
8.	Does the vendor offer a reliable résumé for all project team members?	
9.	Does the vendor fit into your organization or culture?	
10.	Are the training results guaranteed by the vendor?	
11.	Does the vendor inspire personal and professional acceptability?	
12.	Does the vendor have the correct level of rapport and credibility for you to do business with him or her?	
13.	Is the vendor ready with a risk assessment report, identifying any high-risk areas?	
14.	Does the vendor have training results on job performance changes from previous jobs?	
15.	Does the vendor require active involvement from your training manager before, during, and after the training events?	
16.	Does the vendor insist on getting support from management?	
17.	Does the vendor demonstrate interest in seeing joint participation between the student and his or her manager before and after the training event?	
18.	Does the vendor require that both student and manager identify job-improvement areas prior to the training event?	
19.	Does the vendor ask the student's manager to motivate the person enrolled?	
20.	Does the vendor plan that the training be followed by a learning-related project?	
21.	Does the vendor commit to a follow-up evaluation process?	
22.	Does the vendor commit to present a report of training results?	
23.	Does the vendor require that the sponsor's reaction to the given training be reported back to him or her?	
	Total points	

Test Development Checklist

Item	Requirement	✓
1.	The test items match the course objectives.	
2.	The test items relate to what was actually taught.	
3.	The test items measure important concepts rather than trivia.	
4.	The test items measure complex behavior like understanding basic principles, and the ability to practically apply those principles, rather than simply measuring recall.	
5.	The test items are free from vaguely defined problems, ambiguous wording, extraneous or irrelevant information, and unintentional clues to the correct answer.	
6.	The test directions specify how the items are scored and how the students record answers.	
7.	The items are presented in the same format and grouped together logically.	
8.	The test items and pages are numbered consecutively.	
9.	There is sufficient time for students to complete the test.	
10.	The test is long enough to provide a valid, reliable estimate of the students' achievement.	
11.	If the test were given again, the results would be consistent with current test scores.	
12.	I have considered student input regarding ambiguity and problems with specific test items.	
13.	The items are spaced so they can be read, answered, and scored efficiently.	
14.	Each answer space is clearly associated with its corresponding item.	
15.	I established a grading key for all items, even essay questions.	

Sample Forms

This appendix contains sample forms to be used in the development of a training program. Each of the forms is referred to in the appropriate chapter, and completed samples are shown in the case. Each form can be adapted as needed to a particular program or organization. These forms can also serve as the foundation for a database of training project information in a groupware product such as Lotus Notes.

Software Feature/Function to Business Task Matrix

Item	Function	Screen	Module	Business Task	Organization Unit
1.					
2.					
3.					
4.					
5.					
6.					
7.					
8.					
9.					
10.					
11.					
12.					
13.					
14.					
15.					
16.					
17.					
18.					
19.					
20.					
21.					
22.					
23.					
24.					
25.					
26.					
27.					
28.					
29.					
30.					
31.					
32.					
33.					
34.					
35.					
36.					
37.					
38.					
39.					
40.					

Software Feature/Function Difficulty Level by User Type

Item	Function	Screen	Product	Lever/User Type
1.				
2.				
3.				
4.				
5.				
6.				
7.				
8.				
9.				
10.				
11.				
12.				
13.				
14.				
15.				
16.				
17.				
18.				
19.				
20.				
21.				
22.				
23.				
24.				
25.				
26.				
27.				
28.				
29.				
30.				
31.				
32.				
33.				
34.				
35.				
36.				
37.				
38.				
39.				
40.				

Job/Position to Feature/Function to Business Task Matrix

Item	Job/Position	Function	Screen	Module	Business Task
1.					
2.					
3.					
4.					
5.					
6.					
7.					
8.					
9.					
10.					
11.					
12.					
13.					
14.					
15.					
16.					
17.					
18.					
19.					
20.					
21.					
22.					
23.					
24.					
25.					
26.					
27.					
28.					
29.					
30.					
31.					
32.					
33.					
34.					
35.					
36.					
37.					
38.					
39.					
40.					

Training Needs Summary by Software Module

Item	Software Module	Software Function	Screen	Job	Org. Unit	Est. Classes	Est. Hours
1.							
2.							
3.							
4.							
5.							
6.							
7.							
8.							
9.							
10.							
11.							
12.							
13.							
14.							
15.							
16.							
17.							
18.							
19.							
20.							
21.							
22.							
23.							
24.							
25.							
26.							
27.							
28.							
29.							
30.							
31.							
32.							
33.							
34.							
35.							
36.							
37.							
38.							
39.							
40.							

Current Skills Assessment Form for Software Packages

Name:
Title:
Organization Unit:
Date:

Item	Software Module	Software Function	Screen	Years of Experience	Skill Level: 1–5 (1=Beginner, 5=Expert)				
1.					1	2	3	4	5
2.					1	2	3	4	5
3.					1	2	3	4	5
4.					1	2	3	4	5
5.					1	2	3	4	5
6.					1	2	3	4	5
7.					1	2	3	4	5
8.					1	2	3	4	5
9.					1	2	3	4	5
10.					1	2	3	4	5
11.					1	2	3	4	5
12.					1	2	3	4	5
13.					1	2	3	4	5
14.					1	2	3	4	5
15.					1	2	3	4	5

Current Skills Assessment Form for Computer Skills

Note: Additional items can be added as needed. This is only a starting point.

Name:
Title:
Organization Unit:
Date:
Years of Overall Computer Experience:
Overall Skill Level Beginner   Expert 1   2   3   4   5
Years Legacy Computer Experience:
Legacy Computer Skill Level Beginner   Expert 1   2   3   4   5
Years PC Experience:
PC Skill Level Beginner   Expert 1   2   3   4   5
How comfortable are you learning new software? Very uncomfortable   Very comfortable 1   2   3   4   5

Training Needs Summary by Staff Member

Item	Software Module	Software Function	Screen	Person(s)	Org. Unit	Est. Classes	Est. Hours
1.							
2.							
3.							
4.							
5.							
6.							
7.							
8.							
9.							
10.							
11.							
12.							
13.							
14.							
15.							
16.							
17.							
18.							
19.							
20.							
21.							
22.							
23.							
24.							
25.							
26.							
27.							
28.							
29.							
30.							
31.							
32.							
33.							
34.							
35.							
36.							
37.							
38.							
39.							
40.							

Class/Needs Work Estimates Sheet

Item	Software Module	Software Function	Screen	Org. Unit	Est. Classes	Est. Days	Est. Start	Est. Complete
1.								
2.								
3.								
4.								
5.								
6.								
7.								
8.								
9.								
10.								
11.								
12.								
13.								
14.								
15.								
16.								
17.								
18.								
19.								
20.								
21.								
22.								
23.								
24.								
25.								
26.								
27.								
28.								
29.								
30.								
31.								
32.								
33.								
34.								
35.								

Task Group Total Worksheet

	Task group	Task	Days	Est. Start	Est. Complete
1.	**Design**	Develop objectives			
2.		Develop metrics			
3.		Select/sequence content			
4.		Create groups/tracks			
5.	**Choose delivery options**	Investigate options			
6.		Decide delivery method(s)			
7.	**Make-or-buy decision**	Capability assessment			
8.		Decide on trainer versus SME			
9.	**Purchasing training**	Decide what you need			
10.		Find vendors			
11.		Evaluate courseware			
12.		Select packages/vendors			
13.		Select handout sources			
14.		Select book(s)			
15.		Get bids and negotiate			
16.	**Customizing training**	Refine the needs analysis			
17.		Do gap analysis			
18.		Design perfect solutions			
19.		Work with vendors			
20.	**Implementation**	Get the best trainers			
21.		Find internal trainers			
22.		Design trainer evaluations			
23.		Install CBT software			
24.		Assign support tasks			
25.	**Rollout communication**	Build enthusiasm			
26.		Track attendance			
27.		Develop incentives			
28.	**Creating evaluations**	Design evaluations			
29.		Conduct evaluations			
30.		Continual improvement			

Training Labor Budget Worksheet

Task	Labor Type	Hours	Cost/Hour	Total Cost
Develop objectives				
Develop metrics				
Select/sequence content				
Create groups/tracks				
Investigate options				
Decide delivery method(s)				
Capability assessment				
Decide on trainer versus SME				
Decide what you need				
Find vendors				
Evaluate courseware				
Select packages/vendors				
Select handout sources				
Select book(s)				
Get bids and negotiate				
Refine the needs analysis				
Do gap analysis				
Design perfect solutions				
Work with vendors				
Get the best trainers				
Find internal trainers				
Design trainer evaluations				
Install CBT software				
Assign support tasks				
Build enthusiasm				
Track attendance				
Develop incentives				
Design evaluations				
Conduct evaluations				
Continual improvement				
Total				

Training Program Overall Budget Worksheet

Item	Cost
Labor	
Travel, lodging, meals	
Facilities	
Hardware	
Software	
Purchased instruction materials	
Salary/lost job time	
Grand total	

Needs/Objective Work Sheet

Item	Software Module	Software Function	Level	Need	Objective(s)
1.					
2.					
3.					
4.					
5.					
6.					
7.					
8.					
9.					
10.					
11.					
12.					
13.					
14.					
15.					
16.					
17.					
18.					
19.					
20.					
21.					
22.					
23.					
24.					
25.					
26.					
27.					
28.					
29.					
30.					
31.					
32.					
33.					
34.					
35.					
36.					
37.					
38.					
39.					
40.					

Course Description/Syllabus Form

Course Title:

Course Purpose
Enter specifics of course—why is it necessary?

Prerequisite
What must the student know prior to the class?

Instructor
Name, background, contact info

Objectives
Upon the completion of this course, the student will be able to:
◆ ?????

Course Approach
Lecture? Lab? CBT? Approach to learning (e.g., individual versus team)?

Course Schedule
Schedule summary, including parts if multiple.

Course Policies
Breaks, attendance, etc.

Tentative Schedule of Assignments and Activities
Day 1:
1. Goal/activity

Day 2:
1. Goal/activity

Testing, Grading, and Evaluation Policies and Procedures
How will the students be measured? How will they know if they learned?

Training Class Delivery Method Assessment Matrix

Class	Audience	Factors	Delivery Method(s)

Training Capability Decision Matrix

Item	Factor	Priority (1–5)	Develop Internally	Outsource	Either
1.	Staff salaries				
2.	Train-the-trainer costs				
3.	Material purchase costs				
4.	Material licensing costs				
5.	Facility costs				
6.	Media costs				
7.	Equipment costs				
8.	Consulting costs (for internal)				
9.	Current staff skill levels				
10.	Staff skill acquisition time				
11.	Program complexity				
12.	Audience credibility				
13.	Project deadline(s)				
14.	Access to leading-edge expertise				
15.	Risk mitigation				
16.	Development process control				
17.	Delivery process control				
18.	Quality control				
19.	Service-level agreements				
20.	Documentation management				
	Total for each column				

Staff Capability Matrix

Staff Name	Department	Area of Expertise	Skill Level (1–5)

Training Make-or-Buy Matrix

Software	Function	Class	Assigned To	Make or Buy

Courseware Evaluation Form

Item	Characteristic	Strength (1–5)
1.	Concentrate on teaching concepts and solid skills	
2.	Have a uniform design and consistent format	
3.	Use short sentences appropriate to the student level	
4.	Use simple English and avoid unnecessary jargon	
5.	Be technically accurate	
6.	Be free of distracting errors (such as spelling errors)	
7.	Be tested prior to release by independent trainers	
8.	Table of contents	
9.	Index	
10.	Glossary	
11.	Course preview detailing topics covered	
12.	Explanation of how to use the book	
13.	States any assumptions about the student's knowledge	
14.	Summary at the end of each day of training	
15.	Case study at the end of each day of training	
16.	Preview of topics to be covered on the next day	
17.	Review at the start of the second day of training	
18.	Lesson objectives at the start of each lesson	
19.	Summary at the end of each lesson	
20.	Case study at the end of each lesson	
21.	Revision questions at the end of each lesson	
22.	Full explanation of each feature	
23.	Hands-on exercise for each feature	
24.	Numerous short exercises throughout the lesson	
25.	Screen shots illustrating each feature	
26.	Tips and shortcuts	
27.	Screen shots in exercises, particularly at the end of the exercise	
28.	Simple instructions	
29.	Clear step-by-step process with numbered points	
30.	Starting points from a supplied file to avoid excessive typing	
31.	Exercises relevant and meaningful to students	
32.	Clear, uncluttered style	
33.	White space, especially at sides	
34.	Meaningful headings and subheadings	

Courseware Evaluation Form (Continued)

Item	Characteristic	Strength (1–5)
35.	Easy to tell where hands-on exercises start and finish	
36.	Text is broken up with screen shots, diagrams, tables, and other illustrations	
37.	Easy-to-identify menu commands and other special text items	
38.	Uses icons and buttons from toolbars and dialog boxes	
39.	Motivates students by explaining why features benefit them and are relevant	
40.	Satisfies the course objectives	
41.	Logical progression of topics	
42.	Active learning (questionnaires, practical exercises, etc.)	
43.	Multiple-sense learning (text, screen captures, diagrams, hands-on exercises)	
44.	Caters to different learning styles	
45.	Important points first	
46.	Summaries	

Book Evaluation Form

Item	Characteristic	Strength (1–5)
1.	Are a table of contents and divisions of each chapter listed under the chapter title?	
2.	Does the author provide an outline of the book in the table of contents?	
3.	Do topics correspond to objectives for the course?	
4.	Is there adequate and balanced coverage of the content area as prescribed by the course description?	
5.	Are topics arranged in a usable sequence?	
6.	Can they be adapted without disrupting the usefulness of the book?	
7.	Preface. Does the author give a good overview in the preface regarding where the book is going and the type of audience he or she is addressing?	
8.	Do introductory statements or paragraphs begin each chapter or major section?	
9.	Are there clear and well-marked divisions of content within chapters?	
10.	Are there titles, headings, and subheadings to help the student visualize the organization and relationship of content?	
11.	Are there summary sections or paragraphs at the end of each major division or chapter?	
12.	Reading level. Does the textbook contain readable language that is suitable for the reading level of the students who will be using it?	
13.	Do students have a sufficient background to understand the author's material?	
14.	Illustrations. Are these accurate, and are they properly captioned and placed?	
15.	Are the illustrations clear and culturally relevant?	
16.	Are there study questions or quizzes at the end of chapters?	
17.	Does the author include discussion and review questions and/or examination items related to the content and concepts as presented in the chapter?	
18.	Are there lists of related readings at the end of chapters and/or a comprehensive bibliography at the end of the book?	
19.	Are there study aids? Do they help students generalize, apply, and/or evaluate content, simulate critical thinking, or require problem solving?	

Book Evaluation Form (Continued)

Item	Characteristic	Strength (1–5)
20.	Do appendixes, where applicable, contain additional helpful information closely related to the book's content?	
21.	Is there an index at the end of the book? Is there a glossary of terms as used in the text?	
22.	Does the author provide an index with keywords and important terms?	
	Total score	

Content to Course Objective Matrix by Course

Item	Course	Objective	Content
1.			
2.			
3.			
4.			
5.			
6.			
7.			
8.			
9.			
10.			
11.			
12.			
13.			
14.			
15.			
16.			
17.			
18.			
19.			
20.			
21.			
22.			
23.			
24.			
25.			
26.			
27.			
28.			
29.			
30.			
31.			
32.			
33.			
34.			
35.			
36.			
37.			
38.			
39.			
40.			
41.			
42.			
43.			
44.			
45.			

Audience Analysis Summary Form

Audience Member	Department/Area	Software Functions/Modules	Skill Level (1=Beginner, 5=Expert)

Vendor Course Fit Summary

Item	Course Module	Vendor Course Module	Goodness of Fit (1=Bad, 10=Perfect)
1.			
2.			
3.			
4.			
5.			
6.			
7.			
8.			
9.			
10.			
11.			
12.			
13.			
14.			
15.			
16.			
17.			
18.			
19.			
20.			
21.			
22.			
23.			
24.			
25.			
26.			
27.			
28.			
29.			
30.			
31.			
32.			
33.			
34.			
35.			
36.			
37.			
38.			
39.			
40.			

Gap Detail Form

Gap	Course Module	Vendor Course Module	Required Improvements	Required Additions	Potential Misses
1.					
2.					
3.					
4.					
5.					
6.					
7.					
8.					
9.					
10.					
11.					
12.					
13.					
14.					
15.					
16.					
17.					
18.					
19.					
20.					
21.					
22.					
23.					
24.					
25.					
26.					
27.					
28.					
29.					
30.					
31.					
32.					
33.					
34.					
35.					
36.					
37.					
38.					
39.					
40.					

Gap Work List

Gap	Deliverables Affected	Modification Task	Assigned To	Assigned Date	Estimated Done Date	Completed Date
1.						
2.						
3.						
4.						
5.						
6.						
7.						
8.						
9.						
10.						
11.						
12.						
13.						
14.						
15.						
16.						
17.						
18.						
19.						
20.						
21.						
22.						
23.						
24.						
25.						
26.						
27.						
28.						
29.						
30.						
31.						
32.						
33.						
34.						
35.						
36.						
37.						
38.						
39.						
40.						

Consultant Evaluation Form

Item	Characteristic	Strength (1=Poor, 5=Excellent)
1.	Trustworthy	
2.	Inspires confidence	
3.	Commitments kept	
4.	Is open and honest	
5.	Is objective	
6.	Sells solutions, not disjoint pieces	
7.	Is creative	
8.	Offers fresh ideas	
9.	Shows a willingness to confront new challenges	
10.	Exercises good judgment	
11.	Takes initiative	
12.	Adheres to your standards or exceeds them	
13.	Has patience	
14.	Focuses on goals and on getting results	
15.	Is energetic and enthusiastic	
16.	Communicates effectively	
17.	Establishes rapport quickly	
18.	Works well with people in your organization	
19.	Primary concern is for you and your organization	
	Total score	

Trainer Evaluation Form

Trainer Name: Class Name:		Date: Location:				
Item	**The trainer**	**1=Strongly Disagree, 5=Strongly Agree**				
1.	Sets goals and objectives for training	1	2	3	4	5
2.	Develops lesson plans	1	2	3	4	5
3.	Keeps current and up to date	1	2	3	4	5
4.	Conducts needs assessments	1	2	3	4	5
5.	Provides advice to students	1	2	3	4	5
6.	Designs instruction so it is easily understood	1	2	3	4	5
7.	Provides positive reinforcement	1	2	3	4	5
8.	Blends different training techniques	1	2	3	4	5
9.	Uses questioning to involve participants	1	2	3	4	5
10.	Facilitates group learning activities	1	2	3	4	5
11.	Clearly explains concepts	1	2	3	4	5
12.	Presents training in a logical sequence	1	2	3	4	5
13.	Recognizes and attends to individual differences	1	2	3	4	5
14.	Explains complex ideas so they are easily understood	1	2	3	4	5
15.	Evaluates effects and impact of training	1	2	3	4	5
16.	Is flexible and can guide the training as needed	1	2	3	4	5
17.	Is honest and open with participants	1	2	3	4	5
18.	Is sincere	1	2	3	4	5
19.	Manages the classroom in an orderly manner	1	2	3	4	5
20.	Is prompt	1	2	3	4	5
	Total points					

Training Monitoring Log

| | | | No. of Hours | | Course ID | Comment |
Date	Location	Training Description	Off the Job	On the Job		

Name of trainee:

Training Session Sign-Up Sheet

Name	Department	Time In	Time Out	Late? (Y/N)	Late By? (Minutes)

Course and Instructor Evaluation Form

Course: _____   **Instructor:** _____

Date: _____   **Facility:** _____

Training facility:

Effectiveness of the training site for comfort:
Excellent _____   Good _____   Fair _____   Poor _____   Unacceptable _____   Not Applicable _____

Effectiveness of the training site for accessibility:
Excellent _____   Good _____   Fair _____   Poor _____   Unacceptable _____   Not Applicable _____

Effectiveness of the training site as a training forum:
Excellent _____   Good _____   Fair _____   Poor _____   Unacceptable _____   Not Applicable _____

Quality of the training equipment for efficiency:
Excellent _____   Good _____   Fair _____   Poor _____   Unacceptable _____   Not Applicable _____

Level of error-free operation of the training equipment:
Excellent _____   Good _____   Fair _____   Poor _____   Unacceptable _____   Not Applicable _____

Speed of the equipment used for training:
Excellent _____   Good _____   Fair _____   Poor _____   Unacceptable _____   Not Applicable _____

Timely coordination for delivery of the training service:
Excellent _____   Good _____   Fair _____   Poor _____   Unacceptable _____   Not Applicable _____

Courtesy and timeliness of project driver:
Excellent _____   Good _____   Fair _____   Poor _____   Unacceptable _____   Not Applicable _____

Usefulness of projects website for user-friendliness:
Excellent _____   Good _____   Fair _____   Poor _____   Unacceptable _____   Not Applicable _____

Usefulness of project website as an interesting information source:
Excellent _____   Good _____   Fair _____   Poor _____   Unacceptable _____   Not Applicable _____

Training:

Usefulness of curriculum:
Excellent _____   Good _____   Fair _____   Poor _____   Unacceptable _____   Not Applicable _____

Relevance of curriculum:
Excellent _____   Good _____   Fair _____   Poor _____   Unacceptable _____   Not Applicable _____

Ease of learning of curriculum:
Excellent _____   Good _____   Fair _____   Poor _____   Unacceptable _____   Not Applicable _____

Relation of training to my job:
Excellent _____   Good _____   Fair _____   Poor _____   Unacceptable _____   Not Applicable _____

Course and Instructor Evaluation Form (Continued)

Training (*Continued*)

Quality of materials:
Excellent ____   Good ____   Fair ____   Poor ____   Unacceptable ____   Not Applicable ____

Reading ease:
Excellent ____   Good ____   Fair ____   Poor ____   Unacceptable ____   Not Applicable ____

Match of curriculum to software:
Excellent ____   Good ____   Fair ____   Poor ____   Unacceptable ____   Not Applicable ____

The objectives for this class were clearly explained.
Strongly Agree ____   Agree ____   Don't Know ____   Disagree ____   Strongly Disagree ____

The information was presented in a logical and understandable manner.
Strongly Agree ____   Agree ____   Don't Know ____   Disagree ____   Strongly Disagree ____

The documentation was helpful.
Strongly Agree ____   Agree ____   Don't Know ____   Disagree ____   Strongly Disagree ____

The background information presented at the beginning of the class was useful.
Strongly Agree ____   Agree ____   Don't Know ____   Disagree ____   Strongly Disagree ____

I know how to log in to the system.
Strongly Agree ____   Agree ____   Don't Know ____   Disagree ____   Strongly Disagree ____

The log-in instructions are clearly written.
Strongly Agree ____   Agree ____   Don't Know ____   Disagree ____   Strongly Disagree ____

I understand the functions and purposes of the processes covered in the training class.
Strongly Agree ____   Agree ____   Don't Know ____   Disagree ____   Strongly Disagree ____

The class should cover more material.
Strongly Agree ____   Agree ____   Don't Know ____   Disagree ____   Strongly Disagree ____

Instructor:

Instructor timeliness:
Excellent ____   Good ____   Fair ____   Poor ____   Unacceptable ____   Not Applicable ____

Instructor subject knowledge:
Excellent ____   Good ____   Fair ____   Poor ____   Unacceptable ____   Not Applicable ____

Instructor communication skills:
Excellent ____   Good ____   Fair ____   Poor ____   Unacceptable ____   Not Applicable ____

Instructor training preparation:
Excellent ____   Good ____   Fair ____   Poor ____   Unacceptable ____   Not Applicable ____

Course and Instructor Evaluation Form (Continued)

Participant:

Did you attend all the sessions? Y N

Did the tutorials and handouts help you learn the materials? Y N

Is this the first time you learned the materials? Y N

Would you recommend this workshop to others? Y N

Was help available when you needed it during the hands-on session? Y N

Was the instructor/assistant available to answer questions? Y N

Was the hands-on session long enough? Y N

Additional Comments:

1. What have you enjoyed about the class so far?

_____

2. What could be improved about the course?

_____

3. What do you like most about the instructor?

_____

4. What could the instructor do to improve?

_____

5. What do you like most about the subject matter expert?

_____

6. What could the subject matter expert do to improve?

_____

Performance Plan Form

| PERFORMANCE PLAN FOR: **Name Here** | | POSITION: | |
| DATE OF PLAN: **MM/DD/CCYY** | | PERIOD ENDING: **MM/DD/CCYY** | |

Objectives	Target time frames	Change allowances

Signatures:

_____   _____   _____   _____
Employee   Date   Supervisor   Date

Performance Review Form

| PERFORMANCE REVIEW FOR: **Name Here** | | **POSITION:** | |
| DATE OF REVIEW: **MM/DD/CCYY** | | **PERIOD ENDING: MM/DD/CCYY** | |
Objectives	Target	Result	Comments

Signatures:

_____   _____   _____   _____
Employee   Date   Supervisor   Date

PERFORMANCE RATING KEY:

EXCEPTIONAL

Significantly exceeded all goals and values of performance.

SUPERIOR

Consistently met and frequently exceeded goals and values of performance.

FULLY COMPETENT

Met overall goals and values of performance—100%.

DEVELOPMENTAL/NEEDS IMPROVEMENT

Met some goals; with further development likely to meet overall values of performance.

UNSATISFACTORY

Did not meet goals, values of performance; requires significant overall improvement to achieve goals.

INCOMPLETE

Through no fault of the employee, the goal or objective could not be achieved.

Job/Training Performance Comparison

Employee: _____   **Department:** _____

Job/Position: _____   **Rating Date:** _____

Class(es): _____   **Class Date(s):** _____

Item	Course	Objective	Class Performance (1=Bad, 7=Good)	OTJ Performance (1=Bad, 7=Good)
1.				
2.				
3.				
4.				
5.				
6.				
7.				
8.				
9.				
10.				
11.				
12.				
13.				
14.				
15.				
16.				
17.				
18.				
19.				
20.				
21.				
22.				
23.				
24.				
25.				
26.				
27.				
28.				
29.				
30.				
31.				
32.				
33.				
34.				
35.				

Course Review Scheduling Matrix

Item	Class	Development Complete Date	Last Taught Date	Scheduled Review Date	Review Team Members
1.					
2.					
3.					
4.					
5.					
6.					
7.					
8.					
9.					
10.					
11.					
12.					
13.					
14.					
15.					
16.					
17.					
18.					
19.					
20.					
21.					
22.					
23.					
24.					
25.					
26.					
27.					
28.					
29.					
30.					
31.					
32.					
33.					
34.					
35.					
36.					
37.					
38.					
39.					
40.					

Course Review Form

Class: _____   **Last Review Date:** _____
Course Evaluation Average: _____
Trainer Evaluation Average: _____
Test Average: _____

Course Modified By:
Course Modifications:

Trainer:
Trainer Improvement Instruction:

Test Modified By:
Test Modifications:

Task Training Troubleshooting Matrix

Item	Task	Hardware Variables	Software Variables
1.			
2.			
3.			
4.			
5.			
6.			
7.			
8.			
9.			
10.			
11.			
12.			
13.			
14.			
15.			
16.			
17.			
18.			
19.			
20.			
21.			
22.			
23.			
24.			
25.			
26.			
27.			
28.			
29.			
30.			
31.			
32.			
33.			
34.			
35.			
36.			
37.			
38.			
39.			
40.			

Software Feature/Function Training Priority Matrix

Item	Priority	Software Module	Software Feature/Function	Requests	Usage Difficulty
1.					
2.					
3.					
4.					
5.					
6.					
7.					
8.					
9.					
10.					
11.					
12.					
13.					
14.					
15.					
16.					
17.					
18.					
19.					
20.					
21.					
22.					
23.					
24.					
25.					
26.					
27.					
28.					
29.					
30.					
31.					
32.					
33.					
34.					
35.					
36.					
37.					
38.					
39.					
40.					

ABOUT THE AUTHOR

Charles Trepper has spent 20 years in the I/T industry and is a resource for organizations that need help training and organizing their I/T work forces. A frequent speaker at conferences, Mr. Trepper has also appeared on radio and television, providing commentary and insight on solutions to the I/T staffing shortage. As an advisor to I/T executives, he has helped many organizations reorganize and retrain their I/T groups to more efficiently use their human resources. He also champions organizational training budgets, which are often on the chopping block.

Mr. Trepper started his training career teaching organizations how to streamline systems development processes, improve staff utilization, and create training programs to make I/T groups more effective and efficient. He has taught professional courses for I/T and training experts and was on the faculty of Purdue University for two years.

Mr. Trepper writes for several I/T industry trade magazines and is the author of several books. He earned his B.S. in Management Information Science and his M.S. in Technology Management at Purdue University.